Denmark and the European Union

This book offers an accessible, coherent and comprehensive analysis of the recent, contemporary and future challenges and possibilities facing Denmark in the European integration process.

The book traces the formal as well as the informal ways of influence and adaptation in Denmark's relations with the European Union. In doing so, it also offers a contribution to our understanding of Europe as a differentiated political arena. Topics covered include:

- Identification of the challenges and opportunities of Danish EU membership, via the policies pursued by Denmark in Europe.
- The ways in which Denmark adapts to the European integration process.
- The consequences of EU integration for citizen rights, democracy, policy coordination and implementation efficiency.

Denmark and the European Union will be of interest to students and scholars of European Union and integration politics.

Lee Miles is Professor at Loughborough University, UK and also Professor at Karlstad University, Sweden.

Anders Wivel is Associate Professor at the University of Copenhagen, Denmark.

Europe and the nation state
Edited by Michael Burgess
Centre for Federal Studies, University of Kent
and
Lee Miles
Centre for the Study of International Governance, Loughborough University

This series explores the complex relationship between nation states and European integration and the political, social, economic and policy implications of this interaction. The series examines issues such as:

- The impact of the EU on the politics and policy-making of the nation state and vice-versa.
- The effects of expansion of the EU on individual nation states in Europe.
- The relationship between the EU and non-European nation states.

1 **Poland and the European Union**
   Edited by Karl Cordell

2 **Greece in the European Union**
   Edited by Dionyssis G. Dimitrakopoulos and Argyris G. Passas

3 **The European Union and Democratization**
   Edited by Paul J. Kubicek

4 **Iceland and European Integration**
   On the edge
   Edited by Baldur Thorhallsson

5 **Norway outside the European Union**
   Norway and European integration from 1994 to 2004
   Clive Archer

6 **Turkey and European Integration**
   Prospects and issues in the post-Helsinki era
   Edited by Mehmet Uğur and Nergis Canefe

7 **Perspectives on EU–Russia Relations**
   Edited by Debra Johnson and Paul Robinson

8 **French Relations with the European Union**
  Edited by Helen Drake

9 **The Geopolitics of Euro-Atlantic Integration**
  Edited by Hans Mouritzen and Anders Wivel

10 **State Territoriality and European Integration**
   Edited by Michael Burgess and Hans Vollaard

11 **Switzerland and the European Union**
   A close, contradictory and misunderstood relationship
   Edited by Clive Church

12 **Romania and the European Union**
   Dimitris Papadimitriou and David Phinnemore

13 **The European Union and the Baltic States**
   Changing forms of governance
   Edited by Bengt Jacobsson

14 **The Czech Republic and the European Union**
   Dan Marek and Michael Baun

15 **Europeanization and Domestic Policy Change**
   The case of Italy
   Paolo Roberto Graziano

16 **Denmark and the European Union**
   Edited by Lee Miles and Anders Wivel

Denmark and the European Union

Edited by Lee Miles and Anders Wivel

LONDON AND NEW YORK

First published 2014
by Routledge
2 Park Square, Milton Park, Abingdon, Oxfordshire OX14 4RN

Simultaneously published in the USA and Canada
by Routledge
711 Third Avenue, New York, NY 10017

First issued in paperback 2014

Routledge is an imprint of the Taylor & Francis Group, an informa business

© 2014 Lee Miles and Anders Wivel for selection and editorial matter; individual contributors their contribution.

The right of Lee Miles and Anders Wivel to be identified as the authors of the editorial material, and of the authors for their individual chapters, has been asserted in accordance with sections 77 and 78 of the Copyright, Designs and Patents Act 1988.

All rights reserved. No part of this book may be reprinted or reproduced or utilized in any form or by any electronic, mechanical, or other means, now known or hereafter invented, including photocopying and recording, or in any information storage or retrieval system, without permission in writing from the publishers.

Trademark notice: Product or corporate names may be trademarks or registered trademarks, and are used only for identification and explanation without intent to infringe.

British Library Cataloguing in Publication Data
A catalogue record for this book is available from the British Library

Library of Congress Cataloging in Publication Data
Denmark and the European Union / edited by Lee Miles and
Anders Wivel. – 1 Edition.
    pages cm. – (Europe and the nation state; 16)
    Includes bibliographical references and index.
    1. European Union–Denmark. 2. Denmark–Politics and government–21st century. 3. Europe–Economic integration. I. Miles, Lee, II. Wivel, Anders.
    HC240.25.D4D46 2013
    341.242'209489–dc23   2013004278

ISBN 978-0-415-61134-3 (hbk)
ISBN 978-1-138-89813-4 (pbk)
ISBN 978-0-203-79807-2 (ebk)

Typeset in Times New Roman
by Wearset Ltd, Boldon, Tyne and Wear

Contents

List of illustrations	ix
List of contributors	xi
List of abbreviations	xii
Preface	xiv
LEE MILES AND ANDERS WIVEL	

1 Introducing Denmark and the European Union   1
LEE MILES AND ANDERS WIVEL

2 Denmark's relation to the European Union: a history of dualism and pragmatism   14
MORTEN KELSTRUP

3 The Internal Market Policy and the Common Agricultural Policy: the normalization of EU policy-making in Denmark   30
PETER NEDERGAARD

4 Denmark and the Euro opt-out   47
MARTIN MARCUSSEN

5 Justice and home affairs: Denmark as an active differential European   65
REBECCA ADLER-NISSEN

6 A pace-setter out of sync? Danish foreign, security and defence policy and the European Union   80
ANDERS WIVEL

7 Denmark and the Council of Ministers   95
RASMUS BRUN PEDERSEN

8	**Denmark and the European Commission: entering the Heart of the Union** CAROLINE HOWARD GRON	109
9	**Denmark and the European Parliament** ANNE RASMUSSEN	126
10	**Prospects and limits of European interest representation: the shipping and wind turbine industries** KARSTEN RONIT	145
11	**The European 'rights revolution' and the (non) implementation of the citizenship directive in Denmark** MARLENE WIND	159
12	**EU-phoria or -phobia? Danish public opinion about the EU** ANDREAS R. T. SCHUCK AND CLAES H. DE VREESE	175
13	**Public administration, civil servants and implementation** DORTE SINDBJERG MARTINSEN	189
14	**EU coordination processes in Denmark: change in order to preserve** PETER NEDERGAARD	203
15	**Not quite a painful choice? Reflecting on Denmark and further European integration** LEE MILES	217
16	**A smart state handling a differentiated integration dilemma? Concluding on Denmark in the European Union** LEE MILES AND ANDERS WIVEL	228
	Appendix A: the results of the Danish Parliamentary Elections 1971–2011	239
	Appendix B: the composition of Danish governments 1971–2011	241
	Bibliography	243
	Index	270

Illustrations

Figures

1.1	Denmark in a differentiated Europe	8
2.1	Danish attitudes to EU membership	25
4.1	Basic structures of EU-governance in the area of economic policy	59
4.2	Basic structures of EU-governance in the area of monetary policy	61
8.1	Stages of influence and decision-making in the European Commission	117
11.1	Scale of compliance	165
11.2	The Metock case	170
12.1	EU membership support in Denmark and EU-wide	176
12.2	Trust in the European Parliament and national parliaments in Denmark and EU-wide	177
12.3	Satisfaction with the democracy in the EU and in one's own country in Denmark and EU-wide	178
12.4	Mediation model for the effect on vote intention ('no')	183
13.1	Infringement procedures against EU member states in 2008	193
13.2	Infringement procedures against Denmark 2004–2008	194
14.1	Model of Danish EU coordination	207

Tables

2.1	Danish referenda on EC/EU questions	16
2.2	The Danish opt-outs from the Treaty on the European Union	18
2.3	Results of Danish elections to the European Parliament	24
3.1	Distribution of Danish exports 1960–2009 (percentage)	31
3.2	Danish goods and services 1960–2009 (percentage)	33
3.3	CAP-support to farmers in selected member states 1973–2008 (million ECU/euro)	35
3.4	Distribution of CAP expenditures to selected member states in 2009 (million euro)	36
6.1	Danish participation in international military operations since the Second World War	90

6.2	Military operations conducted by the EU	91
7.1	Support for government's request for mandates in the EAC	98
7.2	Support for ratification of 'EU-initiated legislation' in the Folketing 1998–2010	99
7.3	Formal voting power in the Council of Ministers under the Nice Treaty and Lisbon Treaty	103
8.1	The Danish Commissioners	113
8.2	Findings of the pre-formulation phase	119
8.3	Findings of the formulation phase	121
8.4	Findings of the phases	123
9.1	Results of the European Parliament elections in Denmark	129
9.2	Attitudes towards extending the powers of the European Parliament	132
9.3	Attitudes towards representation	133
9.4	Official committee assignment in July 2004	135
9.5	Negative binominal regressions of report allocation from July 1999–31 January 2007	137
9.6	MEP contacts	139
9.7	Voting recommendations	140
9.8	How often do Danish MEPs toe the EPG line? (roll call votes from July 2004–May 2006)	142
12.1	OLS regression predicting Euro-scepticism (Model 1) and logistic regressions (Models 2a and 2b)	182
13.1	Transposition form of EU directives (percentage)	196

Contributors

Rebecca Adler-Nissen is an Assistant Professor at the Centre for European Politics, Department of Political Science, University of Copenhagen

Claes H. de Vreese is Professor and Chair of Political Communication and Scientific Director of The Amsterdam School of Communication Research, Department of Communication Science, University of Amsterdam

Caroline Howard Grøn is an Assistant Professor at the Centre for European Politics, Department of Political Science, University of Copenhagen

Morten Kelstrup is Professor Emeritus in the Department of Political Science, University of Copenhagen

Martin Marcussen is Professor in the Department of Political Science, University of Copenhagen

Dorte Sindbjerg Martinsen is Professor with special responsibilities in the Department of Political Science, University of Copenhagen

Lee Miles is Professor in the Department of Politics, History and International Relations, Loughborough University

Peter Nedergaard is Professor in the Department of Political Science, University of Copenhagen

Rasmus Brun Pedersen is an Associate Professor in the Department of Political Science and Government, Aarhus University

Anne Rasmussen is Professor with special responsibilities at the Department of Political Science, University of Copenhagen

Karsten Ronit is an Associate Professor in the Department of Political Science, University of Copenhagen

Andreas R. T. Schuck is an Assistant Professor in the Department of Communication Science, University of Amsterdam

Marlene Wind is Professor and Director of the Centre for European Politics, Department of Political Science, University of Copenhagen

Anders Wivel is an Associate Professor in the Department of Political Science, University of Copenhagen

Abbreviations

ALDE	Alliance of Liberals and Democrats for Europe
CAACE	The Comité des Associations d'Armateurs des Communautés Européennes
CAP	Common Agricultural Policy
CFSP	Common Foreign and Security Policy
COREPER	Committee of Permanent Representatives
CSDP	Common Security and Defence Policy
DG	Directorate General
DR Congo	The Democratic Republic of Congo
EAC	European Affairs Committee (of the Danish parliament)
EC	European Community
ECB	European Central Bank
ECC	European Economic Community
ECJ	European Court of Justice
ECR	European Conservatives and Reformists
ECSC	European Coal and Steel Community
ECU	European Currency Units
EEA	European Economic Area
EEC	Treaty on the European Economic Community
EFC	Economic and Financial Committee
EFD	Europe of Freedom and Democracy
EFTA	European Free Trade Association
EMI	European Monetary Institute
EMSA	European Maritime Safety Agency
EMU	Economic and Monetary Union
EP	European Parliament
EPC	European Political Cooperation
EPG	European Parliament Party Group
EPP-ED	European People's Party-European Democrats
EREC	European Renewable Energy Council
ERM	Exchange Rate Mechanism
ECSA	European Community Shipowners' Association
ESCB	European System of Central Banks

ESDP	European Security and Defence Policy
EU	European Union
EUL/NGL	European United Left–Nordic Green Left
EWEA	European Wind-Energy Association
FPA	Foreign Policy Analysis
FYR Macedonia	Former Yugoslavian Republic of Macedonia
GATT	General Agreement on Tariffs and Trade
G/EFA	The Greens–European Free Alliance
GWEC	Global Wind Energy Council
IMCO	Intergovernmental Maritime Consultative Organization
IMF	International Monetary Fund
IMO	International Maritime Organization
IND/DEM	Independence/Democracy
IR	International Relations
IRENA	International Renewable Energy Agency
JHA	Justice and Home Affairs
MEP	Member of the European Parliament
MP	Member of Parliament
NA	Non-Attached Members
NATO	North Atlantic Treaty Organization
NGO	Non-Governmental Organization
NORDEK	Nordiskt Ekonomiskt Samarbete
PES	Party of European Socialists
PR	Permanent Representation
OECD	Organisation for Economic Co-operation and Development
QMV	Qualified Majority Voting
S&D	Progressive Alliance of Socialists and Democrats
SEA	Single European Act
SEM	Single European Market
SNE	Seconded National Experts
TCN	Third Country National
TEU	Treaty of the European Union
UEN	Union for Europe of the Nations
UK	The United Kingdom
UN	The United Nations
UNSC	The United Nations Security Council
WEU	Western European Union
WSC	World Shipping Council
WTO	World Trade Organization

Preface

Denmark has been a member of the European Union for 40 years; yet the Danish population and, to some extent, the political elite as well continue to be seemingly uneasy with some of the most fundamental aspects of the European integration process. Thus, whereas it is widely acknowledged that almost all areas of Danish policy have developed and incorporated some sort of EU dimension, Denmark is still widely considered as an outlier that defends its political bastions with opt-outs and – sometimes rather vocally – disputing the political and institutional development of the EU. At the same time, the Danish electorate is one of the most positive towards EU membership among member states' electorates, and Denmark continues to rank among the most complying member states when it comes to implementing decisions made at the EU level. Denmark has even occasionally worked to increase the pace of, and to 'pace-set' EU integration in some issue areas.

Rather than this being regarded as evidence of a 'split personality', this can be viewed as reflecting a pragmatic balancing act between the preservation of national autonomy and maximizing influence through institutional engagement. All EU member states need to engage in this balancing act. Yet for small member states, their limited agenda-setting power often forces a rethinking of strategies by their respective political elites if they are to maximize their respective country's influence in an institutional setting. After all, they have many opportunities to influence small decisions and the day-to-day politics and workings of the EU, but relatively little power in practice to challenge the course set by representatives of larger EU member states or even to participate in their discussions.

This volume offers a coherent and accessible analysis of Denmark and the EU written by leading experts on the various aspects of Danish EU membership. The volume describes and unpacks the most important political and administrative aspects of EU membership and seeks to explain the past trajectory and current decisions of Danish policy-makers in regard to EU developments. By doing this, it tells the story of how Denmark's relationship with the EU was gradually normalized by developments in Denmark, and in the EU, and explores how this small member state tackled the uploading and downloading of policies in a heavily institutionalized environment such as the EU.

We would like to thank a number of people who helped us at various stages during the writing and editing of the book. In particular, we would like to express our gratitude to Martin Marcussen for his contribution in the early stages of the editing process. Martin played a key role in the initial formulation of the project and contributed substantially to discussions on how to frame the book. Also, we are grateful to Ian Manners and Knud Erik Jørgensen, who acted as discussants at an authors' workshop at Schaeffergaarden, Denmark. Both of them offered many valuable points on individual draft chapters as well as on the volume in general. At Routledge, Heidi Bagtazo and her team offered support and feedback throughout the editorial process. Thanks also to Kristian Frey Jensen and Oscar Buhl for their competent research assistance at various stages of the editorial process. A generous grant from the Centre for European Politics at the Department of Political Science, University of Copenhagen, was instrumental in underpinning the project financially, including paying for research assistance, a one-day kick-off workshop and a two-day authors' workshop.

Last but not least, we would like to thank the contributors to this volume. It has been a pleasure to work with all of them, and we have learned a lot about Denmark's past, present and future challenges and opportunities in an ever-changing European Union. We sincerely hope that the readers of this volume will feel the same way.

Lee Miles and Anders Wivel
Loughborough and Copenhagen, 18 October 2012

1 Introducing Denmark and the European Union[1]

Lee Miles and Anders Wivel

Denmark eventually became a full member of the European Union (EU) on 1 January 1973, more than 40 years ago and thus, it has been long time since the country could be accurately categorized as a 'new member state' undergoing a 'normal' transitional phase to the obligations and demands of EU accession. There is a 40-year track record of full membership status worthy of detailed and comprehensive investigation. Moreover, general perceptions are that Denmark's relations with the EU have been somewhat problematic at times, and indeed, largely as a result of the outcome of debates on the Treaty of the European Union (TEU) in the early 1990s, Denmark has enjoyed a rather distinctive institutional and legal set of circumstances pertaining to the characteristics of its continued full membership status, and its participation in further European integration. Phrases, such as 'reluctant European' and 'intergovernmentalist', and the description of Denmark as a state suffering from an 'integration dilemma' (Kelstrup 1993) – have all become part of the universal language that scholars, and even practitioners, regularly use to describe Denmark's experiences as a full EU member since 1973.

Nevertheless, despite the relatively long period as a full member, comprehensive studies of Denmark's complex relationship with the evolving European Community (EC)/European Union have been relatively sparse on the ground, especially those written in English that can be accessible to 'non-Danish' and 'non-Scandinavian' audiences and interested parties as well.[2]

The objective of this text is therefore to, at least for the most part, offer an accessible, coherent and comprehensive analysis of the recent, contemporary and future challenges and possibilities facing Denmark in the European integration process. Particular attention is placed upon tracing the formal as well as the informal ways of influence and adaptation in Denmark's relations with the EU. In doing so, the book seeks to provide a fresh contribution to our understanding of Europe, and more specifically, the EU as a differentiated political arena.

Furthermore, the book specifically aims at identifying the challenges and opportunities of Danish EU membership, past and present, by undertaking a five-fold approach, namely: (1) thematic discussions and historical analysis of the years and phases of Denmark's full membership (first two chapters) and; (2) selective policy evaluations of key specific EU domains in order to provide a balanced assessment of Danish attitudes and perspectives towards the 'mixed' policy portfolio of the evolving EU (Chapters 3 to 6) and; (3) institutional analyses of 'Denmark in Europe' and more specifically, Danish participation in, and relations towards, key EU institutions such as the Council of Ministers/European Council, European Commission and European Parliament (Chapters 7 to 10) as well as; (4) thematic investigations of the impact of European integration on Denmark – 'Europe in Denmark' (Chapters 11 to 14) and finally; (5) the added dimension of scholarly reflections on Denmark as a 'small state' in the EU, where considerable work has already been done, and thus is worthy of particular inclusion (Chapters 15 and 16).

By taking this 'five-fold' approach' – covering historical assessments, policy-analyses, institutional evaluations, thematic domestic politics and small state approaches – this book aims to provide the reader with a comprehensive view of Denmark's complex relationship with the EU. The editors have also been fortunate enough to recruit some of the leading scholars working on the EU and/or Danish politics and public administration so the book will be fit for purpose.

Thematic assumptions and conceptual starting-points

Given the comprehensiveness and complex nature of this text, the editors have refrained from requiring contributors to adopt one single approach and/or theory. They remain convinced that working to such strict theoretical remits would only end up producing a largely unconvincing text, where the credibility of one single approach would be stretched to the limit in a largely fruitless attempt at making 'one size fit all'. The tension between the need for rigorous theoretical application and the nature of this project as a comprehensive 'belts and braces' study of Denmark and the EU would simply be too much.

However, the editors also wished to avoid the almost routine accusation of critics associated with edited books – namely that they have such diverse missions, that such texts suffer from very real dangers of fragmentation and incoherence. In order to balance these competing tensions, the editors have preferred to establish a set of conceptual tools that contributors can apply within the context of their specific chapters and, at the same time, provide cross-cutting reflections valuable for comparative analysis across the various chapters of the book. By taking this approach, the text should be more than the sum of its parts. The book aims at making a contribution to the knowledge of European integration and the ways in which a small state navigates within the European political and economic arena. It analyses how Denmark adapts to European realities, and contributes to constructing a differentiated Europe. Thus, its analysis synthesizes three clusters of theory: theories of Europeanization, theories of foreign policy analysis and theories of (differentiated) European integration.[3]

Europeanization

'Europeanization' as a concept 'is essentially contested as to its usefulness for the study of European politics' (Graziano and Vink 2007: 3) and to some,

'Europeanization' is not regarded as a separate 'theory', but rather as a phenomenon or problem that should be explained (Bulmer 2007; Featherstone and Radaelli 2003: 34). If this is the case, then it is important that Europeanization is not portrayed as a distinct theoretical or conceptual school of thought, but rather as being closer to a phenomenon that needs to be explained. Indeed, this view is largely assumed in the context of this book, which includes Europeanization concepts related to the fact that some of its component literature focuses on how the 'downloading' of EU affairs, business and acts takes place in the national context, the nature of 'cross-loading' among Danish actors, and the furthering of transnational activity between actors in Denmark and those in other countries, as well as the 'uploading' of national interests and preferences to the EU level, and within the EU domain.

It is pertinent to outline these concepts in a little more detail. Schmidt (2006) argues, for example, that Europeanization is essentially about these three dimensions. There is a vertical 'downloading' process by the EU, that broadly relates to the actions of EU institutions, for example: the outcomes of the EU policy cycle, (e.g. the consultation and implementation work of the European Commission), EU (largely secondary) legislation (like regulations and directives) and even decisions of the European Court of Justice (ECJ), that result in EU business being disseminated 'down' to the national and sub-national domains (which usually require a response from national and sub-national actors and institutions). For the most part, such downloading can lead to (largely) 'top-down' changes, such as increasing *attention* and *awareness* on the part of domestic actors towards monitoring EU-related business and legislation, as well as the *adaptation* of domestic institutional structures and processes as a consequence of rising demands from EU policy-making.

In addition, there is a horizontal 'sideways' process of 'cross-loading' where responding to (and handling) EU business, policy outcomes and legislation encourages and shapes cooperation among national actors and institutions and, even below this, at the sub-national domain of regional and local government. Moreover, this cross-loading activity can have both *internal* (i.e. within the nation state – say between national actors in the Danish government and those of the parliament (the Folketing)) and/or *external* (between actors across transnational borders – for instance, Nordic cooperation between Danish institutions and those in other Nordic countries) characteristics. Finally there is an 'uploading' process, whereby national and sub-national actors and institutions develop and then seek to transmit their preferences and positions on EU questions to the supranational level (e.g. to EU institutions like the European Commission or European Council). Such uploading activities can take the form of, for example, lobbying activities by national or sub-national actors in Brussels, and/or the participation of Danish (national and regional) actors in EU Committees and working groups, where Danish preferences may be transmitted upwards from Denmark to the supranational domain of the EU. According to Börzel (2002: 196), such national and sub-national uploading is sought since the respective national and sub-national actors wish to: (1) reduce the need for legal and administrative adaptation in downloading EU policies and legislation into domestic structures that may imply financial and political costs and a reduction in any gains arising from participation in the EU; (2) prevent competitive disadvantages appearing for domestic industries that may be used to operate under existing national and even regional regimes; and (3) enable national and subnational actors and institutions to address problems that continue to preoccupy domestic constituencies, yet can no longer be dealt with effectively at the domestic level.

Alongside these useful, and rather utilitarian concepts of downloading, crossloading and uploading, which provide contributors and the reader with a useful comparative tool with which to gauge aspects of the Danish relationship with the EU across institutional, policy and even legalistic settings, Europeanization concepts are also useful in providing tools for explaining variations in the commitment of respective actors and institutions in Denmark towards aspects of European integration. Above all, Europeanization concepts can offer ways and means to understand for example why, in some areas, such as in environmental policy, Danish preferences towards European integration can be ambitious and can lead to large acceptance of the supranational benefits of EU governance, while in other realms, such as those of Justice and Home Affairs (JHA), Danish reluctance and caution is more substantial, leading to at least the premise of intergovernmental preferences for European cooperation.

Among the most useful is Börzel's idea that national and sub-national actors and institutions engaged in European cooperation, as part of Europeanization, can adopt differing types of strategies when seeking to upload preferences in particular. As Börzel (2002) argues, national and subnational actors and institutions can pursue strategies that are broadly akin to 'pace-setting', 'fence-sitting' and 'foot-dragging'. In simple terms, *pace-setting* equates to when national and subnational actors and institutions actively promote and push policies at the EU level that largely reflect domestic policy preferences and it represents, in most instances, 'the exporting of domestic policies at the European level' (Börzel 2002: 197). On this basis, these actors and institutions may, for instance, articulate that national (in this case, Danish) policies are examples of 'best in class' or 'best-practice' that the rest of the EU should adopt as the EU norm. In contrast, *fence-sitting* behaviour by national and subnational actors and institutions is usually governed by the desire for Denmark to be viewed as a mainstream member state and as a 'good European' by others. When fence-sitting, Danish actors and institutions do not overtly champion issues or policies; they merely prefer to remain engaged because they perceive that there will be political and/or economic advantages from such participation. When fence-sitting, Danish actors and institutions neither systematically push respective issues or policies towards EU action, nor do they block them altogether, and thus do not prevent the attempts of others to do so (see Börzel 2002: 206). Where such actors and institutions are involved in *foot-dragging*, the main focus is for them to overtly defend Danish interests, even if this requires Denmark to be placed on the periphery of EU development. The main aim is largely to stop, delay, or at least contain, the attempts of other member states to upload their domestic preferences and policies to the EU level (see Börzel 2002: 203). Actor and institutional rationales for such foot-dragging are largely based on factors such as negative estimations about the implementation costs upon Denmark arising from such EU business or outcomes. However, it is also important to note that foot-dragging is seldom able to prevent the development of EU policies altogether, nor to prevent these having impacts on Denmark, and thus foot-dragging can result in compensatory measures being agreed, such as, side payments, package deals, derogations, opt-outs and opt-ins, that may enable Denmark to remain peripheral or even outside the respective EU development.[4]

Europeanization thus offers contributors a useful set of general concepts that provide tools for establishing the types, degrees and variations of Danish activity when handling questions of European integration. In the context of this book, they also provide the means to compare the activities of Danish national and subnational actors and institutions across the respective domains of Denmark's relationship with the EU, as addressed by the various contributors in this volume.

In addition, Europeanization concepts can also provide, albeit limited, ways of understanding the mechanisms by which Europe is discursively constructed in Denmark among political and administrative elites as well as in the public policy arena. Hence for this book, Europeanization occurs through a variety of mechanisms that are also largely dictated by the form of European integration being discussed, and/or taking place. A first mechanism is related to what can be referred to as *negative integration*, i.e. the gradual completion of the internal market by removing barriers to the free movement of goods, services, capital and people across the borders of the EU member states. This creates the condition for new structures of competition between national markets and institutions. A second mechanism of Europeanization is more related to *positive integration*, i.e. the formulation of new Europe-wide regulatory frameworks that underpin and expand the scope of the European market. Hard, as well as soft, law is produced in the European political arena and then transferred to and implemented in a national context. A third mechanism of Europeanization that is included in the analysis relates to the *learning processes* that unfold in the routinized encounter between national and European civil servants. For all mechanisms, it is expected that a number of sector-specific intervening variables will work either as contributing factors for domestic change or as barriers to change. In consequence, it is expected that there will be considerable variation in the dependent variable – the national policies, politics and polity. Some aspects may be very robust in their encounter with Europe. In other sectors, considerable change, bordering on transformation, may be detectable.

Foreign policy analysis

A second source of conceptual ideas that help to inform some of the respective chapter evaluations stems from the realms of Foreign Policy Analysis (FPA), not least because elements of FPA can be employed to study, for example, the various ways in which a small state such as Denmark 'uploads' its interests, ideas and identities to a European level (see Hill 2003), especially if the definition of FPA developed by Hudson (2005: 2) is adopted – namely that FPA approaches examine 'not a single decision, but a constellation of decisions taken with reference to a particular situation ... modified over time, requiring an examination of sequences of decisions'. Hence FPA approaches in the context of this volume on Denmark may help us to understand and 'consider *how* certain goals arise and *why* certain behaviour result' (Neack 2003: 26).

More specifically, and drawing from its 'strategic-relational approaches' (see Brighi and Hill 2008: 119), FPA contributes to discussions in this volume in three specific ways. First, by stressing that Denmark's relationship with the EU can be seen as 'a dialectic interplay' (Brighi and Hill 2008: 119) between the strategies of national and subnational actors in Denmark on the one hand, (where Danish actors are *strategic* in orientation towards achieving certain goals at the EU level) and the relational environment of the EU, that not only influences such strategic actors in Denmark, but also has to be analysed from a relational context of how such Danish actors also perceive the EU in a Danish context. In simple terms, to understand how Denmark operates in the EU (Denmark in the EU), there is also a need to recognize the importance of how the EU is seen in, and impacts upon, actors and institutions in Denmark (the EU in Denmark). Hence, FPA approaches in this volume provide us with a means of understanding the constant interplay between *actors* and *context*.

Second, FPA approaches highlight the importance of balancing the 'domestic' and the 'international' (Brighi 2005) since it has long been recognized that in the EU context, the distinction has become blurred (Manners and Whitman 2000), and even 'fused' (Miles 2005a). Above all, FPA scholars, such as, Hanreider (1971) have highlighted the need for a 'compatibility-consensus' or, as Putnam (1988) would argue, a viable 'win-set', where it is explicitly recognized that in order to be successful at the EU level in achieving goals and objectives, actors need to pursue policies beyond the state that are compatible with, and are supported by, a reasonable degree of agreement and consensus within the state. Put simply: Danish policies that are uploaded to the EU will only have a very short shelf life and, indeed, will probably fail, unless they also enjoy a fair degree of domestic support (at least at the elite level as a bare minimum). Where no (or only limited) 'compatibility consensus' exists, Danish positions on EU questions will most probably be ineffective over the medium to long term. FPA approaches thus help us to understand how Danish actors and institutions balance the 'inside' and the 'outside' of the nation state as part of Denmark's complex relationship with the EU.

Third, FPA approaches offer additional insights into the *resources, capabilities* and *instruments* that Danish actors and institutions utilize when handling EU questions and issues, and thus provide extra understanding that compliments the concepts of uploading, cross-loading and downloading, and strategies of pace-setting, fence-sitting and foot-dragging proffered by Europeanization literature. Put simply, *resources* correspond to the 'basic forces' underpinning Danish positions towards

Introducing Denmark and the European Union 7

the EU and vice-versa, such as, geography (bordering Germany, being part of Northern Europe), Denmark's (small) size as a national state in international terms, population size and (prosperous and advanced) level of economic development. These resources help to shape Danish perspectives of itself within the EU as a small, Nordic, economically-advanced, post-industrial nation state and as a full EU member (see Mouritzen and Wivel 2005). *Capabilities* are, in general terms, 'resources that are made operational, but which are not yet translated into the specific instruments which may be applied in practical politics' (Brighi and Hill 2008: 130). These often represent elements that national and subnational actors will seek to improve for the benefit of (Danish) society, in order to give a better chance of implementing effective policy and institutional outcomes, but they are often seen more as long-term investments than as providing an immediate pay-off, such as, the strength of international currency (and the continuation of the Danish krone), the size and proficiency of (Danish) armed forces (in the context of the Common Security Defence Policy (CSDP)) and the skills of its people (and thus Danish involvement in say, Europe 2020 initiatives). It is in the context, for example, of the capabilities domain, that Danish discussions of whether it is better to 'be in' or 'out' of the EU, or indeed the eurozone, often transpire. Hence, capabilities include issues of armed forces, industrial and technology skills, reputation and prestige, GDP growth, quality of civil service, strength of currency, agricultural productivity and even notions of a vigorous civil society. *Instruments* relate to the forms of pressure and influence available to decision-makers and represent something akin to the spectrum from soft to hard power in the discussion of international politics (Nye 2004). In simple terms, instruments relate to forms and types of diplomacy and negotiation being employed and the array of economic and political measures available, such as positive sanctions (like aid, trade agreements and public diplomacy) compared to negative sanctions (like boycotts, embargoes, restrictions on, and degrees of, cooperation and cultural contact between civil societies, to name just a few).

Utilising these general FPA conceptual tools provides the reader with a clearer understanding of the *what* in Denmark's relations with the EU that complements the *how* (uploading, cross-loading and downloading) and the *why* (pace-setting, fence-sitting and foot-dragging) provided by the aforementioned Europeanization concepts (see Figure 1.1).

Differentiated integration

Third, the evaluations in this book are also based on a shared understanding of the European Union as a political and economic arena that fosters unitary integration as well as differentiated integration of all sorts.[5] Dyson and Sepos (2010a: 19–21), for instance, refer to differentiated integration as having four dimensions – *institutional-legal* forms (concerned with the sharing and delegating of competencies between countries and institutions), *geo-strategic* (referring to variations in the susceptibilities of states, actors and institutions to external pressures, threats and leverages), *political-economic* (focusing on differences between and within transnational economic spaces that lead to the integration of economic activities across borders), and *socio-cultural* (characterizing the phenomenon of socialization, belonging and identity that shape 'insiders' and 'outsiders' in the EU).

On the one hand, the founding fathers of the European Economic Communities (EEC), as well as a series of supranational institutions such as the ECJ and the European Central Bank (ECB), promote a unified vision of a harmonized European integration process in which all member states at some point are moving towards the same objective, although with different speeds. On the other hand, as the EU expands in scope – both in terms of membership and issue areas – various more or less permanent patterns of transverse differentiation come to characterize the European edifice. These patterns of diverse integration processes are not bound to go away. Their permanent or semi-permanent character requires us to start theorizing the EU as a more multifaceted process resulting in more multifarious outcomes. Indeed, such a process has begun with Kölliker (2010) highlighting that differentiated integration has a functional (such as forms of institutional settings), Keating (2010) stressing a spatial (such as changing boundaries and the opening up of new territories) and Goetz (2010) identifying the temporal (such as the importance of differing time periods as drivers) dimensions of differentiated integration, which means that Denmark's place in the EU has changed over form, scope and time.

The study of Denmark's role in this integration process is particularly interesting, not least because as Miles (2010a: 188) identifies, differentiated integration relations with the evolving European integration process has been the norm in the Nordic region, with notable differences in approach and speed between the respective Nordic states. Most notably, in the case of Denmark, the country has obtained a number of special opt-outs from central European policy areas, such as the Economic and Monetary Union (EMU), the Common Foreign and Security Policy (CFSP) and JHA. The question that arises is how this special relationship to Europe contributes to shaping Danish domestic and international profiles in the context of a European political arena characterized by new forms of differentiation. The different levels of analysis are illustrated in Figure 1.1.

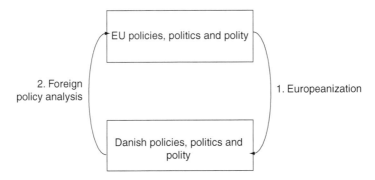

Figure 1.1 Denmark in a differentiated Europe.

Introducing four key dimensions

Using this line of reasoning, a formal level of interest aggregation can be identified, and Denmark's official strategies in the European political and economic arena will be spelled out in this book. However, the contributors go one step further in identifying and classifying more informal, unregulated and deliberative ways of pursuing interests, enacting identities and diffusing ideas in Europe. In order to do this, the book suggests a conceptual framework for understanding small state behaviour in the EU. Building on recent research on the challenges and opportunities of EU member states, four dimensions are outlined, enabling a comparison of the Danish experience as an EU member state across policy areas and institutions. These are:

1. *Autonomy vs. influence*: drawing upon ideas first developed in Kelstrup's *integration dilemma*, (Kelstrup 1990, 1992, 1993; Petersen 1998; Wivel 2005a) this dimension stresses that Danish actors and institutions, under the auspices of Danish EU full membership, constantly negotiate and chart a path that seeks to ensure that, on the one hand, Denmark is neither 'entrapped' within forms of integration that it does not want, (and thus would seek major reductions in Danish autonomy) nor is sufficiently 'isolated' outside the realms of key integration dialogues, thereby causing Danish influence to be peripheral or minimal, and Denmark to become 'isolated' from key discussions and decisions shaping the future of European integration.[6] In simple terms, Danish actors and institutions seek to balance the challenges to Danish autonomy and potential and real entrapment in further integration trajectories against the benefits of securing influence in the EU as a full Member State, which reduces possible isolation from key decisions that will affect Denmark's future. Of course, it should be noted that this is a conceptual tool and that, in reality, the autonomy vs. influence dimension is not a stark autonomy; there is a substantial grey area among and even within Danish perspectives and positions towards aspects of European integration, where Danish actors and institutions seek both autonomy and influence and balance entrapment and isolation considerations at one and the same time.

2. *Formal vs. informal channels of autonomy and influence*: this dimension encapsulates the recognition that Danish actors and institutions will utilize differing channels and forms in order to manage the aforementioned integration dilemma. In particular, Danish actors and institutions will pursue either or, most usually, in combination with formal channels and informal channels. To any member state, the ideal mix of formal and informal policy instruments varies with the institutional characteristics of the policy area in question as well as the particular competences and capabilities available to the state in question (Wivel 2010). In the context of this volume, formal channels include, among others, vertical aspects associated with downloading and uploading, such as Danish membership of official EU institutions

and bodies, Danish participation in the official cycles and processes of EU decision-making (like relations with, and participation in, the formal working groups and committees of the EU institutions) as well as national and subnational actions (like the development and delivery of national and subnational position papers associated with the transmitting of official Danish views to the EU institutions) in the Council of Ministers, European Council and even towards the ECJ. In addition, formal channels also include cross-loading dimensions, including official 'horizontal' discussions within Denmark among Danish actors and institutions, and official relations and contact between Danish actors and institutions horizontally with national and sub-national actors in other countries. Much of this can be associated with what Wolfgang Wessels calls participation in the 'legal constitution' of the EU (see Wessels 2001; Miles 2009). Alongside this, Danish actors and institutions may pursue informal channels, such as lobbying activities, off-the-record discussions, and informal negotiations (both vertically and horizontally) as part of intelligence gathering, interest formulation and articulation, and coalition building (part of what Wessels (2001) calls the 'living constitution' of the EU). In this way, this dimension links to how informal and formal channels can be used to help pursue both formal and informal pace-setting, fence-sitting and foot-dragging on the part of respective national and subnational actors towards respective EU questions and issues.

3 *Change vs. continuity*: traditionally, small states have safeguarded their interests by institutional binding of the great powers, restraining the actions of the strong and providing voice opportunities for the weak. Danish policy-makers saw these formal institutional safeguards primarily as instruments for defending national autonomy and often, therefore, the institutional status quo. However, the effectiveness of the binding strategy has gradually been undermined by increased intergovernmentalism (including increased legitimacy of informal ad hoc great power cooperation), a revised balance of power between EU institutions (challenging the position of the Commission), and the development of new policy areas thereby rewarding informal, multifaceted and proactive member state strategies (Grøn and Wivel 2011; Wivel 2005a). However, there is considerable variation across policy areas. The perspectives, attitudes and positions of Danish actors and institutions towards European integration are highly differentiated according to the respective aspect of European integration under consideration. Hence, within this dimension is an explicit recognition that Denmark is involved in a process of differentiated European integration that has two major impacts in relation to notions of continuity and change. First, there is an aspect of *assessment when it comes to change vs. continuity*, requiring Danish actors to assess and decide where European integration will incur 'change' upon Denmark and vice versa, and where this will simply represent continuity of Danish positions and of existing Danish policy. Hence, in this regard, and drawing upon 'logics of appropriateness', Danish resources, capabilities and

instruments may be incompatible with those at the EU level, leading potentially to Danish change in some instances, whereas in others, they may be compatible and thus represent more semblance of continuity for Denmark. Second, there is the aspect of *articulation when it come to change vs. continuity*, and here contributors will be focusing on where prior assessments have lead, or may lead to, change and/or continuity in the articulation of Danish perspectives, attitudes and policies upwards and downwards within the formal and informal channels of the EU decision-making system.

4 *Policy change vs. structural change*: this fourth dimension complements the prior dimension of change versus continuity by also seeking to acknowledge degrees and types of change in Denmark's relations with European integration. In particular, acknowledgement that assessments and articulation of change, (as previously described), may lead simply to changes in Danish policy positions (*policy change*) at either the supranational, national and sub-national levels, and that may affect one, some or all of the Danish menu of policy interests and preferences transmitted upwards and downwards within the EU system. Examples, of policy change, could include minor aspects, such as changes in Danish policy positions towards Europe 2020 or the EU Innovation Union, or even more instrumental policy change, such as the development and/or termination of EU policy domains; it may even include rather significant ones, such as changes in policy positions towards, say, Danish opt-outs relating to the EMU. In addition, assessment and acknowledgement of change may include more deep-seated *structural* change in Denmark's relationship with the EU, and this would signify where Denmark's relations with the EU have structurally altered, which would affect not just policy but also institutional dimensions of the EU. Aspects could include scenarios, whereby Denmark was to completely reject formal EU Treaties in national referenda that would mean that Denmark is entirely excluded from aspects of European integration. Of course, as the evaluations (such as the contribution of Adler-Nissen) included in this book will verify, the two aspects of policy and structural change are not mutually exclusive but are in fact highly inter-related; yet this dimension encapsulates the desire to be able to mark emphases in the forms and types of change affecting Denmark's relationship with the EU.

Hence, these four dimensional pairs of concepts do not represent dichotomies; instead they perhaps represent something closer to ideal-type ends of four continua. Thus guarding autonomy and maximizing influence coexists, and so do informal and formal channels of autonomy and influence, change and continuity and policy change and structural change. The interesting question is how they co-exist and if it is possible to identify different patterns of coexistence across policy areas and institutions.

The content of the book

The book focuses on the present and on the recent past of Denmark's relationship with the EU (since the end of the Cold War). Authors include references to the more distant past only when it is relevant for understanding the challenges, opportunities and politics of the present. A central goal of the book is to explore how the EU has influenced Denmark as well as the Danish influence on the EU, both formally and informally. In addition, the book uses the Danish case to illustrate how interesting patterns of differentiation unfold in the European political arena.

To fulfil these objectives the first and second chapters explain the volume's conceptual and theoretical set-up, positions it in relation to the existing literature in the field and explains the historical experience of Denmark in the EU. The existing literature on Europeanization, FPA and European integration is drawn upon to establish a heuristic framework that constitutes the framework for analysis in the following chapters.

Chapters 3 to 6 evaluate some of the most central policy areas affected by Danish EU membership: the internal market and agriculture as well as the three policy areas on which Denmark has obtained an opt-out: JHA, EMU and defence policy. It is argued that it is especially in these policy areas that one can obtain a deep understanding of Denmark in Europe as well as of Europe in Denmark. Furthermore, it is the study of these policy areas that will help us to understand the ways in which Denmark contributes to establishing a differentiated political space in Europe.

Chapters 7 to 10 explore how Denmark operates on the European political arena. Thus, the contributors adopt a so-called inside-out perspective. By focusing on the Danish policies and strategies in the Council of Ministers and in relation to the Commission and the Parliament, we get insight into the various ways in which a small state operates in a complex European political arena, inside and between European institutions. In addition, a chapter on Danish lobbyism in Brussels is included, to highlight the increasingly important function that private actors have in European policy-making. Again, a specific small state perspective is adopted to analyse these policy-processes on the margin.

Chapters 11 to 14 move attention to the effects of the EU on Danish and political and administrative processes and institutions. These include the construction of citizen's rights, parliamentary oversight and the Europeanization of legislation and administrative functions and structures. Through this outside-in perspective a number of discursive and material dimensions are identified. In addition, a chapter is included which pays particular attention to public opinion in Denmark and the main cleavages that have existed or have appeared over almost 40 years of EU membership.

Chapter 15 adopts FPA perspectives as a means of explaining the country's opt-outs and reflects on Denmark's future in the EU. In Chapter 16, Danish relations with the European Union are compared and discussed in the context of the different issue areas analysed in the book. This concluding chapter draws together notable observations included in the volume and, more specifically, discusses Danish participation as a small, possibly 'smart' state in an evolving differentiated EU. Particular attention is placed on reflecting on the potential for examining Danish relations with the EU in handling a 'differentiated integration dilemma'.

Notes

1 Thanks to Martin Marcussen for his contribution to a preliminary version of the ideas presented in this chapter and Knud Erik Jørgensen and Ian Manners for comments on an earlier draft.
2 The most prominent examples are Branner and Kelstrup (2000), Kelstrup (1992) and Larsen (2005).
3 Of course, it is contested as to whether any of the three areas can be labelled as 'theories' or even groups of theories in their own right. Various authors have for example, challenged the theoretical rigour of 'Europeanization' (see Bulmer 2007). Others (see Carlsnaes 2002) have challenged whether Foreign Policy Analysis (FPA) is merely a obsolete sub-field of International Relations (IR), while there has been a long-standing discussion over whether it is accurate at all to talk about 'theories' of European integration that are downsizing away from grand theorizing to more middle of the range conceptual ambitions (see Miles 2005a, 2011a). Nevertheless, all can be clearly identified as broad conceptual churches or schools of thought in the literature with potential overarching concepts that both provide some degree of coherence within, and between, these broad churches.
4 Miles has applied these concepts to the case of Sweden under the alternative titles of 'championed policy priorities' (pace-setting), normative policy priorities (fence-sitting) and policy dilemmas (foot-dragging) – see Miles (2001, 2005a).
5 For convenience, this book adopts the definition of 'differentiated integration' offered by Dyson and Sepos (2010a: 4); namely that:

> Differentiated integration is the process whereby European states, or sub-state units, opt to move at different speeds and/or towards different objectives with regard to common policies. It involves different formal and informal arrangements (hard and soft), inside or outside the EU treaty framework (membership and accesssion differentiation), alongside various differentiated forms of economic, trade and security relations). In this way relevant actors come to assume different rights and obligations and to share a distinct attitude towards the integration process – what is appropriate to do together, and who belongs with whom.

6 All member states experience an integration dilemma, but the integration dilemma of small member states is typically more severe than that of the bigger members, because big member states are in a better position to halt or even jeopardize the integration process by refusing to take part if they face initiatives perceived as contradictory to their national interests (Wivel 2005a).

2 Denmark's relation to the European Union
A history of dualism and pragmatism

Morten Kelstrup

Introduction

Denmark's relations with the EU have been influenced by a basic dilemma between, on the one hand, a desire to seek the preservation of national autonomy and, on the other hand, the pursuance of economic and political interests through participation in the EU.[1] As a result, Danish policy towards the EU has been characterized by different ways of managing this dilemma, utilizing mainly different forms of dualistic policies and pragmatic adaption when and where necessary. This Danish dilemma in relation to the EU can be said to be a Danish variant of the so-called '*integration dilemma*'. The integration dilemma can theoretically be described as:

> [t]he dilemma which an actor, possibly a state, experiences when it is confronted with a new important step towards further integration. The situation might be that it has to choose between *either* at the one hand participating in the more intensified integration (with the possible risk of being 'entrapped', being forced to accept decisions which it would otherwise reject) *or* at the other hand rejecting the new integration step (with the risk of being 'abandoned', left outside the integration process or losing influence within this).
> (Kelstrup 2000a: 431)[2]

It could be said that Denmark has been reluctant towards participation in, and the prospect of, supranational political integration, but also not interested in being left outside international and European cooperation, especially not from economic integration; and therefore has experienced the integration dilemma in a rather severe form.

This chapter provides a brief historical overview of Denmark's relationship to the European integration process. It shows how there has been a persistent dilemma between autonomy and influence, which also lies behind the Danish opt-outs.[3] However, the interpretation on the basis of the integration dilemma is not used in any mechanical way. External and internal developments have formed the ways in which Denmark has lived with and modified the dilemma, and there have been important changes over time. Danes are today much more positive to the EU than earlier, and Denmark is now solidly integrated in to the EU in spite of the Danish reservations.

Historical background of Denmark's EU membership and the main phases in Danish membership[4]

Denmark gave a relatively low priority to its European policy in the first decades following the end of the Second World War in 1945 (Petersen 2004; Branner 2000). Denmark had a long tradition of being a small, adaptive and neutral state, and the main preference of Danish politicians after the war was to reconstitute Denmark as an independent and democratic state, which could participate in a liberal world economy and in further international cooperation. The dominant policy was to strive for an open and peaceful world, and the Danish post-war governments were eager to participate in the new international organizations, i.e. the UN-system. In continuation of former Danish neutrality, the government had a clear preference for keeping an all-European option open. Yet, the emergence of the Cold War undermined this policy. Consequential to its Western orientation, Denmark, in 1949, chose to become a member of the Atlantic Alliance and to integrate its defence within the North Atlantic Treaty Organization (NATO). Reminiscences of Denmark's preference for broad European cooperation and avoidance of supranational organizations can be found in later Danish policies, i.e. in Denmark's somewhat reserved policy within NATO, in the decisions to join the United Kingdom in applying for EC membership in 1961 and 1967, in Denmark's participation in European Free Trade Association (EFTA) when the broadening of the EC proved impossible and in Denmark's participation in the failing attempt to establish a stronger Nordic cooperation (NORDEK – Nordiskt Ekonomiskt Samarbete) at the end of the 1960s.

Dominant in Denmark's policy in this period was the decision-making elite's emphasis on economic advantages and concrete results, and a Danish disinclination for political, in particular supranational, EC integration. Because of economic interest in access to a greater market, not least for agricultural products, the Danish government in 1971 decided to apply once more for membership of the EC together with the United Kingdom, Ireland and Norway. The decision was domestically controversial, and in 1972 it was decided to hold a referendum on the Danish membership. The heated debate about consequences of a Danish membership of the EC showed a strong cleavage between, on the one hand, the dominant, pragmatic and economic-based policy and, on the other hand, Danish Eurosceptics who mainly argued in identity terms, seeing participation in the EC as a threat towards Danish national autonomy and sovereignty. The referendum in 1972 had an exceptionally high turnout: 90.1 per cent, with 63.3 per cent voting yes to Danish EC membership (see Table 2.1). Denmark became a full member of the EC from 1 January 1973.

The first phase of Denmark's membership of the EC can be said to last from full membership in 1973 to 1985. In accordance with the pre-accession debate, Denmark joined the EC with a highly selective identification with EC goals.

Table 2.1 Danish referenda on EC/EU questions

Date	Topic	Participation (%)	Yes (%)	No (%)
2 October 1972	Danish Membership	90.1	63.3	36.7
27 February 1986	Single European Act	75.8	56.2	43.8
2 June 1992	The Maastricht Treaty	83.1	49.3	50.7
18 May 1993	The Maastricht Treaty and the Edinburgh Agreement	86.5	56.7	43.3
28 May 1998	The Amsterdam Treaty	74.8	55.1	44.9
28 September 2000	Adherence to the Euro	87.6	46.8	53.2

Source: EU-Oplysningen 2006a.

Most leading politicians advocated membership, and they, together with the Danish administration, focused almost entirely on the economic advantages of joining, including not least the benefits for Danish agriculture, which – in contrast to EFTA – was included in the EC. Denmark was sceptical about supranational and federalist elements in the EC and had a clear preference for intergovernmental structures. Denmark's priority in regard to security and defence was that these matters should be handled within NATO and not in the EC. Thus, from the beginning of membership, Denmark pursued a reluctant EC-policy. It could be said that the stagnation in the 1970s, and first part of the 1980s, of the EC's plans for faster integration helped Denmark in pursuing its policy of economically fast, but politically slow, integration without major problems. An exception was the introduction in 1978 of direct election to the European Parliament (EP). Denmark was, in principle, against this reform, but accepted it on largely pragmatic grounds. The first EP direct election in 1979 demonstrated clearly that there still was a strong Euro-scepticism in Denmark.[5] In general, Denmark's policy toward the EC in this period was characterized by 'limited engagement', 'fragmentation' and 'pragmatism' (Branner 2000). The many problems in the EC's own integration path in this period weakened the supranational pressure on Denmark, and this made it possible for Denmark to follow a pragmatic adaptation without major problems at this time.

The second phase of Denmark's membership of the EC lasted from 1986 until the Danish referendum on the Maastricht Treaty in 1992. The EU experienced a 'new dynamism' in the mid 1980s, partly because of Jacques Delors' new leadership of the Commission and partly because the détente in the late 1980s created a new and more favourable international context. The prospects for a more open Europe had important effects in Denmark. The EC's plans for the Single European Market (SEM) in the mid 1980s provoked Danish Euro-scepticism and led to a Danish referendum in 1986. The result was, though, that 56.2 per cent voted *for* an acceptance of what in Denmark was referred to as the 'EC package' (the Single European Act (SEA) and the formalization of the European Political Cooperation (EPC)) and thus for an acceptance of some supranational elements.

On the basis of the referendum in 1986 and under influence from the international détente there was, in particular from 1988, an emerging consensus among the bigger political parties (The Conservative Party, The Liberal Party, the Social Liberal Party and the Social Democratic Party) around a more positive Danish attitude towards the EC's development. This was, in particular, due to a change of attitude within the Social Democratic Party. The single market plans in the 1980s constituted, in the view of the Social Democratic Party (and also of the Social Liberal Party and parts of the Socialist People's Party) an important societal change that established new international conditions (Haahr 1993). Formulated and somewhat simplified, it was recognized that in a more globalized and neoliberal world, market forces could not be regulated sufficiently on a national basis. This led these parties, in contrast to earlier, to be somewhat more favourable to European regulation and to support the introduction of majority voting in new areas of the EC. The new domestic agreement between the Conservative-Liberal Government and the opposition formed an important part of the background for the acceptance in 1991 of the Maastricht Treaty by the major political parties. In accordance with one of the themes outlined in this book, there is evidence of a direct interplay between Danish *actors* and the changing EU *context*.

Also in this period, Denmark's priority was focused on securing advantages stemming from economic integration within the EC. But by the end of the 1980s, the growing political will within Denmark to take part in the political part of the EC project resulted in there being near unanimity among the government and the opposition on a relatively pro-integrationist policy in the negotiations up to the Maastricht Treaty. The main interpretation was that Denmark should seek economic advantages and influence in the EU, and that the problems related to autonomy and Danish Eurosceptics should not be decisive. Yet, the Maastricht Treaty involved so many supranational elements that a referendum was necessary.

The third phase of Denmark's membership of the EU was the rather short, but decisive, development from the referendum on the Maastricht Treaty (2 June 1992) until the new referendum on the Maastricht Treaty and the Edinburgh Agreement (18 May 1993). The outcome of the referendum on the Maastricht Treaty in 1992 was 50.7 per cent voting 'no'. The referendum result was a shock to the Danish 'establishment' (not only to the major parties, but also to major interest groups, i.e. Danish industry, Danish agriculture and the major part of Danish labour, which had supported a 'yes' vote). In a basic way, the result indicated that there was insufficient popular backing behind the new and relatively more pro-European policy of the Danish government. The referendum was followed by a short period of extreme confusion, since it was very unclear what the alternatives were; although what was evident was that most of the population perceived the possible prospect of having to leave the EC/EU as very threatening. Domestically it was considered important to reach some kind of compromise that would include at least some of the Eurosceptics. The result was the so-called national compromise of October 1992. This was an agreement between all of the important parties, including the Eurosceptic Socialist People's Party. The compromise formulated a Danish EC/EU policy, which, on the one hand, would accept the Maastricht Treaty yet, on the other hand, specified four 'reservations' or 'opt-outs', which should be accepted (and were also formally binding) by the EC member states (see Table 2.2). The negotiations with other EC states after the 'no' vote were also notable in demonstrating the great flexibility shown from the EC-side. Acceptance by the EC partners of the Danish reservations was secured at the December 1992 European Council Summit in Edinburgh. A new referendum was held in May 1993 on the combined Maastricht Treaty and Edinburgh Agreement, including the four Danish reservations, and 56.7 per cent of the Danes voted 'yes' in this 1993 plebiscite.

The 'no' in 1992 made it politically necessary to change Denmark's shortly held, yet more active, EC policy from the last part of the earlier period. The 'no' showed, it could be said, that it had been an illusion to think that Denmark had moved beyond the integration dilemma. The new codification of the Danish policy in the national compromise marked an important step towards a balance between, on the one hand, an economically based policy of continued participation in a more integrated EU, and, on the other hand, a policy which preserved at least a 'formal' autonomy in selective areas. The compromise was an agreement between all major parties, importantly also including the Socialist People's Party, which had been advocating a 'no' at the Maastricht referendum. The compromise included an 'active part' that laid a foundation for a Danish integration policy, which accorded high priority to democracy, openness, subsidiarity (in its Danish interpretation: nærhed), environmental concerns and employment. It included the four Danish reservations: four policy areas in which Denmark should avoid participation: the single currency, defence cooperation, common citizenship, and supranational cooperation in JHA. These reservations have since, because they were included in the referendum in 1993, gained a special status as a kind of 'dogma' within the confines of Denmark's EU policy:[6] as they

Table 2.2 The Danish opt-outs from the Treaty on the European Union

Area of European co-operation	
Economic and Monetary Union	Denmark does not participate in the euro, the third phase of Economic and Monetary Union
Common Defence	Denmark does not participate in the elaboration and implementation of decisions and actions that have defence implications.
Justice and Home Affairs	Denmark only participates in EU judicial cooperation at an intergovernmental level.
Union Citizenship	Denmark holds that union citizenship is a supplement to national citizenship and not a replacement. (The Danish opt-out on citizenship has been embodied in the Amsterdam Treaty).

Source: EU-Oplysningen 2012a.

were accepted in a referendum, there has been a broad and solid agreement between the parties that they can only be changed through a new referendum. While the 1992 'no' vote stopped the more positive and active Danish EU policy, one might claim that the national compromise and the subsequent referendum on 'Maastricht and Edinburgh' in 1993 sedimented Denmark's status into that of a 'member with reservations'. The referendum on the Maastricht Treaty made the integration dilemma very visible, and it is, in particular, in the period after this referendum that we can refer to a 'dualism' not only in attitudes in Denmark towards the EU but also in Denmark's relation to the EU. The subsequent policies developed the dualism of, at one and the same time, pursuing advantages and influence through membership and preserving Danish autonomy, at least formally, in relation to special positions and, not least, in relation to Danish voters.

The fourth phase can be said to last from 1993–2001, i.e. from the referendum in 1993 (and the formation of the EU the same year) and until important external and internal changes in 2001. The basis for the Danish policy in this period was the agreement reached in the national compromise. This represented, as described, a delicate balance between a policy of continued participation in the EU and a policy of reservation, not least oriented towards calming Danish Euro-scepticism. Euro-scepticism in Denmark had become stronger after, and directly because of, the victory in 1992 but subsequently, the Danish Eurosceptics split into two movements: The People's Movement against the EU (which still wanted Denmark to leave the EU) and the June Movement (which was named after June 1992 and had a sceptical EU-policy, based on the Danish reservations, as their main policy). In hindsight it is clear that there were, during this phase, two very different interpretations of Danish reservations (Dansk Udenrigspolitisk Institut 2000: 261). One was that the reservations gave Denmark a 'time out' to allow for the possibility of cancelling the reservations at a later date (perhaps one by one, depending on circumstances). This interpretation was clearly supported by the Liberal Party and the Conservative Party, and at least in part by the government (which since 1998 was led by Poul Nyrup Rasmussen and composed of the Social Democratic Party and the Social Liberal Party). The other interpretation, which was supported by the Socialist People's Party and the two 'no' movements, understood the reservations as representing permanent conditions that underpin and shape Denmark's participation in the EU. The reservations were, according to this interpretation, not regarded as something temporary that could easily be changed, but rather as a basis for Denmark's general policy within the Union.

Basically, after 1993, Denmark returned to the earlier policy of limited engagement, fragmentation and pragmatism, and this illustrates the key dimension of 'change and continuity' in Danish policy outlined in the Introduction of the volume. The reservations are per se an indication of limited engagement. The reservation in regard to defence (wanting defence issues to be treated in NATO) can also be seen as a policy of fragmentation. The construction of the national compromise, which was a compromise not only between parties, but also between orientations, can in itself be seen as a very pragmatic approach. Yet, the compromise in the national compromise was not completely stable, as indicated already above in the description of the two different interpretations. From the mid 1990s, the government of Poul Nyrup Rasmussen introduced new and more active elements in the Danish EU policy. The government stressed that they accepted the four reservations, yet within the confines of this restriction, Danish involvement in EU affairs went nearly as far as it could in terms of representing active participation within the EU. In 1996, the government accepted, with the support of most parties, Denmark's participation in the Schengen Agreement, and in 1996–1998, it took active part in the negotiations of the Amsterdam Treaty. In 1998, a referendum was held on Danish acceptance of the Amsterdam Treaty, resulting in 55.1 per cent voting 'yes'. The campaign had this time given priority to political aspects, and the victory for the pro-EU parties was understood as a confirmation of the government's more active EU-policy. It could be suggested that the period from 1993 to 2001 was marked by a dualist policy, which was at least formally oriented at preserving Danish autonomy in selected areas, especially with reference to the four reservations and which, at the same time, particularly in the later part of the period, tried to maximize Denmark's influence in the EU.

The re-emergence in the mid 1990s of an active Danish engagement in the EU led the government, under Nyrup Rasmussen, to attempt, in 2000, to remove the Danish reservation about non-participation in the euro through a new referendum. The polls before the referendum indicated a clear majority favouring those parties supporting full Danish participation in the euro. Yet, a heated debate was mobilized once again by the national oriented Eurosceptics, and the result of the referendum was that 53.2 per cent voted 'no' to full Danish euro-participation. This was a major defeat for the pro-EU parties that resonated because it, in some ways, represented a repetition of the situation in 1992, although it was not this time necessary to enter into a renegotiation of Denmark's position. The referendum re-established the former balance between pragmatic participation and a reserved policy towards further integration, mainly focused on a formal respect for the four Danish reservations.

The fifth phase in Denmark's relation to the EU runs from 2001 and until the time of writing of this article. The changes in 2001 were both external and internal. The international scene altered, i.e. because of the terrorist attack on the US in September 2001 (that led to a new priority within security policy), and because EU (and euro) cooperation entered a new phase. In Denmark, an important change took place in the fall of 2001 when a Liberal-Conservative minority government led by Prime Minister Anders Fogh Rasmussen came to power with the parliamentary support of the Danish People's Party. The new government claimed that it would pursue a more active Danish EU policy. This must be seen in the light of the traditional pro-EU-position of the Liberal Party. Yet, the government relied on the parliamentary support of the EU-sceptical party, the Danish People's Party. This soon led to a more defensive policy. In the fall of 2002, the priorities of the Danish EU Council Presidency were focused on enlarging the EU and not on intensification of EU's institutional integration. In 2004, the EU's continuing pursuit of agreeing and ratifying a new constitutional treaty enabled the government to return to an old, well-known, consensus-orientation within its EU policy. All major parties (i.e. all parties in the Folketing except the Danish People's Party and the Unity List – the Red–Green Alliance) in November 2004 signed a new political agreement on 'Denmark in the enlarged EU', which specified common views relating to an EU Constitutional Treaty (EU-Oplysningen 2004). The agreement, which in the press was called the 'new national compromise', signified that the government, when confronted with new attempts at further EU integration, was, once again, caught in a tension between a desire for active participation and influence in the EU and the need to preserve a high degree of Danish autonomy (at least symbolically) towards the Danish population.

During the Anders Fogh Rasmussen governments (2001–2009), the so-called 'active' Danish EU policy developed into a mainly rhetorical position. In the more securitized international context after 2001, Denmark actively supported American and British intervention in Iraq, and in opposition to major EU countries such as Germany and France. In some areas (for instance environment and climate), Denmark accepted a high degree of 'Europeanization' of national policies (see Introduction of this volume). In other areas, in particular with regard to asylum policies, the government was reluctant to accept European regulation. In areas of 'identity politics', the Liberal-Conservative Government partly adapted to the nationalism of the Danish People's Party. It could be said that the de facto response to the persisting integration dilemma was partly a differentiation of policies, and partly the adoption of a rather passive EU policy. The government's declared ambition of having a new referendum on a cancellation of all the four reservations was modified with regard to the reservation on JHA, and a referendum was postponed until 'the time was ripe'. Of course, an explanation for this development was that the Liberal-Conservative Government was in cooperation with the Eurosceptic Danish People's Party to form a relatively stable parliamentary majority. This difference between the government and its parliamentary support party as regards their views on EU integration made it rather uncomfortable for the government to have, and further, domestic debates on EU policies; so EU policy was given low priority by the Liberal-Conservative Government.

As regards the negotiations about the Constitutional Treaty, and from the perspective of 'uploading', the primary Danish priority was to ensure that the Danish reservations were preserved. In 2005, the government prepared for a referendum on the Constitutional Treaty that would also combine with holding a referendum on modifications to the Danish reservations. Yet this was abandoned when it became clear that the Constitutional Treaty was rejected in the Netherlands and France. Later it was decided *not* to have a referendum on the Lisbon Treaty. In 2008, as it became obvious that Denmark, as a result of the Lisbon Treaty, would have increased problems continuing with the reservations, there was a renewed ambition to hold a future referendum on at least two of the reservations (the opt-outs on JHA and on Denmark's participation in EU's common defence policy).[7] Yet the situation – and also the attitudes of the public – changed during the summer of 2008 because of a ruling of the ECJ in the so-called 'Metock case'. This ECJ ruling challenged Danish policy towards foreigners (family reunification). The dominant response from the government, and also from the Social Democratic Party and the Socialist People's Party, was to support a national policy towards family reunification, although Denmark had to adapt again in line with EU rules in the end. Clearly, the prevailing interpretation was that a referendum on the reservations could not be won against the Eurosceptic position of the Danish People's Party. Prime Minister Lars Løkke Rasmussen, who in April 2009 followed Anders Fogh Rasmussen as leader of the Liberal-Conservative Government, continued a policy which, on the one hand, declared that it gave high priority to Danish participation in the EU, but which on the other hand, accommodated the Eurosceptic viewpoints of the Danish People's Party, not least in regard to policy towards foreigners. The agreement between the government and the Danish People's Party in summer 2011 on the reintroduction of permanent border controls, an agreement that was part of a much greater compromise on economic policies between these parties, demonstrates clear evidence of the influence of the Danish People's Party upon Denmark's EU policy.

The major picture is that the Danish EU policy in the phase after 2001 has been a low priority for government and been dominated by considerations of domestic politics. The actual policies have been differentiated, in some areas following the EU and in others being reserved towards Europeanization. The tendencies to become dualistic in the sense of having some declared goals, but other practices, have grown. The government has, in its declarations, retained its positive attitude towards the EU and has declared that Denmark should remove the reservations (after a new referendum). Yet, in reality, the government hardly took any initiatives in the EU, and there was not a serious policy for getting rid of the Danish reservations (see also Chapter 15). The main reason for this has, of course, been that government's wish to please its parliamentary support party, the Danish People's Party. In several cases, the government agreed with the Danish People's Party on a stronger policy towards family reunification even when it had, later, to adapt to the EU's rules for free movement. One might say that the EU issue has been severely politicized, but also that the government – because of the parliamentary situation – pursued a policy that could prevent further politicization.[8]

Long-term trends in Denmark's relation to the EU and Danish dualism

The main perspective in this analysis of Denmark's relation to the EU has been that Denmark, on the one hand, has had a basic economic interest in participation in the EC/EU, but, on the other hand, that the Danish attitudes towards the EC/EU have been divided between a pragmatic orientation (which has been positive towards Danish participation) and a more Eurosceptic orientation that places greater emphasis on the preservation of Danish identity and autonomy. Yet, the perspective that Denmark has experienced permanent political problems in its relationship to the EU should not hide the fact that rather much has changed over the years of Denmark's relationship with the EC/EU. Of course, this is partly due to: (1) developments in the EU itself, and partly due to; (2) other changes in the international context, and also; (3) changes in Denmark. This chapter only offers a brief summary of the important changes.

Prevailing, yet changed economic interest in EU-participation

Denmark had a very strong interest in becoming a member of the EC in the late 1960s and the beginning of the 1970s. This was at that time primarily because of the importance of securing access to the European market for Danish agriculture. Denmark secured such access, and for many years was a net recipient in the EU, mainly because of the EU's agricultural policy, and EU payments to Danish agriculture. Since then, agriculture has lost relative importance both in Denmark and within the EU's budget. In 2000, Denmark became a net contributor to the EU's budget, and in 2008, Denmark paid the fifth highest net-contribution to the EU's budget in percentages of BNP per capita. The Danish economic interest in participation in the EU has not, though, diminished. Denmark's dependence of the European market has actually increased. EU expansion with the eurozone has meant that Denmark, although not a member, has seen its primary interest as being to secure a special arrangement with the eurozone that would link rather closely the Danish 'kroner' to the euro. Danish willingness, in spring 2011, to participate in the EU's permanent rescue fund not only represents active 'uploading' of Danish preferences to the EU, but also demonstrates that Denmark pursues an economic policy that seeks to have, and has, close links to the eurozone. Thus, the character of Denmark's economic interest in being in the EU has changed over time, although Denmark still places a high economic priority on EU membership.

Continued, but weakened and changed Euro-scepticism

Denmark had, as has been shown, a very strong Euro-scepticism in the beginning of the 1970s. As mentioned, the People's Movement against the EU secured more than 21 per cent of the votes in the first 1979 EP direct election, and had four out of 15 Danish MEPs (the results of Danish election to the EP are contained in Table 2.3). This was remarkable, not only because of the size of the representation, but also because it was a representation of a movement and not of an ordinary, national political party. Generalizing, it could be said that Danish Euro-scepticism has been politically strong during the entire period of Danish membership. It has – at least compared to Euro-scepticism in other EU countries – and, to an exceptional degree, been based on national identity and sovereignty (Sørensen 2007a). Yet, several observations are important: (1) the political movements of Eurosceptics have lost influence in later years. The representation

Table 2.3 Results of Danish elections to the European Parliament

	1979	1984	1989	1994	1999	2004	2009
The Social Democratic Party	21.9 (3)	19.5 (3)	23.3 (4)	15.8 (3)	16.5 (3)	32.6 (5)	21.5 (4)
The Social Liberal Party	3.3 (0)	3.1 (0)	2.8 (0)	8.5 (1)	9.1 (1)	6.4 (1)	4.3 (0)
The Conservative Party	14.1 (2)	20.8 (4)	13.3 (2)	17.7 (3)	8.5 (1)	11.3 (1)	12.7 (1)
Centre Democrats	6.2 (1)	6.6 (1)	8.0 (2)	0.9 (0)	3.5 (0)	–	–
The Socialist People's Party	4.7 (1)	9.2 (2)	9.1 (2)	8.6 (1)	7.1 (1)	7.9 (1)	15.9 (2)
The June Movement	–	–	–*	15.2 (2)	16.1 (3)	9.1 (1)	2.4 (0)
The People's Movement against the EU	21.0 (4)	20.8 (4)	18.9 (4)*	10.3 (2)	7.3 (1)	5.2 (1)	7.2 (1)
The Danish People's Party	–	–	–	–	5.8 (1)	6.8 (1)	15.3 (2)
The Christian Democrats	1.8 (0)	2.7 (0)	2.7 (0)	1.1 (0)	2.0 (0)	1.3 (0)	–
The Liberal Party	14.5 (3)	12.5 (2)	16.6 (3)	19 (4)	23.4 (5)	19.4 (3)	20.2 (3)
Progress Party	5.8 (1)	3.5 (0)	5.3 (0)	2.9 (0)	0.7 (0)	–	–
Liberal Alliance	–	–	–	–	–	–	0.6 (0)
Participation (%)	47.8	52.4	46.2	52.9	50.5	47.9	59.5

Source: EU-Oplysningen 2009.

Notes
The figures show the percentage of votes and the numbers of seats are in parentheses. The Single-Tax Party and the Leftist Socialists have been left out of the table due to the fact that two parties only participated in respectively one and two of the elections.
* Three of the four elected representatives from the People's Movement against the EU chose to join the June Movement in the period.

of the movements in the EP is now down to one representative (out of 13), and one of the movements, the June Movement, dissolved itself in 2009. Euroscepticism has gradually become less important and has, to a large degree, been absorbed by the Danish People's Party; and (2) in addition, the content of Danish Euro-scepticism has changed in character. In the first decades, it was mainly the leftist parties that were against the EU. Denmark did not – as other EU states – have a Eurosceptic party on the right of the political spectrum. In the 1990s, the Socialist People's Party gradually moved to become an EU-positive party. In the same period, the Danish People's Party, in spite of its early roots in the ultra-right and EU-positive Progress Party, became a major right-wing party to represent national or even defensive nationalist Euroscepticism.

In general a more positive attitude towards the EU

The strong articulation of Euro-scepticism in Denmark might give a misleading picture as regards the overall state of the general attitudes of Danes towards the EU. Several analyses show that, over the years, there has been a growing acceptance by the Danish population of the EU (Andersen 2002; Togeby *et al.* 2003). Figure 2.1 shows, according to the Eurobarometer, how the Danes over time have increasingly accepted the EU and, in fact, score well *above* the EU average. In Danish debates, it is hardly ever argued as a serious policy that Denmark should leave the EU. Even for Danish Eurosceptics, the prevailing view seems to be – alongside all kinds of criticism – that Denmark should stay in the EU.

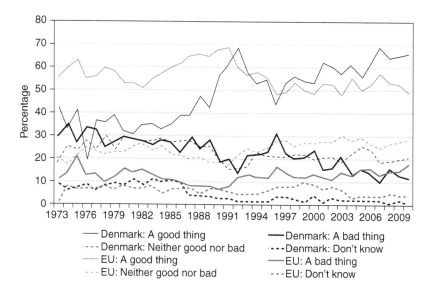

Figure 2.1 Danish attitudes to EU membership (source: European Commission 2012a).

A practice of referenda in EU-matters, but a 'lock-in' as regards the Danish reservations

Denmark is the country in the EU that has held the most referenda in relation to EU-policy (six in all – see Table 2.1). As described above, two of these (in 1992 and 2000) resulted in majorities for the 'no-side'. One of the reasons for the numerous Danish referenda is specifically legal, i.e. that paragraph 20 of the Danish constitution prescribes that under certain conditions a referendum shall be held when authority is transferred to an international body. Yet, it should also be noted that the 1986 referenda was *not* obligatory. In general, it can be claimed that, in Denmark, a special legal *and* political tradition concerning referenda on EU matters has developed. Not least, it was the very difficult situation in 1992–1993 that contributed to this development. The acceptance of the four Danish reservations in the referendum in 1993 can be said to have established a political obligation to respect these reservations until they are changed through new referenda. In some ways, and reinforced by the experience from 2000, this has created a 'lock-in' situation in which it has become very difficult and decidedly risky for any government to try to change the reservations (see also Chapter 15).

It is no exaggeration that, since 1993, the four Danish reservations have played an important – perhaps even dominating – role in relation to Danish debates about the EU. The 'no' in 1992 and the subsequent national compromise represent a deep and comprehensive politicization of Denmark's relation to the EU. Since then, there has been a kind of 'stop-go' evolution as regards the politicization of Danish EU policy. Around the times of EU referenda and the EP direct elections, there has been heated public debate about EU issues (and in particular about the appropriateness of the Danish reservations). Between these events, there has been very little debate, and European issues have hardly had any role in normal parliamentary elections. Indeed in the last decade, there has been a marked tendency *not* to discuss Denmark's EU policy.[9] The reason for this has, of course, been the special constellation operating within Danish domestic politics in which the government has depended on the parliamentary support of the Danish People's Party.

Conclusions

The general picture of Denmark's relationship with the EU in the last four decades indicates a remarkable continuity, in spite of the underlying changes. Denmark has, in all the years, had strong economic interests in EU-participation, although the character of Denmark's interests has altered. During most of the history of Danish EU membership, there has been a majority in the population with a positive attitude towards Danish participation in further European integration; yet, there has also persistently been a strongly articulated Eurosceptic minority that has successfully presented itself within, and in terms of, mainly defensive, national discourses. The governments have tried to handle or adapt to these tensions in different ways. One form of pragmatic adaption was the national compromise in 1992–1993. Another form was the attempt in the 1990s to pursue what could be called an offensive kind of dualistic policy: the policy which, at one and the same time, is active in the EU and still respects the reservations. Since 2001, the government has mainly followed a more passive form of dualism: that of declaring that it adheres to the EU principles, but in practice (not least under influence of the nationalistic policy of the Danish People's Party) pursues other policies either actively or through lack of implementation. Thus, in relation to the Danish public, the government has followed a rather strong national policy; in particular with regard to the policy towards foreigners, while it at the same time has claimed that its policies are within the general rules of the EU.[10]

The main interpretation presented in this chapter has been that Denmark's policy towards the EC/EU, its complexity and numerous tensions, can be understood on the basis of the 'integration dilemma'. Yet, in thinking about the integration dilemma, it should also be recognized that we are – normally – *not* dealing with a 'real' dilemma in the sense that the actor, here Denmark, has to choose *either* participation *or* withdrawal. The very basic reason for this is that the EU is a complex and flexible system of multi-level governance, which does not push the states towards an either/or choice in relation to influence/autonomy tensions (Kelstrup 2000b). Rather, the most interesting aspect in applying such thinking about the integration dilemma is to use it to describe *ways in which a state can either avoid the dilemma, live with it, 'manage' it or even transform it.* After all, Denmark has – in spite of many difficulties – managed to live with the integration dilemma for a rather long time. One might interpret the Danish reservations, the Danish policy of 'partial' active engagement in positive integration[11] and Danish offensive and defensive dualism as attempts to avoid the dilemma in any radical form. The basic dilemma has not led the Danish state to a clear choice of either full participation or non-participation. Rather, the choices have – sometimes even in very creative and/or contradictory ways – been postponed and diluted.

A special way of avoiding the integration dilemma is to pursue a policy of dualism. Dualism can be understood as the simultaneous pursuance of two (or more) different policies that – at least in important aspects – are in conflict with each other, but where the conflicts or contradictions are hidden or blurred. A typical dualism is a formal and declaratory adherence to specific policies, but lack of implementation of these policies.[12] Another form is discrepancies between policy formulations towards different scenes, for instance with some formulations on the EU-scene, but other formulations oriented towards the domestic political scene. A third form refers to formulations of policies, which are in (hidden) conflict with already established treaty obligations.

Basically, the integration dilemma can be used to understand the different forms of dualism within Danish EU policy. Denmark has clearly – also when reservations were formulated – been very afraid of being 'abandoned', and being left out of further integration. Yet, on the other hand, there has also, since the early 1970s, been a fear of being 'entrapped' in the EU, of being forced to accept decisions that are seen not as produced by Danish democracy, but through a decision-making process in which the Danes only have little influence. The various Danish governments have – in the different phases of Danish membership of the EC/EU – tried to 'manoeuvre' as regards to the integration dilemma. In the first phase (1973–1985) there was a rather strong Euro-scepticism, but the relative stagnation in the integration process made it possible to 'live with' the tension. In the second phase (1986–1992) the demands for EC participation were intensified (i.e. because of the 'new dynamism'). Danish policy in the late 1980s could be seen as an attempt to place greater priority on participation in the (supranational) integration process. Yet, the referendum in 1992 was a manifest sign that scepticism was very strong and thus can be seen as a 'correction'. In the third phase (1992–1993) some balance was found in the national compromise and confirmed with the referendum in 1993.[13] In the fourth phase (1993–2001) there was a dualism in the interpretations of the four reservations, and there we might also see what this author has called an *active dualism* in the late 1990s. Then in the present phase (2001–to the present) the way of handling the integration dilemma has changed. The politicization of the policy towards foreigners, the so-called 'value policy' of the governments since 2001 and the special parliamentary situation (in which past governments have been dependent on the Danish People's Party), has resulted in a high priority being given to considerations of domestic politics. Thus, it seems that the government has gone a long way towards pursuing a kind of *passive dualism*, particularly in relation to its policy towards foreigners, claiming that it adheres to the EU's rules, but in practice – in certain areas – following policies of non implementation.

Perspectives considering Denmark's relation to the EU are, of course, very dependent both on the EU's development and on future domestic politics in Denmark. On the one hand, when the EU absorbs the full consequences of the Lisbon Treaty, the problems related to the Danish reservations, in particular the reservation in JHA, is almost certain to increase. In addition, a more effective EU might well create greater problems for the different kinds of Danish dualism. On the other hand, if the EU continues to be in crisis, this will most likely make it easier for Denmark to continue its special 'balance' (and different dualisms) in regard to participation in the EU. Domestic political developments in Denmark might also have a decisive influence. If nationalist issues and traditional populism continues to have an important role in shaping public debate in Denmark, it will be very difficult for any Danish government to give a high priority to EU policies and to transform traditional and national Euro-scepticism in the country. Yet, if there is a public debate that can focus on future challenges – for Denmark and the EU – and avoid traditional populism, it might be possible to define and pursue an EU-policy which more openly places Denmark as a critical, but also active, participant in the future Europe.

Notes

1 To simplify the text, the term of 'EU', when nothing else is specified, is used to cover the European Community (EC) as well as the EU as appropriate.
2 The integration dilemma has some parallel to the security dilemma in alliance politics (Snyder 1984). For discussions of the integration dilemma see Kelstrup (1993, 2000b, 2006), Mourtizen and Wivel (2005), Petersen (1998) and Wivel (2005a).
3 By focusing on the importance of autonomy and influence factors on Danish perspectives, this chapter addresses one of the key thematic dimensions outlined in the Introduction of this volume.
4 Other studies of Denmark's historical relationship with the EU include Branner and Kelstrup (2000), Hansen (2002), Petersen (2004), Sørensen (2007b), and Kelstrup *et al.* (2008).
5 The People's Movement against the EC received 21 per cent of the votes and secured four of the Danish parliamentary members in the first European Parliament (out of 15 Danish members), cf. Table 2.3.
6 These comments also highlight how the compromise allowed for a potential realignment of the capabilities and instruments underpinning Danish positions towards the EU – aspects also accorded importance in the Introduction of this volume.
7 The Danish Institute of International Studies published a report on the developments since 2000 on the Danish opt-outs (Dansk Institut for Internationale Studier 2008). This was designed to be in preparation for a new referendum that never materialized.
8 Because of the dualism between, on the one hand EU membership and, on the other hand, a very nationalistic policy for the Danish People's Party, the government and administration have been engaged in the rather problematic implementation of a series of EU directives on family reunification (see, for instance, Bøegh-Lervang and Madum 2010).
9 An exception was the debate in the summer of 2008 on the ruling of the ECJ in the Metock case.
10 The latest example of this kind of dualism is that the Liberal-Conservative Government (in May 2011) agreed with the Danish People's Party that Denmark shall reintroduce border controls. This was celebrated by the Danish People's Party as a historic victory. Yet, at the same time, the Danish Minister of Integration declared that the intended border control would not violate the rules within the Schengen Agreement.
11 See Introduction to this volume.
12 A dualistic policy could be seen as a special kind of Europeanization.
13 Whether the national compromise was in itself a kind of dualism that contained internal contradictions might also be worthy of discussion.

3 The Internal Market Policy and the Common Agricultural Policy

The normalization of EU policy-making in Denmark

Peter Nedergaard

Introduction[1]

With regard to Danish governmental policy,[2] this chapter represents a comparative analysis of the development of two areas of EU policies that are seldom compared even though they are both cornerstones of European integration, namely the Common Agricultural Policy (CAP) and the Internal Market Policy, which respectively aim at the creation of free movement within the EU for agricultural goods and industrial goods and services. In addition, both policies are flagship supranational projects of the EU in which Denmark has been fully engaged since the beginning of the country's membership in 1973.

However, the instruments used for these two free trade projects are fundamentally different: one uses external protectionism and high budgetary expenditures; the other uses regulations and low budgetary expenditures. These differences are due to the fact that the CAP is a multi-dimensional policy (Knudsen 2009) rooted in the French Quesnayian state planning tradition, whereas the Internal Market project is a more one-dimensional policy rooted in the neoliberalism of the 1980s, even though the concept of a Common Market was already embedded in the Treaty of Rome in 1957.

The aim of the CAP was to establish a Common Market for agricultural goods, but also to create an adjustment of the balance between rural and industrial Europe, taking into account the perceived unfairness experienced as a result of industrial modernization in the agricultural sector employing approximately 20 per cent of the workforce in the EC[3] in 1960 (Knudsen 2009; Olesen and Laursen 1994: 110–112).

The Internal Market Policy was a much more single-minded liberalization project with, however, huge implications for the political economies of the EU member states (Sandholtz and Zysman 1989). At the same time, there are connections between the two policy areas. The Internal Market project for industrial goods and services certainly took lessons from the CAP, where an internal market for agricultural goods had already been established in the 1960s even though periods of monetary instability had temporarily led to some degree of breakdown in this.[4] Finally, both policies have substantial implications for the Danish export of goods that mainly go to neighbouring countries as seen in

Table 3.1, which illustrates an overview of Danish exports of goods from 1960 onwards.

Both the CAP and the Internal Market Policy created their own path dependencies after their establishment. Hence, they have often been quite difficult to change at the EU level in spite of shifting priorities in the member states as to the structure and content of the two policies. As far as Danish governmental policy is concerned, these changed priorities have mainly been within the field of the CAP. In other member states there might also have been some shifts in their position vis-à-vis the Internal Market Policy. There are, however, probably only a few examples of such a profound change as in the case of the Danish government's policy towards the CAP. Normally, and also at the level of member states, it seems to be very difficult to step aside from the logic of the once-created path.

What is interesting to follow is the fundamental change in the Danish governmental position towards the CAP compared with a generally (but far from always consistent) positive attitude towards the Internal Market project. This also reflects one of the central themes of this volume, where 'change and continuity' in Danish policy is also differentiated according to policy fields. In the following, the Danish governmental position on both the CAP and the Internal Market Policy are analysed first. These two important policy areas of the country's economy will then be compared in order to identify explanatory factors as far as the Danish governmental position is concerned. In this section, the subject of this chapter is seen in the broader context of the four dimensions of the book enabling comparison of the Danish experience as a member state across policy areas: (1) autonomy vs. influence; (2) formal vs. informal channels of autonomy and influence; (3) change vs. continuity; and (4) policy change vs. structural change. The conclusion follows.[5]

The method of historical process tracing will be used in the analysis of the development of the Danish governmental position on the CAP and the Internal Market Policy. The causal pathway will be reconstructed by identifying incidences and actors in the different historical stages.

Table 3.1 Distribution of Danish exports 1960–2009 (percentage)

	1960	1970	1980	1990	2000	2009
Germany	22	13	19	18	20	18
UK	27	19	15	11	10	8
Sweden	9	17	11	11	11	12
Netherlands	2	2	4	5	4	5
USA	7	8	5	5	6	10
Japan	0	0	2	4	4	2
Other countries	34	40	45	46	46	45

Source: Danmarks Statistik 2011.

Note
Due to rounding off, the figures do not always add up to 100 per cent.

The Danish governmental position on the CAP

During the negotiations on the creation of a Common Market in the EC in the mid 1950s, it became clear that agriculture had to be included in this market. France was an efficient and a major exporter of agricultural goods and feared the country's market would fail to benefit from its comparative advantage in this sector if it were to be flooded with German industrial goods. Therefore, France not only demanded a Common Market for agricultural goods but also a special common agricultural policy regulated in the Treaty and based on minimum prices and with partly common EC financing of the fund responsible for intervening in the agricultural markets, FEOGA (Fonds Européen d'Orientation et Garantie Agricoles) (Molle 2006; Johnson and Turner 2006).

Germany gave in to the French demands, not least because of an eagerness to obtain the trade benefits of the customs union. At the same time, Germany also wanted the political benefits accruing from becoming a fully accepted partner within the EC. Hence, the CAP has also been interpreted as a simple bargain between French agriculture and German industry. Simultaneously, the objectives of the original CAP reflected the traditional German agricultural policy based on high prices of agricultural products (Nedergaard 1995: 114). However, new research claims that this is too simple a narrative of the origin of the policy. For example, based on a historic scientific account of original documents behind the CAP, Knudsen (2009) argues that it encompassed far more than a French–German bargain. Rather, it was a broad agreement related to national welfare policies that were being introduced all over Europe around 1960; this time, however, aiming to improve incomes for farmers. Interpreted in that way, the CAP was the first pan-European welfare policy.

No matter the reason, from the very beginning, safeguarding the farmers' incomes through guaranteed prices was an important aspect of the CAP. In consequence, the policy was basically protectionist, and export subsidies (called 'export restitutions' in CAP jargon) were an essential factor in maintaining high prices on agricultural products within the EU's customs union, due to the fact that excess production can by definition either be destroyed (which was in practice for a number of years for some products, but became increasingly politically unacceptable) or exported out of the bloc. Internally, the common price level was set well above world market prices.[6]

The CAP was a primary reason for Danish membership of the EC in 1973. Even though the importance of agriculture for the country's membership had been declining in terms of export and employment vis-à-vis Danish industry and services, the agricultural sector was (in the 1960s) and still is (in 2011) of significant importance for the Danish economy, employment and export market (see Table 3.2).

The situation in Danish agriculture before 1973 was gloomy. Since the CAP had been established at the beginning of the 1960s, Danish agriculture had lost shares in the export markets in the EC, especially in Germany and Italy, and the farmers received low prices for the exports that actually took place due to the import levies imposed on them by the EC in order to protect its high price system. A phrase was coined to illustrate the situation for Danish agriculture before 1973: that of being in a 'waiting-room' (Nedergaard 1992: 109). In the perception of Danish agricultural interest organizations and key political decision makers, sooner rather than later, Danish agriculture would have to leave this room if it was to survive.[7]

Denmark applied for membership of the EC together with the United Kingdom the first time in 1961 (Olesen and Laursen 1994: 133). Until that year, most of Denmark's exports came from agriculture. Still in 1961, from a total export of 10.5 billion kroner, 4.6 billion kroner originated in agriculture, and nearly 300,000 people were employed in the sector (Olesen and Laursen 1994: 128). At the same time, 88 per cent of the agricultural export went to EFTA (mainly bacon and butter to the United Kingdom) or the EC (mainly cattle and beef to Germany) (Olesen and Laursen 1994: 129). Table 3.2 shows the distribution of Danish exports from 1960 onwards.

The perception among key decision-makers in Denmark was that the construction of the CAP and the external customs union in the EC would hit Danish agricultural exports hard. At the beginning of the 1960s, Denmark, (and as an example of active Danish 'uploading'), pressed for long term guarantees for its exports to Germany; however, no promises were given as long as internal EC negotiations on the CAP continued (Olesen and Laursen 1994: 137).

The Danish governmental policy towards the EC in the 1960s was steered by the decision in the parliament (the Folketing), in 1961, that the country should enter the bloc together with the United Kingdom (Olesen and Laursen 1994: 142). The two vetoes by the French president Charles de Gaulle towards the United Kingdom's membership in the 1960s meant that Denmark was put in a very difficult position.

From the mid 1960s onwards, the CAP and the erection of the customs union around the EC member states began to take its toll on Denmark's agricultural exports. There was a sharp decline in the export of poultry and eggs to the EC. Initially, other agricultural commodities more or less kept their market share in the bloc, but they were hit by the EC's import duties, which led to severe income losses for Danish farmers. At the same time (in the 1960s) the Danish economy

Table 3.2 Danish goods and services 1960–2009 (percentage)

	1960	1970	1980	1990	2000	2009
Agriculture etc.	48	31	29	23	16	9
Energy	0	2	3	3	6	5
Industrial goods etc.	28	39	42	46	46	49
Services	24	29	26	28	33	37

Sources: Danmarks Statistik 2008; Danmarks Statistik 2011.

Note
Due to rounding off, the figures do not always add up to 100 per cent.

more than ever needed an influx of foreign currency from exports for the sake of societal modernization, and the country suffered from a more or less permanent problem of too little foreign currency (Olesen and Laursen 1994: 143).

Finally, after the change of president in France in 1969, when Georges Pompidou replaced Charles de Gaulle, the door opened for British membership of the EC. The United Kingdom was still interested, and so, therefore, was Denmark. The negotiations between Denmark and the representatives from the EC on possible membership began in June 1970 and went on until January 1972. As far as the CAP is concerned, Denmark wanted as short a transition period as possible to ensure that the country's agricultural exports could enjoy the benefits of the Common Market as quickly as possible (Olesen and Laursen 1994: 150).

In the period of time up to the referendum on Danish EC membership on 2 October 1972, the economic arguments in favour of membership were stressed both by leading politicians and many experts. In particular, the increasing export incomes in the case of a 'yes' vote, and the deterioration of the balance of payments that would result from a 'no', were pointed out as important arguments in favour of membership. On the other hand, the political implications were downplayed. The result of the referendum was 63.3 per cent in favour of EC membership and 36.7 per cent against; 90.1 per cent of the electorate participated in the vote.

After securing membership of the EC, the representatives of the Danish government were, for a long time, strong defenders of the basic principles of the CAP and the traditional high price support policy regime. It was argued that the price support mechanisms were 'neutral' in the sense that they were beneficial for each farmer according to the farmer's production. At the same time, this also signified enhanced economic terms for Danish farmers, as they were relatively efficient producers. Even the excess supply resulting from the price support policy was defended, as the Danish Minister of Agriculture confirmed in 1978: 'After all, it's better to have a little too much than to lack' (Folketinget 1978: column 10046).

This policy line is reflected in a report from 1983 in which the official Danish governmental position towards the CAP was said to rely on the following points of view (Ministry of Agriculture 1983): 'to uphold the fundamental principles of free trade together with the Community preference, common finance, and free competition on equal terms...to uphold the price support policy as the main instrument in securing the farm incomes'. Until the years after 2000, this governmental stance represented a broad consensus of agricultural interest organizations and shifting (social democratic centre-left or conservative-liberal centre-right) governments and the attitude clearly mirrored the Danish benefits of the CAP in terms of annual income transfers and net welfare induced. However, from 2000 onwards, criticism of the CAP began to surface from leading decision makers. This development also reflected the fact that Danish agriculture had lost some of the huge benefits from the CAP relative to other member states, cf. Table 3.3. This table indicates the 'classical subsidies' (i.e. storage costs, export restitutions and direct payments) of the CAP from the

FEOGA's guarantee section for which Denmark originally wanted EC membership and not, for example, subsidies due to rural development (these had been on the rise over the years), where Denmark had never been a great recipient, cf. Table 3.4.

In Table 3.3, all member states (except Luxembourg) from 1973 onwards are represented with the annual payments from FEOGA's guarantee section (i.e. the classical subsidies cf. above).

At the same time, international pressure had increased as far as the traditional set-up of the CAP was concerned. This pressure materialized through the international trade negotiations under the auspices of GATT and later WTO. As a result of the Uruguay Round of trade negotiations at the beginning of the 1990s – when agricultural trade was for the first time a serious matter on the agenda – the EU was forced to adapt part of the traditional CAP. Hence, in the years following, the so-called MacSharry reform[8] of the CAP came into being in 1993–1994 with less of the budget spent on upholding price support and more on direct payment to farmers, no matter the future production levels (Nedergaard 1995). In 2003–2004, the so-called Fischler reform[9] was negotiated and adopted by the Council of Ministers. This further strengthened the direct payment system at the cost of the traditional high price policy system, where the support levels were coupled to the actual level of production. However, neither the MacSharry nor the Fischler CAP reforms denoted a reduction in the CAP budgetary expenditure (Nedergaard 2006).

The MacSharry reform of the CAP resulted in a radical change in the way agriculture was subsidized. Before, subsidies were overwhelmingly provided for through markets in the form of market support through subsidies for intervention, storage and export. After the reform, these channels for subsidies decreased. Instead they were, to a much larger extent, given directly to the primary producers (Ministry of Agriculture and Fisheries 1995: 13), cf. also Table 3.4.[10]

Table 3.3 CAP-support to farmers in selected member states 1973–2008 (million ECU/euro)

	Denmark	Belgium	Germany	France	Ireland	Italy	Netherlands	UK
1973	346	210	791	1,195	87	545	594	155
1978	806	602	2,489	1,739	552	747	1,274	439
1983	684	612	3,078	3,569	623	2,823	1,714	1,697
1988	1,212	721	4,904	6,210	1,081	4,350	3,828	1,993
1993	1,335	1,299	4,976	8,135	1,650	4,765	2,328	2,738
1998	1,154	851	5,553	9,007	1,633	4,129	1,373	4,314
2003	1,220	1,017	5,846	10,419	1,945	5,370	1,360	3,973
2008	970	560	5,673	8,859	1,299	4,256	903	3,213
Increase (%)	280	267	717	741	1,493	781	152	2,073

Sources: European Commission 2005; and own calculations.

Note
The figures are in nominal terms.

Table 3.4 Distribution of CAP expenditures to selected member states in 2009 (million euro)

Member state	Direct payments	Market measures	Rural development	Total
Denmark	972	90	66	1,128
Belgium	560	294	64	919
Germany	5,496	209	1,187	6,892
Ireland	1,276	178	355	1,809
Spain	4,921	1,017	1,278	7,216
France	8,081	911	942	9,934
Italy	3,813	1,406	1,135	6,355
Netherlands	794	227	73	1,093
Poland	1,248	206	1,933	3,386
Sweden	718	55	277	1,050
UK	3,422	74	645	4,141

Source: European Commission 2010a.

The introduction (in the MacSharry reform) of a general hectare premium combined with an obligatory set-aside scheme implied that there had to be direct support paid out to all farms in Denmark, which in the mid 1990s totalled 70,000–80,000. Hence, the number of cases handled by the administrative authorities would be much higher than before, also because it was impossible to establish one single system for the case handling of all schemes (Landbrugs- og Fiskeriministeriet 1995: 14).

It was only after the change in government in 2001 when a centre-right liberal-conservative government took over office from a centre-left social democratic-led government that the Danish governmental position towards the CAP changed profoundly.[11] The defence of this new line is characterized as a shift towards the support of a market liberalization of the common agricultural market, implying a reallocation of resources towards research and innovation as opposed to the traditional instruments such as the price support policy and direct payments (at least if the direct payments were not conditioned on certain standards being met as far as animal welfare, the environment, the landscape etc. are concerned) (Nedergaard 2006).

The year 2003 seems to have been the turning point for this new governmental stance on the CAP. In a report from the Danish parliament's Committee for Food, Agriculture and Fisheries from that year, it is noted that a majority of the committee (the majority was constituted by the parties in opposition as well as the representatives from the Danish People's Party, which otherwise normally supported the government) had adopted the resolution that the government should withdraw its support for the introduction of new so-called export restitutions (i.e. export subsidies) for pork. This was interpreted by the Danish government as a general demand by a majority of the parliament to oppose all new proposals for export restitutions suggested by the Commission. At all the meetings in the management committees after the report mentioned above, the

Internal Market Policy and the CAP 37

government officials therefore always opposed the introduction of new export restitutions (Folketinget 2003a). Hence, the Danish representatives since then have normally voted against all payments for new export restitutions and have usually been the only member state to do so. According to the author's informants, other pro-reform member states, such as Sweden, are much less fundamentalist than Denmark on this matter.

In 2007, the non-governmental parties further strengthened their opposition vis-à-vis the existing CAP. In a parliamentary debate, important and clear cleavages became apparent, although several of the viewpoints from the 'old' approach were also represented. According to political parties representing a majority of the parliamentarians, the policy of price support should be replaced with spending the financial means available from the CAP on new knowledge, innovation and sustainability in the agricultural sector (Folketinget 2007c: 5814). In a resolution by a majority in parliament, the government was given the task of preparing a strategy on ways of actively dismantling the EU's agricultural support (Folketinget 2007b). The resolution adopted by the Danish parliament in 2007 followed a recommendation by the parliament's European Affairs Committee (EAC) just a week earlier (Folketinget 2007a). According to the author's informants, this resolution has since acted as 'the Bible' for all Danish decision-makers (politicians and civil servants alike) vis-à-vis the CAP. In 2010, the government put forward a paper entitled 'Towards a new Common Agricultural Policy' (Ministry of Food, Agriculture and Fisheries 2010). This was a 'pace-setting' attempt (see Introduction to this volume) to come up with a proposal for a new CAP in accordance with the majority of the Danish parliament. According to this paper, the CAP should be 'focusing on research, development and innovation in the agricultural sector'.

The reason for the radical shift in the official Danish governmental attitude vis-à-vis the CAP is not clear-cut, but could be accounted for by a combination of several factors. As indicated by the Minister of Food and Agriculture in 2007, the increasing consumer demand for good quality and sustainable products means that an allocation of agricultural expenditure towards research and innovation should favour Denmark (Folketinget 2007c: column 5814–5). However, this might be true only in the long run.

In the short term, the more the price support mechanism is weakened, and the more agricultural expenditure is allocated to alternative purposes (cf. Table 3.4), the less beneficial the CAP is for Denmark even though the country has lost ground when it comes to 'classical' subsidies from the CAP compared to other member states, as shown in Table 3.3. In addition, the new found 'idealism' of the Danish parliament came at this time because Denmark had already lost out on the latest CAP reforms (the MacSharry reform and especially the Fischler reform) as more of the CAP funding went to rural development (called 'modulation' in CAP jargon, and from which Denmark does not benefit much, cf. Table 3.4) instead of export restitutions (where Denmark traditionally gained a lot). At their highest in the 1980s, Denmark received six billion kroner[12] per year in export restitutions, and in 2003 Denmark was still receiving three billion kroner[13] per year. In recent years this has decreased further to much less than one billion kroner per year.

The Danish position concerning the CAP has become ever more unrealistic due to the fact that, since the Lisbon Treaty, the European Parliament is now part and parcel of the CAP decision-making process, and according to the author's informants this will certainly contribute to the upholding of the status quo as far as the policy is concerned. Hence, a radical change (i.e. a dismantling as wished for by a majority of the Danish parliament) is more difficult to achieve than ever before.

The Danish governmental position on the Internal Market Policy

The Internal Market of the EU should be seen as a continuation of the EC's Common Market policy. After massive disappointments as far as the implementation of the Common Market for industrial goods and services were concerned, market integration was revitalized in the mid 1980s under a new name: the Internal Market. This time, there was a precise programme with a new and more flexible strategy and an exact deadline: 31 December 1992. However, this initiative did not take place in a vacuum, but was nourished over a period of time with neoliberalism in a hegemonic ideological position (Sandholtz and Zysman 1989).

The export of industrial goods and services was never the reason for Denmark's first application for membership of the EC in 1961. On the contrary, generally, the industry of the EC member states was perceived to be much more competitive than Danish industry. In 1958, the government published a report on the impact of a quick reduction of tariffs of relevance to Danish industry, which was part of the economic integration in the customs union of the EC. The report pointed out that 40 per cent of Danish industry would, as a result, be exposed to hard and severe competition in its home market. In particular, German industry was generally perceived to be more competitive than its Danish counterpart (Sørensen 1994: 82). The report on the lack of competitiveness of Danish industry was named the 'shock report' and it had an enormous impact on both political decision-makers and on broad public opinion.

A new governmental report on the economic consequences of EC membership in the mid 1960s painted a more optimistic picture of the competitiveness of Danish industry. Within four years, industrial production would increase by 30 per cent, industrial export by 20 per cent and industrial investments would double. Still, however, approximately 20 per cent of Danish industry would face difficulties in the case of EC membership. It seemed as if Danish membership of EFTA (from 1960) had already exposed Danish industry to outside competition to a degree and made it more fit for the purpose (Olesen and Laursen 1994: 138).

In the negotiations between the Danish government and EC officials, Denmark still sought to obtain exemptions for certain sectors of industry – or at least longer periods of transition, in contrast to the export of agricultural products, where a short period of transition and no exemptions were preferred, as mentioned above. However the EC officials were sceptical, as all new member states should accept the aquis communautaire.

The Danish governmental appetite for EC membership increased after 1964, when the United Kingdom introduced an extraordinary import duty of 15 per cent on all imported goods due to a severe balance of payment crisis (Olesen and Laursen 1994: 143). This was a sharp violation of EFTA obligations and would have led to an ECJ ruling had it happened within the more rule-of-law- based cooperation of the EC.

In the aftermath of the global oil crisis in 1973, the EU suffered from euro sclerosis, i.e. permanent low economic growth, high unemployment and high inflation. Many EC member states adopted pure 'beggar thy neighbour' national solutions to the crisis, for example, through devaluations that improved the competitiveness of national firms, but impaired that of companies from other member states.

In addition, there was a paralysis of the EC in the 1970s, due to new British demands on renegotiations of the entry terms into the EC and reform of the EC budget in order to decrease the British financial contribution to the bloc. The last demand increased after Margaret Thatcher came into power in 1979 (Rüdiger 1994: 171). This problem was not solved until the so-called British rebate was accepted by other member states at the European Summit in Fontainebleu in 1984.

Hereafter things began to change as far as European integration was concerned. A new visionary president of the European Commission (Jacques Delors) arrived in Brussels, and France, with a socialist president (Francois Mitterand), was ready for a neoliberal solution to the country's economic problems after a failed state interventionist attempt right after the socialist-communist government took over in 1983.[14]

The most authoritative expression of the concrete steps that were planned for the 1980s, was the Commission's White Paper of 14 June 1985 on the completion of the Internal Market (Commission of the European Communities 1985). This included nearly 300 proposals as to how the Internal Market should become a legal reality.

The Danish centre-right government was strongly in favour of the Commission's White Paper. As the opposition parties in the parliament continued to resist the integration of the Internal Market into the new EC Treaty (the SEA), the Danish government called for a referendum on the issue in 1986. The referendum on the so-called 'EC Package' was won by the government with an overwhelming majority.[15] Afterwards, the opposition parties accepted the Internal Market in principle, but they often had some strong reservations concerning specific elements of the programme.

In the debate in the Danish parliament in November 1988 (Folketinget 1988: columns 2605–2666), the spokesman for the Social Democratic Party, Ivar Nørgaard, explained these reservations. First, the market liberalization of the Internal Market should be supplemented with an expansive economic policy by the government in order to offset the negative impacts stemming from increased unemployment in certain sectors due to the restructuring process in the aftermath of the implementation of the Internal Market (Folketinget 1988: column 2621). Second, he was sceptical about the degree of harmonization needed as far as excise duties and consumer taxes were concerned. He also foresaw that it was necessary to maintain the so-called two-day rule (the free import of consumer goods is only allowed after 48 hours in another member state). He explained that these were necessary for upholding the Danish welfare system (Folketinget 1988: columns 2623, 2639 and 2640). Third, Nørgaard was also critical about the consequences of the liberalized public procurement of the Internal Market for the system with collective agreements concerning wages that dominate the Danish labour market (Folketinget 1988: column 2624).

Among the critical points made by Nørgaard, the third one became a recurrent issue in the public discourse on the Internal Market. This was also a reason for the later Danish scepticism on the Services Directive in the mid 2000s (see below). It is debatable whether a traditional expansive Keynesian economic policy recommended by Nørgaard would have changed much of the restructuring process as a result of the Internal Market Policy. In any case, the plan for EMU soon followed the Internal Market programme, and therefore the focus in the member states shifted in the direction of avoiding huge public deficits. As far as the point about harmonization of excise duties, indirect taxes and the two-day rule was concerned, it was a social democratic-led government that, later on in 1992,[16] made the decision to harmonize exactly that as part of the implementation of the Internal Market programme (Retsinformation 2010).

In spite of certain criticism made about the liberalization of the Internal Market, there has been broad support for the project among all the potential government parties (The Conservative Party, the Liberal Party, the Social Liberal Party, and the Social Democratic Party) since the late 1980s. The Internal Market has been recognized as an integral part of the EU, with sizable 'downloading' and 'uploading' implications for Denmark. In particular, the Social Democratic Party and also, to a lesser extent, the Socialist People's Party, have fully accepted the idea behind the project. It has been seen as a precondition for growth, in order to stimulate the Danish business climate, and aid the creation of a positive external balance of payments through the country's export market. 'More is better' catches the overall Danish position on the Internal Market. An indicator of this is the fact that for many years, the Commission's 'scoreboard' on the member states' implementation of Internal Market directives has shown that Denmark has always featured among those with the best records (European Commission 2010b).

The general support for the Internal Market does not mean that there has been no criticism of it from mainstream political parties, but this is directed towards individual directives and never the project as such (as was sometimes the case for the Social Democratic Party in the 1980s and even for the Conservative Party concerning the EC's Common Market[17] in the 1950s and 1960s). This criticism of individual directives now also comes from centre-right parties

(The Conservative Party and the Liberal Party) that in the 1980s were normally fully-fledged ideological supporters of everything that came out of the Brussels (perceived neoliberal) Internal Market machine.[18] According to the author's informants, the Danish government's stance has changed from 'idealistic support' to 'realistic support' for the Internal Market initiatives. The Services Directive is an illustrative case in this regard.

The Services Directive is an example of where a broad spectrum of Danish political parties (including the traditional hard core Internal Market fans) has been rather critical of the Commission's original proposal. This was debated in the Danish parliament in 2005, when (according to the Minister of Business Affairs, Bendt Bendtsen), one of the main reasons behind the government's scepticism towards the policy was the so-called Country of Origin principle (Folketinget 2005).

Initially, according to the author's informants, the Danish government was very positive and enthusiastic in its support for the Commission's original proposal for a Services Directive. Then a widespread consensus took root among top officials dealing with the issue, that the Country of Origin principle meant that everybody covered by the Directive could come to Denmark and offer their services according to the rules and regulations in their home country. Soon they found, however, that there were several exemptions from this general principle, but there was still anxiety that it would potentially undermine the Danish labour market model in which wages and working conditions are negotiated among social partners (trade unions and employer associations) and not regulated by law (the same fear that was pointed out by Ivar Nørgaard in 1988, cf. above). Labour unions were particularly afraid that this would happen, whereas the employers' associations (although in principle also supporters of the non-state interventionist labour market model) were also eager to see cheaper suppliers of services in the Danish market.

The reduced Danish tendency to accept the proposals for Internal Market directives upfront has opened up a democratic window for more political debate about the content of these proposals. The Danish parliament (especially via its EAC) has become much more involved in the debates over Internal Market directives at an earlier stage in the decision-making process. The parliamentarians now demand involvement in the discussions over the directives almost right from the beginning, and ministers now sometimes need mandates before debates in the Council of Ministers, and long before the final decision-making phase. When approaching the final meetings in the Council of Ministers with a specific directive on the agenda, a new mandate from the EAC of the parliament is sometimes required.[19] This is a new situation compared with just five years ago.

The fact that the Internal Market directives are now scrutinized much more carefully in Danish institutions, however, does not mean that the governmental support for 'more' Internal Market directives is necessarily less strong. In June 2010, for example, the government put forward a new paper with an action plan on 'A More Open and Safe Single Market' (Ministry of Foreign Affairs 2010b). Here, the Danish government proposes 12 quite concrete initiatives in order to see that happen: more uniform national rules, further opening of the services market, simpler and more uniform EU rules, effective implementation of EU rules in Denmark, a strengthening of the Internal Market Centre of the Danish state, better application of the CE[20] marking, improved knowledge and application of the Internal Market rules, the setting up of a surveillance committee, strengthened planning and prioritization efforts, increased cooperation between authorities, international cooperation on market surveillance and improved enforcement in the services field (Ministry of Foreign Affairs 2010b). In general, the 2010 action plan is a reaffirmation of Denmark's positive position vis-á-vis the Internal Market project.

The CAP and the internal market in comparison

In this section, the CAP and the Internal Market Policy are comparatively analysed with regard to four dimensions which are the *leitmotif* of the book: (1) autonomy vs. influence; (2) formal vs. informal channels of autonomy and influence; (3) change vs. continuity; and (4) political change vs. structural change.

As far as the autonomy versus influence dimension is concerned, both analysed policies are common EU policies. Hence, member state autonomy is limited and, generally, member states have to rely on influencing the new directives and regulations through coalitions with other member states and connections with the European Parliament. However, there are still some differences as to the question of autonomy. The CAP is mainly run through regulations (especially the market governance side of the CAP), whereas the Internal Market is mainly governed by directives, which, (in contrast to regulations), have to be implemented in the various member states. The implementation process opens up for a degree of member state autonomy as to the mode by which the directives are integrated into national law even though the national administration of regulations is also often a problem seen from a European integration perspective (Monti 2010).

At the same time, the post-MacSharry CAP has led to greater national autonomy, especially at the administrative level, due to the fact that the administrative tasks have become so much more onerous. It should therefore also be expected that bureaucratic politics, as far as post-MacSharry CAP is concerned, are stronger than before.

For both the CAP and the Internal Market Policy, the formal channels of influence go through the Council of Ministers' decision-making system. Since the Lisbon Treaty came into force, both have come under the remit of the European Parliament's decision-making powers. The formal channels of influence are important for both policy areas. However, the formal autonomy of the member states is somewhat greater as far as the Internal Market is concerned due to the fact that directives allow for the possibility of influencing the implementation process.

The informal channels of influence are characterized by strong interest organizations in both the CAP and the Internal Market Policy-making processes.

There are also some differences here, however, as the CAP is characterized by strong agricultural interest groups and rather weak consumer organizations (Nedergaard 2009). This is also the case in Denmark. Internal Market Policy-making, on the other hand, is denoted by a myriad of interest organizations from all kind of sectors and businesses even though some are more important than others.

In Denmark, as well as in the EU, interest organizations are important factors in accounting for the Danish position regarding the CAP and Internal Market Policy-making. However, the agricultural organizations have been weakened over the years. As the shift in the Danish position on CAP reform has shown, a position can change radically even though business interest organizations prefer to maintain the status quo. On the other hand, the change in the Danish position has no impact on the actual CAP policy, which benefits the country's farmers (even though to a lesser degree relative to other member states and to the situation before). The reason is that the Danish position comprises an insignificant minority position among the EU member states.

As far as the CAP is concerned, many more environmental non-governmental organizations (NGOs) are now interested in the policy, and these informal channels of influence are partly responsible for the changing the Danish governmental position on reform even though pure parliamentarian factors are probably more decisive, cf. below.

The third dimension to be considered deals with change and continuity as far as the two analysed policies are concerned. The Danish position on the CAP since 1973, when the country became a member of the EC, can only be characterized as an example of remarkable change. Denmark entered the EC for the very same reasons (a CAP with high prices on agricultural products) for which it is now among the few member states with a strong wish to drop the policy.

The changing role of the Danish governmental position from a hard core traditional CAP supporter (and always in alliance with France in order to keep the traditional high price arrangements as intact as possible) to a hard core CAP reformer (always on the opposite side of France in order to dismantle the traditional high price arrangements as much as possible) is a remarkable change of a policy position within the EU that should be further investigated. In this chapter – based upon documents and interviews – some explanations have been offered, namely: (1) the CAP became less and less favourable to Denmark (however, the traditional CAP *is* still beneficial to Danish farmers); (2) it is an attempt to bait the government (this has certainly been seen before) and this became possible because of an alliance between the opposition parties and the EU-sceptical Danish People's Party normally supporting the government; and (3) it is purely symbolic politics with no impact whatsoever on the ground as long as Denmark is regarded as an outsider in its strong opposition to the traditional CAP. However, a majority of parliamentarians in the Danish parliament pay tribute to the environmental and third world NGOs that have become much more outspoken about the CAP in the last 10–15 years.

As for the Internal Market Policy, seen from a Danish governmental perspective, this is much more characterized by continuity than the CAP. Overall

Danish support for the EU's Internal Market was, and is, strong. The general opposition (from the 1980s) among social democrats is long gone. All potential government parties are committed supporters of the policy. However, in spite of the overall support, the character of it has changed. From an idealistic or perhaps even ideological backing for the Internal Market and the ideas behind it, support has become what one informant calls much more 'realistic'. As he said: 'Yes, we do support the Internal Market, but we also point out rather quickly and bluntly when and where we have any reservations'. In other words, compared to the governmental position on the CAP, the change in the stance on the Internal Market is more a question of a variation in style. This is perhaps in contrast to some of the other member states, where resistance toward the Internal Market is also a matter of substance (according to Monti (2010)).

The fourth dimension in this section's comparative analysis concerns the question of policy change versus structural change. As far as the CAP is concerned, the variation in the Danish governmental policy position is probably influenced by the structural change in the Danish economy, where the agricultural sector was once a very important sector; it is still important today, but much less so than in 1973.

As for the Internal Market Policy, the minor policy change (from idealism to realism) is probably a sign of a more mature way of dealing with EU matters among Danish policy-makers. Policy-making is now much less influenced by the old 'yes' and 'no' discourses regarding membership of the EU. Most political parties are fully in favour of EU membership and so is the large majority of the electorate, where opposition to membership has almost disappeared. This has also led to a more 'relaxed' attitude towards proposals coming out of Brussels, (i.e. towards downloading'), where even strong pro-EU parties are often against certain aspects due to national interests, party ideology, the party's base among the voters etc. In that sense, EU policy-making in Denmark has become 'normalized'.

Conclusion

This chapter has compared Danish policy positions on the CAP and on the Internal Market Policy, and identified a sharp change in the Danish policy position concerning the CAP, and a much smaller shift in the policy position towards the Internal Market.

As far as the CAP is concerned, the Danish governmental position has changed from strong support of the traditional CAP mechanisms to strong support for a radical reform of the traditional CAP mechanisms. So far, however, the Danish policy change (influenced by a majority in the Danish parliament outside the minority government) has had no impact on the policy and the support that Danish farmers obtain from the CAP. Hence, there is speculation over whether this was mainly a way of baiting the government.

The Danish government's policy position concerning the Internal Market has been much more marked by continuity. The support for it was, and still is, very strong. However, some changes can be identified which represent a shift from an 'idealistic position', to a 'realistic position'. This change has been accepted at the elite level by the responsible ministers (see the case above on the Services Directive). From there it has been trickling down to bureaucracy. This is also a sign of normalization in Danish EU policy-making.

This 'normalization' has, at the same time, opened up an opportunity for politicization and, hence, greater democratization of the EU policy-making process in which the Danish parliament has become much more strongly involved at a much earlier stage compared to just a few years ago. So, finally, after four decades of EU membership, the EU is beginning to be part of the normal workings of Danish democracy, and alongside this, Denmark has begun to act as something more akin to being a 'mainstream' member state in an evolving EU.

Notes

1 This manuscript has certainly benefitted from the discussions and comments made in the seminar at Schæffergården on 29–30 September 2010.The author appreciates not least the comments made by Ian Manners, Knud Erik Jørgensen, Lee Miles, Rebecca Adler-Nissen, Caroline Grøn and Anders Wivel. Lena Brogaard has been a research assistant on this project.
2 The focus of this chapter is on Danish governmental policy as far as the Internal Market and the Common Agricultural Policy is concerned. The role of NGO's and interest groups are only included in the analysis if and when they contribute to explaining the Danish governmental policy in these two areas.
3 Before the Maastricht Treaty, the name of the EU was the EC. In this chapter, the EC is used for the historic EU before the Maastricht Treaty.
4 The devaluations of the EC currencies in the 1970s led to a system of 'green' currencies and monetary compensation in order to avoid distortions of the CAP, which necessitated strict border control etc.
5 The data collected for this piece stems from a large number of public documents from the Ministry of Food, Agriculture and Fisheries, from the Danish parliament, as well as from the Ministry of Business and Economics. Some are mentioned in the list of references at the end of the chapter. In addition, a number of interviews have been carried out with key informants about the subject: EU Special Advisor Jens Hauge Pedersen (Ministry of Food, Agriculture and Fisheries), Head of Division Stig Uffe Pedersen (Ministry of Business and Industry), Head of Division Martin Bresson, Ministry of Business and Industry (June 2010), Chief Consultant Lene Bøgh Hansen, the Ministry of Foreign Affairs (September 2010) and Chief Consultant Lotte Linnet, Ministry of Food, Agriculture and Fisheries (September 2010).
6 In some cases, the world market prices for agricultural products have actually been higher than the internal EU prices.
7 The main Danish agricultural interest organization, Landbrugsraadet, (The Agricultural Council) (now: Landbrug & Fødevarer, i.e. Danish Agriculture and Food Council) was the first major interest organization to work in favour of Danish EC membership at the beginning of the 1960s.
8 Named after the Agricultural Commissioner Ray MacSharry.
9 Named after the Agricultural Commissioner Franz Fischler.
10 E.g. the male premium scheme (in Danish: handyrspræmieordningen).
11 This can be taken as an example of 'change' as discussed as a key thematic dimension for understanding Danish policy in the Introduction of this volume.

12 Approximately €0.8 billion.
13 Approximately €0.4 billion.
14 E.g. a 'solution' that involved a reduction of the weekly working hours to 35 hours only contributed to increasing costs for French firms and, thereby, increasing unemployment.
15 56.2 per cent voted 'yes', while 43.8 per cent voted against the EC package (EUoplysningen 2006b).
16 As a consequence of the EMU and the establishment of the Internal Market, several directives harmonizing the excise duties were adopted in 1992 and put into force on 1 January 1993 (Retsinformation 2010).
17 The Conservative Party in the 1950s and 1960s was the main representative for the non-agricultural business interests that would be hit by EC membership according to the shock report.
18 Still, the Danish People's Party is quite critical of many EU initiatives as well as the supranational character of the EU, but it normally takes a positive stand toward the Internal Market's free movement of goods (and also towards services, to a lesser extent).
19 See Chapter 14 on Danish EU coordination in this book.
20 CE: Communauté Européenne/Conformité Européenne. The CE logo has become a symbol for free marketability of industrial goods within the EEA (European Economic Area) without any literal meaning. By affixing the CE marking to a product, the manufacturer – on his or her sole responsibility – declares that it meets EU safety and health and environmental requirements.

4 Denmark and the Euro opt-out

Martin Marcussen

After almost two decades of experience with the Danish opt-out from the euro, it has not become much easier to evaluate its consequences for Denmark. There are a number of unresolved economic as well as political issues to consider in that regard, with the political elite favouring influence in European decision-making and the electorate leaning towards Danish economic autonomy. In addition, the future development of the EMU-project seems increasingly uncertain and Denmark's place in the global and European economy as a model country is no longer a given. Therefore, it is fully understandable if politicians adopt a wait-and-see attitude towards the future of the opt-out.

The referenda

Plans for a European Economic and Monetary Union (EMU) were presented in parallel with the adoption of the Treaty for the European Economic Community (EEC). The question of one day introducing a common currency in Europe has constituted a guiding theme throughout the entire European integration process (Dyson and Quaglia 2010). The path through which the euro was finally introduced, first as an electronic means of payment in 1999 and then as coins and notes in 2002, has been long and cumbersome and filled with obstacles. This probably contributes to the common perception that the EMU is the greatest leap forward in the history of European integration.

In Denmark, the question about the country's relationship to European economic cooperation has been characterized by what looks like a paradox. On the one hand, since the beginning of the 1990s a broad political consensus has developed that the Internal Market (see Chapter 3 of this volume) fully reflects the basic ideas in Danish foreign economic policy. Danish politicians have traditionally supported liberalized markets that are underpinned by a strong competition policy and an inclusive social dimension, including a European structural policy. In addition, a firm political consensus has developed according to which the sound policy doctrine – low price inflation, a stable currency, low public debt and deficits, as well as an independent monetary authority – constitutes the basis for discussing other political issues. The stability-oriented philosophy, originally predominant in Denmark's southern neighbour, Germany, labelled 'die Stabilitätskultur' (Dyson 1994), has obtained hegemonic status in Denmark. On the other hand, however, and despite this apparent leaning towards European economic policies and philosophies, it has become increasingly clear to the political elite that the question about a common currency in Europe threatens to split almost all political parties in Denmark into two blocs – one bloc in favour of introducing the euro, the other one sceptical towards the euro.

The paradox is that it would be technically unproblematic for Denmark to sign up for the euro-philosophy, -institutions and -policies, but that the issue remains highly controversial among political elites as well as in the population. The consequence of this paradox is that a very particular praxis regarding Denmark's sovereignty in the European framework has developed according to which sovereignty issues, irrespective of the attitude of the majority of the parliament, ought to be discussed in public and eventually put out for a referendum. For that same reason, the then Prime Minister Poul Schlüter and Minister of Foreign Affairs Uffe Ellemann-Jensen made sure that the final draft of the Maastricht Treaty from December 1991 contained a clause stipulating that Denmark would use a referendum to decide whether to adopt the common currency or not. Consequently, a referendum was called for in spring 1992. The referendum concerned the entire Maastricht Treaty and it resulted in a narrow 'no' on 2 June 1992. Prior to the referendum, the population was met with bleak prophesies, which would be realized if it chose to reject the Treaty. For instance, EU-Commissioner Henning Christophersen argued that a 'no' to the Treaty would probably cost something in the neighbourhood of 200,000 jobs and lost exports amounting to 40 billion Danish kroner (Politiken 19 May 1992, quoted in Bonde 1993: 87–88). In his budgetary outlook, Minister of Finance, Henning Dyremose, argued in a similar vein that a 'yes' would result in 20,000 additional jobs, while a 'no' would cost about 30,000 jobs over the following few years (Børsen 28 April 1992, quoted in Bonde 1993: 87–88). Minister of Foreign Affairs, Uffe Ellemann-Jensen added that 'a "no" could result in higher interest rates, increased unemployment and welfare as we knew it 20 years ago' (Politiken 19 May 1992, quoted in Bonde 1993: 87–88). In contrast to these doomsday prophesies, the Governor of the Danish central bank, Erik Hoffmeyer, maintained that it would not imply an economic catastrophe for Denmark if the vote turned out to be negative. However, he would personally recommend a 'yes' to the Treaty (*Berlingske Tidende* 29 February 1992, quoted in Bonde 1993: 87–88). The spring report from the Danish Economic Council – the so-called Wise- Men – argued along similar lines.

At an early stage in the campaign leading up to the referendum, Jens-Peter Bonde from the People's Movement against the European Community held that a rejection of the Maastricht Treaty would not lead to a renegotiation of the entire Treaty. In contrast, a Danish 'no' to the Maastricht Treaty would allow for the possibility that the Danish government could 'make a list of stipulations from the Treaty which should not have legal effect in Denmark' (citation from Ryborg 1998: 24). The No-movements and the Socialist People's Party then started to make lists of the type referred to by Bonde. These various lists all contained a wish to be exempted from the planned EMU. On 22 October 1992, partly based on these lists with controversial issues, the Social Democratic Party, the Socialist People's Party as well as the Social Liberal Party agreed on the so-called national compromise. The national compromise was formulated as a plan B, now that the Danish population had rejected plan A (the full adoption of the Maastricht Treaty). Officially the plan was entitled 'Denmark in Europe' and it rapidly gained support from all parties in the Danish parliament except from the Progress Party. On top of the list of policy areas from which Denmark should try to obtain opt-outs from the Treaty was the single currency. The document also emphasized, however, that 'Denmark ascribes participation in European currency cooperation such as the existing European Monetary System (EMS) immense importance' as a result of which the 'no' to EMU should not be seen as a no to close European cooperation on the matter.

After dramatic and intense diplomatic negotiations with the other EC member states, in an example of what the Introduction highlights as the importance of Danish 'uploading' of national preferences, a summit at Edinburgh, on 11–12 December 1992, adopted a protocol that should be attached to the Maastricht Treaty. The protocol included an opt-out from the third stage of EMU. 'We are now able to call for a new referendum in April or May [1993]', a relieved Danish Prime Minister told the press after the summit. Indeed, 'we have succeeded in integrating all the major points from the national compromise in the Treaty', Poul Schlüter concluded (citation from Bonde 1993: 4).

The referendum took place on 19 May 1993 and resulted in a clear 'yes' to the protocol. During the campaign leading up to the referendum, it seemed to be of particular importance for the Social Democratic Party to emphasize that the opt-out from EMU did not preclude Denmark from actively participating in and contributing to European economic cooperation. The Socialist People's Party chose to emphasize that the EMU opt-out may be seen as a safeguard mechanism, which prevented the EU from developing towards a veritable European federation. Thus, while using quite different arguments, the two parties recommended their electorate to support the protocol with the EMU opt-out. The Liberal Party also recommend a 'yes' vote, but it never tried to hide the fact that it hoped that the opt-out would be merely a temporary hindrance for Denmark's full participation in the EMU. Arguments for a 'no' to the protocol adopted in Edinburgh came among other places from the Progress Party, which was not convinced that the opt-out would prevent Europe from developing into a federation (Jensen and Jespersen 2003).

Those positions were maintained relatively unaltered until 1998–1999, when the EMU-project began to materialize. In the beginning of 2000, opinion polls occasionally indicated that the Danes had started to regard the EMU with more positive lenses. In combination with the fact that the third stage of EMU had started on 1 January 1999, the Prime Minister Poul Nyrup Rasmussen decided that the time had come to call for another referendum on the euro. At the extraordinary Social Democratic Party congress on 30 April 2000, Poul Nyrup Rasmussen obtained full and almost unconditional support for his plan to call for a referendum on the euro. Never before, and never since, has the Social Democratic Party been so united regarding such an important EU-issue. In addition, the majority of the labour market organizations, the largest political parties and most of the national media were united in their support for the euro. Thus the prospectus for a successful campaign looked bright prior to the campaign (Marcussen and Zølner 2001).

During the 2000 referendum campaign, the Social Democratic Party argued that the Danish EMU opt-out could be seen as a threat to the Danish welfare state, and indeed would continue to have serious economic consequences for Denmark. The Liberal Party added that the opt-out excluded Denmark from having political influence in Europe. Denmark would become increasingly marginalized. In contrast, the Socialist People's Party continued to regard the EMU opt-out as a guarantee that Europe would not obtain federal characteristics. The party also argued that the opt-out had not had any serious economic consequences at all. The Danish People's Party added that the opt-out should first of all be seen as a guarantee that Danish political and economic sovereignty and identity would not be gradually undermined in Europe (Jensen and Jespersen 2003).

Just as in 1992, the 2000 campaign was characterized by gloomy predictions about the state of the Danish economy if the Danes decided to maintain the opt-out from EMU. Two major private banks – Unibank and Danske Bank – predicted that unemployment would increase by 10,000–15,000 persons if the opt-out was maintained (*Berlingske Tidende* 2000b). The largest labour organization (LO) thought that it would be rather in the neighbourhood of 35,000 additional unemployed if the Danes voted 'no' in the referendum (*Berlingske Tidende* 2000a), whereas the labour market think tank The Economic Council of the Labour Movement (Arbejderbevægelsens Erhvervsråd) predicted that the number of additional unemployed over the next four years would be 21,000 (Politiken 2001). At a press conference a few days in advance of the referendum the Minister of Economics, Marianne Jelved, and the Minister of Finance, Mogens Lykketoft, claimed that a 'yes' would create at least 15,000–20,000 new jobs in Denmark, whereas a 'no' would cost the Danish society some 20 billion Danish kroner a year over the next decade (Information 22 September 2000).

In contrast to those bleak economic prophecies, the Danish Wise-Men's institution, Det Økonomiske Råd, declared that full participation in the third stage of EMU would only have small and uncertain economic advantages and disadvantages for Denmark (Det Økonomiske Råd 2000: 7). In combination with the fact that the value of the euro had plummeted in relation to the dollar throughout the entire campaign and that many Danes thought that the EU campaign against the newly elected right-wing government in Austria was unsympathetic, the conclusion from a scientific authority with broad legitimacy such as the Wise-Mens' institution had dramatic effects. The initial quite positive popular attitude towards the euro immediately turned negative and stayed there until the final 'no' vote was a reality. In the end, a minority of 46.8 per cent of the voting population supported full participation in the EMU.

The 'no' vote in 2000 meant that Denmark would stay in the so-called Exchange Rate Mechanism II (ERM II) that it had joined in 1999 with the start of the third stage of EMU. The ERM II differs from ERM I in that it is not a multilateral system based on a bilateral parity-grid. Each participating currency in the ERM II has a central parity vis-à-vis the euro but not vis-à-vis the other participating currencies, as was the case in the ERM I. Inside the ERM II, the fluctuation band is set to ±2.25 per cent around the euro. Concretely, this means that the Danish krone can fluctuate between 762,824 kroner per €100 and 729,252 kroner per €100. In reality, the Danish central bank has literally pursued a fixed exchange rate policy almost as a currency board with immediate and automatic adjustments to underpin the parity irrespective of domestic considerations. Since 1997, the Danish central bank's key interest rates have shadowed the interest rates of the Bundesbank, and from January 1999 the interest rates of the ECB. Occasionally the Danish central bank changes its rates unilaterally when the krone is exposed to upward or downward pressure, for instance in connection to the global financial turmoil in 1998, in the autumn of 2000 when the Danes voted 'no' to the euro, and during the financial crisis of 2008–2009.

Since the end of 2008, fewer and fewer Danes are of the opinion that the Danish euro opt-out ought to be abolished. Even though the Danish economy, like the economies of most other European countries inside or outside the Euro Area, is being challenged by the economic recession emanating from the financial crises of 2008 and 2009 the crisis-awareness and -sensitivity of the Danes seem to be rather limited (*Berlingske Tidende* 2009b). The level of welfare in Denmark is high, unemployment is low, income taxes have been reduced, the general price level has fallen and interest rates on real-estate loans have reached a historical low. Overall, the average Dane expects that the Danish economy will continue to develop positively – at least compared to its continental-European neighbours. At the same time, the majority of the Danes are of the opinion that the debt crisis of the Euro Area periphery is symptom of a larger structural problem of the Euro Area, which cannot be solved with the present constellation of Euro Area members. In addition, the Danes seem to be sceptical towards the Euro Area's ability to make efficient decisions that would guarantee the stability-oriented nature of European economic cooperation. In other words, the Euro Area is no longer associated with German economic virtues.

In February 2009, the share of euro-opponents (42 per cent) was equal to the share of euro-supporters (*Berlingske Tidende* 2009a). Since then, the number of euro-opponents has risen gradually, reaching an all time high in February 2011: 50 per cent against the euro, 41 per cent in favour (*Berlingske Tidende* 2011). This pattern in opinion did not prevent then liberal Prime Minister Lars Løkke Rasmussen from talking about the need for referendum in the near future. In May 2009, he talked about organizing a euro-referendum before the next parliamentary election in November 2011 at the latest (Børsen 2009). In February 2011, when commenting on German and French ideas about a European Competitiveness Pact, the Danish Prime Minister aired the possibility of having a referendum about the euro before the Danish EU-presidency in spring 2012 (Børsen

2011). Overall, the major contenders of parliamentary power – the Conservative Party, the Liberal Party and the Social Democratic Party – are all in favour of abolishing the euro opt-out. At the same time, they are parties with seeping popular support. This stands in sharp contrast to the Socialist People's Party, the Liberal Alliance and the right-wing Danish People's Party who, for different reasons, are in favour of maintaining the opt-out for the time being. Thus, the next referendum, whether it lies in the near future or far away on the horizon, seems to split both the government and the opposition. In this regard, the major cleavages would resemble those from earlier referenda, with the autonomy/influence dilemma remaining unresolved – it would be business as usual (Marcussen and Zølner 2001).

The economic dimension of the opt-out

Both before and after the financial crisis, there seems to be broad agreement in Denmark about the fact that it is not primarily economic considerations that are decisive for whether Denmark should one day choose to join the Euro Area. This does not mean, of course, that the EMU-project has been completely without economic significance for Denmark. As a small and open market-economy that trades primarily with other EU-countries, Denmark has traditionally been very dependent on economic conjunctures on the European continent. The near completion of the Internal Market (see Chapter 3 in this volume), and the creation of the Euro Area, has brought about considerable trade- and investment- related advantages, including more extensive financial integration across borders. Despite the euro opt-out, Denmark has reaped considerable benefits from European economic integration. In almost the entire period in which Denmark has been exempted from the Euro Area the Danish economy has prospered to the extent that it has been common to talk about the 'Danish model economy' (Pedersen and Campbell 2007; Schwartz 2001). This development has been fostered by Internal Market and European monetary integration, but also by global processes of liberalization, technological development and other features related to globalization, which have played a role. Over the preceding two decades, Danish politicians from the left as well as from the right wing have generally exploited the economic development to undertake considerable structural reforms that have improved the country's institutional competitiveness (Marcussen and Kaspersen 2007) – including providing the conditions for a more flexible labour market, a well-functioning financial system, and, not least, an effective and reliable public sector.

In the decade 1998–2008, Denmark has been at the absolute top of almost all international comparisons regarding international competitiveness and innovation (Marcussen 2010). Thus, in 2008–2009, Denmark was in a favourable position to deliver the kind of expansionary economic policies required to curtail the challenges emanating from the financial crisis. Because of its fixed exchange rate policy inside the framework of the ERMII, Denmark was not able, like Sweden, to let the national currency decline to more competitive levels. Thus, during the financial crisis, Denmark had to rely on structural reforms and costly fiscal expansion. Consequently, like most other countries in the EU, Denmark is no longer able to fulfil the convergence criteria. Today, Denmark's international competitiveness suffers from low levels of productivity and growth (Andersen 2011). However, the overall impression is that Denmark has not been impacted harder by the financial crisis as a result of its position as a euro-outsider. If anything, the financial crisis has highlighted the tensions within the Euro Area between the so-called PIIGS (Portugal, Italy, Ireland, Greece and Spain) and particularly Germany as a result of which the average Dane is less inclined today than ever before to vote in favour of Denmark's full participation in the EMU.

Interviewing Danish stakeholders (such as central bankers, civil servants in the economic ministries, university professors and representatives of employers' and employees' organizations) about the economic dimensions of the euro opt-out, it seems to be the overall perception that the basic conclusions made in the spring 2000 Wise-Men report mentioned above still hold true. Thus, in its spring 2009 report, the Danish Wise-Men conclude that considerations about Denmark's relationship to the Euro Area are still, despite the financial crisis, primarily a political issue. If there is an economic benefit to be reaped from giving up the euro opt-out, it would be modest (Det Økonomiske Råd 2009: 304–313). The general opinion seems to be that, in retrospect, it cannot be argued that the Danish economy has suffered or profited from not having introduced the euro, and that predictions of the opposite have shown to be wrong or exaggerated. Being asked which priorities they have in Europe, and which visions they have for European cooperation, the Danish euro-stakeholders mention the further calibration and optimization of the Internal Market with free movement of labour, services, goods, capital and knowledge. In that regard, and as instances where Danish policy-makers may seek to upload preferences to the EU level, free and fair competition and further cooperation with regard to financial supervision, trade union matters, environmental matters and science are being mentioned as areas in which Denmark could play an enhanced role.

Interestingly, before the financial crisis, a considerable portion of Danish business managers concluded that it does not make a difference for themselves and their companies whether Denmark does or does not have the euro (Sentio Research July 2008 quoted in Danish Broadcasting Corporation 2008). Today, with the financial crisis somewhat at a distance and the euro crisis very present, Danish business leaders in exporting companies are even more sceptical towards the euro (Jyllands-Posten 2012).

However, it is fair to say that only few of the interviewed euro-stakeholders have fundamentally altered their point of view with regard to Denmark and the euro. For them, being inside the Euro Area would still imply that Denmark is less vulnerable to future financial and currency crises. A more direct exposure to international currency crises, such as those experienced back in 1992 and 1993 when Sweden and the United Kingdom chose to leave the stable currency regime as defined by the ERM, can also be envisaged in the future. Basically, a euro-outsider such as Denmark that has chosen to link its currency to the euro within the framework of the ERM II has three options in case of serious economic and financial difficulties. First, the European System of Central Banks (ESCB) may chose to employ the 'guarantee' that was offered to Denmark back in 1999 when it entered the ERMII: that it automatically and without limitation would support the Danish stable currency regime in case of a currency crisis provided that such an action would not violate the overall objective of the euro-system, which is price stability. The financial crisis of 2008 and 2009 has illustrated that the ECB is actually willing to apply this 'guarantee'.

A second option concerns the possibility of temporarily letting the Danish currency float like the Swedish krone. A series of other countries that are normally used for comparison, and applied as a Danish benchmark in other contexts, such as Switzerland, Norway and New Zealand, have adopted a floating currency regime. Thus, a situation like the Swedish one is not unforeseen in the global economy. However, for most of the interviewed Danish euro-stakeholders such an option seems to be speculative, but nevertheless an option that could be applied in a situation of very serious crisis. To maintain the stable currency regime is clearly the most preferred option, as a result of which the option of letting the Danish currency float should be seen as the very last possibility employed when everything else has proven to be in vain. Interestingly, some interviewees feel that just to talk about such an option could seriously weaken the credibility of the Danish stable currency regime.

Finally, talking about the position of a euro-outsider in a situation of a serious currency crisis does not imply that Denmark should join here and now. The timing has to be right. Most euro-stakeholders, taking everything into account, prefer a wait-and-see option. While waiting, however, there are other matters that are higher on the agenda of Danish euro-stakeholders such as the Internal Market, the Europe 2020 project and the Pact of Competitiveness/Euro Plus Pact.

The political dimension of the opt-out

It is inherently difficult to isolate the economic dimensions from the political dimensions of the EMU. One political dimension refers to the intergovernmental negotiation process that finally led to the adoption of the EMU as part of the Maastricht Treaty in 1992. In that perspective, the EMU is a political compromise that satisfies different national interests and perspectives. Similar intergovernmental dimensions have been decisive in crisis-management situations during 2008 and 2009 and in the gradual construction of a European Stability Mechanism in 2010. A second political dimension is related to a debate about whether Frankfurt and the ECB ought to have a political counterweight – so-called 'gouvernance économique' – in the European Parliament and/or in the framework of the Council of Ministers. Such a point of view is based on the idea that the EMU is an asymmetric structure that leaves essential political decisions to unaccountable technocrats without a public mandate. Most recently, a European Semester and a Europe-wide banking supervisory system have been suggested as elements of European economic governance. A third political dimension refers to the idea that EMU de facto is a stepping stone or even a catalyst for further political integration in Europe into sensitive areas such as taxation, social and distributive issues, and, not least, labour market-related issues. Just as the Internal Market can be seen as the basis on which the EMU was founded, the EMU can be seen as a foundation for integration into areas that so far have been primarily reserved for national decision-making. In spring 2011, a Competitiveness Pact/Euro Plus Pact had been proposed in that regard, involving policy areas hitherto excluded from systematic European cooperation and decision-making.

A fourth political dimension is related to the political functions of the euro. In that perspective, the euro is not only a means of payment. A currency can be seen as an expression of national identity and sovereignty. In this way, the euro is just one element that is helping to constitute the EU as one of the two real superpowers in the world. A fifth political dimension refers to the day-to-day political administration of the euro, including political decisions about how and when to apply the excessive deficit procedure, whom to chose for the post of Euro-group president, and generally how to establish procedures, institutions and norms through an essentially political decision-making process. Finally, the EMU can be associated with political ideas, either placing the euro-project on the liberal, capitalist side of the party political spectrum or as a project that helps consumers all over Europe to overcome the drawbacks of lacking competition and transparency emanating from monopolistic tendencies within the narrow national economies. In that perspective, the EMU can also be seen as the most important leap towards creating a European federation that once and for all consolidates peaceful exchange on the European continent. In short, there are many political dimensions to the EMU that could be highlighted (Dansk Institut for Internationale Studier 2008: 181–183).

The prestige of euro-outsiders

Talking about the political dimension of euro-outsiderness (see also Miles, 2005b), it seems that two aspects, in particular, are of importance: international prestige and influence. In the world of central banking, for instance, the reference to the quite elusive concept of 'prestige' has played a central role in any kind of international interaction. This has also been the case for the Danish central bank. The archives of the Danish central bank document that central bankers had prestige in mind when first approaching the newly-created Bank for International Settlements in 1929–1930. It was also prestige that entered the discussion about how to relate to the International Monetary Fund (IMF) when that organization was on the drawing board during 1944–1995. The reference to prestige has not been less frequent in recent years when discussing Denmark's relationship to European monetary cooperation (Marcussen 2008).

Clearly, Danish euro-stakeholders have different things in mind when talking about the prestige of Denmark in international forums. Some, such as the central bankers mentioned above, would have their trustworthiness and credibility in mind. Prestige in that sense simply depends on whether the Danish policy is able to perform in full accordance with the international norms of the day. Other euro-stakeholders would argue that we are beyond the point where Danish trustworthiness is at stake. Over 25 years, Denmark has demonstrated an unequivocal commitment to the stability-oriented macro-economic policy agenda and has been loyal to European monetary cooperation. To this group, prestige is a matter of personal authority in international negotiations. The Danish euro-stakeholders are of the opinion that the euro opt-out is the most well-known opt-out among the four opt-outs and that they are constantly asked to explain themselves in international forums. The fact that international counterparts consider the Danish euro opt-out as a curiosity that has no obvious explanation may have an impact on the personal authority of the Danish negotiators. When they fail to convince their international counterparts about the rationale for the euro opt-out they feel that they have lost a little bit of their prestige (Adler-Nissen 2009a).

It is, of course, difficult to conclude with any kind of certainty what prestige means in international contexts. On a general note, however, it can be argued that it need not be the case that small state representatives are blessed with a lower level of prestige in international forums than large state representatives. Due to their geo-strategic location, their natural resources, the personal charisma of their leaders, their ability to enter into winning coalitions or to act as neutral mediators between opposing coalitions, or simply due to their ability to perform on all kinds of parameters, small states can indeed be blessed with a high level of international prestige (Naurin and Lindahl 2008a; Magnúsdóttir 2009). In any case, international prestige depends on a much broader set of factors than just formal features such as a euro opt-out. It could be argued that Denmark, despite its euro opt-out, is indeed considered as one of the more prestigious EU member states. The fact that the EU Commission, as well as the Organisation for Economic Cooperation and Development (OECD), the IMF and other international organizations frequently refer to the Danish labour market philosophy revolving around the concept of flexicurity has paid off quite well on the prestige account. The same goes for its environmental profile.

The influence of euro-outsiders

The interviews conducted with Danish euro stakeholders also help to clarify what exactly is meant by 'influence'. One aspect of influence concerns the ability to form the agenda of the forum in which one participates. Clearly, participation does not guarantee that influence in that sense is assured. The agenda of any political forum depends on a very long series of inter-related factors among which the concrete meeting dynamics is only one. To influence a political agenda would, in any case, require a certain proactive attitude. For small member states, power over the agenda does not come by itself.

A second aspect is related to the fact that participation in certain forums constitutes a short-cut to essential information. This perspective is based on the assumption that there is some information which is exclusive to a certain forum and which cannot be obtained from anywhere else. In a pluralistic political system such as the European system, the amount of information that has these characteristics is probably small. A third aspect has to do with the formal right to vote in these forums. This is, of course, only relevant if decision-making by hand-raising is taking place, which is not the case in the Euro-group, for instance.

In a discussion about whether or not Denmark is losing political influence by its euro opt-out, it should also be noted that, using a historical perspective, Denmark has more often than not acted as a decision-taker rather than a decision-maker. For a short while during the preparation of the European system of monetary governance, the Danish central bank governor formally participated on an equal footing with other EC member states in the workings of the predecessor to the ECB, the European Monetary Institute (EMI). Before that, European economic coordination took place in the monetary committee and the committee of central bank governors (based in the Bank for International Settlements in Basel). In these forums, substantial power was located around Germany and the Bundesbank in particular, as a result of which it became normal to talk about asymmetric governance in European monetary cooperation. Thus, the present situation, in which Denmark clearly is on the receiving side of decision-making, can be seen as a continuation of past practices. However, decision-making routines and power structures are constantly developing, and, in the following, the main forums from which Danish civil servants and ministers are excluded will be presented, and the way that ongoing developments alter the significance of being excluded as a result of the euro opt-out will be discussed.

Economic policy-making in Europe: the Euro-group

Towards the end of 1997, it became clear that France and Germany considered establishing a forum for coordination in the form of a so-called 'euro-council' constituted of euro-insiders. It would exclude from its deliberations countries that had obtained an opt-out and countries that were not yet qualified to be part of the Euro Area. This idea was met with fierce resistance from Denmark, among others. The official Danish position was that it did not want this forum to be created at all, and if it was created, Denmark wanted full access to all meetings. Objections of that kind were met with the assurance that all decisions would still be made in the Ecofin Council to which all countries have access, and that the new forum would merely be an informal coordinating device (Agence Europe 15 September 1997). The acting EU-presidency, represented by the Luxembourg Prime Minister, Jean-Claude Juncker, presented various concrete ideas as to how it would be possible to involve the euro-outsiders in the deliberations of the new euro-council. The French Minister of Finance, Dominique Strauss-Kahn (who, together with his German colleague Theo Waigel, had taken the initiative to create the euro-council) emphasized in a similar vein that it would be completely natural to include all the euro-outsiders provided that the concerned countries fulfilled the convergence criteria and were involved in the ERM II (Agence Europe 17 November 1997).

The Danish Minister of Foreign Affairs, Niels Helveg Petersen, used the occasion to remind the public and his European colleagues about the spirit of the Maastricht Treaty according to which it was assumed that the euro-outsiders should be continuously involved in EMU decision-making (Agence Europe 24 November 1997). All the way up to the beginning of the Luxembourg Summit in December 1997, at which the euro-council was established as an informal forum, it was emphasized by various parties that the euro-outsiders, of course, ought to be closely involved in the deliberations of this forum. The euro-council should under no circumstances replace the work that was taking place in the Ecofin council. Concretely, it was mentioned that the euro-outsiders should have the status of observers in the euro-council, and that agendas for the informal sessions should be forwarded in advance of the meetings (Agence Europe 10 December 1997; see also Agence Europe 11 December 1997 and 12 December 1997).

Today, it is known that the euro-council – which today is referred to as the Euro-group – has undergone a process of increasing formalization, and it functions as a coordinating as well as a decision-making forum in a long series of policy areas of direct relevance to the euro-outsiders. In fact, the formalization of the meetings has on occasions rendered the official meetings in the Ecofin council superfluous. Also, and in contrast to initial expectations, Denmark does not automatically receive the agendas of the meetings or any other form of background information in advance of the meetings. This is a development that has taken place gradually. In 2000, the Euro-group started to assemble prior to the meetings in the Ecofin council (Agence Europe 17 July 2000), as a result of which ministers (and not least the press) tended to turn their attention away from the Ecofin meetings, which were organized the following day. In 2003, a very exclusive forum referred to as the Euro-group Working Group was established. It did not include the euro-outsiders. This was a major step towards the total exclusion of euro-outsiders from EMU deliberations. Until then, all preparations for meetings in the Euro-group had taken place in the so-called Economic and Financial Committee (EFC) to which all euro-outsiders had access (Crooks and Parker 2003). In 2004, it was decided that the Euro-group should have a permanent chairperson, Jean-Claude Juncker, who represents the Euro-group in external forums and streamlines the internal procedures. This too is a major step towards the formalization of the group (Agence Europe 10 September 2004). Finally, in 2008 it was formally mentioned in the Lisbon Treaty that the Euro-group is an informal forum. This clearly is an important recognition of the Euro-group and its role in EMU decision-making. There is no indication that this process of formalization will end here. Almost all propositions for economic reform in Europe contain a clause indicating that more competences and responsibility ought to be placed in the Euro-group. During the French Presidency, Nicolas Sarkozy suggested that the Euro-group ought to have its own permanent secretariat, a clear mandate to strengthen economic policy-coordination, and establish closer contact with the ECB (*Financial Times* 2008). At the outset of the financial crisis, Members of the European Parliament suggested that the

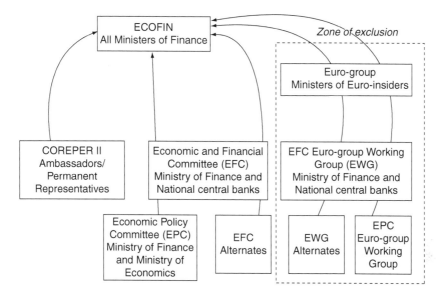

Figure 4.1 Basic structures of EU-governance in the area of economic policy.

Note
In formal terms, all EMU-related decisions are made in the Ecofin Council. With time, however, a parallel system of meeting forums that only include the Euro-insiders has taken form. The Euro-group is central in that parallel system of deliberation. The dotted line indicates a 'zone of exclusion' to which the euro-outsiders are prevented access.

Euro-group should be the centre of a new European economic architecture (Agence Europe 24 October 2008). Towards the end of the financial crisis, the president of the EU, Herman van Rompoy, presented a proposal for a new economic governance structure in Europe in which the Euro-group played an important role (October 2010). In general, the Euro-group is seen as a major catalyst for European economic integration. This also goes for its efforts to coordinate structural reforms in the Euro Area and for its role in representing the EU in the international arena (see, for instance, Cohen and Subacchi 2008; European Commission 2008a; and Pisani-Ferry *et al.* 2008).

This does not mean that the Euro-group is flawless. Over the years, the Euro-group members have learned the hard way to stick to discipline when making public statements about the euro. However, when it comes to almost all other areas, the Euro-group members take very dissimilar positions. For instance, the group rarely takes a common position when evaluating national budgetary situations. The same goes for interpretations of the stability and growth pact and its application in practice. The Euro-group members also differ as regards the content and usefulness of gouvernance économique and whether the Euro-group constitutes an element of such a practice or not. Until the beginning of 2011, the Germans had consistently rejected any mention of a political counterweight to the Frankfurt-based ECB because this would violate the independence of the bank. With Angela Merkel's ideas of a Pact of Competitiveness, elements of economic governance were introduced in order to maintain European economic integration on a stability-oriented course. The French, however, see the Euro-group and possibly also the euro-Summit constituted by Euro Area Heads of State and Government as a political accountability mechanism needed to make economic governance more effective and more legitimate. Since the Euro Area seems to grow almost by the year, the probability that it would come to constitute a unitary actor with one voice on European economic matters is small. It is more likely that coalitions inside the Euro-group, constituted by countries with similar interests and profiles, will pop up from issue to issue. In reality, this means that the continued enlargement of the Euro Area would create a group of core euro-insiders and another group of periphery euro-insiders (Umbach and Wessels 2009). Such a possible fragmentation of the Euro-group would make it easier for the euro-outsiders to navigate inside the European economic governance structure and probably also help to make the distinction between euro-outsiders and euro-insiders less relevant as regards obtaining strategic and technical information (Marcussen and Dyson 2010).

Monetary policy-making in Europe: the ECB's Governing Council

Another institutional development of importance for the euro-outsiders takes place at the ECB in Frankfurt. Three issues are of particular importance for the role of euro-outsiders in the ESCB: first, that the ECB Governing Council is a collegial body; second, that the Euro Area is enlarging; and third that the functions of the ECB seem to expand.

Decisions about interest rates are made in the Governing Council. These decisions are emulated by the Danish central bank. Over the years, and particularly during EU-related referenda, it has been common to argue that Denmark ought to have a member in the Governing Council that could somehow promote Danish interests. However, the Governing Council is a so-called collegial body in which all members have one vote each. Their presence depends on their personal skills. They speak on their own behalf and in their own personal capacity. This means that if a Danish central bank member should get a seat on the Governing Council, he or she would not be able, expected or even allowed to place Danish interests first. All the members of the Governing Council have as their primary objective the promotion of the interests of the Euro Area. Developments in one single Euro Area country are only relevant in so far as these developments have an impact on the entire Euro Area economy. Based on this principle, the 2009–2010 Greek and Irish debt crises have been object of a number of discussions in the Governing Council, since the outcome of these crises is decisive for the euro economy overall. In praxis, the principle of collegiality is taken very seriously inside the ECB Governing Council. Any attempt to promote national interests is considered as a threat toward ECB independence (Howarth 2009).

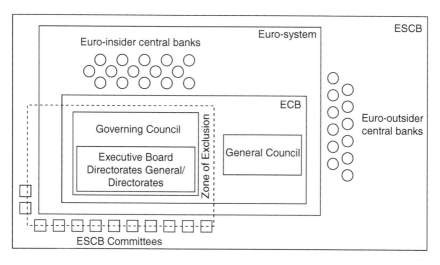

Figure 4.2 Basic structures of EU-governance in the area of monetary policy.

Note
The European System of Central Banks (ESCB) consists of the European Central Bank (ECB) and the National Central Banks of the EU including the central banks that have not introduced the euro. As a direct consequence of not having adopted the euro, the euro-outsiders are excluded from participating in the work of the Governing Council and partly excluded from preparatory work in a series of ESCB Committees. This constitutes a 'zone of exclusion', which is indicated by the dotted line. All EU member states participate in the work of the General Council.

That Denmark would never get 'its own' representative in the Governing Council has been clear from the beginning of the EMU. However, what remained undecided until a few years ago concerned the situation in which the number of members in the Governing Council grew as a result of continuous enlargement of the Euro Area. Are decisions about interest rates to be made in a similar manner when the number of euro-insiders is 11 as when the number is 17 or 22? Having adopted the Nice Treaty, back in March 2003, the Heads of State and Government decided to ask the ECB to formulate an appropriate decision-making system based on some form of rotation principle. Initially the system should start working when the number of Euro Area members reached 16. This happened on 1 January 2009. However, just days before, the ECB Governing Council decided to continue its functioning voting regime and to introduce the rotation system only when the number of euro-insiders exceeds 18. Once up and running, the rotation system means that two groups of countries are formed. Countries within each group will then have to vote in turns. When the number of euro-insiders reaches 22, a third group will be formed, which functions in the same way. In reality this system of rotating voting rights means that new Euro Area countries are not assured a right to vote on all issues. Some have argued that a system of A, B and C members will be developing inside the Governing Council (Umbach and Wessels 2009).

A final issue, which is of importance for the euro-outsiders, concerns the competences of the ECB in various areas. In principle, monetary policy-making is centralized in Frankfurt, whereas issues related to payment systems and financial market supervision is decentralized in the member states. This does not mean that the ECB is not active in these areas. On the contrary, the financial crisis has worked as a catalyst for cooperation in exactly these areas, but the kind of cooperation we are talking about is intergovernmental. This concretely means that Denmark is fully involved in all matters relating to building up a new financial supervision structure for the EU.

Overall, with regard to the new programs and governance systems that have to do with financial supervision and payments, these do not belong to the zone of exclusion to which Denmark has no access. In both areas of cooperation, the European central banks and private banks are free to engage as much as they wan,t irrespective of their national currency.

In conclusion, it would be too simple to argue that Denmark is simply excluded from European economic decision-making as a result of its euro opt-out. The picture is more complicated, underlining that European economic governance is elusive (Dyson 1994).

A wait-and-see strategy

With 20 years of experience, it has not become easier to evaluate the costs and benefits of being a semi-permanent euro-outsider (Miles 2005b; Marcussen 2005). The difficulty arises from the fact that various undecided issues are at stake at this very moment.

A first undecided issue concerns the *fate of the Euro Area*. In the history of European integration, the EU has gone through one crisis after another, each of which has led to a more integrated European edifice. With the EMU it may be different. It is now common to discuss the crisis of the EMU as a struggle for survival, not only of the EMU as such, but also of the EU overall. According to an *optimistic scenario*, the Euro Area will continue its growth. Year after year, new members will join the Euro Area and all of these countries will seek to fulfil the basic criteria for membership as described in the Stability and Growth Pact and possibly in the Competitiveness Pact/Euro Plus Pact. While undertaking structural reform with a view to enhancing productivity and international competitiveness and creating the right conditions for innovation and growth, focus is directed at the level of price-inflation in order to create the right conditions for enduring monetary and financial stability. In this scenario, the Euro Area can be seen as a 'harmonization project' according to which its members will increasingly come to look like Germany in form and content (Marcussen 2009). At any time, the European interest rate established by the ECB will be the most optimal interest rate for all parties involved. Finally, an outcome of such a scenario will be that the Euro Area will come to constitute one unitary actor on the world stage, representing one consistent voice in the IMF, WTO and other forums in which the global rules of the game are being formulated.

According to the more *pessimistic scenario*, it will become increasingly difficult to convince euro-outsiders to sign up for membership of the Euro Area. Countries like Poland and the Czech Republic, which are currently taking a more hesitant and even sceptical position with regard to their future relationship to the euro, will become a model for other euro-outsiders to emulate. The same can be said about Denmark, Sweden and Great Britain, who have demonstrated that their euro-outsiderness has not prevented them from realizing their basic political and economic objectives (see Miles, 2005b). According to this scenario, we will probably also observe the euro-insiders continuing to be reluctant in their willingness and capacity to undertake necessary reforms, as a result of which the existing tensions between the core export-led economies and the periphery economies will be aggravated. The Euro Area is best described as a 'differentiation project' in which national economic and political structures, processes and cultures will continue to exist, making it difficult to coordinate policies across the Euro Area. On the international scene there will never be anything like a single Euro Area voice in central decision-making forums.

On a quite simplistic level, it could be argued that the Danish position towards the Euro Area depends on whether the euro-project turns out to be a harmonization project or a differentiation project. In this way, Danish policy towards the euro reflects some of the themes of differentiation identified in the Introduction to this volume. If the euro turns out to be a fully-fledged success on all parameters, it will function as a pull factor for Denmark. In that case it will be an advantage for Denmark to join the euro – or at least to maintain its fixed currency policy. If the Danish population chooses not to join the euro, the Danish economy will gain from a dynamic Euro Area anyway, constituting one of the largest single markets in the world. A dynamic and prosperous Europe is a win–win situation, whether Denmark has a euro opt-out or not. In contrast, a Europe characterized by internal tensions, quarrels and lack of coordination will help to push Denmark and the Danes farther away from the Euro Area. Denmark does not gain much by taking part in a zone of conflict nor does it gain much from staying outside the eurozone. A prolonged period of crisis is a situation in which both insiders and outsiders will be losers.

If the first undecided issue concerns the fate of the euro-project, the second issue to notice concerns the *state of the Danish economy*. According to an *optimistic scenario* the Danish decision-makers will exploit the current crisis to undertake reforms that will bring the Danish economy into a new stage in which knowledge, ideas, design, values and culture will create the right conditions for future innovation and production in the public as well as in the private sector. Gradually, the Danish economy will become less and less dependent on oil and gas from the North Sea and more and more reliant on alternative and more sustainable sources of energy. Denmark will become a role model for others to follow on the forefront of globalization. According to the more *pessimistic scenario*, economic, political, social and environmental sustainability is put at risk and the currency will become a target for speculation. Internationally, the entire collective of credit institutions will rate the country, its economy and its future prospects at junk level. On the way to the abyss, international economic institutions will gradually take over control of the major economic institutions and basic democratic principles will consequently be dismantled.

With the basis of these two extreme scenarios for the Danish economy, it would be reasonable to argue that the better able the country is to reap the benefits from globalization, the less dependent it is on the Euro Area. In other words, the healthier and more dynamic the Danish economy is, the less dependent the country is on seeking shelter in the Euro Area, disregarding whether the Euro Area turns out to be a success or not. If, in contrast, the Danish economy runs down a less fortunate avenue, towards recession, Danish politicians and private businesses will be urged by electorates and shareholders alike to reconsider the euro opt-out. Such reflection is, of course, more likely to lead to Euro area membership, if the Euro area – in contrast to the Danish economy – turns out to be a success.

On the basis of this, the question can be asked whether Danish politicians, in the short to the medium term (where the Danish economy seems to be overcoming the international recession with less pain than most of its Euro Area neighbours) dare to take the risk of calling for yet another referendum on the euro? The risks involved can be quite high because yet another 'no' to the euro will not only recreate a position as a semi-permanent euro-outsider, but, rather, tend to create an entirely new position in which Denmark is de facto a permanent euro-outsider – or at least considered to be a permanent euro-outsider. Despite numerous public discussions about a forthcoming euro-referendum in Denmark, it is most likely that Danish politicians from both the opposition and those in charge will adopt a wait-and-see attitude. After all, this is what a pragmatic, small country can afford to do, and what it has historically always done.

5 Justice and home affairs

Denmark as an active differential European[1]

Rebecca Adler-Nissen

Introduction

In 2011, Denmark's right-wing government announced the deployment of over 40 additional customs control officers to be permanently stationed at the border with Germany. Critics at home and abroad, especially the European Commission and southern neighbour Germany, cautioned that this move undermined the idea behind the Schengen border-free zone. Commission President José Manuel Barroso warned that the Commission 'would not hesitate to intervene' if the principle of free movement was endangered. The Danish Foreign Minister, Lene Espersen, defended the move, which was the result of a deal with the government's far-right ally – the Danish People's Party. Espersen insisted the new border checks complied fully with the Schengen Agreement and the aim was 'to fight the entry of illegal goods and drugs' into Denmark, not to control people (EUbusiness 1 July 2011). Denmark is a member of Schengen, but, ever since the opening of the Danish borders in 2001, this membership has been a controversial issue in domestic politics.

In October 2011, a few months before Denmark assumed the rotating EU Presidency, the newly elected Prime Minister, Helle Thorning-Schmidt, abolished her predecessor's border control plan and reintroduced normal Schengen procedure. Yet Schengen is still a hot potato. With the Arab Spring in 2011 and the arrival of North African refugees and migrants, France and Italy debated the possibility of opting out of the Schengen zone altogether to make it possible for them to protect their own borders. Schengen, however, remains a cornerstone in the EU.

Denmark appears to be a reluctant participant in JHA, but in reality it contributes actively. While Denmark has a formal opt-out from the common migration and refugee policy, Danish officers still participate in operations by Frontex, EU's border control agency. Moreover, despite a Schengen protocol, Danish police officers use the Schengen Information System on a daily basis. In 2010–2011, Denmark even deployed police officers to the 'Joint Operation Poseidon' at the border with Turkey in north-eastern Greece, which is a major point of entry into the EU for illegal immigrants. This highlights the importance of *differentiated* and *informal* integration.

This chapter analyses Denmark's puzzling position on European cooperation with JHA (which in EU treaty language is now labelled 'Freedom, Justice and Security'). To understand the rapid development of this particular policy area, it is necessary to recall the dramatic structural and policy changes in Europe from the 1990s and onwards. From the mid 1990s, and particularly since 11 September 2001 and the resulting global war on terror, the EU has been eager to intensify cooperation with JHA. The Arab Spring in 2011 has only reinforced this eagerness.

This fast-growing and high-profiled area covers the free movement of persons, immigration, visa and asylum policy and external border policy as well as judicial cooperation in police, criminal and civil law matters. An analysis suggests that on average 10 new legislative proposals on JHA are tabled every month (Monar 2007). While the rest of the Union pushes for deeper integration, Denmark's approach to EU cooperation in JHA is profoundly ambivalent. On the one hand, Denmark actively supports collective EU measures to fight transnational crime and terrorism. On the other hand, the Danish government and population seem almost allergic to participation in the fast-developing EU policies on refugees and immigration. With the entry into force of the Treaty of Lisbon in 2009, the task of managing Denmark's position in the JHA has become even more difficult. Due to *structural* changes, i.e. treaty changes, Denmark will be prevented from participating in cooperation on police matters and criminal law in the future. However, the treaty also presents Denmark with a fresh opportunity to transform its current opt-out into a 'pick and choose' model.

Exploring Denmark's apparent outsider-position, this chapter demonstrates that the Danish position in this politically sensitive field has undergone profound policy changes over the last two decades despite the permanent legal opt-out from all supranational cooperation. The chapter argues that Denmark is an *active differential European* and provides an overview of the inbuilt tensions in the Danish position. The focus is on the most controversial and debated aspects of Denmark's cooperation in JHA. Empirical illustrations therefore concentrate on Denmark's opt-out and the cooperation on migration, asylum and border policy rather than on civil and criminal law, which is less debated. The chapter focuses on the Danish government and does not cover the role of companies, interest groups or civil society, which are to a large extent sidelined from the concrete decision-making process. Indeed, EU cooperation on JHA has developed partly in isolation from broader domestic constraints. For instance, pro-migrant non-governmental organizations have been rather unsuccessful in influencing what Andrew Geddes calls a 'bureaucratic epistemic community' (Geddes 2000: 150).

The analysis is organized as follows. The subsequent section explains the Danish JHA opt-out in more detail. The following sections detail the Danish position in relation to Schengen, the difficult negotiation of parallel agreements, asylum and migration policy and, finally, the consequences of the Lisbon Treaty and other structural transformations. The chapter ends by setting out the policy dilemmas that Danish decision-makers face or are likely to face in the years to come.

Maastricht and the quick-fix opt-out

Since the Danish rejection of the Maastricht Treaty in a referendum in 1992 and a subsequent negotiation of protocols, Denmark has had a controversial opt-out from JHA. While few Danes understand the technical details, the opt-out remains an important symbol of autonomy for large parts of the Danish population (see Hansen 2002).[2] The opt-out is seen to constitute a bulwark against European integration; underpinning an image of the state with full political and legal authority over people and territory. Consequently, when shifting Danish governments claim that the opt-out harms Denmark's position (see also Chapter 15), they still have to assure the Danish public that they respect the protocol (Adler-Nissen 2008).

One of the paradoxes of the Danish position is the remarkable contradiction between the original motivation behind Denmark's reluctance towards community competence within the area of asylum and immigration policy, and its current motivation to maintain its opt-outs. In the beginning of the 1990s, Denmark (together with the Netherlands) was among the most liberal countries and feared that community competence within asylum and immigration policy would threaten the high level of protection given to asylum seekers in Denmark (Manners 2000: 98). However, from the late 1990s, the Danish asylum and refugee policy has become stricter than similar rules in the other EU states. This has resulted in special requirements concerning the rules on family reunification and requirements of attachment to Denmark. Today, the Danish rules on asylum and immigration represent significant barriers to the perceived inflow of immigrants, asylum-seekers, criminals and terrorists. In the media and public debates, Eurosceptic politicians, such as the influential Danish Member of the European Parliament (MEP) Morten Messerschmidt, from the Danish People's Party, claim that protocols protect national sovereignty and may serve as a model for other member states. Danish pro-European governments and administrative elites argue that they lose political influence when they 'are sent outside' the door, but see Adler-Nissen (2009b) for a discussion of this.

When Denmark voted 'no' to the Maastricht Treaty in 1992, the 'no' was carefully interpreted as a rejection of 'the United States of Europe', not as a refusal of European cooperation as such.[3] The opt-out from JHA was therefore designed as an exemption to supranational cooperation, leaving Denmark free to participate as long as cooperation remained intergovernmental. Supranational cooperation implies among other things that EU legislation has a direct effect in member states and a direct effect for EU citizens – this implies substantial EU *downloading* (see the Introduction to this volume). In contrast, intergovernmental cooperation (which is the traditional form of treaty-based international cooperation between states) legislation has to be transposed into national law via national parliaments (and arguably, therefore, implies less EU *downloading*). Due to the insistence on intergovernmentalism, the JHA protocol is 'activated' by the particular *mode* of cooperation rather than the political *content*. The basic logic is that Denmark is out when cooperation is supranational, but participates when it is intergovernmental. Throughout the 1990s, most member states were reluctant to surrender sovereignty on politically sensitive areas such as border control, asylum policy and police cooperation. German plans for the full communitarization of immigration and asylum policy had been successfully blocked (Geddes 2000: 89; Givens and Luedtke 2003: 305). Consequently, when the Danish JHA opt-out was introduced after a second referendum on Maastricht in 1993, it did not have any practical significance. Instead, at the outset, Denmark participated fully in all aspects of JHA cooperation because it remained intergovernmental.

With the Amsterdam Treaty in 1997, however, member states took a drastic choice towards the integration of their asylum, immigration, border control and civil law policies. Substantial parts of the JHA portfolio were transferred to ordinary EC cooperation with the entry into force of the Treaty in 1999.[4] The supranational move 'triggered' the Danish opt-out for border control, civil law and asylum and immigration policy (Title IV, Treaty establishing the European Community). Only criminal law and police cooperation remained intergovernmental, which is why Denmark could continue to participate in these policy areas on an equal footing with all other member states. In sum, while national control and authority may still be important concerns for the 27 member states, cooperation in JHA has shifted from taboo to totem in less than two decades.[5] Meanwhile the Danish opt-out has remained in force.

Beyond the integration dilemma

A driving motivation behind the opt-outs was to avoid Europeanization and accommodate domestic Euro-scepticism. As Helen Wallace puts it, an opt-out may guarantee 'immunity from disliked European legislation' (Wallace 1997: 682), but the price for autonomy is a loss of influence in the policy-making process. This intuitively convincing account of a peripheral status due to opting out lends itself easily to the concept of an 'integration dilemma'. It implies that every state (and especially a small state) faces a dilemma when reaching a certain stage in the process of supranational, political integration. This involves an uncomfortable choice between becoming entrapped in the integration system by surrendering substantial parts of its political authority and being abandoned by the integration system by insisting on preserving formal state-based sovereignty (Petersen 1998: 35ff.).[6] The basic idea is that a state cannot have both *autonomy* and *influence* (see also the Introduction to this volume). However, as we shall see, the trade-off between autonomy and influence is far from straightforward.

With the entering into force of the Lisbon Treaty in 2009, the consequences of the Danish opt-out have grown dramatically. As the treaty abolishes the so-called pillar structure (the division of the EU and EC treaties into intergovernmental and supranational pillars); most legislation under JHA is now covered by the Danish opt-out and Denmark will gradually be excluded from all cooperation on police and criminal matters. This leaves the Denmark with a profound dilemma: Should it abolish the opt-out in order to remain part of police cooperation and fight against terrorism (popular with the Danish population) in exchange for giving up autonomy and refugee and immigration law (more controversial with the Danish population)? Or should it accept a situation where Denmark is completely excluded not only from sensitive policies of immigration, but also from police and security cooperation? The stakes are growing when it comes to Denmark's position on JHA – with the prospect of structural change in Denmark's relationship with the EU possibly now on the cards.

Denmark as an active copycat

This section argues that – beneath the surface – Denmark is an *active differential* European in JHA.[7] Denmark, that is the Danish government and administration, seeks to compensate formally and informally and prepare for its gradual (and self-imposed) exclusion from the high-profiled area. Consequently, a well-established, but publicly unknown policy of shifting Danish governments is to keep Danish legislation consistent with EU legislation in almost all aspects of JHA – notwithstanding the opt-out. Denmark engages in systematic mimicking and copying of EU legislation in areas covered by the opt-outs. Hence, this chapter will first analyse the peculiar Danish Schengen position and second, the negotiation of parallel agreements in relation to asylum and civil law cooperation.

Schengen

Today, all EU policies on border control and large parts of illegal immigration are categorized as developments of the Schengen framework (in EU language: the Schengen *acquis*). Moreover, a substantial part of police cooperation is equally considered a development of Schengen cooperation. Yet because this latter area has hitherto remained intergovernmental, this has not had any consequences for Danish participation in practice.

Denmark was initially reluctant to share authority on border control with the other member states; the domestic debate centred on German police officers entering Danish territory and the EU influencing Danish criminal law. Yet Denmark accepted the surrender of its national border controls by signing the Schengen Agreement in 1996. When Schengen was later integrated in the Amsterdam Treaty in 1997, part of it was inserted into the supranational Title IV. A protocol was drafted to assure ensure that Denmark could accede to any future supranational EU rules that might be introduced on the basis of the original Schengen cooperation while continuing to respect the opt-out from 'supranationality' in the field of JHA. The protocol states:

> Denmark shall decide within a period of 6 months after the Council has decided on a proposal or initiative to build upon the Schengen acquis under

the provisions of Title IV of the Treaty establishing the European Community, whether it will implement this decision in its national law.[8]
(Article 4 of the Schengen Protocol)

At first glance, it appears as though Danish autonomy has been formally secured. However, the protocol also states that if Denmark decides *not* to implement such a Council initiative, the other member states will consider which 'appropriate measures' should be taken. This is a diplomatic way of saying that Denmark will be thrown out of Schengen if it does not implement a Council initiative (Vedsted-Hansen 2008: 117). The Council has never had to consider such measures because Denmark has so far transposed all such initiatives into national law. Despite the often domestically sensitive legislation, Danish governments have loyally stood up for Schengen; at least until now. It remains to be seen whether this copycat arrangement can withstand a situation where the Danish permanent custom control arrangement is judged to violate Schengen obligations. If, for instance, the ECJ finds that Denmark is in breach of the Schengen rules, the rather odd intergovernmental construction in a supranational system might also be put into question. For some Danes this would finally create a welcome opening for leaving the border-free zone.

Parallel agreements on asylum and civil law

A second – and perhaps more bizarre way – of copying takes place through *parallel agreements*. If an EU measure is based on a reciprocity principle, Denmark cannot just copy EU legislation. Instead, it needs a parallel agreement. For example, the Dublin system is based on a reciprocity principle that commits all member states to receive asylum-seekers referred under the Dublin criteria from another member state. Denmark is of course free to copy parts of the regulation into Danish law and itself decide to receive asylum-seekers from other member states, but it has no way of ensuring that, for example, Greece accepts asylum-seekers referred from Denmark. These more advanced forms of cooperation, such as EU agencies and supranational funding structures, have increased over the last years. Today, reciprocity mechanisms are applied to everything ranging from recognition of divorces to court rulings regarding terrorism (Peers 2006: 76).

The Danish government has only asked for a parallel agreement on areas considered to be of 'vital interest to the country' (Vedsted-Hansen 2004: 67). If granted, Denmark copies the EU measure into a Danish law, which is then subsequently passed by the Danish parliament (the Folketing). So far, Denmark has applied for six parallel agreements, but the Commission has only granted three, two on civil law and one on asylum. The Commission refused to grant Denmark parallel agreements with respect to the Regulation on insolvency proceedings and the Regulation on jurisdiction and the recognition and enforcement of judgments in matrimonial matters (Bruxelles II Regulation). The most important of these is probably the latter, which concerns the Dublin system, considered the cornerstone of EU cooperation on asylum.

Both the Schengen *acquis* and the parallel agreements effectively constitute 'exemptions to exemptions', allowing Denmark to participate in certain measures despite its opt-out. Importantly, these exemptions have been pushed for by both liberal-conservative and social democratic governments. Of course, while Denmark is allowed participation it has no right to vote on new Schengen measures. In practice, Denmark is thus de facto forced to accede to all new Schengen measures, but formally retains no power to influence their content

With regard to parallel agreements, Denmark is similarly bound to accept any changes to the EU rules or else give up the agreement entirely. Denmark can obviously voice such concerns during negotiations, but it has no voting powers in the Council, which, all other things being equal, leaves member states freer to ignore the Danish position (Dansk Institut for Internationale Studier 2008: 333). For the civil law measures covered by the parallel agreements, it is also the case that Denmark has ceded its right to negotiate on these matters in other international fora, such as the Council of Europe. The political price for these association instruments – getting an exception to the exception – is considerable.

Moreover, the EU is very reluctant to extend such agreements. Basically, the very idea that the EU should enter into a treaty with one of its own member states appears absurd. Negotiations on the existing three agreements took several years. According to the Commission, the following conditions apply when Denmark is granted a parallel agreement:

1   Parallel agreements should only be of an exceptional and transitional nature.
2   Such an interim solution should also only be accepted if the participation of Denmark is fully in the interests of the Community and its citizens.
3   The solution in the longer term is that Denmark gives up its protocol on JHA.

On this basis, Denmark will have a hard time negotiating additional parallel agreements over the next couple of years. Whether agreements will be granted or not depends entirely on the Commission (Europaudvalget 2003). Denmark is not a rule-maker, but a rule-taker. Overall, however, this copying suggests that formal opt-outs do not necessarily equal exclusion. This proves interesting in light of Lee Miles' analysis of how states with euro opt-outs behave in the EU. According to Lee Miles, '[...] exclusion from the single currency does not create a clearly delineated division of EU member states into permanent sub-groupings that can affect national perspectives on all areas of EU policy making' (Miles 2005b: 6). The perspective is clearly also relevant when it comes to understanding Denmark's position and strategies within JHA.

Civil law under the radar of public attention

In civil law cooperation, Denmark *can* choose to stand outside, but in practice it has done much to align its national legislation generally with EU measures and, in a number of areas it has applied for parallel agreements. While civil law cooperation generally passes below the radar of public attention, it has become increasingly important for the EU as goods and persons move freely across borders. As border controls disappear, the need for member states to work together in avoiding the abuse of open borders arises. If for instance, a company in one member state becomes insolvent, it must be possible to take legal action across borders. Likewise, if two parents from different member states divorce and cannot reach an agreement on child custody, common legislation is needed to solve the dispute fairly and prevent one parent from hiding with the child in his/her home country. Cooperation in the area of civil law has been developed to solve precisely these kinds of problems. Due to the opt-out, however, Denmark has been excluded from a number of civil law initiatives.

The Brussels II Regulation (also called the divorce Regulation) is one example. This Regulation ensures that rulings in cases about child custody in one country are automatically in force in all other member states, if the father and mother come from different member states. While civil law matters remain peripheral to migration and asylum issues, they are of growing concern to the Danish family law administration. Structural changes in the way international civil law is governed, with the EU codification of an increasing number of international law instruments, may make civil law yet another challenge for Danish EU policy. It is, however, mainly with regard to the harmonization of *asylum legislation and legal immigration*, in particular family reunification, that Denmark has gradually taken a different political course than the rest of the EU.

The illusion of autonomy

As mentioned, the opt-out arguably presents Denmark with the freedom to pursue different policies than that of the other member states. So far, however, Denmark has mainly used this freedom with regard to asylum and legal immigration. The influential populist, right-wing Danish People's Party explains the 'value' of the opt-out:

> No supranational or international body should impose a particular refugee and immigration policy on Denmark. Who and how many we wish to let into our country are to be entirely the internal affairs of Denmark. The Danish People's Party will fight to ensure that refugee and immigration policy remains an area where the Folketing is sovereign.
> (Dansk Folkeparti 2004; author's translation)

However, serving the symbolic purpose of legitimizing Danish EU membership to the population, the exemption from cooperation on immigration, asylum and civil law actually works very differently from how it is presented in the Danish public debate.

Protecting the strict Danish asylum and immigration legislation

If Denmark were to abolish its JHA opt-out tomorrow, this would imply substantial changes to Danish asylum and immigration legislation (*Udlændingeloven*). The EU's directive on family reunification does not permit member states to maintain provisions such as the Danish 24-year rule, the association requirement, the housing requirement and other special Danish requirements for obtaining family reunification. Under the EU directive, member states may – if special needs demand it – impose a 21-year rule, but the ordinary requirement under the directive for the family reunification of couples is 18 years. Incorporating the EU's current rules into Danish law would also imply that foreigners with permanent residence would be able to demand family reunification and a range of other rights on a par with Danish citizens earlier than is the case at present (Kjær 2004).

With regard to asylum, member states have thus far only been able to agree on a set of directives setting out minimum standards on who qualifies for protection, asylum procedures and reception conditions.[9] Against this background, it is difficult to assess whether Danish asylum law is substantially more restrictive than asylum policies in other EU member states. If or when the EU succeeds in adopting the new directives on asylum, the chances are that the current Danish asylum policy will appear more restrictive than that of the rest of the EU.

Already today, however, Denmark's freedom to pursue an independent asylum and immigration policy is limited in practice. As Chapter 11 notes, this is partly due to the much-debated right to family reunification that flows from the EU's general rules on the free movement of EU citizens (Directive 2004/38/EC of 29 April 2004). The ECJ has established that if free movement within the Union is to be effective, this must include the right for EU citizens to take their family and spouses along with them. It is important to stress that these rules do not pertain to EU cooperation on JHA, even though in reality they also concern family reunification. The Danish opt-out does not cover the rules regarding free movement, and Denmark is obliged to process all family reunification cases for EU citizens exercising their right to move (Gammeltoft-Hansen 2009; Lassen 2007).

The more liberal rules have induced a number of Danes to exercise their right to free movement and take up work in, for example, Sweden for a period, and then subsequently return to Denmark and claim family reunification under the EU procedure. Judgments from the ECJ mean that more and more Danes are likely to claim the special right to family reunification under the EU procedure (Starup 2008). As should be clear from the above, the opt-out does not guarantee that Denmark can decide over its own immigration or asylum policy. Structural changes, in the form of new treaties and 'external shocks' such as terrorist attacks or the Arab Spring, clearly trump such national aspirations.

An unwanted goodbye to Europol

Has the Danish government lost control over its participation in JHA with the Lisbon Treaty? As more and more policy areas have moved from intergovernmental to supranational cooperation, the Danish opt-out now covers all parts of EU cooperation on JHA. Denmark is thereby excluded from participating in a still growing part of EU cooperation. Denmark has had little control over the treaty changes that have moved policy areas from the (now historical) third to the first pillar. Denmark is formally committed to avoiding hindering the rest of the EU in moving cooperation forward. This clause was inserted in the Danish opt-out protocol in 1993 to ensure that Denmark would not attempt to block or sabotage political developments. When a new policy has gone over to supranational first pillar cooperation, Denmark has therefore been prevented from voicing opposition or opposing it in other ways. Changes in the legal framework of the EU have had enormous consequences for Denmark.

In 1999, Denmark was suddenly excluded from all EU cooperation on civil law, an area in which Denmark had been an active participant and driving force for international cooperation since the 1960s. With the Treaty of Lisbon now effective, this case of abrupt exclusion is set to repeat itself. The treaty abolishes the last remaining parts of the old third pillar, thereby 'normalizing' police and criminal law cooperation within the supranational EU framework. As new measures are now being adopted, Denmark is prevented from participating. Moreover, Denmark's participation in the current range of intergovernmental measures will gradually be abolished as new supranational legislation is set to replace the existing third pillar instruments over the next five years. Denmark will then be barred from participating in EU cooperation on issues such as human trafficking, international crime and the fight against terrorism, issues where Denmark has so far been a full and active participant.

This will have important effects on Denmark's cooperation in the areas police cooperation and criminal law. Hitherto Denmark has been able to participate in Europol, the European Law Enforcement Agency, which aims at improving the effectiveness and cooperation of the competent national police authorities in preventing and combating terrorism, unlawful drug trafficking and other serious forms of organized crime. Moreover, Denmark participates actively in building up Eurojust, a special unit composed of national prosecutors, magistrates and police officers that help the member states coordinate difficult cases and prosecutions across borders. Both institutions, located in The Hague, are vital tools in the fight against international crime. Europol and Eurojust are playing an increasingly important role in facilitating interaction between the respective national law enforcement and judicial authorities. Joint Investigation Teams set up by Europol are used to reduce obstacles to cross-border operational cooperation through non-legislative measures such as training, identifying best practice and operational and technical support. Mutual recognition of judicial decisions, the European Arrest Warrant, the execution of orders freezing property or evidence and rules on the confiscation of crime-related proceeds has fundamentally changed the way police officers cooperate in the EU today, in effect extending the 'reach' of national internal security measures to the territories of other EU member states. If the opt-out is not changed, Denmark will be forced to leave both Europol and Eurojust when these are eventually amended or replaced by new supranational legislation.

It is uncertain whether Denmark will manage to secure some sort of special association agreement with regard to some of the more important police and criminal law measures. Unless the opt-out is abandoned or changed before new legislation is adopted, this would be a likely strategy to pursue with regard to, for example, the EU's police agency, Europol, where maintaining Danish presence would no doubt be considered of the utmost importance. On the one hand, the other member states may well be interested in securing Denmark's continued participation in order to 'avoid a white spot on the map' when it comes to combatting international crime. On the other hand, there is continued reluctance to extend any further special association agreements among both the Commission and those member states that wish to see Denmark eventually abandoning its opt-out. Furthermore, hoping for parallel agreements is not an effective strategy to secure continued Danish participation in police and criminal law cooperation more generally. Even if Denmark is granted such arrangements on a par with Norway, an agreement of this sort does not amount to full participation when it comes to ensuring influence on the legislative proposals and management of Europol or other EU agencies.

From a Danish perspective, parallel agreements are not necessarily attractive because they bind Denmark without giving it influence over how the legislation develops. When a new policy area is established or made supranational, it is tricky to foresee what content it will be given and how quickly new measures will be adopted. Until recently, few had probably imagined that the EU would have a common border agency that coordinates border operations in the Mediterranean. It is characteristic of large parts of JHA cooperation that, despite widespread concerns and political sensitivities, policies have tended to develop a lot faster than most people had expected. As JHA cooperation has been growing, so has the Danish opt-out. Precisely because the legal anatomy of the opt-out relates to the mode and not the content of the cooperation, Denmark has had few possibilities to influence this process.

To the extent that new measures are believed to go against Danish interests, the opt-out is obviously a guarantee that Denmark is not bound against its will. But the opt-out also works the other way around: Denmark cannot accede to new measures even though there is a Danish political majority in the Folketing that wishes to do so. In these cases, the Danish government can only watch as Denmark is gradually excluded from parts of EU cooperation that it hitherto participated in.

If the introduction of the Danish opt-out on JHA in 1993 was meant to signal to other member states that they should support Denmark in keeping this policy area intergovernmental, the opt-out today (instead) prevents Denmark from following the rest of Europe in this area of cooperation (Adler-Nissen and Gammeltoft-Hansen 2008). Undeniably, the opt-out provides Denmark with the freedom to pursue a different policy on certain issues. This autonomy has been used above all in the area of asylum and immigration, where in principle the opt-out guarantees the relatively strict Danish policies regarding asylum and family reunification. As this chapter has sought to demonstrate, however, this autonomy has its price. This is mainly because the opt-out in JHA has turned out to be highly inflexible when it comes to securing Denmark's interests in other areas of cooperation.

The Lisbon Treaty and the opt-in possibility

The Treaty of Lisbon gives Denmark the possibility to transform the opt-out into a so-called opt-in, and may pave the way for a (formal) structural change in Denmark's relationship with the EU. Conscious of the perspective of complete exclusion from JHA, including cooperation on police matters and criminal law, the Danish government used much of its goodwill during the negotiations on the Constitutional Treaty to secure this opt-in possibility, which is similar to the supposedly more advantageous British and Irish protocols (Dansk Institut for Internationale Studier 2008: 371–376). Importantly, this opt-in possibility can only enter into force following a Danish referendum.

Winning such a referendum will be extremely difficult for any Danish government. Not only is the opt-in possibility complicated to explain (as this chapter illustrates). Broader trends in European politics visible in the last few years also provide a difficult backdrop for holding a referendum. The euro crisis and austerity measures imposed on indebted euro member states from 2009 and onwards proved to many Danes, right or wrong, that the opt-outs (and particularly the euro opt-out) protect Danish interests. Moreover, the growth of Euro-scepticism in many European states, apparent during the European Parliament elections in June 2009, indirectly legitimizes the Danish opt-out position.

Meanwhile, the rest of Europe anticipates that Denmark *will* make use of the opt-in possibility. Attached to the modified Danish protocol is a declaration of particular importance. It states that Denmark *will* make use of the opt-in possibility, that opting out should not be permanent, and that the Commission expects Denmark to participate fully in all parts of JHA cooperation with time. The preamble to the protocol on the Danish opt-in position attached to the Treaty of Lisbon is very precise in this regard:

> Conscious of the fact that a continuation under the Treaties of the legal regime originating in the Edinburgh decision *will significantly limit Denmark's participation* in important areas of cooperation of the Union, and that it would be *in the best interest of the Union* to ensure the integrity of the acquis in the area of freedom, security and justice;
>
> Wishing therefore to establish a legal framework that will provide an option for Denmark to participate in the adoption of measures proposed on the basis of Title IV of Part Three of the Treaty on the Functioning of the European Union and welcoming the intention of Denmark to avail itself of this option *when possible in accordance with its constitutional requirements*;
>
> Noting that Denmark will not prevent the other member states from further developing their cooperation with respect to measures not binding on Denmark.
>
> (Preamble to the Protocol on the Position of Denmark, author's emphasis)

Note that two purposes are invoked for granting Denmark the possibility to adopt the opt-in possibility: Denmark's participation is significantly limited, and it is in 'the best interests of the Union'.

Contrary to the current situation, an opt-in will provide Denmark with the ability to choose on a case-by-case basis whether it wishes to participate in new EU proposals or not. The opt-in possibility guarantees Denmark three months to decide whether or not to participate in discussions once a proposal for legislation is formally presented to the Council; if Denmark decides to participate, negotiations will continue with its full participation. As another option, Denmark can choose to await the results of the negotiations and only opt in to adopted legislation later on if it changes its mind, provided this meets with the approval of the European Commission.

On paper, the opt-in possibility should provide Denmark with much more flexibility, giving it the power to decide when to participate and when to remain outside new EU legislation. Moreover, if Denmark chooses to opt in early in the process (before the three-month deadline), it will have the same influence as the other member states and will be able to leave Danish fingerprints on new EU legislation. Last but not least, Denmark will regain control of the scope and content of the opt-out, as it can choose on a case-by-case basis, irrespective of whether measures are supranational or intergovernmental. Denmark arguably gets the best of both worlds: freedom to remain outside, as well as freedom to participate.

Notwithstanding these possibilities, if comparable British and Irish experiences are examined in closer detail, it is evident that the opt-in possibility is not without its challenges. Thus, a number of potential issues might make the otherwise attractive model somewhat difficult to handle.[10] First, the national decision-making procedures in the Danish government, parliament and administration will be put under pressure to construct a national position more rapidly. Under the opt-in system, Denmark must consider whether to opt in or out each time a new proposal is put on the table. The time constraint of three months is stressful (Adler-Nissen forthcoming: 199).

Second, Danish decision-makers will have to calculate risk. Under the qualified majority voting system, a member state needs to form a blocking minority in order to prevent the legislation from being adopted. This is now the normal practice in nearly all fields of European cooperation. An opt-in possibility means that if Denmark opts in to discussions in which qualified majority voting applies and all of a sudden does not approve of the proposal, it might not be able to construct a blocking minority. In short, this means that exploiting the opt-in possibility is risky. Just as in 'normal' areas of European cooperation, the Danish government may not be able to influence the proposal 'enough', will have to accept being out-voted and will, in principle, be forced to accept legislation it dislikes.[11] In addition, an important part of the opt-in possibility is that, once Denmark's opts in, it will be obliged to opt in to all future changes of the given piece of legislation, as well as related proposals which are directly affected by it.

Third, the decision to opt in or not is not merely a question about the concrete proposal, but also about how Denmark wishes to position itself. If Denmark chooses to opt in to the majority of all new measures, it will most likely be perceived to be more or less an 'ordinary' member state within JHA (despite its special position). In contrast, Denmark may well be met with disapproval by the rest of the Union if it chooses to remain outside large parts of JHA. If Denmark systematically pulls out when it comes to cooperation that involves a large degree of political and/or financial concessions, this will also be seen as a sign of lack of solidarity. Several member states already have difficulties in understanding the need for a special Danish position in the area of asylum and immigration. Whereas the current opt-out simply prevents Denmark from participating today, it may be more difficult to explain to the other member states why Denmark should still wish to remain outside specific areas of cooperation with an opt-in possibility.

Conclusion

This chapter has argued that Denmark is an active differential European in JHA. Denmark adapts to new EU legislation even in politically sensitive areas covered by its formal opt-out protocols. Far from being an ardent intergovernmentalist or a reluctant European, shifting Danish governments have worked hard to keep Denmark highly involved in this policy area. The Danish government pragmatically circumvents the Danish sovereignty claims in the consensus-oriented EU. The *autonomy* vs. *influence* dilemma is thus far from a zero-sum game. Sometimes Denmark gets both influence and autonomy and sometimes it achieves neither autonomy nor influence. The trade-off is not clear.

It is difficult to predict how the Danish opt-out in JHA will be handled in the future. What is more certain is the continued development of JHA cooperation, i.e. structural changes will continue, resulting in increasingly more dramatic implications of opting out. Denmark can choose to introduce an opt-in possibility with a referendum. However, winning such a referendum will be extremely difficult for any government due to the political sensitivity of JHA policies. For instance, leaving the Schengen zone would have seemed out of the question a few years ago, but today this is an attractive scenario for an increasing number of Danish parliamentarians.

With the Treaty of Lisbon, Denmark will be formally excluded from participating in most JHA cooperation, from immigration to police matters and criminal law. While none of the other member states are interested in kicking Danish police officers out of the Europol headquarters, Denmark is set to be excluded from all police and criminal law cooperation within the coming decade. Even with an opt-in possibility, however, Denmark is not certain to be fully part of the game. For those politicians who would like Denmark to push above its weight within JHA, the option of completely abolishing the opt-out remains a more attractive, albeit domestically unrealistic, alternative. As long as Denmark keeps its strict immigration policy, and in particular the 24-year rule on family reunification, we are unlikely to see a total abolishment of the opt-out.

Differentiation has hitherto enabled a deepening of the integration process even though not all governments (or populations) were fully on board. For the member state in question, however, the consequences of an opt-out are often difficult to predict and politically challenging to manage. The unintended consequences of the JHA opt-out lead to a murky picture with very few clear winners. Originally constructed as a quick-fix solution, the Danish opt-out has today become just as much a straitjacket as a guarantee of national sovereignty. JHA is sensitive for all member states. However, the Danish position appears extreme in comparison with most other member states, which cooperate wholeheartedly on, for example, combatting international crime and illegal immigration.

Notes

1 This chapter builds on Adler-Nissen and Gammeltoft-Hansen (2010) and Adler-Nissen (forthcoming).
2 In addition, this dimension reflects one of the themes of the Introduction, namely, and using a FPA perspective, the need for Danish domestic factors to be (partly) balanced alongside Danish views of international commitment to the EU, either formally or informally.
3 For details regarding the debate leading up to the Maastricht referendum, see Adler-Nissen (2008), Møller (2003) and Petersen (2003).
4 The United Kingdom, Denmark and other reluctant member states attempted to resist the communitarization of asylum, immigration and border control up until the last weeks before the Amsterdam Summit, but they failed (Moravcsik and Nicolaidis 1998: 29).
5 For a discussion of differentiation in JHA, see Papagianni (2001).
6 See also Kelstrup (2006: 278) or Archer (2005).
7 See also Miles (2010a).
8 This special procedure is criticized by legal scholars for being 'complex [and] illogical' (Tuytschaever 1999: 101).
9 Refugee lawyers and NGOs have further pointed out that these minimum standards in many ways represent a black letter reading of international refugee and human rights instruments that in practice may easily result in member states falling below this threshold (Gammeltoft-Hansen 2007; Peers 2006: 352).
10 For a more detailed comparison of the United Kingdom and Denmark in this respect see Adler-Nissen (2009a).
11 Steve Peers notes that the United Kingdom has already been out-voted twice in relation to the Refugee Fund and the Return Fund. However, the United Kingdom only voted against the legislation because the House of Commons had a scrutiny reserve, not because of any objections to the two measures as such (Peers 2006: 5).

6 A pace-setter out of sync?
Danish foreign, security and defence policy and the European Union

Anders Wivel

According to most accounts – political and scholarly, critical and celebratory – Danish foreign, security and defence policy has changed dramatically since the end of the Cold War. During the Cold War, Danish foreign policy in general was pragmatic and reactive. Denmark has been a member of NATO since 1949 and the EU since 1973, but did not play a significant role in shaping the policy direction of either of these organizations, and membership was seen more as a necessary evil for protecting security (NATO) and trade (EU) interests than an opportunity for shaping international relations. This reactive pattern was also a notable characteristic with regard to the 'progressive' Nordic foreign policy agenda, where Denmark was largely a follower of the Swedish lead (Mouritzen 1995). Even on foreign policy issues where there was a distinct Nordic profile, such as human rights and solidarity with the Third World, Denmark played it safe. The country took care only to cooperate with countries in the Third World that would not upset the United States and, while voicing its general support of human rights, various Danish governments were reluctant to condemn specific human rights abuses (Holm 2002: 24–25).

By the end of the Cold War, the priorities of Danish foreign policy changed considerably. Despite initial confusion on what to make of the end of the Cold War and, in particular, the ensuing European dynamics fostering a deepening of European integration (Wæver 1992), and a general reluctance towards German unification (Mouritzen 1996), consensus soon emerged among the Danish foreign policy elite that Europe's new security order should be seen as 'a unique window of opportunity' allowing a new foreign and security policy based on so-called 'active internationalism' (Holm 2002: 21, 22–23).

Denmark's overall position in foreign and security policy changed from 'repressed atlanticism' (NATO member with reservations and stipulating no US military installations in Denmark) to 'mainstream atlanticism' (resembling other European states with an atlanticist foreign policy position that promoted a strong role for the United States in Europe and close transatlantic cooperation) before settling on a 'super atlanticist' position offering strong support to US policy post-11 September, even when this was controversial (Mouritzen 2007). Denmark supported the United States' foreign and security policy on a number of high profile and often controversial issues (including the strikes against Iraq in 1998). It participated in the war in Kosovo in 1999 (without a clear mandate from the UN) and the military mission in Afghanistan in 2002 and – more controversially – was also involved in the invasion of Iraq in 2003 and the ensuing efforts by the United States to fight the Iraqi insurgents (Larsen 2009; Wivel 2005b).

In the context of alliance politics, Denmark transformed itself from a reluctant – even latently neutral (Holbraad 1991) – NATO member into an impeccable ally, delivering exactly:

> the kind of output that NATO kept calling for: deployable expeditionary forces that were sustainable in terms of national logistics and reinforcement and that could be put in harm's way in the combat zones where NATO now needed to be engaged.
> (Ringsmose and Rynning 2008: 55–56)

This was made possible by a reform of Danish defence forces, where a territorial defence of the state by a combination of professional officers and reserves was replaced by a combination of deployable forces aimed at international missions and a so-called 'total defence' combining military and non-military measures against terrorism (Heurlin 2007: 71). Using the concepts of the Introduction to this volume, Denmark transformed its alliance policy from foot-dragging, to fence-sitting to pace-setting.

In terms of the EU's foreign, security and defence policy, Denmark has been less active, less international and by no means impeccable. An opt-out from the TEU excluded Denmark from participating in the elaboration and implementation of EU decisions and actions with defence implications. In contrast to Danish NATO policy, and Danish post-Cold War foreign policy in general, Denmark's approach to the EU's security and defence policy remained one of foot-dragging. Denmark was excluded from participating in the military missions that have so far been carried out in the Balkans, Africa and Asia (see Dansk Institut for Internationale Studier 2008). Moreover, when Europe was split over controversial issues, such as Iraq and missile defence, Denmark sided with the United States, e.g. Denmark was a co-signatory of the letter of eight in January 2003 supporting the American position on Iraq and effectively undermining the prospects for any common EU position on the issue.[1]

This is puzzling in the context of 'the widespread perception that the EU foreign policy framework provides unique access to the scene of world politics for small member states' (Larsen 2005: 1).[2] This chapter explores this puzzle by utilizing the concepts discussed in this volume's introductory chapter in order to explore the recent history of Danish foreign, security and defence policy in the context of the EU.

Stuck in the middle: Denmark between the EU, NATO and the Nordic region

Denmark has traditionally maintained a strong coherent national position in Council meetings with the Foreign Ministry, functioning as the central coordinator (Soetendorp 1999: 54). Although occasionally hailed as a 'leader state', because of its ability to maintain strong bastions of formal independence in some policy areas (including defence), while pushing for greater EU regulation in others (Eliason 2001: 192), Denmark is most often viewed as a 'fringe country' located outside the EU centre of gravity, politically as well as geographically (Soetendorp 1999: 45).

This fringe position has been particularly dominant in relation to foreign, security and defence policy. During the Cold War, Danish foreign policy was based on a functional compartmentalization between four so-called 'cornerstones', each identifying a central area of foreign policy and for each area an international organization, which Denmark could use as a platform for promoting its foreign policy interests: Security policy/NATO, economic cooperation/EU, identity politics/Nordic Council, value promotion/UN (Due-Nielsen and Petersen 1995: 38; Hækkerup 1965). These cornerstones reflected the delicate balancing of domestic and international demands on foreign policy-makers: NATO and the EU were primarily viewed as institutions of necessity, whereas the Nordic Council and the UN were viewed as institutions of choice. Using the concepts from the Introduction to this volume, NATO and the EU were mainly viewed by both the electorate and the political elite as sources for downloading policies on security and trade, whereas the Nordic Council and the UN were viewed as institutional forums ideal for uploading small state policy and value promotion, even though uploading remained symbolic in most instances. In reality, this was more a triangle than a quadrangle as the UN was used mainly as a platform for projecting Nordic and, to a lesser extent, European interests and values on to the global arena. Although foreign policy cooperation took place across the four areas, security policy was primarily a matter of Atlantic cooperation and secondarily a matter of global or all-European cooperation (Due-Nielsen and Petersen 1995: 39).

Within these frameworks, Denmark pursued three long-term priorities viewed as essential for promoting Danish security interests (Heurlin 2001). The first priority was the military defence of Denmark. In the first part of the twentieth century, this priority was pursued by a strategy of neutrality, but like a number of other European small states (see Wallace 1999), Denmark changed its strategy after the Second World War, when the country – after a brief period of relying on the United Nations and flirting with the option of a Scandinavian Defence Union – became a NATO member in 1949. NATO membership was seen as a necessary evil in the context of the Cold War (Wivel 2009), and defence expenditure as an admission fee for entry into the collective defence organization and thereby access to military protection by stronger military powers (Ringsmose 2009). Danish policy-makers remained committed to NATO membership, but, at the same time, refused US military installations on Danish territory, questioned the relevance and utility of armed forces, except for peace-keeping missions (Browning 2007), and kept Danish military expenditures consistently below the NATO average resulting in a yearly criticism of Denmark in NATO's defence planning apparatus (Ringsmose 2009: 81–82). The second priority was to promote international rules and norms of behaviour. Like other small states with limited military capabilities, Denmark has an obvious interest in an international legal system constraining the actions of all states rather than a system where power decides alone. Accordingly, Denmark promoted a rule-governed international system, from the establishment of arbitration to solve interstate conflicts in the late nineteenth century, to regulation of disarmament from the early twentieth century and participation in the United Nations from the mid-twentieth century and onwards. The third priority was cooperation and integration. Denmark pursued a security strategy emphasizing cooperation even among enemies. During the Cold War, Denmark supported détente and peaceful relations with the Soviet Union and became a member of the UN, NATO and the EU.

The three essential long-term priorities were in accordance with Denmark's 'Nordic' foreign policy identity. During the Cold War, Denmark and the other Nordic countries were often viewed by themselves and others as a bloc with a similar approach to international relations. This bloc was characterized, internally, by being a security community and, externally, by its unique approach to world politics promoting what the Nordic countries themselves (and sometimes other countries as well) saw as a progressive foreign policy agenda of peace, disarmament, cooperation, human rights, ecologically sound development and solidarity with the Third World. Creating a strong international society characterized by adherence to universal rights rather than great power politics was one of the fundamental issues promoted by all Nordic countries during the Cold War. International cooperation and peaceful relations were central as well. The Nordics tended to see their own security community as exemplary and actively promoted peaceful relations between East and West. Even the Danish military defence priority was in accordance with its Nordic affiliation as the Nordic countries made effective use of their different security policies to promote the concept of a particular 'Nordic balance', which was not to be upset by either of the superpowers if the region was to stay peaceful and characterized by low tension (Brundtland 1965; Noreen 1983).

This view of security policy left very limited room for a direct role for the EU in Danish foreign and security policy. Danish policy towards the EU was generally referred to as 'market politics' by the Danish policy elite and media, thereby signalling that European integration was viewed primarily as an economic issue (Pedersen 1996: 87), and as a pragmatic choice, in order to increase Danish economic capabilities (see the Introduction to this volume). However, Danish foreign, security and defence policy was related to the development of the EU in at least two respects.

First, the functional compartmentalization characteristic of Danish foreign policy was conditioned on a European security order, where European institutions played a fundamental role. France, the United Kingdom and the Benelux countries established the Western European Union (WEU) in 1948, via the Treaty of Brussels, as a forum for defence policy coordination and in response to the Communist coup in Prague and the fear of German military revival. In 1951, the European Coal and Steel Community (ECSC) – which merged with the European Economic Community (ECC) in 1957 – was established in order to prevent another world war on the European continent by placing French and German production of the two most important raw materials for war making, coal and steel, under a common authority (see Adler-Nissen 2009c: 56; Wivel 2000: 231). This development was an important factor in providing the geopolitical stability upon which Danish foreign policy compartmentalization rested. Paradoxically, security concerns were of vital importance for Denmark's decision *not* to join the ECSC, in particular the fear of being absorbed by Germany and a reluctance to become an insider while leaving all other states in its Anglo-Nordic geopolitical environment as non-members (see Pedersen 1996: 85). Accordingly, Denmark reacted to the new institutionalization by a pragmatic 'wait-and-see' attitude, but still benefitted from the geopolitical stability that followed from cooperation among the European great powers.

Second, the institutional order was conditioned on US support, both political and military. In this context, Nordic identity politics and value promotion in the UN was a 'luxury good', only affordable because the Nordic countries were allowed to free ride on a security order created by the presence of an American security guarantee to Western Europe and the institutionalization of the European continent. Also, the Danish reliance on NATO was left unchallenged by the institutionalization of Europe, since NATO continued as the primary collective defence alliance for Western Europe throughout the Cold War. With the United States guaranteeing security through NATO, the EU refrained from developing its own security and defence policies and capabilities (Adler-Nissen 2009c: 56).

In addition to these indirect effects of European institutionalization on Danish foreign and security policy, the establishment of the EPC in 1970 directly influenced Danish foreign and security policy after Danish accession to the EU in 1973 (Larsen 2000: 40–42). On the one hand, Denmark focused on maintaining the intergovernmental character of the EPC, keeping it distinct from the rest of the EU and ensuring that only political and economic aspects of security, and not military security, could be discussed. On the other hand, Denmark 'downloaded' policies, e.g. on the Middle East, from the EPC and 'uploaded' policy preferences to the European level in particular, with regard to the Nordic countries, and with lesser impact on the United States and South Africa. In the UN, Denmark generally continued to vote with the Nordic bloc, but at the same time tended to follow the EPC line in many policy debates (Strömvik 1998). Although occasionally portraying itself as a bridge builder between the Nordic countries and the EU, Denmark was, at most, maintaining bridges built before the Danish accession to the EU: Denmark did not defect from the Nordic bloc in the UN as a consequence of EU membership, but in cases where no other member state was prepared to break unanimity among EU member states, Denmark was unwilling to do it alone and chose to vote with the rest of the EU (Wiberg 1989).

In general, Denmark behaved pragmatically and reactively in Atlantic, European and Nordic forums, allowing others (NATO: the United States; the EU: big member states; the Nordic region: Sweden) to take the lead and positioning itself as 'allied with reservations' in relation to European, Nordic and Atlantic multilateralism.[3] Pragmatically focusing on preserving autonomy, Denmark opted for the 'selective downloading' of policies compatible with Danish interests and identity.

In sum, the EU played only a marginal role in official Danish foreign and security policy during the Cold War. After joining the EU, Denmark participated in the EPC, but with an emphasis on preserving its intergovernmental and non-military nature, i.e. focusing on protecting national autonomy rather than gaining international influence. However, below the radar, Danish foreign and security policy was conditioned by the reconstruction of the European security order after the Second World War, i.e. on the US security guarantee coupled with the construction of the ECSC, and later the EU, and the division of labour between the EU and NATO. For these reasons, Denmark's simultaneous reliance on NATO, the EU and the Nordic dimension in foreign and security policy during the Cold War was less of a problem than it might seem at first.

Free to choose? Danish foreign and security policy and the EU after the Cold War

The end of the Cold War made the EU seem an almost ideal security organization for Denmark (see Wivel 2005a). It was the only organization covering almost all aspects of security and the only significant weakness was its military capabilities. However, with a new all-European and multidimensional security agenda dominating not only academia but official statements across Europe, the non-military security identity of the EU now seemed less of a liability than ever. For Denmark, the soft nature of the EU as a security actor presented an opportunity for avoiding political marginalization, while preserving its traditional Atlantic security identity embedded in NATO. The EU created incentives for non-violence and the peaceful resolution of conflicts in most parts of the European region. Prospective member states were likely to observe norms of human rights, protection of minorities and peaceful resolution of conflicts with other states, because this was a requirement for membership (Mouritzen *et al.* 1996; Mouritzen and Wivel 2005). All West European great powers were member states, and to the extent that the values and goals of a European approach to security were made clear, they coincided with traditional Nordic priorities such as the spread of democracy, peace and human rights. The institutionalization of great power relations in the EU seemed to replace 'a Europe of many centres with a Europe of a single centre' (Wæver 1998: 54), where Germany and France constituted the engine of integration in a cooperative hegemony, providing a bulwark against the instability and conflict characteristic of European great power relations prior to the Cold War (Pedersen 1998). The continuation of Franco-German cooperation after the dissolution of the Soviet Union was an important indication of the importance of the EU for the region's stability and it contrasted with the post-Second World War period and Denmark's fear of being absorbed by Germany.

More specifically, the TEU raised the perspective of a common defence for the first time and incorporated the objective of a 'common foreign policy', but stated the foreign policy goals of the Union in a tentative and rather vague language, pointing to its intention to assert its identity on the international scene. The goals of the Common Foreign and Security Policy (CFSP), as stated in the Treaty of Amsterdam, were only slightly more specific. They stressed the ambition to strengthen the security of the Union in all ways, i.e. to safeguard common values as well as the fundamental interests, independence and integrity of the Union, and even more ambitious goals such as the desire to preserve peace and strengthen international security and cooperation, and to develop and consolidate democracy and respect for human rights and fundamental freedoms. The Treaty bound the member states legally to the so-called Petersberg tasks, which had been politically embraced by the Foreign and Defence Ministers of the WEU. However, 'on paper, the Petersberg tasks include virtually any military operation not undertaken as a result of a collective-defence commitment, since they embrace peacekeeping, humanitarian intervention and peace-establishment' (Heisbourg 2000: 6). In essence, the EU took care of important security functions in the region, but remained a civilian power without an army and the ability to act effectively in military affairs. Only in 1999, were military capability targets set for European Security and Defence Policy (ESDP) missions in the Helsinki Headline Goals and only in 2003 was a European Security Strategy agreed upon. These developments reflected a rapid development of the EU as a foreign and security policy actor after the Cold War: the collapse of the Soviet Union meant that Europe was now less central to US security interests than in the past and the break-up of Yugoslavia, and the ensuing wars in the Balkans, revealed deep divisions among EU member states as well as the inability of the Europeans to secure stability and order in their own neighbourhood, eventually leading the United Kingdom and France to take the lead in the development of the EU as a security actor.

Denmark reacted to the transformed security order faster and more radically than most other states in Europe (see Elbjørn and Wivel 2006). A new 'activist' policy was initiated by the end of the Cold War as a successful Danish attempt to help the three Baltic countries to rebuild their states and become integrated in European and transatlantic institutional structures; it was subsequently developed as a new foreign policy doctrine, making common security and the spread of democracy and human rights the foundation of Danish foreign policy from 1993 and onwards. The general Danish approach to foreign and security policy had gone from foot-dragging to pace-setting.[4] As noted in the 1997 Danish Defence Commission's 1998-white paper, 'Fremtidens Forsvar', after the end of the Cold War, Denmark now enjoyed unprecedented security in a highly institutionalized security environment, which allowed Danish foreign policy decision makers to focus on the 'indirect' threat to Danish security stemming from instability in

Europe in the absence of a 'direct' threat, which had disappeared with the Soviet Union (Danish Defence Commission 1998: 17). Soon, the country 'involved itself to an unprecedented degree in international peacekeeping, peace-building and peace-making operations' (Rasmussen 2005: 28–29).

In a few years, Denmark effectively transformed itself from what was often considered the weakest link in NATO to a Nordic and European avant-garde in defence policy. Denmark sent combat forces abroad and reformed its defence forces '[e]ven before the new security environment had been fully realized', and the goal of taking full advantage of the new security environment was shared by foreign policy-makers as well as the Danish Armed Forces, who 'enthusiastically embraced expeditionary military operations as the new *sine qua non*, and pushed actively for greater professionalization and internationalization of the Services' (Saxi 2010: 416). The events of 11 September 2001 accelerated this development. Danish defence was transformed into a two-tier system focused on internationally deployable forces combined with 'total defence', which was aimed at preventing terrorist attacks on Denmark and cushioning Danish society from the consequences in the event that it should happen (Heurlin 2007: 71–72). Territorial defence forces were finally abolished in 2004 and conscription was reduced to four months, now serving primarily as a means to education in total defence and as a way of recruiting for professional forces (Saxi 2010: 417).

European integration was to play a major role in Denmark's new foreign policy characterized by 'active internationalism', and in 1993 the Danish government outlined a radically transformed role for the EU in Danish foreign and security policy. According to a government white paper on the 'principles and perspectives in Danish foreign policy', the EU was now the most important platform for Danish foreign policy influence (Danish Government 1993). For the Danish foreign policy elite, the four cornerstones, which had served as a compass for Danish foreign and security policy during the Cold War now seemed to be exactly the pillars underpinning European integration.[5] As summed up by Foreign Minister Niels Helveg Petersen in 1996:

> Today we need the Union for three main reasons [...]. First, we need it for reasons of security [...]. The theory of 'Peace through Integration' has stood the Test of History. Today, war is literally unthinkable among members of the EU [...], second, [...] to produce common solutions to common problems [...]. More and more policy problems have international aspects that demand international action [...] thirdly, we need the Union to promote our values and defend our interests at the global level.
>
> (Niels Helveg Petersen quoted in Larsen 2000: 43)

This signalled what was already a fact: the Nordic bloc in the UN had been subsumed by a larger and more influential European bloc promoting many of the same issues of peaceful co-existence, environmental issues, human rights and development (Laatikainen 2003). Also, Denmark participated actively in the CFSP. On the civilian aspects of the CFSP in particular Denmark, Sweden (especially) and Finland successfully influenced policy content (Miles, 1998), even in the face of big member state opposition (Jakobsen 2009). Viewing EU enlargement as an important instrument of securing and stabilising Denmark's geopolitical environments, the Danish government played an active and successful role in the Eastern enlargement finally decided at the Copenhagen summit in 2002. In sum, the EU is the most important framework for Danish foreign policy across policy areas (Larsen 2005).

Danish commitment to the EU as the central institutional framework for Danish foreign and security interests seemed robust even in the wake of the terrorist attacks on New York and Washington on 11 September 2001, and in the aftermath of the cartoon crisis in January–March 2006. The fight against terror and the spread of weapons of mass destruction were (predictably) moved to a more prominent place on the foreign policy agenda and explicitly mentioned as specific foreign policy priorities in the new foreign policy agenda published by the Danish government in 2003. However, the comment was relatively brief and official statements continued to emphasize the importance of the EU, which was seen as the central forum for fighting terrorism (in close cooperation with the UN and the United States), while the United Nations was seen as the key instrument in preventing the spread of nuclear weapons (Danish Government 2003: 20–21). In 2004, this was followed up by a government white paper on terrorism underlining the continued importance of the UN, EU and NATO (Danish Government 2004). Moreover, despite what is sometimes described as late lukewarm European support for Denmark during the cartoon crisis in 2006, later that same year in its new globalization strategy, the Danish government stated that 'the EU is and will increasingly be the most important international framework for Denmark in the management of the challenges of globalization' (Danish government 2006: 11). In addition, Danish policy-makers put their words into action by participating actively in Council of Ministers discussions on foreign, security and defence affairs, (which could also be taken as notable instances of 'uploading' by Danish policy-makers – see Introduction to this volume).

Political commitment to the EU has been followed up by the Europeanization of Danish foreign, security, and defence administration. A number of civil servants in the Ministry of Foreign Affairs work full time with ESDP-related topics, and the Ministry of Defence 'has allocated almost as much manpower to take care of Denmark's relationship to the ESDP as the Ministry has allocated to take care of Danish interests in relation to NATO's defence planning' (Olsen 2011: 22). Moreover, Danish civil servants are actively involved in approximately 30 working groups in Brussels on CFSP-related topics including all groups on defence issues, with the exception of the group on the European Defence Agency (Olsen 2011: 21).

Despite this seemingly strong commitment to the EU, there were important limitations to the European integration of Danish foreign and security policy. After initially rejecting the Maastricht Treaty in a referendum in 1992, Denmark chose to stay outside EU cooperation on defence policy as one of four exemptions from the treaty granted to Denmark at the European Council meeting in

Edinburgh in December 1992, and ratified in a Danish referendum in May 1993.[6] For this reason, Danish military foreign policy activism has since taken place under the auspices of NATO, the UN and coalitions of the willing, and Danish influence within the ESDP has been limited. Militarization was an important aspect of Denmark's active internationalism, and contributing to military operations was viewed by the foreign policy decision-makers as an important means to international influence (Wivel 2012). Outside the ESDP, NATO, the UN and coalitions of the willing allowed Denmark to do this. During the Cold War, the UN had provided the institutional framework for Danish military missions but, from the mid 1990s, Danish participation in international military operations was increasingly conducted in the context of NATO and coalitions of the willing (see Table 6.1).

This development was unrelated to the actual content of EU military missions. Looking at the purposes of the military operations conducted by the EU since 2003, these are highly compatible with Danish foreign policy priorities as they focus on reducing the dangers stemming from 'indirect threats' and furthering stability and integration (see Table 6.2).

Thus, paradoxically, the transformation of Danish defence since the end of the Cold War would fit very well with a role as an active participant in EU defence policy. Denmark is now a producer of security, rather than a consumer, and has embraced the idea of denationalization of defence (allowing for specialization), and the militarization of Danish foreign policy allows for the combination of military policies with civilian policies, which could provide a strong platform for Danish influence on EU policy (see Heurlin 2007: 72; Olsen 2011: 20–21). The policy goals of ESDP missions have been almost identical to official Danish foreign and security goals, and Danish troops have been training for exactly these kinds of missions since the early 1990s (Dansk Institut for Internationale Studier 2008: 110; Larsen 2000: 102–104). In this respect, Denmark is in an ideal position for uploading policy preferences to the European level. However, at the same time, Danish participation in military missions under the auspices of the EU is precluded by the Danish exemption from the Maastricht Treaty, according to which Denmark cannot participate in the 'elaboration and implementation of EU decisions and actions which have defence implications' (EU-Oplysningen 2012b) This excludes Denmark from participation in EU military operations as well as EU planning and cooperation on development and acquisition of military capabilities.

Exclusion from EU defence policy has not excluded military activism. Most controversially, Denmark has supported the US position on a number of military issues and was a co-signatory of the letter of eight in January 2003, supporting the American position on Iraq and effectively undermining the prospects for any common EU position on the issue. Subsequently Denmark joined the American-led coalition in Iraq despite the lack of authorization from the UN Security Council. The Danish government has consistently supported the invasion of Iraq and the ensuing efforts by the United States to fight the Iraqi insurgents. Even though human rights concerns have been central to Danish foreign policy in the

Table 6.1 Danish participation in international military operations since the Second World War

Operation	Period	Location	International framework	Legal framework
The Danish Command in Germany	1947–58	Jever and Itzehoe	British Zone of Occupation in West Berlin	N/A
UNEF I	1956–67	Gaza and the Suez	UN	UNSC Resolution 1001 (ES-I) (of 7 November 1956)
ONUC	1960–4	DR Congo	UN	UNSC Resolution 143 (of 14 July 1960)
UNFICYP	1964–94	Cyprus	UN	UNSC Resolution 186 (of 4 March 1964)
UNTAG	1989–90	Namibia	UN	UNSC Resolution 435 (of 19 September 1978)
UNPROFOR I and II	1992–5	Various locations in the Balkans	UN	UNSC Resolution 743 (of 21 February 1992)
UNCRO	1995–6	Croatia	UN	UNSC Resolution 981 (of 31 March 1995)
UNPREDEP	1996–9	FYRO Macedonia	UN	UNSC Resolution 1982 (of 26 November 1996)
UNMEE	2000	Ethiopia and Eritrea	UN	UNSC Resolution 1312 (of 30 June 2000)
IFOR	1995–6	Bosnia and Herzegovina	NATO	UNSC Resolution 1013 (of 15 December 1995)
SFOR	1997–2006	Bosnia and Herzegovina	NATO	UNSC Resolution 1088 (of 12 December 1996)
AFOR	1999	Albania	NATO	N/A
OPERATION AMBER FOX	1999–2002	FYRO Macedonia	NATO	The North Atlantic Council's approval of the Operational Plan (of 26 September 2001)
KFOR	1999–	Kosovo and FYRO Macedonia	NATO	UNSC Resolution 1244 (of 10 June 1999)
ISAF	2003–	Afghanistan	NATO	UNSC Resolutions 1386 (of 14 November 2001), 1413 (of 23 May 2002), and 1444 (of 27 November 2002)
OPERATION ENDURING FREEDOM	2002	Afghanistan	Coalition	Beslutningsforslag B37 by the Danish Parliament (of 14 December 2001)
DANCON/IRAQ	2003–2007	Iraq	Coalition	Beslutningsforslag B118 by the Danish Parliament (of 18 March 2003)
Intervention in Libya	2011	Libya	NATO	UNSC Resolution 1973 (of 17 March 2011)

Sources: Hærens Operative Kommando 2008; Folketinget 2011.

Table 6.2 Military operations conducted by the EU

Operation	Period	Location	Purpose	Legal framework
ARTEMIS	2003	DR Congo	Stabilization of the security conditions and improvement of the humanitarian situation in Bunia	UNSC Resolution 1484 (of 30 May 2003)
CONCORDIA	2003	FYRO Macedonia	Contribution to the stabilization of a secure environment with regard to the implementation of the Ohrid Framework Agreement (of August 2001)	N/A
EUFOR ALTHEA	2004–	Bosnia and Herzegovina	Security contribution to facilitate the progress of further European integration in Bosnia and Herzegovina	European Council's decision 2004/570/CFSP (of 12 July 2004
SUPPORT TO AMISS II	2005–2006	Sudan/Darfur	Contribution of military and civil assistance to mission AMISS II conducted by the African Union	European Council's decision 2005/55/CFSP, OJ L 188 (of 20 July 2005)
EUFOR RD CONGO	2006	DR Congo	Military assistance to the UN mission in the Democratic Republic of the Congo	UNSC Resolution 1671 (of 2006)
EUFOR TCHAD/RCA	2008–2009	Chad and the Central African Republic	Protection of civilians, refugees and the wide distribution of humanitarian assistance	UNSC Resolution 1778 (of 2007)
ATALANTA	2008–	The Coast of Somalia	Military protection of vessels from WFP and preventive actions against piracy off the coast of Somalia	UNSC Resolutions 1814 (of 2008), 1816 (of 2008), 1838 (of 2008), 1846 (of 2008), and 1897 (of 2009)
EUTM SOMALIA	2010–	Somalia	Education and training of Somali security forces	European Council's decision 2010/197/CFSP (of 31 March 2010)

Source: European External Action Service 2011.

post-Cold War era, the government's critique of the US policy of keeping prisoners at its military base at Guantanamo Bay, Cuba, were relatively mild and low-key. During the post-Cold War era, Denmark has continuously committed a relatively high level of troops to international operations, and the 'extensive Danish willingness to deploy a significant number of forces in high-risk areas in Afghanistan has been met with much appreciation and applause inside NATO' (Ringsmose and Rynning 2008: 62). In Libya in 2011, Denmark deployed six F-16 fighters and one Hercules transport plane along with corresponding ground crews and was one of the most active and efficient participants in the coalition (see Saxi 2011).

Danish support for American security policy in general, and the Iraq war in particular, was in conflict with Denmark's continued emphasis on the importance of a rule-governed international society with a prominent place for the United Nations, which is promoted through the EU. These conflicting aspects of Danish security policy exposed a Danish dilemma between activism and influence and between a strategy mainly tied to the United States and a strategy mainly tied to the EU. Since the end of the Cold War, Denmark has pursued an activist foreign and security policy in contrast to the reactive and pragmatic policies of the past. Initially designed to maximize Danish influence, this policy has increasingly been decoupled from the international institution defined by Denmark itself to be the major arena for Danish influence on international affairs – the EU – and instead tied to the security policy of the United States. This dilemma has been ameliorated by the return of the United States to more traditional *Realpolitik* after neoconservatism and the transformation of the 'either NATO or EU' discussion into a 'how should we combine the EU and NATO' debate (Ringsmose and Rynning 2008: 79). For Denmark, however, this might prove to be an even more difficult challenge than the strained transatlantic relationship during the George W. Bush presidency, because the Danish defence opt-out prevents Denmark from participating fully in this development.

In addition, two developments within the EU challenge the ability of Denmark to pursue its foreign, security and defence policy within the EU successfully. First, the development of the EU as a foreign policy actor has accelerated the informal negotiations between the large states. Examples include the informal negotiations over the response to the wars in the former Yugoslavia in the 1990s, the terrorist attacks on Washington and New York in 2001, the Iraq War in 2003, the global financial crisis in 2008 and the war in Libya in 2011. Whether the big member states agree or not, small member states like Denmark are typically sidelined when the going gets tough and big decisions need to be made. Second, the Lisbon Treaty's introduction of the European Council President (Article 9b §6, Lisbon Treaty) and the creation of a 'High Representative of the Union for Foreign Affairs and Security Policy', which combines the posts of the Commissioner for External Relations and the role of the High Representative, merging the Commission and Council expertise on the issue of foreign affairs (Article 9e, Lisbon Treaty) is slowly altering the game of foreign and security making in the EU. For Denmark, this accentuates the need for a more coherent foreign, security and defence policy strategy integrating the military and civilian aspects of Danish foreign policy activism.

Conclusion

By its activism and its radical transformation of its armed forces, Denmark has, in some respects, been a pace-setter among small states in post-Cold War Europe. Paradoxically, it has been a pace-setter out of sync with the development of the EU as a military actor. To be sure, the EU plays a central role in Danish foreign and security policy, both as a forum for discussing foreign and security policy challenges with other EU member states and as a platform for influence beyond the normal sphere of interest for a small state. During the Cold War, European institutionalization provided an important condition for Danish foreign policy compartmentalization. After the Cold War, the EU became the most important multilateral framework for Danish foreign and security policy, but even though the EU initially presented itself as an ideal and comprehensive security institution, compartmentalization continued in the EU and NATO as a consequence of the Danish defence opt-out.

The defence opt-out limited Danish participation in the development of the EU as a military actor and reduced Danish action space with regard to pursuing an activist foreign policy agenda more generally. The effects of this development have been cushioned by the permissive interpretation of the Danish defence opt-out by Danish foreign policy-makers. This interpretation has allowed them to engage in debates in the Council of Ministers with possible implications for defence, allowing (and expecting) civil servants to engage actively in EU security and defence discussions on all issues except those with direct consequences for the operational level. Thus, the Danish political and administrative elite has continued to focus on influence by allocating resources for active participation in EU foreign, security and defence policy-making, and by using the formal channels for influence available in the EU system (such as working group participation) despite the domestically induced priority given to autonomy. The result has been a structural change in day-to-day Danish political and administrative practices, which have been Europeanized in the sense that EU policies have been downloaded (as defined in the Introduction), increasing attention and awareness on the part of domestic actors towards the EU as well as adaptation of domestic institutional structures and processes.

At the same time, Danish foreign policy has been 'Americanized' as a consequence of the Danish defence opt-out. This is as much of a structural change as administrative Europeanization, and is a paradox considering that the close Danish partnership with the United States in military affairs has been a political consequence of the reluctance of the Danish electorate to contribute to the creation of a European superpower with defence capabilities. Facing a Eurosceptic electorate domestically, and having only limited influence on the development of the EU as a security actor in general, as well as being cut off from contributing actively to ESDP missions despite their compatibility with Danish foreign and security policy priorities, Danish policy-makers have chosen to cultivate the country's bilateral relations with the United States. Current NATO-EU rapprochement points to the possible end of a meaningful division between Europeanized and Americanized elements of Danish foreign policy, but also to the continued challenges following from the Danish defence opt-out in a security environment, which rewards flexibility and the ability to cross over old institutional dividing lines.

Notes

1 The letter of eight was published on 30 January 2003, in a number of international newspapers. The letter was signed by the Prime Ministers of the United Kingdom, Italy, Spain, Portugal and Denmark (all EU members) and the governments of Poland, Hungary and the Czech Republic in support of the US position on Iraq. See Global Policy Forum (2003).
2 One potential explanation for this might relate to the past shadow of neutrality, which has constituted the core of a Danish foreign policy tradition according to the majority of historical research on the subject (Branner 2000: 186). However, Finland, another small state with a history of neutrality, has actively used the EU in its security policy (see Arter 2000).
3 For the original 'allied with reservations' argument concerning NATO, see Villaume (1995).
4 Not all aspects of Danish foreign and security policy during the Cold War may be considered foot-dragging. Danish development policy and the Danish contribution to superpower détente during the Cold War may be considered activist (Wivel 2012).
5 I owe the general point to Larsen (2009).
6 See also Morten Kelstrup's contribution to this volume.

7 Denmark and the Council of Ministers

Rasmus Brun Pedersen

Introduction

The Council of Ministers has been the primary focus of attention for Danish EU policy for a long time. It has always served as the central platform for Danish interest representation in the EU, with considerable uploading of Danish interests (see the Introduction to this volume) taking place via the Council. A main characteristic of Danish Council policy has been the presentation of intergovernmental preferences as well as a reluctant position towards further institutional integration while, at the same time, actively participating in the everyday policy of the Council.[1] Danish Council politics have often been characterized as a dilemma between gaining influence and maintaining national autonomy. In Chapter 2, Morten Kelstrup defines this as an 'integration dilemma' experienced by actors confronted with a new important step towards further integration. The situation might be that the actor has to choose between either: (1) participating in more intensified integration with the risk of being entrapped or being forced to accept decisions, he would otherwise reject; or (2) actually reject further integration entailing the risk of being abandoned, left outside the integration process or losing influence within this (see also Kelstrup 2000a, 2000b, 2006; Petersen 1998; Wivel 2005a). As Kelstrup notes, the integration dilemma has been most visible in the Danish Council policies, especially regarding the question of institutional reforms of the Community, where Denmark has often fought to maintain (and uploaded preferences advocating) the institutional status quo and aimed at participating actively in the institutions' everyday policy.

The Danish status quo orientation in the Community has long been secured by, and via, relatively rigid policies towards further institutional reforms in order to combat steps toward further transfer of institutional integration resulting in an erosion of the position of the small states in the Community. Preservation of the Council institutions has been seen as a central platform for the protection of Danish autonomy and as a vehicle for interest representation. Danish Council policy has thus traditionally been built around a defence of the principle of unanimity and a fierce rearguard opposition against reform addressing in the way the Council works in the everyday policy-making – including the preservation of the rotating presidency.

This status quo position has often had the character of erecting certain 'bastions' by which the Danish government has sought to defend the institutional status quo (Mouritzen 1988, 1995; Mouritzen and Wivel 2005: 36). One particular bastion influencing Danish Council policy has been to fight reforms that would alter the balance between small and large member states and between the institutions where Denmark traditionally has favoured the centrality of the Council and the preservation of unanimity. Another bastion of Danish Council policy has been to defend equal representation between small and large member states via the rotating presidencies in the Council structure. The main problem for Danish governments – especially Social Democratic ones – has, throughout the Danish participation in the EU, been the question of institutional development of the EU institutions. The Danish viewpoint has been that problems within the EU were related to the lack of political will rather than dysfunctional institutions or the lack of formal procedures (Petersen 2006: 654).

However, the picture of a reluctant Danish attitude to institutional reforms of the Council and the Community is supplemented by a more pragmatic attitude to the work of the Council. Denmark has traditionally aimed at being actively involved, both formally and informally, in the everyday negotiations in the Committee of Permanent Representatives (COREPER) and the working groups in order to benefit via active participation and exploitation of the existing institutional structures of the Council.

Danish Council policy has therefore maintained a dualistic character, and this has particular resonance in the light of the themes identified in the Introduction of this volume. On the one hand, Danish Council policies have traditionally been characterized by rearguard (sometimes foot-dragging) action and an attempt to build and defend political bastions in order to fight further institutional integration (such as changes in voting procedures and the change of balance between small and large states and between the institutions). On the other hand, Danish officials have uploaded Danish preferences and participated actively in the everyday politics of the Council and attempted to exploit the existing institutional framework.

Successive EU enlargements, as well as the evolving EU constitutional debate over the last decade, have put pressure upon the respective intergovernmental positions apparent in Danish Council policies. The demand for greater democratic legitimacy in the Community has further underlined the need for a gradual revision of central elements in the Danish Council policy. A gradual change of central Danish positions and an abandonment of bastions on institutional issues in order to 'manage' the dilemma of integration can therefore be detected. This, coupled with the Danish ambition throughout the 1990s and the 2000s to first, conduct a more active foreign policy, second, to have the ambition to further integrate Denmark so that she is regarded as part of the European mainstream, and finally, to 'maximize' Danish influence within the community has resulted in a gradual removal of the Danish resistance towards institutional reforms of the Community and the Council structures. This has most notably concerned the question about qualified majority voting in the

Council, the increase of European Parliament involvement and the question of the role of the Council presidencies. However, this gradual revision has passed by and has been remarkably unnoticed by the literature as well as Danish public debates, which is surprising given the controversial character of the questions involved.

This chapter argues that the traditional Danish Council 'bastions' have gradually been eroded over the last decades of constitutional bargaining and successive rounds of EU enlargements in order to manage the dilemma of integration and to avoid marginalization of Denmark in the Community. A substantial part of this change can be explained by a gradual adaptation to the integration dynamics by Danish actors, but also by a change in the coalition patterns of the parties traditionally negotiating Danish EU policy. Growing pragmatism predominated throughout the 2000s, compared to the orthodoxy that otherwise characterized Danish Council policy in the 1980s and 1990s.

Parliamentary foundation of Danish Council policy

The Danish parliament (the Folketing) and the political parties play a crucial role in formulating Denmark's Council policies. A general explanation is that, normally, Denmark is governed by minority governments with relatively weak parliamentary bases (Damgaard 2000). This problem is often mitigated by a tendency to form broad consensus coalitions regarding EU-policy since minority governments need external support from the opposition to form majorities in order to pass legislation (Benz 2004; Christiansen and Pedersen 2011). While Chapter 14 focuses on a presentation of Danish EU-coordination, this chapter primarily deals with the relevance of the interparty mode of Danish EU-coordination (Damgaard 2000; King 1976).

Danish EU policy is normally decided between a permanent coalition of political parties consisting of the Liberal Party, the Conservative Party, the Social Liberal Party and the Social Democratic Party and in addition, since 2004, the Socialist People's Party. Table 7.1 shows that successive Danish governments enjoyed relatively broad and stable coalitions of political parties behind their bargaining positions in the Council of Ministers in the period from 2001–2009. It is interesting to note that the Socialist People's Party is also highly supportive – 86.6 per cent on average – when the government has required a mandate. The Eurosceptic Unity List (the Red–Green Alliance) supports in 55.6 per cent of the cases, while the Danish People's Party is supportive in 71.3 per cent of the cases.

The group of mandate parties also favours EU-initiated legislation in the Danish parliament. Table 7.2 shows the rather large majority supporting legislation that originates from the EU and that has been negotiated by the government in the Council. This suggests that the EU is not debated in a consistent way and at the same level and in a similar fashion to regular domestic politics. It seems that the degree of consensus supporting EU-initiated legislation is higher when compared to that of normal domestic politics (Green-Pedersen 2012).

Table 7.1 Support for government's request for mandates in the EAC

	2001	2001–2005	2005–2007	2007–2009	Average
The Unity List – the Red-Green Alliance	48.6	58.7	48.9	58.5	55.6
The Socialist People's Party	90.5	88.0	85.9	84.4	86.6
The Social Democratic Party	100	96.4	92.7	91.8	94.4
The Social Liberal Party	100	97.2	95.0	87.1	94.7
The Christian Democratic Party	96.2	–	–	–	–
The Conservative Party	99.4	100.0	100.0	100.0	100.0
The Liberal Party	99.4	100.0	100.0	100.0	100.0
The Danish People's Party	79.0	74.7	64.9.	72.1	71.3
N (Total no. of mandates)	105	392	262	147	906

Source: Christiansen and Pedersen 2011.

Note
The percentages are calculated as the share of votes that are not against the government's negotiation mandate. The numbers for 2001 cover the 2001–2002 session and parts of the 2000–2001 session.

The figures suggest that Danish EU-coordination is negotiated between a rather broad and stable coalition that seems to support the mandates and the positions of the Danish government in the Council negotiations.

Including the opposition parties in the formulation of the government's bargaining mandates, and the stability thereby achieved, seems to serve two effects. First, it secures the existence of a stable majority behind the government's bargaining mandate in the Council and thereby enables a minority government to pass legislation initiated by the EU without the fear of having a majority against it. Second, it ensures that the coalition parties have the opportunity to influence the content of the bargaining mandates of the Danish government, and enables them to maintain a tight parliamentary control over the government's bargaining strategy in the Council negotiations (Christiansen and Pedersen 2011).[2]

When a party participates in providing a mandate in the Committee, they apparently also, more or less directly, commit themselves to secure the ratification in the parliamentary vote on the legislative bill later on – provided that the government has done its utmost to represent the mandate during Council bargaining. There is a political price to such a parliamentary commitment. The price of stability is political influence on the mandates, and the minister is, in turn, forced to incorporate wishes from the coalition members in the positions and mandates for the upcoming negotiations in the council (Christiansen and Pedersen 2011; Nielsen and Pedersen 2011).

This procedure for negotiating governmental mandates and bargaining positions gives the coalition parties excellent opportunities to influence and direct the content of the mandates and the overall strategy of Danish policy in relation to the 'high politics' of the intergovernmental conferences where the Union's institutional politics are negotiated (See Chapter 14 for a discussion of the benefits of a centralized EU-coordination system). This implies that formal Danish

Table 7.2 Support for ratification of 'EU-initiated legislation' in the Folketing 1998–2010

	The Unity List – Red-Green Alliance	The Socialist People's Party	The Social Democratic Party	The Social Liberal Party	The Conservative Party	The Liberal Party	The Danish People's Party
1998–2001	55.5	86.4	100.0	100.0	89.1	88.2	73.6
2001–2005	43.3	67.0	90.7	90.7	100.0	100.0	89.7
2005–2007	46.0	80.7	93.2	93.2	100.0	100.0	86.4
2007–2010	62.4	84.7	90.6	90.6	100.0	100.0	91.8

Source: Christiansen and Pedersen 2011.

Note
Support is measured by the share of 'yes' votes (percentage) in the individual parties.

Council policy is negotiated between a broad coalition of parties including more traditional pro-European parties like the Liberal Party, but also includes talks with more intergovernmental-minded parties like the Social Democratic Party (especially in the 1980s and early 1990s) and the Socialist People's Party (Pedersen 2009). Petersen (1995) has pointed out that these coalition dynamics for Danish EU policy traditionally placed the Social Democratic Party in a dominant position in Danish EU policy which, ultimately, has led to a Danish Council policy tainted by an intergovernmental and reluctant position toward further insitutional reforms of the structure of the European institutions (Petersen 2006; Pedersen 2009). In this perspective (or at least as part of it), the traditional reluctant positions of the Danish government in the context of EU-policy can be explained by the domestic coalition dynamics resulting from the Danish tradition of having minority governments, as well as the inclusion of a broad coalition centred around a dominant Social Democratic Party when the Danish bargaining positions are to be negotiated in the Community.

Therefore – in order to understand how Denmark chose to react to the integration dilemma identified by Kelstrup – future research on Danish EU policy should turn its attention to a study of how the coalition partners subscribed to, and were weighted between, perspectives relating to autonomy vs. influence argumentation. Recent studies seem to suggest that, due to an increased pragmatism among the pivotal actors in this coalition, a gradual acceptance of institutional reforms of the Council structure (as part of EU decision-making) have developed (Hug and König 2002). Comparing Danish bargaining positions from the 1980s and 1990s, with the positions from 2000 and onwards, clearly indicates that Denmark has abandoned many traditional bastions in its Council policy and seems to have prioritized participation over maintaining national autonomy (Pedersen 2009; Laursen 2002, 2008; Petersen 2006). Danish acceptance of the institutional terms and arrangements provided by the Lisbon Treaty[3] suggests that Denmark, as small state, has become more pragmatic in its Council politics. Danish policy-makers have consistently argued that Denmark maintains sizable and positive interests in (further) EU enlargement and is a regular proponent of well-functioning and efficient institutions in order to maximize the economic benefits from membership. This interpretation might exaggerate the role of domestic factors as the determinants on Danish Council policy, since EU developments during the respective period forced Denmark, and its policy-makers, to reorient its policies and principles on the institutional issues in many respects.

Danish Council policy

Calls for greater efficiency and an interest in an increased market after the enlargement means that, in general terms, small states face a growing pressure to alter the Union's institutional structure in order to secure well-functioning institutions in the EU. Many of these reform changes seem to favour the larger member states, since their formal position in the Council is strengthened with the Lisbon Treaty. Studies of the legislation process in the Council show that the larger member states obviously dominate much of the legislation (Thorhallsson and Wivel 2006; Napel and Widgren 2010). At the same time, research of the Council's everyday policy also shows that small countries like Denmark have many opportunities to compensate for their relative size and often gain more influence over the shape and form of legislation that far exceeds their formal positioning and relative size within the EU. This in turn indicates that formal voting power is not all that matters in Council negotiations.

Traditionally, Denmark has been sceptical towards further institutional reforms and has conducted an *arrière-garde* fight against them; it has aimed at enjoying the economic benefits from membership through an active participation in the Council's everyday politics and has attempted to exploit the existing institutional framework. Where the 'bastion politics' on the institutional issues primarily took the form of 'negative' bastions in order to maintain national autonomy, the Danish strategy in the everyday policy of the Council has been more nuanced since Denmark has tried to form 'positive' bastions and engage in coalition building with like-minded countries in order to gain influence on the legislation adopted by the Council (Mouritzen 1988, 1995; Mouritzen and Wivel 2005). The ability to form coalitions has become more important given (and alongside) the gradual removal of unanimity; the predominant voting principle in the Council means that veto threats from sceptical intergovernmentalist countries no longer have the same weight and/or bearing upon ongoing EU negotiations.

While it is relatively easy to estimate the formal power of the member states in the Council, it is much more difficult to define their informal bargaining power and ability to influence the legislation process (Thorhallson and Wivel 2006). Recent studies suggest, and the Introduction to this volume also highlights, that it is equally important to look at the 'informal' power of the member states in the negotiations. Informal power is difficult to define, but can be understood as a combination of the material resources of a country (e.g. size of the economy and the population), and other non-material resources, such as diplomatic skills, the activity of the country's ministers and officials in negotiations in the Council and the negotiators' social network capacity.

Formal influence in the Council

In recent years, most legislation adopted by the Council is, as earlier mentioned, by Qualified Majority Voting (QMV). The word 'qualified' refers to the fact that not all states have equal voting power. By definition, the use of QMV reduces the influence of the smaller states in Council voting since, formally, they cannot cast a veto.

The question of the extension of QMV in the Council has long been central to Danish Council politics. QMV now applies to most policy areas, and has largely replaced unanimity and simple majority voting. The two traditional voting methods of unanimity and simple majority voting favour the smaller member states in the EU as each state has the same weight regardless of their size;

however, it has only been applied to procedural matters in a limited number of policy areas (Westlake and Galloway 2004). The unanimity voting method requires the approval of all members of the Council – or at least the acquisition of all members, since abstention does not prevent unanimity. The unanimity voting method thereby, in theory, provides the small member states with the same possibility to prevent proposals from being adopted as the large member states, since, formally, they have the same bargaining power in areas decided with unanimity in the Council (Thorhallsson and Wivel 2006). In theory, this meant that a single small member state or a coalition of smaller member states could block legislation in the Council. The gradual introduction of QMV, induced by the Nice and the Lisbon Treaties, has formally clearly favoured the larger member states because the voting powers of member states have been altered in their favour.[4] In theory, the extension of the QMV method into more policy fields seems to weaken the small member states' position in the Union's decision-making process. However, as generally acknowledged in the literature, the small states' veto power is limited in practice and the threat to veto is an option mainly used by the larger member states (Moravcsik 1993). Still, the question of introducing QMV has been a central element in Danish Council policy. Some Danish reservations can be interpreted as an attempt to formulate barriers to this adaptation, and as examples of 'foot-dragging' (see Introduction to this volume) – or at least to institutionalize certain inertias in the adaptation process within an institutional power structure in which Denmark has only had limited influence as a small state (Kelstrup 2000a: 424). However, comparing Danish positions since 2003 with traditional Danish positions during earlier treaty reform negotiations, suggests a willingness to accept more QMV and an increase in the co-decision procedure (Laursen 2008: 257). It seems that Denmark, as a small dependent state, is realizing that it must swim with the current, as the costs of exit would be high (Laursen 2008: 264). This indicates that an increased pragmatism in Danish Council policy has prevailed in the last decade, and that Denmark gradually has abandoned some of the traditional bastions (or 'foot-dragging') relating to the general introduction of QMV as part of EU decision-making (see for instance Pedersen 2009; Petersen 2006; Haahr 1992, 1993). Denmark seems to have accepted a loss of formal powers in order to be able to secure well-functioning institutions after successive EU enlargements.

If the rules of the Lisbon Treaty are examined, especially those that will come into force in 2014, small countries are secured representation in one part of the double-majority procedure according to which a winning majority must contain 55 per cent of member states. Country population size is represented in the second part of the procedure, where a winning majority must include 65 per cent of the EU population.

One way of showing the formal effects of the change in Danish bargaining power, before and after the Lisbon Treaty, is to calculate a power index that presents the possibilities for a given country to convert a losing majority to a winning majority (this index is also known as the Shapley–Shubik index). The

Table 7.3 Formal voting power in the Council of Ministers under the Nice Treaty and Lisbon Treaty

Member state	SSI – Nice Treaty	SSI – Lisbon Treaty
Germany	8.7	15.5
France	8.7	11.5
UK	8.7	10.9
Italy	8.7	10.6
Spain	8.0	7.9
Poland	8.0	6.6
Romania	4.0	4.1
Netherlands	3.7	3.3
Greece	3.4	2.4
Belgium, Portugal, Czech Republic	3.4	2.3
Hungary	3.4	2.2
Sweden	2.8	2.1
Austria	2.8	2.0
Bulgaria	2.8	1.8
Denmark, Slovakia, Finland	2.0	1.5
Ireland	2.0	1.3
Lithuania	2.0	1.2
Latvia, Slovenia	1.1	1.0
Estonia	1.1	0.9
Cyprus	1.1	0.8
Luxembourg	1.1	0.7
Malta	0.8	0.8

Source: Beach 2010.

Note

The Shapley-Shubik Index (SSI) shows a country's share of the total power. The figures have been rounded to one decimal place. Due to this, the figures do not always add up to 100 per cent.

index has been applied in Table 7.3 on both the existing rules of the Nice Treaty and the new rules of the Lisbon Treaty's double-majority procedure, which applies from 2014.

Table 7.3 shows – not very surprisingly – that, formally, the large member states are the most powerful in the Council. Under the current rules, the four largest countries are equally likely to have the casting vote (8.7 per cent) in turning a losing majority into a winning majority. The table also shows that the smaller member states are over-represented relative to their population size.[5] This present over-representation is reduced with the Lisbon Treaty. Here we see that Germany's formal power is estimated to increase from 8.7 per cent to 15.5 per cent and we see a similar but weaker tendency for the other large member states. Conversely, the formal weight of the smaller countries will be weakened in the new system. After 2014, the Danish weighting power will drop to 2 per cent (or relative from 23 per cent of Germany's weight to 13 per cent) (Beach 2010). Formal power is of course significant if a country wants to stop unwanted legislation in the Council. But it is one thing to talk of formal power – another is who decides in reality and how the member states gain influence in the Council.[6]

Informal influence in the Council

Recent research shows how the larger member states with the largest voting power dominate the legislation process in the Council. In a study of 60 different EU-directives, Thomsen *et al.* (2006) have demonstrated that the largest member states were the most powerful. Similarly, Naurin and Lindahl (2008b) show that when governments are asked which countries they most often work with they often refer to Germany, France and Great Britain. The result of these studies seems to indicate that the largest member states dominate the cooperation pattern in Council negotiations.

However, recent research also shows that the smaller member states have other opportunities, exceeding their formal power, to influence the legislation process in the Council of Ministers. Studies suggest that countries like Denmark, Sweden and the Netherlands have much more influence on EU legislation than should be expected relative to their formal power. Three factors in particular, enable small countries to achieve a relatively greater impact than their formal size.

Council presidencies

The rotating presidency of the Council of Ministers is often an opportunity for smaller countries to set the agenda for a while, and negotiate compromises that favour their own interests (Tallberg 2006). In a set of statistical analyses, Arregui and Thomson (2009) and Schalk *et al.* (2007) have shown that countries holding the presidency are able to put their stamp upon laws adopted by the EU. It is therefore a potentially important change in the conditions for small-state influence that the larger member states have been successful in establishing a long-term chair of the European Council and a long-term Union Minister of Foreign Affairs, who chairs the Foreign Affairs Council.

The changes introduced by the Lisbon Treaty constitute a fundamental shift from the rule of rotating presidencies of the European Council and the Foreign Affairs Council. Small countries have fought hard to minimize the power of the chair of the European Council because they were concerned that the new permanent chair would become an instrument for the larger member states' preferences. This push by larger states to increase the power of long-term chairs is problematic for the smaller member states, because they have traditionally used the presidency to increase their influence and prestige within the Community. Even though the rotating presidencies of the other Council formations will continue, and small states will seek to reduce the power of the long-term chairs, the respective presidency will have comparably less power and influence than the respective leader of the country holding the rotating presidency under the current system (Magnette and Nicolaïdis 2005), the small member states are likely to face increased pressure to amend the rotating presidencies further and to give increased power to the long-term chairs.

Denmark – together with other small states – has traditionally seen the presidency as a means to increase its international prestige (see Miles 2003a), because it provides small states with a valuable opportunity to play a major international role. This was clearly visible during the last Danish presidency in 2002, when the Danish chairmanship successfully negotiated the terms and conditions for the enlargement of the EU (Thorhallsson and Wivel 2006). Moreover, the most recent enlargement of the EU means that each state would have to wait more than 12 years between presidencies – a gap set to increase with future enlargements.

While it should have been expected that Denmark would defend the continuation of the rotating presidency in the Union, the Danish government (influenced by its experiences from its presidency in 2002) sought – during the negotiations of the convention in 2003 and later on at the IGC on the Constitutional Treaty and the Lisbon Treaty negotiation – to argue for a more flexible arrangement to run the EU (Laursen 2008). Denmark therefore supported the idea of a group presidency, to solve the problems of continued representation of the existing model. But, following the experiences with the Danish presidency in 2002, the then Danish Prime Minister, Anders Fogh Rasmussen, after admitting that the coordination across the council formations was essential, was more sceptical. As he noted, 'the very question of coordination across Council formations is the Achilles' heel of the group presidency' and therefore a group presidency would be paralyzed in an enlarged EU and would not be able to function (cited in Laursen 2008: 253). Instead, Denmark pragmatically started to support the idea of an elected Council President in order to secure 'continuity, clarity and balance in relation to the Commission'. Further, the Danish government now argued that a permanent chair would present a solution to the problem of the national presidencies' increased workload. However, Fogh Rasmussen saw two risks with the new system: (1) It would potentially disrupt the balance between large and small member states in the Community; and (2) it would lead to unfortunate conflict with the Commission. If the model were to be adopted, it should therefore include some institutional safeguards to ensure equal status of large and small member states in the Community.

In the final negotiations of the Constitutional Treaty, and later the Lisbon Treaty, the proposal to introduce a permanent European Council President was accepted, while the rotating presidency would be maintained. Denmark further accepted the idea of a Common EU Foreign Minister. The construction was now seen as a means to maintain efficiency in the Council, with a close coordination between the permanent President and the national presidency. The question of reforming the Union presidency reveals a central element of the dilemma of integration; the introduction of a permanent EU President, on the one hand, would mean a decrease in national autonomy and opportunities to influence the EU. On the other hand, it is of strong interest to Denmark that both the EU and the institutions function well. In an enlarged EU, with a broad group of small member states without the capacity to lift the burdens of an EU presidency, the new model would provide the EU with some continuity and stability, which is in the Danish interest. Over time, Denmark seems to have solved the dilemma by accepting a reduced autonomy in order to secure (well-) functioning institutions in an enlarged EU.

The changing nature of the presidency is an important challenge for the small states to have influence, but it should be weighed against the potential gains in the efficiency of institutions. As small states benefit the most from an international environment characterized by strong international institutions, they have an interest in the continued and increasing effectiveness of EU policy-making.

Consensus culture

The culture of resolution in the Council of Ministers is characterized by a certain kind of 'club atmosphere'. In public, and in the Danish debate, the ministers often give an impression that it is 'us against them', but behind the closed doors of the Council of Ministers the norm for consensus in Council negotiations is strong (Westlake and Galloway 2004). The norm says that great efforts are often made to ensure that countries agree on legislation with unanimity. Often negotiations in the Council continue long after a majority is found to ensure that all member states' specific interests are met. This norm also secures that smaller countries' views are often heard in negotiations over legislation.

Activity and engagement in the Council negotiations

Recent research indicates that small countries are often very active in Council negotiations, and they are often better prepared and have more well-coordinated and detailed bargaining positions, which seems to help the smaller member states to gain influence beyond their formal bargaining power (Panke 2010a). Studies of cooperation patterns in the Council have shown that although the three large countries are most central in negotiations, small states like Denmark, the Netherlands and Sweden are the second most central actors (Naurin and Lindahl 2008b; Mattila 2008; Arregui and Thomson 2009). The effect of the gradual abandoning of unanimity in Council negotiations seems to have forced the member states to alter their negotiation behaviour. The literature suggests that this has impacted upon Danish Council policy, as it apparently has changed from negative to positive bastion building in order to become more active in promoting Danish interests. In Council history, Danish positions were, for a long time during the 1970s and 1980s, closely linked with other intergovernmental-minded countries like France and the United Kingdom in order to defend their autonomy and influence over what were considered 'national policies' (Petersen 2006; Pedersen 2009).

After the accession of Sweden and Finland, Denmark soon found new allies that shared many of their preferences and priorities in the community, for instance on environmental, employment and consumer policies. This suggests that Denmark has tried to form alliances with like-minded countries in an attempt to form positive bastions in its Council policy, on selected policy areas (Mattila 2004, 2008: 31; Zimmer *et al.* 2005). The general impression of the research on the Council is that northern member states more often communicate and vote together with other northern member states (Mattila 2008: 31; Mattila and Lane 2001; Naurin and Lindahl 2008b). This implies that the Nordic countries are more likely to vote together than with southern members and vice versa. However, previous analyses show that, on average, larger member states (Mattila 2004) and northern member states (Hayes-Renshaw *et al.* 2006) are more likely to abstain or vote against than smaller member states or southern member states (Mattila 2008: 29). In a recent study, Mattila shows that Sweden (together with Denmark, Poland and Lithuania) tops the list of 'no' votes and abstainers in Council voting. Mattila also provides a more detailed analysis of the most frequent dissenting coalitions in the Council. The analysis shows the most active country pairs that together have contested proposals on the Council's table. Naurin and Lindahl's (2008b) results are especially interesting, since they seem to support what many politicians and commentators claim, i.e. empirical evidence indicates that the Danish opt-outs must be removed if Denmark is to play a key role in the EU. Paradoxically, this seems to be quite the opposite, since the reservations seem to force Danish – and Swedish – ministers and officials to be more active and better prepared than their counterparts in order to gain influence (see also Adler-Nissen 2009a).

Conclusions

One of the central challenges for Denmark as a small state has been to react to the continued pressure from larger member states to change the institutional structure in their favour. The Council has, in this respect, always served as the central platform for Danish interest representation. The Danish status quo orientation in the Community has long been secured by relatively rigid policies towards further institutional integration in order to ensure that the balance between small and large member states was not disrupted. This has historically resulted in a Danish Council policy traditionally built around a defence for the principle of unanimity and a fierce opposition against attempts to reform the institutional structure of the Community. Enlargements of the EU, combined with the Danish ambition to pursue an active and committed alliance strategy throughout the 1990s and 2000s, have resulted in a change in Danish Council policy. The traditional reluctant Danish attitude towards institutional reforms has been seen as a limitation that has duly constrained Danish ambitions of seeking greater influence in the EU, and as inhibiting future EU enlargement; consequently, Denmark has gradually abandoned its opposition towards reforms of the Council's structure. In terms of the integration dilemma identified by Kelstrup, Denmark seems to have chosen influence over autonomy in its Council policies.

A reluctant attitude to institutional reforms of the Council and the Community was always supplemented by a more active attitude to the Council's work. Denmark has traditionally aimed at being actively involved in everyday negotiations in COREPER and the working groups in order to benefit from any cooperation through active participation and exploitation of existing, institutional Council structures. Danish Council policy has therefore had a dualistic character.

On the one hand, Danish policies towards the Council have been characterized by rearguard actions, elements of 'foot-dragging' and an attempt to build and defend political bastions in order to fight further institutional integration; on the other, they have represented a serious effort on the part of Danish actors to participate actively in the everyday politics of the Council and to exploit the existing institutional framework. The adoption of the Lisbon Treaty has, in many respects, been influenced by Denmark's opportunities to formally influence Council legislation but has, on the other hand, highlighted the need for a more active profile in the Council's everyday policy-making.

Notes

1 The term 'Danish Council policy' has been adopted in the context of this chapter to mean all Danish (informal and formal) policy positions and preferences adopted by the Danish government in relation to the workings of the Council of Ministers, and towards issues relating to the EU that are being discussed within the specific institutions of the Council of Ministers (including COREPER). This term therefore implies (and, indeed, incorporates) dynamics relating to uploading, cross-loading and downloading, as well as pace-setting, fence-sitting and foot-dragging, as outlined in the Introduction to this volume.
2 This interpretation is supported in Nedergaard's discussion in Chapter 14 of this volume. He further argues that the centralized character of the Danish coordination system seems to have served as a political instrument for EU-sceptical parties to gain influence on Danish EU policy and to secure an intergovernmental position often used to build Danish bastions in the community.
3 The Lisbon Treaty provided for three big reforms of the Council structure: (1) a permanent President to chair the European Council for a two and a half year period, renewable once. The President is to represent the EU in international affairs together with the new foreign minister; (2) from 2014 onwards, the qualified majority will represent a so-called 'double majority', which may require 55 per cent of the member states, representing 65 per cent of the population. In the existing 27 EU countries, these Lisbon rules would allow three big member states and a small one to block a decision desired by the remaining 23 countries. Certain key decisions still require unanimity, for example the admission of new member states, tax matters and major foreign and security issues; and (3) a system of team presidencies is introduced, meaning that three countries will chair all council compositions for 18 months together. But they will all get to chair each council for six months.
4 In some particularly sensitive areas, such as common foreign and security policy, taxation, asylum and immigration policy, Council decisions still have to be unanimous. In other words, each member state has the power of veto in these areas.
5 For example, Denmark has a 2 per cent likelihood of converting the majority that is approximately a quarter of Germany's formal power (8.7 per cent) even though the Danish population is only 6.7 per cent of the German.
6 It is notoriously difficult to measure power, and even harder to estimate who has had the greatest influence on a specific legislation and why. For example, if the outcome corresponds to a country's position, it may reflect the fact that the country has had an impact on the outcome, but it can also be said that a government without special interest in a topic has taken a position similar to what they *expected* most countries to want (Beach 2010). But if the outcome still corresponds to its position, it cannot automatically be concluded that the country has had an impact.

8 Denmark and the European Commission

Entering the Heart of the Union

Caroline Howard Grøn

Introduction

This chapter examines how Denmark and key Danish actors relate to the European Commission (Commission). While Denmark might be broadly interpreted to mean all Danes, the focus in this chapter will be on how the Danish government relates to the Commission.[1] More specifically, the chapter explores the opportunities for Danish actors to upload preferences and policies to the Commission (as discussed in the Introduction to this volume). Nevertheless, as regards the Commission context, downloads to the Danish national level also take place, typically in the form of ongoing adjustments of Danish positions in the light of, and in response to, Commission positions. First, the chapter will provide a brief history of the relationship between Denmark and the Commission. Second, attention is next focused on the way day-to-day politics are handled in relation to the Commission today. Here, focus is on the ways the Danish government seeks to influence activities inside the Commission. The chapter especially concentrates on two of the four distinctions identified in the Introduction to this volume, namely, questions of formal vs. informal channels of autonomy and influence and change vs. continuity.

The findings of the chapter are drawn from different sources. Twenty-three interviews have been carried out with Danish diplomats in Brussels, Danish civil servants based in Copenhagen dealing with the Commission, as well as Danes working within the Commission, and all covering a wide array of policy areas. The aim of the interviews was generally to provide an overview of the strategies available when influencing the Commission, as well as an evaluation of their impact. Areas affected by the Danish opt-outs, as well as areas not affected by the opt-outs, were covered. Generally, the Danish strategies available in relation to the Commission did not differ substantially as regards this aspect. A small number of interviews were conducted in order to gain a better understanding of Danish policy towards the Commission, since very little of the policy is publicly available.[2,3] Finally, information obtained via interviews is supplemented by numerous other sources such as official statistics, legal documents and other publicly available information.

The Commission – why do they care?

The Commission is centrally placed in the EU (Nugent 2000). Holding the right of initiative as well as being 'guardian of the Treaties', the Commission plays an undeniable role both when legislation is formed and when its implementation is to be evaluated.[4] Significantly, the Commission is traditionally perceived as a friend of smaller member states due to its obligation to defend the European interest (Bunse *et al.* 2005: 12–15), rather than the particular interests of member states. As part of the existing configuration of the Union, the Commission retains the important role of mediating power battles between member states, which are expected to play out in the Council. For Denmark, these power battles are, at least theoretically, hard to enter, let alone win, since Denmark formally constitutes a small state with only seven votes. The enlargement of the EU to 27 member states changed the dynamics in the Council, which, according to the internal guide of the Danish Foreign Ministry, enhances the importance of the Commission and early interest mediation:[5]

> Those days are over where the Council was the central arena for member states. The complexity of the legislative procedure means first and foremost that the framework outlined in the initial proposals put forward by the Commission is even more important than before. It is much easier to fight to maintain a good idea in a proposal than introducing it at a later stage.
>
> (Permanent Representation of Denmark to the EU 2008: 1, author's translation)

The Commission hence constitutes an important access-point for a small member state like Denmark, and duly attracts, and warrants, interest from scholars. However, measuring influence is notoriously difficult. Here, it is operationalized in this chapter via means of a discussion of which strategies are used to affect policies proposed by the Commission and how successful Danish actors themselves evaluate and regard these to be. In the following, a brief overview of the relationship between Denmark and the Commission is provided.

Denmark and the Commission – a reluctant European

Numerous authors have addressed the relationship between member states and the Commission. Either from a 'Commission' perspective (e.g. Coombes 1970; Michelmann 1978; Page 1997; Kassim and Menon 2004; Egeberg 2006; Trondal, Van den Berg and Suvarierol 2008) or by looking at individual member states relations with the EU broadly, including the Commission (for the Nordics: Miles 1996; more generally: Bulmer and Lequesne 2005). Building on this literature, this section gives a broad introduction to Denmark's strategic view with regard to the Commission, and an overview of Danes in the Commission.

Denmark and the delimitation of the Commission

Denmark has traditionally had a rather reluctant attitude towards the Commission. To a certain extent, the Commission, as a supranational EU institution, has represented and embodied what is problematic about the EC/EU in a Danish context; and, from the perspectives of a substantial majority of Danish actors, the difficulties with the supranational element of European integration more generally (Petersen 2006: 86). It is hence obvious, that the general aims of Denmark, and Danish actors, have been to avoid interacting with, and delimiting the role of, the Commission, as well as the EU more broadly, since both are deemed to cause 'trouble' for, and within Danish domestic debates. Hence, as the editors in their Introduction argue, from a FPA perspective, Danish actors often seek to consider international profiles of the EU (and its institutions) within domestic profiles. In the Commission context, this was, for example, reflected in Danish emphasis on financial reforms and checks and balances after the resignation of the Santer Commission in 1999, as well as Danish enthusiasm about the European Transparency Initiative.[6] Transparency and the opportunity for greater control over the Commission, were, for instance, aspects of the Lisbon Treaty related to the Commission, which were specifically mentioned in the Danish political agreement on the Treaty.[7] There was, hence, no publicly formulated Danish opinion on, for example the reduction of the size of the Commission. More broadly speaking, Euro-scepticism among the Danish population (see, for instance, Sørensen 2007a) has led to Danish political elites being very wary of Commission interference in Danish domestic affairs as well as opposing the Commission having a substantial role in steering further EU integration. This, according to some interviewees, facilitates and leads to a rather passive approach on the part of Danish actors towards the Commission, particularly among Danish politicians, viewing the Commission as more of a threat than as an opportunity for enhancing the uploading of Danish policy and preferences (see the Introduction to this volume). Nevertheless, although this is generally the case as regards the way the broad, 'macro'-image of the Commission is perceived in Denmark and by Danish actors, the following section will discuss examples of initiatives deviating from this approach.

Furthermore, from an administrative perspective, Danish policy towards the Commission has basically centered on two things, namely: (1) making the Commission reflect and seem more like the practices of the Danish civil service;[8] and (2) trying to keep the associated costs of running the Commission in check, since it is seen in most Danish political circles as being highly inefficient. From the general Danish perspective, the Commission stands out from the perception of 'proper administrative practices' in two ways. As regards the first aspect, it is extremely hard to fire employees in the Commission resulting in a rather inflexible organization, opposed to the new public management trend dominant in northern Europe (Grøn 2010: 239). Second, salary levels of Commission officials and staff are regarded as being high. Although Commission salary scales were reformed with the 2004 revision of the Staff Regulation (Kurpas et al. 2008: 47), they still largely appear to be too generous from the perspective of the Danish government. Furthermore, Commission staff salaries increase automatically from year to year, attracting controversy and criticism in Denmark (and elsewhere). Most notably, when Commission officials, in the midst of economic crisis all over Europe, were duly awarded sizable pay rises in 2010–2011, the Danish Minister of Finance argued publically that these actions showed a lack of 'respect' among Commission officials, since they did not refuse the pay rises (Politiken 2011). As regards the second aspect, and in line with the general Danish perspective of the Commission, a notable Danish governmental policy aim is to keep Commission costs in check. Here, and in common with other member states, the Danish focus is on major political dynamics relating to the internal functioning of the Commission, especially close examination and auditing of Commission demands for increased budgetary funding and/or of Commission proposals for (often under-) financed reforms.

Danes and the Commission

Danish Commissioners

Clearly, Commissioners play an important role in the Commission. The impact of national allegiances is debated in the literature, ranging from emphasis on the way the College of Commissioners is dominated by national politics (Peterson 1999) to the influence of supranational or dossier interests in shaping the conduct and effectiveness of respective Commissioners (Egeberg 2006). Since accession in 1973, Commissioners nominated by Denmark (henceforth called Danish Commissioners) have generally held important portfolios (see Table 8.1), although this is something that has become increasingly difficult to secure as the number of portfolios available to Commissioners has duly increased.

Following the public debate before announcements, it seems clear that three arguments can be used in explaining why Denmark, as a small country, has succeeded in securing such relatively high profile and prestigious posts and portfolios for Danish Commissioners. First and foremost, the sound and generally high competence of respective Danish Commissioners is mentioned (see, for example, Drachmann 1994; Winther 1999; Østergaard *et al.* 2004; Jessen *et al.* 2009). Looking back, since the days of Henning Christophersen, it is notable that every Danish Commissioner has managed to become the respective Commissioner with the portfolio most closely associated with their respective field of expertise. Except for Ritt Bjerregaard, who had been party spokesperson on the issue of the environment, all Danish commissioners since Henning Christophersen have held ministerial positions in the Danish government, with equivalent portfolio areas to those they went to also hold in their days as a European Commissioner.

Second, Denmark has succeeded in securing posts, at least since Ritt Bjerregaard, where Denmark had a clear policy profile. It has been debated whether this could constitute an obstacle both in relation to environment and agriculture

Table 8.1 The Danish Commissioners

Period	Commission President	Danish Commissioner
1973–7	Ortoli	Finn Olav Gundelach, Internal Market/Customs Union
1977–81	Jenkins	Finn Olav Gundelach, Vice-President, Agriculture and Fisheries
1981–5	Thorn	Finn Olav Gundelach, Agriculture and Fisheries*
1985–8	Delors I	Henning Christophersen, Vice-President, Budget, Financial Control, Personnel and Administration
1989–92	Delors II	Henning Christophersen, Vice-President, Economic and Financial Affairs and Coordination of Structural Funds
1993–4	Delors III	Henning Christophersen, Vice-President, Economic and Financial Affairs
1995–9	Santer	Ritt Bjerregaard, Environment and Nuclear Security
1999–2004	Prodi	Poul Nielson, Development and Humanitarian Aid
2004–9	Barroso I	Mariann Fischer Boel, Agriculture and Rural Development
2009–14	Barroso II	Connie Hedegaard, Climate Action

Note
* Died in January 1981, followed by Poul Dalsager.

(see e.g. Larsen 1994), but has been seen as a strong advantage in relation to both development and climate (Jyllands-Posten 1999; Jessen *et al.* 2009).

Third, proposing women ensures more attractive portfolios (Larsen 1994; Østergaard *et al.* 2004; Jessen *et al.* 2009). For all female candidates this has been an issue, since ensuring some form of equal representation is, typically, a challenge for Commission Presidents (EurActive 2009). This has not been lost on Danish governments, with, for example, Danish Prime Minister Fogh Rasmussen actively using the 'threat' of nominating (and thereby duly sending) a man, to aid the securing of Commission Presidential approval for the allocation of the prestigious agriculture portfolio to female Dane, Fischer Boel.

All in all, it seems clear that Denmark has prioritized sending Commissioners with a clear-cut competence for the job, and thus represents an example of successful Danish 'uploading' (see Introduction). Above all, Denmark, and Danish uploading, has secured the appointment of highly capable women as Commissioners, and for the Commission, which has also been widely appreciated across Europe.

Danes in the Commission

Beyond Commissioners, Danes are also represented in the rank and files of the Commission. The importance of nationality among Commission officials is widely debated (see, for example, Page 1997; Hooghe 2007; Trondal 2008). Commission officials are not supposed to be loyal towards their country of origin, but as will be clear in the following section, centrally placed Danes in the Commission have proved to be a valuable asset when Danish governments and actors have sought to upload and influence the Commission. It is not only the Danes who think so. Elsewhere in the EU system (for example, in terms of numbers of MEPs and of votes in the Council), larger countries have settled for being slightly under-represented. Nevertheless, as regards country-ratios of numbers of respective staff in the Commission, there is a notable concern even for some large states, such as the United Kingdom, as illustrated by the newly elected British Foreign Secretary William Hague's speech in 2010. Hague criticized his British predecessors, as:

> They neglected to ensure that sufficient numbers of bright British officials entered EU institutions, and so we are now facing a generation gap developing in the British presence in parts of the EU where early decisions and early drafting take place.
>
> (Hague quoted in Conservatives 2010)

In the literature on the Commission, the impact of nationality is analysed from different perspectives. Hooghe shows, in her 2007 study, that national socialization is far more important for officials' view on integration than the socialization obtained in the Commission (Hooghe 2007). Similarly, Page argues, that the multinational character of the Commission poses a number of challenges to the organization (Page 1997: 41). On the other hand, studies by, for example, Trondal (2008), highlight the importance of defending dossiers rather than national interests among seconded officials to the Commission, and Georgakakis (2010) argues that the EU career tracks of officials provides them with a particular EU social capital.

In 2009, the attention given to Danes working in the institutions was increased when a full-time position at the Danish Permanent Representation (PR) in Brussels was designed to deal with issues in relation to Seconded National Experts (SNEs).

Broadly, there are two ways into the Commission beyond being appointed Commissioner: through the Concours, (an entry competition) and through a posting as a national expert. At senior levels, especially for new member states, a notable cohort of people has been 'pararchuted' into the Commission (Kassim 2004: 37). This practice is studiously avoided today. While one senior ranking official can be very important for a member state, the focus here will primarily be on Danish functionaries and SNEs.

Denmark has constantly been slightly over-represented compared to the percentage of total EU population, but this is true for a number of smaller member states (Willis 1982: 14–16; Grøn 2010: 33–34). Traditionally, Danes have been less interested in participating in the Concours, and hence entering the Commission, than other nationalities. First, it is argued that salary levels and an attractive Danish labour market generally makes it less attractive to apply for positions in Brussels. Second, the Danish family structure with two-income families, and (for Commission officials typically possessing an academic degree) two-academic-income families, plays a role. Salary levels, while being generous for one-income families are less so if the family are used to two. Furthermore, the spouse of the Commission official could also be expected to want a relevant job in Brussels, which can be difficult to secure in practice. The 2010 Concours, however, saw a steep increase in interest among Danes, which was supported by information events for Danes and courses sponsored by the Ministry of Foreign Affairs together with the Danish Association of Lawyers and Economists (in Danish abbreviated 'DJØF').

Traditionally, nationality plays a role when it comes to career progression for functionaries inside the Commission, especially in relation to positions at the top of the hierarchy (Page 1997: 42). Here the Danes describe their attitude as 'demand driven'. Sometimes individuals inside the Commission address the PR and ask for help. The PR, and the Permanent Representative, can use his or her network to promote individuals. Such back up is, however, valuable capital and is not to be wasted. Furthermore, most Danes in the services prefer to work without the assistance of the PR.

An alternative entry route into the Commission is via placement of SNE's (see also Trondal 2008; Trondal *et al.* 2008). As noted below, SNE's are valuable assets when member states attempt to upload and influence the Commission; this finding as regards the Danish case does, to some extent, question the findings of other studies of SNEs that highlight loyalty towards the dossier as the main loyalty among SNEs (Trondal 2008).

On its website, the Commission writes on SNEs:

> Seconded National Experts (SNE's) have a dual role: they bring their experience of the issues they are used to dealing with to the Commission, and take back to their home administration the knowledge of EU issues which they acquire during their period of secondment.
>
> (European Commission 2012b)

Formally, SNEs work under similar conditions to Commission functionnaires, but not permanently and without being eligible for managerial responsibility (Article 6 in Commission 2008). Their loyalty is to lie with the Commission. Their salaries are paid by the member state, meaning that SNEs maintain and have the salary they received when working in their national civil service, although the Commission offers an additional allowance on top, which makes it economically attractive. For an official situated in Brussels in 2008, this would mean a daily allowance of €119.39 (Article 17, Commission 2008). For a younger (and junior) Danish official, this would approximately mean a post-taxation doubling of his/her monthly income; although this depends of course on their prior salary level in relation to the Danish position.

To become a SNE, three routes are possible. Either the member state can wait for the Commission to propose a position as an SNE in a location where the

Commission would like to have one, or the member state can lobby the Commission to ensure that a position is made for a specific candidate from that country. Finally, empirical examples can be mentioned where certain member states have paid the entire cost of SNEs in order to enable key personnel to secure positions deemed of high strategic importance for the country.

Denmark has not had a strong tradition for placing SNEs in the Commission, although recent years have seen greater acknowledgement of their importance.[9] Due to a lack of comparative data, it is impossible to say if the Danes have been more or less interested in placing SNEs, compared to other member states. The Danish Ministry of Finance set up special funds for which ministries can apply in 2006. In order to increase the number of SNEs, ministries could receive a reimbursement of up to 50 per cent of their costs related to SNEs.[10] There are still vast differences in the use of SNEs among departments and the extent to which this is an active part of respective personnel policy. The Ministry of Economic and Business Affairs is typically presented as a best case; here the Ministry has clearly defined where it is important to have SNEs and postings are an active part of the personnel policy. The Ministry of Foreign Affairs is also very active, but in most other places, placements are described as 'ad hoc', typically a consequence of individual preferences among employees and strongly constrained by the budget departments of the ministries. Not surprisingly, when it comes to SNEs and EU staff in the Ministries in general, there has been a recent upgrade in terms of activity and numbers to accommodate the specific demands associated with the 2012 Danish Council Presidency.

While the section below illustrates that SNEs can be valuable, they are, at the same time, costly, since they retain their national salary while not actually working for the respective national ministry.[11] The Danish PR estimated in May 2010, that Denmark had between 35 and 37 SNEs. No official figures have been available on the overall number of SNEs with respect to the Commission. However, the intention of the Danish government is to see an increase in the number to 50 through the SNE strategy.

Day-to-day politics: strategies for entering the heart of the Union

The decision-making process of the Commission is outlined roughly in Figure 8.1. Of course, a linear model depicting the process is a simplification, but here it is applied to create a structure for analysis. If diagrams of EU decision-making are consulted, typically the first three stages are conflated into the Commission proposing a piece of legislation, with emphasis placed on the phases beyond the Commission.[12] In this chapter, emphasis will be placed rather differently on the process internally within the Commission, the first three stages (see Kurpas *et al.* 2008: 40–41 for a discussion of the internal processes of the Commission).

For each of the stages, a number of tools can be used. In the following, the phases will act as the structuring device, so as to clarify which tools are used, and when. Some tools are useful throughout the decision-making process, while

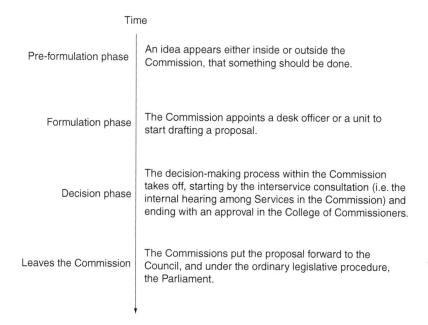

Figure 8.1 Stages of influence and decision-making in the European Commission.

others hold predominance at certain key stages. The dimensions discussed in Chapter 1 will be applied, with a particular focus on the formal/informal and continuity/change dimensions.

Before conducting a detailed discussion of the stages, a few words on the distribution of responsibility between the ministries in Copenhagen and the PR are in order. Copenhagen holds two important responsibilities; namely: (1) Copenhagen based officials have the expertise, and; (2) these officials formulate political opinions. While an attaché at the PR of course acquires and offers extensive knowledge of a policy area, more specific technical arguments that are used as part of Danish uploading of policies and preferences are typically provided by, and delivered from, the respective ministry back home in Denmark. The attachés then have a responsibility, based on the formulation of a Danish viewpoint, to present the views in the right fora, keep track of what is going on and transmit such knowledge back to the appropriate people in Copenhagen.

Pre-formulation phase

In the pre-formulation phase, two things are really important for Danish officials: first, to be able to frame the agenda, furthering issues of Danish interest and suppressing issues that go against it; and second, finding out what is going on in the Commission. These two priorities will be discussed first, and then the Danish 'success-rate' will be evaluated (according to the interview material).

Agenda-setting

Agenda-setting in relation to the Commission can take different forms depending on the policy area. In some areas, like the environment, most legislative action takes the form of the revision of earlier legislation; while other areas, such as JHA, sees mostly new legislation. Furthermore, different channels can be used. The usage of Council conclusions is one way of agenda-setting in relation to the Commission, often formulated in close cooperation with the Commission. The Commission works in accordance with a five-year working programme. When a Commission takes office, it outlines some rather broad goals and then adopts a more specified work programme every year, outlining its main priorities (European Commission 2010c). The work programme can be useful in two ways; first, it can be the basis for enhancing influence on the Commission and second, it can be used for information purposes. The Danish Ministry for Economic and Business Affairs attempted to participate actively in the formulation of the work programme of the Barroso II Commission. In order to improve their ability for doing so, a British civil servant was stationed in Copenhagen for six months to help the Ministry, since the British are quite accomplished in gaining influence at this stage. This is done through consultancy reports, conferences and the like. Here, agenda-setting is seen as a five- to 10-year perspective, and is costly both in manpower and consultancy fees.

Finally, the Commission typically prepares hard legislation, such as directives, regulations, framework decisions and, also, decisions of so-called soft law, like communications, reports, green books and white books. These pieces of soft law allow for a public hearing before any hard law is formulated. Practices on hearings differ widely between ministries. Some ministries have formulated policies on hearings, which emphasise that the ministry should always address such hearings, while others prioritize strongly between cases and some hardly ever react to them.

These are all relatively formal methods of agenda-setting in relation to the Commission. Such strategies are typically combined with informal contacts to the relevant desk officer. Among Danish officials, two things are emphasised: personal relations and delivering text. Personal relations are important in building confidence and to gain information on what is going on inside the Commission. Delivering key arguments in writing is also an advantage. Basically this can either be done as a draft for the particular piece of legislation or just a brief note underlining critical points; for instance in the form of non-papers. However, the strategy is very time consuming and difficult if drafts should be implemented into pieces of legislation. The British are mentioned as having a more proactive approach, writing proposals and having a linguistic advantage.

Obtaining information

One of the main tasks at this stage is to obtain information on what is brewing in the mind of the Commission. While green books, white books and the work programme are all good sources of information, not everything coming out of the Commission is announced in this way, and furthermore, the ability to affect the Commission even before the work programme or soft law is made, is important. As always, the earlier in the process any attempts at influence are made, the better the chances are for really framing legislation.

Several routes into the Commission can be used. The relevant desk officer can be contacted, but to do so it is necessary to know whom he or she is. Typically, the attachés at the PR will have coffee or lunch with desk officers within their area of responsibility every now and then. This is a way of obtaining information on what is going on. In general, the networking activities of attachés are important. Attachés from other PRs can also be useful in gaining information.

'Using the passport' is also a viable strategy. A route to information can be to contact a Dane in the respective Directorates Generals (DGs) of the Commission in order to enquire about what is going on, or whom to ask for further information and intelligence. SNEs can be used in a similar way. To illustrate the importance placed on this, the PR provides employees with a complete list of Danes in the Commission. It is quite often expected that SNEs themselves will contact their home ministry, should something of potential interest arise. While Commission officials are generally described as friendly and very willing to talk to the attachés, contacting a Dane is generally considered to be easier. As one interviewee described it: 'you can skip the first lunch', meaning that the effort required to get to know people informally before you can exchange information, which is typically done over coffee or lunch, is not needed when the person you contact is a Dane. Hence if it is possible, contacting a Dane is the easiest way of obtaining information about where to go to promote Danish interests.

Finally, if lines of communication between the home ministry and the attaché are functioning well, attachés can be informed of what is going on as regards expert groups operating under the auspices of the Commission by policy experts working from an agency in Copenhagen.

Successes?

Early stage interest mediation has been on the political agenda for a while, and there is rising acknowledgement that this is an extremely important phase. Basically, one point is important here: early interest representation is expensive and, for it to work, timing is really important. Providing text, being present and possessing the relevant knowledge requires manpower and considerable effort, and for a small country, this can be difficult to deliver.

Table 8.2 Findings of the pre-formulation phase

Main strategy	Agenda-setting both through formal and informal channels
Type of arguments	Technical
Type of change	Large-scale structural change is possible but expensive

Formulation phase

When the drafting of a policy proposal starts, influencing the Commission slightly changes, but a number of the strategies remain the same. Personal contact at desk-officer level and the delivery of written arguments are still valuable tools. On top, when there is an actual proposal in existence, the hierarchy of both the PR and the ministry in Copenhagen can be activated.

Providing the technical solution

When drafting goes on in the Commission, there is still room for influencing legislation to a large extent. The best way of doing so is by supporting desk officers to do their research and drafting. In some policy areas, like environment, Denmark has a particular advantage in being known for having existing officials with considerable expertise. Technical arguments backed by scientific evidence are valuable. Here, as in the pre-formulation phase, opportunities for 'upload' exist. In areas, such as the Lisbon Strategy or 'better regulation', the Danes succeeded in presenting their own ideas as 'good', viable solutions to common European problems. The Ministry of Economic and Business Affairs, for example, produced a publication together with the British and Dutch governments on 'Smart Regulation' that was duly presented to the Commission. While such an effort is by no means a common approach among Danish ministries, it illustrates the potential of promoting country-specific interests through the uploading of ideas that was neatly presented as, first, a focused technical solution, and second, as furthering the well-being of all Europeans. Contact at lower level of the hierarchy is generally made easier in the few cases where the desk officer is a Dane, functionnaire or SNE.

Getting your hands on the draft

Similarly, Danish officials can be very helpful in another endeavour: getting hold of drafts. In order to target comments and input, draft copies of Commission proposals are invaluable. Due to the limited number of Danish officials, some of which are not too keen on disseminating drafts to Danish diplomats, other channels are also used. These might build on personal relations to the drafting desk officer and on strategically placed SNEs, or they might be obtained through networks with other attachés from different countries. Just as in the pre-formulation phase, knowledge of what is going on inside the Commission is extremely valuable.

The question of loyalty of both functionnaires and SNEs is pertinent in this context. While Commission officials are obligated towards the Commission, there is still a general recognition that they consider the interests of their country of origin. Quite often it was explained that if documents were 'really' confident they would not be leaked, but if they were not, they quite often were – often either by email or by regular mail. It was argued that it is in the general interests of the Commission, at least to a certain extent, to acquire input on legislation early on in the process in order to ensure a smooth ride through the Council and the Parliament. To do so, member states need to know what is going on.

Enter the hierarchy

Yet, the informal contacts at the bottom of the hierarchy can be combined with contacts further up the ladder if the issue is deemed sufficiently important. Here, different notabilities can be activated. These range from policy experts flown in from Copenhagen, sending the Heads of Unit and/or the Permanent Secretary from the respective ministry to the Permanent Representative or the Danish Minister. Sending in various people of course transmits different signals, and no matter who is being sent, it is extremely important that the person meets someone in the Commission at the same level. Sending a policy expert typically means meeting the desk officer and, possibly, a Commission Head of Unit. It might even be that the expert knows the desk officer personally from the Commission working groups that eases contact. Here, the signal is that it is a serious matter for Denmark; yet something which is perceived as representing a technical solution. If the Head of Unit from Copenhagen participates in a meeting, this will typically be with the Commission Head of Unit. Here, issues are marginally more politicized. If there is a need to send a stronger, more politicized signal, the Permanent Secretary or the Ambassador can be utilized. Here, meetings will be at Director General level or with the cabinet. Finally, the Minister can announce his or her appearance in Brussels, meeting (preferably) the relevant Commissioner. Herein lies a very strong political signal, described by some as rather desperate,[13] and this will typically happen after a series of meetings at lower levels. Bringing in the Minister also plays a role in relation to the Danish national debate, because contact then becomes formalized. This could be an advantage, should the Minister have a need to 'show' that something is being done, but could also count negatively should nothing come out of the show of force. While meetings at lower levels of the hierarchy are pretty common, it seems rather uncommon for the Minister to attend meetings with the Commission.

Successes?

The formulation phase still allows for large-scale influence. Yet as noted above, this comes at a cost. Representing a small member state of course affects the weight of the punches that national officials can swing in Brussels, something

Table 8.3 Findings of the formulation phase

Main strategy	Providing technical solutions or using the hierarchy
Type of arguments	Technical, slightly political
Type of change	Large-scale change still possible

that Danish diplomats and civil servants are very much aware of. Hence providing technical input, especially within policy areas where the Danes already have a strong position, is the most successful strategy. This is best done informally. Again, success depends to a large extent on resources, and the ability to prioritize certain areas over others.

Decision phase

Once a proposal has been formulated, it begins its journey through the internal decision-making mechanisms of the Commission. Here, a proposal is first sent to interservice consultation, where those services and actors with a respective portfolio that might be affected by the proposal can submit their views and give their input. Subsequently, the proposal is discussed among cabinet members at a 'Special Chefs' meeting, followed by a discussion among Heads of Cabinets at the weekly 'Hebdo' meeting. Hereafter a proposal enters the agenda of the College for decision (Kurpas *et al.* 2008: 40–41).

The cabinets unfold

In the decision phase, the cabinets take centre stage. Contacts and influence can be attempted through different channels, typically either through the cabinet holding the relevant dossier or through the Danish Cabinet. The interservice consultation is typically a phase with limited diplomatic activity.

Moving on, the cabinet raises its importance. However, time is short. The cabinet will receive a dossier 24–72 hours before it is to be decided upon by the College. This is typically too late for the PR to prepare any real work on a dossier if it is not already known to them. Furthermore, few things can be changed at this stage. A dossier can be temporarily stopped, or, on extremely rare occasions, blocked. None of the interviewees could recall a dossier being taken completely off the table at this late stage due to Danish considerations.

Coordination between the PR and the Danish cabinet appears ad hoc, and to a certain extent builds upon personal relations. The Danish cabinet is sensitive towards Danish perspectives, but is not in a position to defend them recklessly. Generally, it was the perception among interviewees that the Commissioner has 'few shots' in the meetings of the College, and that political capital was wasted if a Commissioner (or his/her staff) was perceived as promoting national interests too strongly. The phrase 'the country I know best' can be used in meetings, but defending national interests too blatantly cannot be regarded as a viable strategy according to the interviewees. One country seen as doing so is the United Kingdom, since the efforts of British Commissioners were often mentioned as being too closely coordinated with those of Whitehall.

A third access route can be respective Danes working in other cabinets. Under Barroso I, several Danes were placed in non-Danish cabinets, primarily due to the lack of experience among nationals originating from the new member states. For the Barroso II Commission, great efforts were made to place Danes in cabinets in a similar manner, but it proved to be much more difficult, partly because new member states nationals now have the relevant experience to fill such positions, and partly because bigger member states lobbied for their candidates more actively. Finally, the placement of a Dane in close proximity to Catherine Ashton, the High Representative of the Union for Foreign Affairs and Security Policy, to form the new External Action Service of the EU, was expensive in terms of diplomatic capital.

Political arguments hit the table

In this phase, arguments are typically political. All technicalities are cleared out earlier in the process, and if the Commissioner is to use his or her political capital and intervene in a dossier with no obvious relations to the portfolio of the Commissioner, this is based on strong political arguments. National political considerations play a role; this was, for instance, the case when the proposal for a common consolidated corporate tax base was taken off the Commission table at the suggestion of Irish Commissioner McCreevy, shortly before the first Irish referendum on the Lisbon Treaty (Kurpas *et al.* 2008: 8). Similarly, there is an understanding within the Commission that certain issues can be shuffled around under consideration of national political agendas. However, this cannot be done too often.

Successes?

In this phase, room for change is very slim and the main strategies go through the cabinets, typically informally. The main arguments brought to bear are political. Being a smaller member state plays a role, since (generally) the Danes do not think they are 'allowed' to be as difficult as larger member states. Furthermore,

Table 8.4 Findings of the phases

	Pre-formulation phase	*Formulation phase*	*Decision phase*
Main strategy	Agenda-setting both through formal and informal channels	Providing technical solutions or using the hierarchy	Blocking through the Cabinet or political intervention, primarily informal
Type of arguments	Technical	Technical, slightly political	Political
Type of change	Large-scale structural change is possible but expensive	Large-scale change still possible	Smaller changes or delay

there seems to be a perception among Danish officials, both inside and outside the Commission, that the Danes play more by the rules than certain other nationalities. Whether this is just a perception or an actual fact is hard to determine.

Denmark and the Commission: trouble in Copenhagen

Denmark and Danish actors attempt numerous different strategies in order to influence the Commission. Looking at the dichotomies framing this volume, it becomes clear that both formal and informal strategies are applied, but at various stages and with different effects. Formal strategies can be used at the beginning of a policy process, yet can also be used as an emergency break at later stages. Informal strategies are generally evaluated as the most efficient overall and throughout the process. Furthermore, it is clear that strategies aiming at delivering technical arguments are usually more efficient than strategies focusing on political arguments. In general, it can be argued that the diplomatic capital expended when delivering technical arguments to the Commission is an investment that will yield a positive return if the quality of input is rather good. There is an advantage in being known, and in being known for delivering high quality input. On the other hand, expending diplomatic capital on promoting political arguments is simply plain spending. Here, there are clear limits to the credit line held by a small country.

Looking at the difference between promoting various kinds of change, the chapter illustrates that the earlier the participation and uploading, the larger the propensity for change that is possible. The Danes, however, generally consider early interest mediation difficult, because it expends considerable resources. Here, a common problem proposed by interviewees is the prioritization of resources in favour of the ministries based in Copenhagen. This problem is acknowledged both in Brussels and Copenhagen, yet the understanding of, and for, the prioritizations is perhaps biggest in Copenhagen. The European Affairs Committee and the Danish system of parliamentary control (discussed in Chapter 14 of this volume) draws huge amounts of resources from the civil service, which, at least as seen from a civil servant perspective, could have been used more constructively in promoting Danish interests. Rather, the focus is on the Minister avoiding 'trouble' in the Committee. In general, the Danish reluctance towards the EU is seen as an issue, where 'Brussels' is largely perceived as primarily being a place that generates trouble for Danish politicians at home. This in turn affects resource allocation with the balance moving from offensive towards defensive strategies. Shortage of resources is a given, and fewer resources held by a small country compared to larger countries, which have the opportunity to follow 'all' cases, is also to be expected. The internal prioritizations are, however, up for discussion. And among the ones aimed at trying to influence the Commission, more resources focused on Brussels rather than Copenhagen seems a wise prioritization.

Notes

1 The important relationship between (Danish) lobby groups and the EU (and its institutions) will not be addressed here, although it is explicitly recognized that this remains highly significant for understanding Danish relationships with the evolving European Commission. See Karsten Ronit's analysis in Chapter 10 of this volume for an analysis of Danish lobby groups in a European context.
2 For instance, the latest political agreement on Danish EU policies (see EU-Oplysningen 2008a), does not contain anything on how Denmark sees the Commission, apart from the statement that the institution should be transparent and Denmark favors more 'democratic decision-making' in the EU.
3 Information obtained in interviews has been validated via other interviews as well as by an evaluation of the status of the interviewee. Interviewees are anonymous and are not quoted directly. Nevertheless, a listing of the respective interviewees can be obtained from the author.
4 Article 17 of the consolidated version of the TEU. See European Union (2010).
5 Which is generally recommended (e.g. Greenwood 2007).
6 The European Transparency Initiative was initiated with a 2006 Green Paper and followed up by a 2007 communication, aimed at improving transparency in EU policy making. In particular, questions pertaining to lobbying of the Commission were addressed. The main result of the transparency drive was a volunteer lobby register for lobbyists dealing with the Commission (European Commission 2006).
7 See EU-Oplysningen (2008a).
8 The main modernization initiative in recent years, the 2000 Kinnock reforms (European Commission 2000a, 2000b), did not receive any official Danish attention, according to interviewees. This reform should, taking into account Danish preferences, have been popular.
9 See Danish Agency for the Modernisation of Public Administration (2011, 2010).
10 See Retsinformation (2006).
11 While SNEs are expensive, in terms of budgeting, they shift across categories from being counted as wage costs to being counted as operating expenses. This means that in a situation where the salaries in a certain ministry are to be reduced, the posting of people to Brussels might be a good idea.
12 For an overview of EU decision-making procedures, consult European Union (2012).
13 It can however also be used proactively to build personal relations between a minister and his/her counterparts.

9 Denmark and the European Parliament

Anne Rasmussen

The European Parliament (EP) is unquestionably the EU institution whose powers have changed most radically over the years. Denmark has been represented in the EP since it joined the EC in 1973, and it has held elections to the EP every fifth year since the first direct elections in 1979. Just as in the rest of the EU, elections to the EP have not always been given a high amount of attention in Denmark and they have often focused more on national issues than issues closely linked to the work of this institution. When the EP has been discussed in the Danish debate, it has often not been portrayed in a very flattering way. Much has, of course, changed since Thatcher and other commentators referred to it as a 'Mickey Mouse parliament' (see for example Information 2009). However, in Danish debate there is still a prominent image of the EP as a big inefficient, bureaucratic assembly consisting of members who receive high salaries, but spend a high amount of their time discussing issues detached from the lives of the general public (see for example Information 1999; Politiken 2009). Moreover, there is no lack of stories of the monthly 'travelling circus' between Brussels and Strasbourg, which is estimated to cost approximately €200 million every year and to have negative environmental consequences (see for example Politiken 2007a, 2007b; *Berlingske Tidende* 2006). In spite of this negative image, Denmark is actually one of a few countries where turnout in EP elections has remained relatively constant whereas it has dropped in most of the EU (Jensen *et al.* 2009). Denmark also distinguishes itself from many other EU countries by making strong efforts to integrate the work of the MEPs with that of the national government and parliament (Fich 2008). In this way, official Danish institutions have put a high emphasis on using the MEPs to ensure that Danish interests and ideas are uploaded to the European level in order to preserve Danish autonomy and influence. Some of these efforts take a relatively formal nature, but most of them are informal and rely on ad hoc contacts between the Danish political system and the MEPs.

Little is known about whether such efforts translate into actual differences between the Danes and the remaining MEPs. The existing literature does not include any information *whether* and *in which ways* Danish MEPs systematically differ from their fellow colleagues in the EP. The aim here is, therefore, to compare the position and strategy of the Danish MEPs to MEPs from other countries. MEP positions are examined by analysing their policy positions on key issues and attitudes towards representation, and MEP behaviour is examined by looking at how frequently MEPs are in contact with and receive voting recommendations from different actors at the national and EU level. Moreover, an overview of important types of offices held by the Danish MEPs and MEPs from other member states is created and voting behaviour is discussed.

Recent literature has underlined how the EP has evolved from its early days as an assembly into an institution, which has a lot in common with the parliaments that are familiar from the national context (Corbett *et al.* 2005; Hix and Lord 1997; Hix *et al.* 2006, 2007; Kreppel 2002; McElroy 2007). This conclusion holds, no matter whether its organizational structure or the behaviour of its members is examined. Similar to national parliaments, the EP is organized into party groups, which have gradually become stronger over time, and the most important policy dimension contested within this institution is the left-right dimension. Regarding the EP as being similar to national parliaments has enabled researchers to use familiar concepts and tools from comparative politics to study it. This has opened up a range of research questions similar to the ones already known from the national context. At the same time, such a research focus may lead us to ignore some of the peculiarities of this institution, which may still affect its day-to-day work. There is a risk that the question of how the different national backgrounds of members affects the dynamics of how the institution works is neglected.

Even if the findings with regard to nationality are mixed, they provide preliminary evidence that there are some differences between Danish MEPs and their colleagues within the EP. Whereas the volume of legislative reports written, or type of committee seats held, does not generally differ between the Danes and the rest of the EP, the attitudes and contact patterns of the Danes *do* differ from other MEPs. Both when it comes to analysing their attitudes to increasing the different powers of the EP and representing different types of entities within it, Danes remain more devoted to preserving national autonomy than the rest of the EP – perhaps signalling that the issue of influence vs. autonomy, as discussed in the Introduction to this volume, has resonance here. Moreover, contact patterns demonstrate that Danes are significantly more in touch with different national actors than their fellow MEPs. Whether these differences in attitudes and contact patterns ultimately affect the policy stances of Danish MEPs in everyday politics remains to be seen. However, the evidence indicates that even if mainstream research on the EP leads us to treat this body like any other parliament, links to the national context still play a role and may be an additional factor to take into account in explaining MEP behaviour.

The chapter starts by providing some background to Denmark and the EP, including information about EP elections, the Danish MEPs and their institutional linkage to the Danish political system. Thereafter, the chapter is devoted to a systematic analysis of whether the Danes in the EP differ from their fellow colleagues. It looks at policy positions of MEPs and compares the behaviour of the Danes to other MEPs by looking at the kind of offices they hold within the legislature, and at their contact patterns.

Denmark and the European Parliament

Denmark has been represented in the EP since the beginning of its EU membership, which means that Danish politicians have been directly elected to this institution ever since 1979. The number of Danes in the EP has varied over time. However, like other small member states, Denmark has always been somewhat over-represented compared to bigger member states, where the number of seats as a share of the population size is generally lower. The current number of Danish members is 13 out of a total number of 736 MEPs. Whereas turnout in EP elections has generally gone down in the EU ever since the first direct elections, it has remained relatively stable in Denmark (Jensen et al. 2009; Nedergaard 2005). After reforms, elections to the EP follow a proportional system in all countries, with smaller discrepancies between them (Farrell and Scully 2007). In Denmark, the method used to calculate proportionality is D'hondt's system, which is also the most commonly used in the EU as a whole (Corbett et al. 2007). Candidates have to be a minimum of 18 years old and run in 92 different regional units (Jensen et al. 2009). However, the country acts as one constituency when it comes to electing its MEPs rather than the smaller units used for national elections (Corbett et al. 2007). In EP elections, in contrast to national elections, a voter in Denmark can thus select any candidate from the country as a whole, even if the norm is that candidates mainly campaign in the regional units where they are nominated.

An overview of the lists and the division of votes in all EP elections is provided in Table 9.1. Within the lists, preference voting takes place for individuals meaning that the individuals with the highest number of personal votes are the ones that get elected, irrespective of what their number is on the party list. The lists are similar to national elections with the exception that, apart from the national political parties, certain special anti-EU groupings (the June Movement and People's Movement against the EU) also run for EP elections (Corbett et al. 2007). These groupings gather anti-EU voters from different political parties and have been quite successful over time, even if their support has recently dropped. The People's Movement against the EU dates back to Denmark's accession referendum in 1972, which was formed to mobilize the Danish 'no' vote. Since then, it has played a strong role in creating opposition in the Danish referenda on new EU treaties, even if its only real success was in the rejection of the first Maastricht referendum in 1992. The June Movement was formed after the first Maastricht referendum and distinguished itself from its sister organization by acknowledging Danish membership of the EU. Instead, its focus has been on restricting EU involvement in several policy areas. In the current EP, only the People's Movement against the EU is represented. One of the reasons for this is that more sceptical attitudes towards the EU have increasingly found their way into the electoral programs of the national political parties, especially those placed at the right-hand side of the political spectrum.

Due to the relatively high threshold for winning an EP seat, some of the small Danish parties have traditionally had a harder time finding representation in this

Table 9.1 Results of the European Parliament elections in Denmark

		7 June 1979	14 June 1984	15 June 1989	9 June 1994	10 June 1999	13 June 2004	7 June 2009
The Social Democratic Party	% of total vote	21.9	19.5	23.3	15.8	16.5	32.6	21.5
	MEPs	3	3	4	3	3	5	4
The Social Liberal Party	% of total vote	3.3	3.1	2.8	8.5	9.1	6.4	4.3
	MEPs	0	0	0	1	1	1	0
The Conservative Party	% of total vote	14.1	20.8	13.3	17.7	8.5	11.3	12.7
	MEPs	2	4	2	3	1	1	1
Centre Democrats	% of total vote	6.2	6.6	8	0.9	3.5	–	–
	MEPs	1	1	2	0	0	–	–
The Justice Party	% of total vote	3.4	–	–	–	–	–	–
	MEPs	0	–	–	–	–	–	–
The Socialist People's Party	% of total vote	4.7	9.2	9.1	8.6	7.1	7.9	15.9
	MEPs	1	2*	1	1	1	1	2
The June Movement	% of total vote	–	–	–	15.2	16.1	9.1	2.4
	MEPs	–	–	–	2	3	1	0
The Christian-Democrats	% of total vote	1.8	2.7	–	1.1	1.3	1.3	–
	MEPs	0	0	–	0	0	0	–
The People's Movement against the EU	% of total vote	21	20.8	18.9	10.3	7.3	5.2	7.2
	MEPs	4	4	4	2	1	1	1
The Danish People's Party	% of total vote	–	–	–	–	5.8	6.8	15.3
	MEPs	–	–	–	–	1	1	2
The Liberal Party	% of total vote	14.5	12.5	16.6	19	23.4	19.4	20.2
	MEPs	3	2	3	4	5	3	3
The Left Socialists	% of total vote	3.5	1.3	–	–	–	–	–
	MEPs	0	0	–	–	–	–	–
The Progress Party	% of total vote	5.8	3.5	5.3	2.9	0.7	–	–
	MEPs	1	0	0	0	0	–	–
Liberal Alliance	% of total vote	–	–	–	–	–	–	0.6
	MEPs	–	–	–	–	–	–	0
Total number of MEPs		15	16	16	16	16	14	13
Participation (%)		47.8	52.4	46.2	52.9	50.5	47.9	59.5

Source: EU-Oplysningen 2009.

Note
* When Greenland left the EC, Denmark's 16th seat went from Greenland to the Socialist People's Party.

body. By contrast, there has been continued support for the old Danish parties in the EU elections, even if there have been some fluctuations in that support over the years. Some of these fluctuations are related to changes in the popularity of the parties in the national scene. As an example, both the Danish People's Party and the Socialist People's Party profited from high popularity in the national polls in the last round of elections. Other positive increases in the votes of a party have depended on its ability to attract prominent candidates. This was, for example, the case in 2004 and 1994, when the Social Democratic Party and the Conservative Party received above average results when they had former prime ministers on the top of their lists.

Even if turnout to EP elections has been relatively stable in Denmark, it has remained considerably lower than in national elections. EP election campaigns have often been dominated by national rather than EU issues and thus have been similar to EP elections in general (Reif and Schmitt 1980). Like other member states, Denmark has been represented in the EP by both relatively junior and senior politicians. A prominent example of an elected MEP who was relatively junior when entering the EP, is the current leader of the Danish Socialists: Helle Thorning Schmidt. She used the EP as a platform for entering national politics. Just like the rest of the older EU member states, Denmark has generally had a lower ratio of MEPs with senior and junior ministerial experience than the new member states (Corbett et al. 2007). However, the EP has not merely been a playground and future training ground for Danish politicians interested in a subsequent career in Danish politics. Many elected Danish MEPs have been well known from the domestic political scene. Examples include former Danish Prime Ministers Poul Nyrup Rasmussen and Poul Schlüter, together with a number of other Danish politicians with long careers in national politics who have entered the EP. Recent examples include Mogens Camre, Margrethe Auken and Gitte Seeberg.

The Danish parliament has traditionally played a relatively strong role in controlling its national government in European affairs (Bergman 1997). One of the instruments used to control the Danish government has been the weekly meeting of the Danish parliament's EAC. Ministers have to attend in order to collect mandates from their parliamentary majority before important votes in the Council of Ministers. Whereas EU policy was primarily regarded as foreign policy in Denmark for many years, a change took place in the mid 1980s, after which politicians became less concerned with debating overall attitudes towards the European construction and focused more on exerting influence on concrete EU policies. As a result, Danish MPs devoted increased attention to their relations with Danish MEPs (Fich 2008). Even though committee meetings of the Danish parliament are normally only open to members of the committee itself, an exception has been made by the EAC with regard to Danish MEPs. Here, they are always invited to participate in the meetings and they also receive all the written background material on the EU dossiers produced by the Danish national government. The former chairman of the EAC, Ove Fich, reports that one reason the national MPs were interested in contact with MEPs was the realization that even if they controlled them tightly, national ministers could still be voted down in the Council of Ministers (Fich 2008). In such a situation, support from the EP was essential in the EU decision-making process. In order to ensure that Danish ideas and interests are uploaded to the European level (see the Introduction to this volume), the Danish government itself has also often used Danish MEPs to further its views on EU matters. Usually, it contacts and assists MEPs in their work on EU matters where vital Danish interests are at stake and the EP has a strong say (Rasmussen and Manners 2008; Fich 2008).

Little is known about whether Denmark acts differently from other member states in the EP. In fact, the trend in recent EP research has been to ignore nationality due to the fact that EP party groups have gradually become stronger over time. Although it is the national and not the EP party groups that control the re-election of MEPs, these party groups control important assets within the EP such as committee positions, rapporteurships for writing legislative reports and plenary speaking time (Lindberg et al. 2009). Several studies emphasize how party politics influence both committee appointment and rapporteurships within the EP (McElroy 2001; A. Rasmussen 2008a; Lindberg 2008a, 2008b; Kreppel 2002; Hoyland 2006). Moreover, when it comes to explaining intra-institutional decision-making within the EP, research also makes clear that partisan, rather than national, alignments matter. Both early work (Attina 1990; Raunio 1997; Kreppel and Tsebelis 1999; Kreppel 2000; Thomassen et al. 2004), and recent works by Hix and his collaborators (Hix et al. 2005, 2007; Noury 2002; Hix 2002) on voting behaviour in this body, shows that the party political left-right dimension dominates in the EP. Moreover, despite frequent criticism of the lack of strength of EP party groups, it is shown that they achieve relatively high and rising levels of cohesion.

Whether there is still a role for nationality to play in such a party-driven landscape remains, of course, to be seen. This issue does not only relate to the discussion of whether the EP is a normal parliament that ought to be studied with the general tools from comparative politics, but also to a more general discussion among European integration scholars. On the one hand, intergovernmentalists see the EU as a construction driven by national elites, which enter into agreements when it is in their national interest. According to this view, EU institutions do not take on a life of their own, but are bodies that facilitate compromise between different types of national interests (Moravscik 1998). The EP is one of several bodies where national parliamentarians can get together to balance their different national views. On the other hand, neo-functionalists emphasize how national elites shift loyalty to the EU level when they move from the national context to Brussels. According to these scholars, the EP is more than a collection of national interests, but a body that develops a European identity of its own (Haas 1958). The question is whether neo-functionalists are right in claiming that such shifts of loyalty occur among Danish MEPs when they arrive in Brussels, or whether there is something different about their preferences and behaviour that distinguishes these MEPs from the rest of the EP.

Policy positions

Two surveys of MEPs, conducted in 2000 and 2006 and generously made available to this author by Farrell et al. (2006), are used to compare the positions of Danish MEPs to that of other MEPs.[1] More detailed examinations of the policy positions of MEPs reveal some interesting differences between the MEPs from Denmark and those from the remaining EU member states. Table 9.2 pools the survey data from the MEP surveys in 2000 and 2006 where MEPs have been asked similar questions about their attitudes towards extending the powers of the EP. In all areas, Danes are more sceptical about extending the powers of the EP than their colleagues, and these differences are highly significant no matter whether we speak about giving the EP initiative power, or about extending its co-legislating powers, its budgetary powers or its power to influence the appointment of the Commission. Only when it comes to the issue of whether the EP should be allowed to remove individual Commissioners from office are the Danes almost as sceptical as other MEPs. It is already known that Denmark has traditionally been one of the most sceptical countries about extending the powers of the EP (Fich 2008). The data here very clearly shows that this sceptical attitude is represented in Brussels by MEPs, who have not shifted their loyalties towards the EU level. In line with the EU sceptical population, Danish MEPs remain more hesitant than their colleagues about extending the powers of this institution. The same picture is conveyed by the research findings of Rasmussen on the voting behaviour of Danish MEPs, from July 2004 to May 2006. She finds that Danish MEPs from the Independence/Democracy (IND/DEM), the Union for Europe of the Nations (UEN) and European United Left–Nordic Green Left (EUL/NGL) are even more critical

Table 9.2 Attitudes towards extending the powers of the European Parliament

Question	Danes vs. remaining members	Sign.
The European Parliament should have the right to initiate legislation	Disagree more strongly	**
The European Parliament should have equal legislative power with the Council in ALL areas of EU policy-making	Disagree more strongly	***
The EP should be able to amend ALL areas of expenditure in the EU budget	Disagree more strongly	***
The Commission President should be nominated by the EP, rather than the national governments	Disagree more strongly	**
The European Parliament should be able to remove individual Commissioners from office	Disagree more strongly	

Source: Farrell et al. (2006).

Note
Mann–Whitney U test, Sign. ***<0.01, **<0.05, *<0.10.

towards further EU integration than their fellow group members (M. Rasmussen 2007: 70).

Moreover, when examining attitudes towards representation, there are some interesting differences between the Danes and the rest of the EP. Previous research has shown that the attitudinal ties between MEPs and their national parties are stronger than to their EP party group (A. Rasmussen 2008b). This is probably not least because national parties have the ultimate sanction over MEPs, i.e. to prevent their re-election (Lord 2006; Bowler *et al.* 1999). Interestingly, there is a detectable tendency for Danish MEPs to attach a higher priority to representing views related to national autonomy than is found among their fellow MEPs. Hence, the Danes attach significantly greater importance towards representing both the people in their member state, the people who voted for their party, and their national party as such in the EP than do the rest of the MEPs who answered the 2000 and 2006 surveys. In contrast, there is no significant difference between Danish and other MEPs in how important they find it to represent all the people of Europe, all the people in their constituency or all the people in their EP party group.

Again this draws a picture of the Danes being more devoted to preserving national autonomy than other MEPs. The findings do not allow us to draw any general conclusions on whether the EP is a body of members who are primarily concerned with preserving national autonomy rather than European views. However, they do suggest, that, relatively speaking, the Danes have quite a strong attitudinal tie to home. Rather than being examples of elitist representatives,

Table 9.3 Attitudes towards representation

Question	Danes vs. remaining members	Sign.
How important is it to you to represent all people of Europe in the European Parliament?	Lower importance	
How important is it to you to represent all people in my member state in the European Parliament?	Greater importance	**
How important is it to you to represent all the people who voted for my party in the European Parliament?	Greater importance	**
How important is it to you to represent all the people in my constituency in the European Parliament?	Lower importance	
How important is it to you to represent my national party in the European Parliament?	Greater importance	**
How important is it to you to represent my EP party group in the European Parliament?	Greater importance	

Source: Farrell *et al.* 2006.

Note
Mann–Whitney U test, Sign. ***<0.01, **<0.05, *<0.10.

whose loyalty has shifted to the EU decision-making level, they demonstrate quite a strong national attachment even after arriving in Brussels.

Behaviour and office

This chapter now moves beyond attitudes, and takes a closer look at whether there is evidence to indicate some differences between the Danes and the rest of the MEPs in the type of offices they hold and their contact patterns. Even if Denmark is a small EU member state, Danes have often held influential positions. Former Prime Minister Poul Nyrup Rasmussen became president of the Party of European Socialists (PES), and Jens Peter Bonde was chair of the IND/DEM group in the EP. However, no systematic research has so far compared the offices held by the Danes and the remaining MEPs. Two crucial types of office held by MEPs within the EP are membership of the standing committees and rapporteurships.

The EP's standing committees prepare the daily business of the EP by drafting reports and opinions on legislative matters before they go to the plenary. Although it has been in existence since the early days, the first direct elections in 1979 marked an expansion of the committee system (McElroy 2001). The number, jurisdiction and size of the standing committees are decided at the beginning of each term and confirmed mid-term. According to the EP rules of procedure, 'The composition of the standing committees shall, as far as possible, reflect the composition of Parliament' (Rule 177), but leave it up to the EP party groups and national party delegations to decide how to fill the committees. In this way, there is (theoretically) some scope for a national delegation with a given EP party group to fight strongly for seats on certain committees if these are perceived as being particularly important to national interests. As an example, we might see a higher representation of MEPs from countries with coastlines on a committee such as the fisheries committee, or of MEPs from countries with poorer regions on a committee such as regional development. At the same time, existing research shows that committee seats are assigned in a way that ensures representative committees. In an early study of the third EP term, Bowler and Farrell (1995) found that the share of standing committee seats is proportional to both nationality and ideological party blocs. McElroy also found that rather than consisting of preference outliers, vis-à-vis the chamber, committees are generally representative of the EP as a whole (McElroy 2006). In contrast, some partisan effects can be found. There is some evidence that parties use committee assignments to control members (McElroy 2002) and that national parties pay more attention to MEP behaviour on powerful committees (Whittaker 2005). However, no research has so far demonstrated that there should be any overall systematic biases between how well a given country is represented on committees and in the full plenary.

To examine MEP behaviour, it is necessary to provide an overview of important types of office MEPs hold, i.e. rapporteurships and committee seats. Here, two datasets collected by Nikoleta Yordanova, from the University of

Mannheim, on the activities of the MEPs are analysed. The first includes information about the official committee assignment in July 2004 (i.e. the beginning of the sixth EP), and the second dataset shows the report allocations under the consultations and co-decision procedures from the start of the fifth EP (i.e. July 1999 until 31 January 2007). Table 9.4 compares the share of Danes on the different committees in July 2004, to the share of Danes in the plenary as a whole. The findings are in line with the previous literature. There is, of course, some variation in the share of Danes on the committees. However, this is unavoidable because the share of Danes within a given party group might deviate from the plenary, and it is clear that committee seats are first and foremost distributed in such a way that proportionality between party groups within the plenary and the committees exists. However, out of 20 committees only two have a significantly different share of Danes than the plenary, i.e. the committees on constitutional affairs and budgetary control. Both of these have a higher share of Danes than the plenary. However, it is important to be careful when interpreting these findings, which may suggest that Danish members felt more strongly about constitutional and budgetary control issues than the rest of the MEPs. They could also simply indicate that Danish MEPs, at the start of 2004, had more

Table 9.4 Official committee assignment in July 2004

Committee	Share of Danes (%)
Foreign affairs	1.9
Development	2.9
International Trade	0.0
Budgets	2.1
Budgetary Control	7.9***
Economic and Monetary Affairs	2.1
Employment and Social affairs	3.3
Environment, Public Health and Food Safety	2.5
Industry, Research and Energy	2.0
Internal Market and Consumer Protection	2.7
Transport and Tourism	3.0
Regional Development	1.0
Agriculture and Rural Development	1.2
Fisheries	3.6
Culture and Education	0.0
Legal Affairs	0.0
Civil Liberties, Justice and Home Affairs	1.0
Constitutional Affairs	5.5**
Women's Rights and Gender Equality	1.8
Petitions	0.0
EP as a whole	1.9

Source: Data from Nikoleta Yordanova, University of Mannheim, of full and substitute committee members.

Note
Mann–Whitney U test, Sign. ***<0.01, **<0.05, *<0.10.

experience and expertise in these areas than the remaining MEPs. Nevertheless, it is an interesting finding that, at least in the July 2004 figures, it looks as if Danes are not particularly strongly represented in the committee jurisdictions relating to the Danish opt-outs of the EU.

Apart from committee seats, rapporteurships are among the most important offices held by MEPs. The institution of the rapporteurship stems from continental Europe. The idea is that a specific MEP acts as rapporteur and prepares a report on a given proposal. He or she is also is responsible for negotiations on the matter, both with the EP and between the EP and other institutions. In this way, acting as rapporteur can give an MEP a unique opportunity to influence policy matters. In fact, the literature points out that even if committee chairs in the EP can exert significant influence on committee agendas, they have generally lost influence over time with the increased use of early agreements in the co-decision legislative procedure. Whereas committee chairs may participate in these informal negotiations with the Council and the Commission, it is the EP rapporteurs that take the lead (Farrell and Héritier 2004). In contrast to committee assignments, report allocation is not regulated by the EP's rules of procedure. This means that there is more scope for lack of proportionality, and for how well MEPs from different party groups or countries are represented in the plenary when it comes to writing reports. The way the process works is that party groups are allocated a certain number of points on each committee to bid for reports based on the size of the party group on the committee. First, a party group's coordinator on the committee competes with other party group coordinators to win a report. Second, once a coordinator has won a report, he decides which of his party members he will allocate the report to (Yordanova 2011).

Existing studies have examined rapporteurship allocation with data at both the aggregate and individual level. Looking at the aggregate data, Kaeding (2004, 2005) concluded that report allocation did not proportionally reflect the composition of the EP. He found differences in both party group affiliation and nationality and between report allocation and the EP plenary. Analysing different datasets and periods, Benedetto (2005) and Mamadouh and Raunio (2003) found that there is (largely) proportionality between rapporteurship allocation and EP party group affiliation, but not between national party delegations within these groups. Using individual level data, Hausemeer (2006) shows that salient committee reports are given to more loyal party members. Lindberg also finds that both the European People's Party-European Democrats (EPP-ED) and the PES appoint rapporteurs with policy positions close to the median position of their party groups, but that only the former is able to sanction members for disloyal voting behaviour when allocating co-decision reports (Lindberg 2008a, 2008b). Other studies find that different individual level characteristics, such as expertise and interest group affiliation of MEPs, also matter in the report allocation process (Kaeding 2005; Yoshinaka et al. 2010).

None of the existing studies specifically examine whether there is any systematic biases between the number of reports written by Danish and other MEPs. In order to avoid drawing inferences from the allocation of reports of minor importance, this chapter only examines the allocation of substantial reports. In examining whether Danes are more or less productive than other MEPs, there are also controls for certain other variables that have been shown to matter in previous research, such as the party group affiliation of an MEP and whether the MEP is male or female. The estimated models are binominal regressions, since the data is, strictly speaking, not interval level, but count data, and it is also not normally distributed.

Table 9.5 shows that the sex of a respondent affects the likelihood of writing co-decision but not consultation reports. Interestingly, women have, on average, written more co-decision reports than men. Most importantly however, some party group effects are found. IND/DEM members have written fewer consultation and co-decision reports than the reference category (i.e. EPP-ED). Moreover, other small party groups seem to have been less active than EPP-ED members. The Greens (G/EFA) have written fewer co-decision reports, and UEN members have written fewer consultation reports. In contrast, there are no significant differences between members of the three big parties of the EP in report allocation. Finally, the dummy, checking whether an MEP is Danish or not, has a positive sign in the co-decision model and a negative one in the consultation model. However, it is insignificant, indicating that it does not matter whether an MEP comes from Denmark or how many reports that MEP has been allocated. No matter whether there is an analysis of committee or rapporteurship assigments,

Table 9.5 Negative binominal regressions of report allocation from July 1999–31 January 2007

	Number of substantial co-decision reports		Number of substantial consultation reports	
	Coef.	Std. Err.	Coef.	Std. Err.
Danes	−0.817	0.770	0.208	0.732
Male	−0.535	0.161***	0.168	0.237
EP party group (ref. EPP–ED)				
PES	−0.160	0.187	−0.191	0.265
ALDE	0.030	0.235	0.303	0.325
Greens/EFA	−0.676	0.391*	−0.153	0.471
EUL/NGL	−0.528	0.389	0.246	0.435
IND/DEM	−1.364	0.615**	−2.342	1.066**
UEN	−0.441	0.470	−1.371	0.821*
NA	−2.371	1.026**	−14.168	407.032
Constant	−0.622	0.160	−1.388	0.244
N	732		732	
Pseudo R^2	0.030		0.0284	

Source: Data from Nikoleta Yordanova, University of Mannheim.

Note
Only substantial reports (i.e. no simplified procedure, codifications, comitology introduction and appointments).

evidence cannot be found that Danes distinguish themselves from the remaining MEPs with respect to office allocation.

The contact patterns of MEPs have also been examined. In the 2000 and 2006 surveys, MEPs were asked how frequently they were in contact with a number of different actors at the EU and national level. As Table 9.6 shows, the contact patterns of Danish and other MEPs are not significantly different when it comes to being in touch with citizens, interest groups, other MEPs from the same member state, Commission officials or national ministers. However, when we look at contacts with other types of actors there are some interesting differences between the Danish MEPs and the rest of the EP, which are in line with the differences in attitudes discussed earlier. Again, there is a tendency for the Danes to have a stronger tie to their national political system compared to other MEPs. Danish MEPs report that they are more frequently in touch with their national party executive and MPs, and with civil servants from their national government, than other MEPs. One explanation of the higher level of contact that the Danes have with their national MPs might be that they actually do use their opportunity to participate in the weekly meetings of the parliamentary EAC. Others secure contacts to their national party by participating in its weekly meetings or by having regular email contact (M. Rasmussen 2007: 44).

Moreover, we see the effects of the work of the Danish government to actively use the Danish MEPs to further Danish views (and uploading) on EU matters of importance to Denmark where the EP has strong say (Rasmussen and Manners 2008; Fich 2008). Important areas have included working conditions, the environment and consumer protection, which were areas where Denmark often found itself in a minority position in the Council (Fich 2008). Qualitative interviews by Rasmussen with all 14 Danish MEPs at the time also confirm that most MEPs are in frequent contact with the Danish Ministries for the Environment and Food, Agriculture and Fisheries (M. Rasmussen 2008). Her research reveals that, over the years, Danish ministries and parties have become more active in maintaining such contacts than they were in the past, due to the increased powers of the EP.

Contact with European and national-level actors is, of course, not mutually exclusive for Danish MEPs. Existing research also very clearly shows that even if MEPs have ties to home, their frequency of contact in everyday politics is (of course) still higher to EP party groups than to national parties at home (A. Rasmussen 2008b). After all, EP party groups are engaged in the daily business of the EP. They control important assets within the chamber, such as committee positions, committee assignments, speaking time and the legislative agenda (Corbett et al. 2007). However, even if contacts with national actors are weaker than those with EU-level ones, they are stronger for the Danish MEPs than for the rest. Interestingly, there is also a difference between the Danes and the remaining MEPs when it comes to looking at contact with their EP party group leadership. Hence, even if the Danes report that they are frequently in touch with the latter, they are significantly less frequently in touch with their EP party group leadership than the rest of the MEPs that answered the survey.

Table 9.6 MEP contacts

Question	Danes vs. remaining members	Sign.	N
How frequently are you in contact with ordinary citizens?	More frequently		401
How frequently are you in contact with organized groups?	More frequently		396
How frequently are you in contact with leaders of my EP party group?	Less frequently	*	397
How frequently are you in contact with MEPs from other parties of my member state?	More frequently		399
How frequently are you in contact with officials in the Commission?	Less frequently		397
How frequently are you in contact with members of my national party executive?	More frequently	***	395
How frequently are you in contact with MPs from my national government?	More frequently	***	395
How frequently are you in contact with ministers from my national government?	More frequently		399
How frequently are you in contact with civil servants from my national government?	More frequently	*	397

Source: Farrell *et al.* (2006).

Note
Mann–Whitney U test, Sign. ***<0.01, **<0.05, *<0.10.

Finally, voting recommendations were analysed. Hence, an important type of contact between MEPs and different types of actors is the exchange of recommendations to MEPs on how they should vote on concrete matters. MEPs receive voting recommendations from a range of different actors. Again, existing research shows that MEPs are, of course, more likely to receive voting recommendations from their EP party groups than from their national parties (A. Rasmussen 2008b). Although national parties care about what is happening in the EP, they have little incentive to constantly monitor and dictate events. It is already known that close monitoring systems between MEPs and national governments are the exception (Messmer 2003). Not all issues are salient to the national parties. Hix and Lord, for example, argue that national parties are less active in monitoring MEPs because they know they will not be penalized in national elections even when MEPs act irresponsibly (Hix and Lord 1997). In addition, Rasmussen (2008) points out how the lag in national attention may mean that Danish political parties are not always aware of the issues when they are debated in the EP.

However, just as with contact patterns in general, there is a difference between the Danes and the remaining MEPs when an analysis is made of how frequently they actually do receive voting recommendations from national level actors. Hence, even if Danes receive such recommendations less frequently from national than EU level actors, they still report that they are more likely to receive

140   *A. Rasmussen*

Table 9.7 Voting recommendations

Question	Danes vs. remaining members	Sign.	N
How often do you receive recommendations on which way to vote from your national party leadership?	More often		395
How often do you receive recommendations on which way to vote from your EP party group leadership?	Less often		396
How often do you receive recommendations on which way to vote from your national party delegation of MEPs?	More often		387
How often do you receive recommendations on which way to vote from the European Commission?	More often		372
How often do you receive recommendations on which way to vote from your national government?	More often	**	385
How often do you receive recommendations on which way to vote from European interest groups?	More often		386
How often do you receive recommendations on which way to vote from national interest groups?	More often		386

Source: Farrell *et al.* (2006).

Note
Mann–Whitney U test, Sign. ***<0.01, **<0.05, *<0.10.

such recommendations from their national government than do the remaining MEPs. Again, this confirms statements in existing research that the Danish government is playing an active role in bringing Danish MEPs on board when important Danish issues are being discussed in Brussels (Fich 2008). Such frequent contacts do not only go to the ministries at home, but also via the PR in Brussels. Rasmussen quotes an MEP for stating:

> I can always contact the permanent administration if I need further information on an issue. We [the Danish MEPs] are regularly invited to meetings with the current ambassador and use each other's expertise. We all know each other and therefore, there is a very strong network.
> (M. Rasmussen 2007: 41)

National interests may also affect concrete voting behaviour. Fich reports how in the first years of the history of the EP, members often voted along national rather than party group lines. Many Danish MEPs saw themselves as 'national representatives rather than representatives of a specific attitude towards society' (own translation) (Fich 2008: 23). In this period it was also common for the national delegations within a given EP party to have their own party programmes, and, in areas such as fisheries and agriculture, national dividing lines were particularly strong. However, over time, party group discipline became stronger and national dividing lines within the party groups became weaker. Despite these developments, Rasmussen and Manners (2008) report, in research from recent years, that in areas such as environment, employment and social affairs, animal rights, food safety and agriculture, the national affiliation has led the Danes to vote along national rather than party group lines on several occasions (Rasmussen and Manners 2008; Auken 2008). Rasmussen's quantitative research of 1,875 roll call votes between July 2004 and May 2006 only finds evidence that Danes systematically vote together on environmental issues, but she points out that national affiliation might still play a strong role in the agricultural and employment votes that are not taken by roll call. This is supported by her qualitative research (M. Rasmussen 2007, 2008), which shows that not only have the Danes fought for tighter environmental standards, but also for more free market measures in agriculture than many of their southern European party group colleagues, irrespective of which party group they came from. She quotes an MEP for explaining:

We are strongly in favour of introducing more free market measures into the Common Agricultural Policy by reducing the EU farm subsidies. However, the French delegation would never dream of changing the current structure of farm subsidies. This creates situations where we vote in a national way rather than voting with the members of our group.

(M. Rasmussen 2007: 40)

In addition to being members of a European institution, this therefore leads Rasmussen and Manners to conclude that Danish MEPs have often served 'as a channel for Danish views' in their daily work within the EP (M. Rasmussen 2008: 50). Moreover, in line with previous research for the EP as a whole (Hix 2002) Rasmussen's quantitative analysis of the voting behaviour of the Danes shows that on issues where the preferences of their EP party groups and national party delegations conflict, Danes tend to follow the opinion of the national party group (M. Rasmussen 2007: 60). Finally, there are some interesting differences in whether Danish MEPs follow their EP party group that are probably not only likely to be related to the issue area debated, but also to their party group membership. Hence, it is known from previous research of the EP as a whole, that the larger EP groups are much more cohesive than the smaller ones (Hix *et al.* 2007).

As shown in Table 9.8, this argument also applies to the Danes. Even if there is some variation among MEPs, the best predictor for explaining differences between them in degree of agreement with their EP party group is the size of the group, rather than whether these MEP's have been re-elected or are freshmen.

Table 9.8 How often do Danish MEPs toe the EPG line? (roll call votes from July 2004–May 2006)

Name of MEP	Seniority	Size of EPG	Agreement (%)	Disagreement (%)	Non-voting (%)
Margrethe Auken	Low	Larger	84	6	10
Ole Christensen	Low	Larger	86	10	4
Dan Jørgensen	Low	Larger	86	10	4
Britta Thomsen	Low	Larger	70	7	23
Poul Nyrup Rasmussen	Low	Larger	77	7	16
Henrik Dam Kristensen	Low	Larger	62	7	31
Anders Samuelsen	Low	Larger	68	9	23
Niels Busk	High	Larger	78	5	17
Anne Jensen	High	Larger	89	6	5
Karin Riis Jørgensen	High	Larger	78	5	17
Gitte Seeberg	Low	Larger	67	18	15
Mogens Camre	High	Smaller	47	37	16
Ole Krarup	High	Smaller	32	7	61
Jens Peter Bonde	High	Smaller	25	54	21

Source: Rasmussen 2007.

Conclusion

Despite the predictions of the EU integration literature, that representatives may lose their national loyalties when arriving in Brussels, there is evidence here that Danish efforts to upload Danish interests and ideas to the EU level via its MEPs have been successful. This, to some extent, verifies the importance attached to uploading dynamics in the Introduction to this volume. Danes distinguish themselves from their fellow MEPs in a number of respects. They tend to be more devoted to issues of national autonomy and be more in touch with national actors than the rest of the EP – that also highlights the resonance of autonomy variables as outlined in the Introduction to this volume. In line with the official Danish attitude and the general position of the Danish population, Danish MEPs are more sceptical towards European integration than other MEPs. They are also more strongly attached to representing views of different national actors than their colleagues. In addition, there is evidence that the special Danish way of handling EU-policy leads to more interaction between Danish MEPs and their national parliament and government than in other countries. The Danish MEPs have more frequent contacts with their national level actors than their colleagues, and they also report that they are more likely to receive voting recommendations from home than do the rest of the MEPs. The Danish political system plays an active role in ensuring that Danish interests and ideas are uploaded to the European level by contacting the MEPs. Some of these contacts take a relatively formal nature through, for example, meetings of the EAC of the Danish parliament, but most of them have an informal character.

The findings here do not contradict the fact that, with the evolution of its power, the EP has gradually come to resemble a national parliament with the left-right policy dimension being the most dominant line of contestation and MEPs primarily voting along party group lines. Relatively speaking, *it is* the EP party groups and not the national parties or the Danish parliament or government at home that control the daily work of the Danish MEPs. Treating the EP as any other national parliament using the comparative politics literature is therefore highly recommended in the vast majority of studies. However, the findings also indicate that there may still be some differences between MEPs from different countries in role orientation, which cannot be explained by traditional party theory. Instead these differences result from the fact that MEPs come from different countries, whose interests sometimes differ irrespective of party affiliation. Qualitative evidence suggests that, for Danish MEPs, such differences do affect their voting behaviour on a number of key issues of special relevance to Danish politics. More systematic evidence needs to be collected on how far these differences in orientation and contact patterns of MEPs affects office allocation and concrete voting behaviour within the EP.

Note

1 The response rates in the 2000 and 2006 surveys are 31.8 and 37.2 per cent respectively. This is no lower than in recent mass and elite surveys (Hix *et al.* 2006). Moreover, the sample and population have been compared with respect to nationality, EP party group and gender. The correlations were very high, indicating that there is little bias between sample and population in these crucial respects.

10 Prospects and limits of European interest representation

The shipping and wind turbine industries

Karsten Ronit

Introduction

Many Danish interest groups have a track record of formal participation in political institutions and enjoy a high degree of recognition. However, patterns of exchange are dynamic and are informed by changes on domestic and international scenes. Historically, Danish interest groups have, to varying degrees, seen interest representation in a broader territorial perspective and have given attention to a number of international bodies that were essential to the shaping of policy and rule-making. With Danish membership of the EEC/EU in 1973, a more systematic effort was initiated by interest groups that were particularly affected by European integration, or by those that anticipated such future scenarios. Many have extended their field of operations, are today present on the European scene and combine different institutional strategies.[1] The dual focus on Danish as well as on European institutions is a base line for key Danish interest groups, but often more so in the economic domains.

Yet, conditions vary enormously across interest groups, and also within business. Business is far from a homogenous category facing equal prospects or limits. In this chapter, the experiences from two different industries will be compared, although it is recognized that the two industries have very different backgrounds: Shipping is an established industry, whereas the wind turbine sector is more of a greenhorn. Shipping has been an important trade in Denmark for centuries and has maintained a strong position in the economy, with A. P. Møller-Mærsk as the primary shipowner but by no means the only player in the industry. The wind turbine industry is of recent origin, dating back to the 1970s and characterized by fluctuating fortunes. In this respective industry, the company Vestas Wind Systems plays a leading role, although at a low level, and the industry comprises many other companies. While major corporations are known to the public at large and in the business community, less recognized is the fact that these industries are organized by representative business associations. The Danish Shipowners' Association and the Danish Wind-Industry Association, however, are important players in each of their fields.

These two sectors display some interesting variations, both in economic and in political terms. It will be interesting to examine, then, whether certain similarities in their behaviour can be observed with regard to their domestic and international strategies. A key issue in the strategy of these industries is the degree to which domestic or European institutions should be approached and interest-group resources allocated. If important decisions are made at the European level, if major rules are adopted by European institutions and if significant financial means are distributed by European bodies, then these developments are likely to affect the strategies of interest groups and turn their attention to the European scene. As referred to in the Introduction, 'uploading' represents an intriguing task, and takes particular forms in the context of interest groups. If, however, Danish institutions remain important for these industries, their work tends to concentrate on the domestic scene. Yet, this does not suggest that a single territorial level is chosen or that prioritizing is simple, nor that choices are consistent across issues; nevertheless, some basic patterns and dynamics of interest representation can be traced.

Studying these must also take account of the role of territorial levels beyond the European scene. In this sense, inspiration can be sought from existing theory ('interpretive case study') with an expectation that some findings may be at odds with existing theory ('deviant case study') (Lijphart 1971: 691–693). Just as it would be problematic to exclude the European processes from an analysis of current Danish business strategies, so also it would be strange to evade the global scene, especially in a time of economic and political globalization. Thus, a study of the Danish shipping and wind turbine industries and their interest representation must include three territorial levels; a domestic, a European and a global arena. Such a study captures how industries and interest groups with economic and political backgrounds may show significant variation in their behaviour, yet also reveal intriguing common approaches because they are embedded in a range of global structures. Indeed, if such different industries display certain similarities in their behaviour, then there are grounds to believe that, more or less, the same kind of behaviour can be found in other industries with a global dimension, and in a comparative perspective presumably not only in Denmark but in other European countries as well.

The following section examines some of the major theories that capture the activities of interest groups in the EU and facilitate the study of how different strategies are combined. Against the backdrop of these theoretical considerations, the chapter examines how the shipping industry and the wind turbine industry have focused on different territorial levels and institutions in the political representation of their interests. In the concluding section, some lessons are drawn for studying organized in business in the EU.

Interest group activity: one level, two levels, and beyond

Several decades ago, interest-group studies in Europe were primarily concerned with how private actors could leverage their own governments, to what degree they were integrated into public policy-making and, occasionally, how they assumed co-responsibility for public policy. The focus was on domestic processes and arrangements that lent themselves to comparison across countries (e.g. Eschenburg 1955; Finer 1966; Meynaud 1958). However, with the gradual development of European policies and European institutions, a special branch of interest-group studies unfolded and came to embrace the European level (Greenwood *et al.* 1992). Accordingly, the studies of interest groups and of European institutions were combined with analyses of multi-level governance, scrutinizing linkages between different territorial levels within the Union (Marks and Hooghe 2001). This theoretical advance corresponds with the actual paths of European integration as authority is transferred to the European level, while the member states remain important entities in the overall European structure. The traditional separation of domestic and European politics is abandoned (see Miles 2011a, 2011b), and associations must adapt to new environments (Grote *et al.* 2008); indeed, challenges are also facing the shipping and the wind turbine industry.

In the midst of new and complex relations linking different territorial levels, a specific European scene with its own players and logics has emerged. A key focus in this field of research is the coordination between private interests and the relations between organized interests and the European institutions: analyses provide insights into both the patterns of associational strategies in the business community and the relative importance of the European institutions (Eising 2007). This has paved the way both for studies of 'uploading', concerned mainly with influencing domestic and European policy-making in the early stages of the policy process, and for studies of 'downloading', focusing on the domestic implementation of EU regulation.

As regards the coordination of interests, however, research provides contradictory evidence of associability. EU-institutions have, for obvious reasons, attracted a rich variety of corporations and associations of all sorts and much interest-group activity is uncoordinated, reflecting the many and diverse interests seeking influence and the different political cultures prevailing in the member states. Although fragmentation exists, many areas are organized in a coherent format, with one major organization per industry. However, the rules and practices guiding decision-making in these more or less coordinated organizations are under-theorized, and the different roles of firms and national associations in European federations are still poorly understood.

As to the interactions between organized interests and the European institutions, research has a better grasp, and official recognition of private interests and their access to institutions, offices and staff is without doubt a great advantage for business (Bouwen 2004). Various modes of contact and participation deserve scrutiny in their own right. In this context, the European Commission is attributed a pivotal role in European integration and has a number of tasks that clearly distinguishes it from ordinary administrations of traditional intergovernmental organizations. For obvious reasons, its pro-active role makes it highly relevant for organized interests to gain access to and influence the Commission, either to assist in the further development of policy or to thwart initiatives. With the Commission singled out as the most relevant institution, exchanges with its various DGs and agencies are important (Pollack 2003).

Less proliferated are research studies of interest groups and the European Parliament and the Council, although for different reasons. Relations between interest groups and the Council are weak and lack substantial institutional underpinning, but the domestic levels feeding into the Council are important. In this perspective, the focus is shifted to domestic politics, although this branch of research is not identical to traditional studies on interest groups since new domestic forms of interest representation are contextualized by the wider European politics. Contacts between interest groups and the European Parliament have historically been of a different nature, mainly because the Parliament in the past was less influential in the overall architecture of the EU and, therefore, less relevant to engage with. These relations have gradually changed with the delegation of increasing powers to the Parliament (Hix 2005), and, as a consequence, interactions have become increasingly regulated and strategies more differentiated (Marshall 2010). Although the Parliament is still, in relative terms, less attractive to interest groups, these groups must combine different strategies and not rely on a single institution.

These variable forms of coordination and institutional orientation also have consequences for the allocation of associational resources over time. In the early days of European integration, even business interest associations, not strongly affected by concrete measures, saw the writing on the wall, anticipated stronger future policy spill-overs and assumed that their interests would one day be systematically addressed by new policy initiatives. Many firms and associations decided to maintain a presence in Brussels and directed their European political work from this vantage point, enrolling in European-wide associations to represent consolidated European interests vis-à-vis European institutions.

Today the strong presence of associations in Brussels is not merely a symbolic act that demonstrates a broad interest in European developments, signifying an ambition to follow agendas with a possible future influence on business. In fact, many interests are today affected in very concrete ways, and greater resources must be invested by associations in order to defend their cases in relation to all European institutions. The old associations slowly upgraded their engagement, new associations have taken up the challenge and new forms of coordination have emerged. Altogether, the study on European interest groups is increasingly recognized as an important element in the analysis of European politics, and, interestingly enough, research has in some ways gone full circle as the role of interest groups was also predicted in early research on European integration (Haas 1958).

Although the knowledge base has expanded considerably with more known about associations and their relations with EU institutions, it is not always clear how business is affected, when there is something to win or lose from public interventions, and when regulation should be encouraged or avoided by business. Currently, further model building is necessary in order to map and theorize on associational strategies and how they are related to public policy. Caution must also be displayed when referring to business; business is not a uniform category and, as this chapter will show, there are interesting variations across industries.

Furthermore, the definition of a joint strategy is not uncomplicated, and the members of European associations – firms and national associations – have different opportunities to define the industries' interests.

Many processes link domestic and European levels, give rise to different forms of associability and lead to different kinds of relations, but a brief overview does not capture all manifestations of interest-group behaviour, especially when activities move beyond European boundaries. Indeed, a key problem currently facing European interest-group studies is that they tend to isolate the role of these actors from global developments and the need of business to work in these contexts. Long ago, it became clear that the domestic scene was getting too narrow, but there is also a great risk that the European scene can become too narrow.

Informed by economic and political globalization, business faces a range of new challenges, and, accordingly, complex strategies are required. Whereas some globalization processes are of more recent origin, others go further back in time, and in a number of cases pre-date European institution building. This is hardly surprising given the uneven globalization of corporate activity across industries, but this perspective is missing in most research on European integration which tends to see European institution building as structuring economic and social processes rather than being the other way round. However, the speed at which business proceeds is related to, but not identical with, the speed of politics, and strong economic forces were set in motion both before and after the European project began in the 1950s. Therefore, it cannot be taken for granted that industries attribute the same importance to the European level and design similar strategies.

In the following, the behaviour of Danish shipping and wind turbine industries are examined, as two industries experiencing different conditions, which may generate varying forms of action. Yet, it is also expected that these industries share some features in the way they operate, triggering a set of certain commonalties in political behaviour.

Business interests are organized and represented at different territorial levels and give different emphasis to these levels, although it is anticipated that the European level is not necessarily the highest and most important one for these industries. Therefore, levels beyond the EU must be built into models of interest representation and link actions at national, European and global levels. Furthermore, business interests are represented in a huge variety of ways reflecting the different preferences of corporations and associations, but we expect that the orientations towards specific markets will be important. Therefore, the economic factors will be key drivers in structuring political behaviour.

Finally, business interests are seeking benefits of a very diverse nature because the goals of business are complex, but there are some general goals to be achieved and principles to be followed. It is therefore assumed that only certain degrees of intervention are encouraged, and it is necessary to also account for the possibility that business has a preference for not involving the EU.

Shipping industry – the EU as stumbling block in a global strategy

Shipping, including merchant shipping, is a very old enterprise, dating back to prehistoric times. At a later stage, shipping activities became systematically organized by states and associations of seafarers and merchants and were further internationalized in medieval times. Moving even further up in history, maritime interests were interwoven with political interests in many countries during the age of Mercantilism and during the sixteenth century to the eighteenth century, shipping was deemed by many governments as an important trade. Although a small country, Denmark in this way became a comparatively large sea power.

However, with the slow disentanglement of the relation between shipping and state in modern capitalism, the need for organizing shipowners in an independent format became apparent (Ronit 2000), and in 1884, the Danish Shipowners' Association was formed. Many other business associations were also formed in Denmark at the eve of the nineteenth century, and in a domestic context it was important for shipping to match other business interests and find a coherent platform to speak for shipping. The association had – and still has – notable Danish shipowners as members: in the early period especially, the DFDS Seaways; later, the East Asiatic Company, and later still, A.P. Møller Mærsk. The association held a prominent position and became highly respected by the Danish government. It was recognized that the industry almost embodied a kind of national Danish interest that should be defended by government in relevant international forums. It was no incident that the authority designated to regulate the industry, established in 1908 as the Ministry of Commerce and Shipping, included 'shipping' in its name. It is clear that many maritime interests came to be represented by the Danish government, a view also valid in a contemporary perspective, but the industry cannot rely on the benevolent actions of government and must represent its own interests in a distinct and uncompromising way.

Although much activity was related to Danish waters, significant interests abroad were represented in the Association. It was only natural for Danish shipowners to give their work an international orientation, and collaborate with shipowners and other major interests in the maritime sector in other countries with the aim of creating a level playing field for the industry. The overriding strategic outlook was based on the principle of 'freedom of the seas'; the proper implementation of this principle has never been uncomplicated, and it enabled Danish shipping, and other shipping interests for that matter, to take part in international trade without being discriminated against. Very importantly, this does not exclude regulation, but it excludes national and regional legislation and measures that run counter to global rules, a key point we shall elaborate upon shortly.

In the late 1800s, the international outlook of the Danish Shipowners' Association led to international cooperation of various kinds, such as joining relevant international private organizations that came to represent shipping. The association joined the International Federation of Shipping, established in 1909 and concentrating on employer issues, and enrolled in the International Chamber of

Shipping, established in 1921 and catering to an array of maritime producer interests. These associations united shipowners from across the world and from different branches of shipping, and, as peak associations, undisputedly came to represent shipping worldwide. With a clear focus on many international issues, the Danish association became embedded in an international environment and, consequently, a set of international principles was guiding its efforts domestically (Danish Shipowners' Association 1984).

It was of primary importance that the private organizations of shipping be established at the global level before shipping was organized in a public framework. In other words, it was possible for private shipping interests to structure the policy field long before agendas, routines and regulatory tools were developed and coordinated in public policy. The early creation of global associations shows that the industry had a rather firm grip on the policy development. With the creation of the Intergovernmental Maritime Consultative Organization (IMCO) in 1948, renamed the International Maritime Organization (IMO) in 1959 and recognized as one of the UN's special agencies, maritime issues were organized by a public body. The IMO was based in London, in fact in the same place where the private organizations were already headquartered.

In our context, it is important to note that private and public organizations together institutionalized maritime and shipping policy at the global level and based their work on a number of norms and practices routed in century-old traditions. However, new challenges also emerged and new pieces of regulation were adopted. The IMO has adopted a large number of conventions, and issued several hundred codes and recommendations to regulate shipping in the areas of safety management, environmental protection, handling of goods and training (International Maritime Organization 2010). Therefore, the private and public organizations of the policy field indicate that shipping policy was firmly structured at the global level many years before attempts were made to streamline shipping policy at the European level.

Indeed, shipping was not immediately embraced through European integration. Major attempts to address maritime policy and shipping issues were not taken until the mid 1980s (Commission of the European Communities 1986a, 1986b, 1986c, 1986d), and the policy initiatives were not particularly welcomed by business. In relation to the 1986 Single European Act, a long list of complaints was actually formulated. It is interesting to note that at that time, a European association was already in place: the Comité des Associations d'Armateurs des Communautés Européennes (CAACE) was established in 1965, but renamed European Community Shipowners' Association (ECSA) in 1990. Although the formation of the CAACE was in some ways related to initiatives by the European institutions, the association was not well developed in its early days, although it could take action if need be. In this way, the formation of the CAACE shows some of the same features that have characterized European association-building more generally, namely, that it is advantageous to have a formal, even if somewhat dormant, organization ready because it can step in, be consulted and otherwise represent the industry. In other words, the shipping industry was pre-adapting. Eventually, it could upgrade and develop into a mature association at a later stage when circumstances permitted. A stronger effort was required when more serious ambitions to regulate shipping were launched or were in the planning stage in the 1980s and 1990s.

From the perspective of the Danish Shipowners' Association, however, this boost was not enough to match the new challenges, and, in 1989, the association decided to establish its own office in Brussels. To reap the benefits of collective action, national associations usually delegate powers and pool resources to represent European-wide interests, and design joint units that understand European politics. In some cases, however, national associations prefer to be present in Brussels, but the position of the Danish Shipowners' Association is in many ways exceptional in the context of European shipping coordination.

In European shipping, the Danish association is not an insignificant partner that seeks to find alternative ways of representation because the European association is dominated by members from major countries. In fact, the Danish Shipowners' Association holds major shipping interests, and is a big player from a small country. National associations in European business federations do not always dispose of equal voting rights and are not involved in the leading bodies on an equal footing, but large countries do not always have large industries and, therefore, do not necessarily dominate European federations.

Furthermore, the Danish association does not draw on specific EU funds or seek other benefits from the coffers of the EU. Many economic, social and regional groups have this goal as their primary *raison d'être* for investing resources and running their own offices in Brussels. Instead, the association prefers to keep the EU out of politics, because any European maritime policy risking the blocking of global rules is not desirable. As the Danish Shipowners' Association stated recently: 'Due to the international character of shipping the efforts of the Danish Shipowners' Association is concentrated on the international rules to avoid regional legislation' (Danish Shipowners' Association 2010: 40).

From the perspective of Danish shipping, it is relevant to influence associational politics on the spot so to speak, and, in some cases, also amplify the power of the ECSA, and, overall, make the concerted European voice in shipping stronger. In business, it is important to ensure that competitors from other countries are not given preferential treatment and special access to European institutions. In this context, establishing an office makes good sense. Also, other business interests related to the maritime sector, such as shippers, have their own preferences, and it is important to both actively build alliances and, occasionally, work to minimize the influence of other groups in the market. Interests are not the same across European shipping or across other parts of the maritime sector.

Strong national interests persist among some shipowners and some countries. Not all segments of the shipping community are decidedly working to support free competition or depart from a global outlook. Typically, there is a division between those operating exclusively in a Mediterranean or European context and those participating in global operations, and when it is difficult to reach agreement in ECSA, Danish shipowners can take independent action to enhance the global perspective. Depending on the issue, another possibility is to let global associations engage in regional politics. Indeed, the opening of an office in Brussels in 2007 by the World Shipping Council (WSC), formed in 2000 and specializing in liner shipping, is meant to present to the European Commission the interests of this global section of shipping.

Today European integration also blankets shipping, and major steps have been taken to institutionalize maritime policy, one of the latest manifestations being the creation of the European Maritime Safety Agency (EMSA) in 2006, and to develop new and integrated maritime strategies (European Commission 2009). In these processes, the Danish Shipowners' Association has strived with notable success to keep the global dimension in sight and let it guide European regulation as far as possible. In the case of shipping policy, the EU is a latecomer and is not in a position to develop a new policy field and influence it in substantial ways when it is transformed into areas of global public policy. When the first attempts were made to develop a European maritime policy, the EU found itself in a pre-existing institutional context where the policy space was filled to a considerable degree – if not completely occupied – by public agencies in the UN system and corresponding private organizations. The logic here was to work on the basis of global agendas and rules. These institutional factors have been crucial to the work of the Danish Shipowners' Association, coming from a small country but representing a global industry.

Wind turbine industry – the EU as one element in a global strategy

The history of the wind turbine industry delivers a fascinating, yet much more recent, account of a business sector and its political behaviour. From being part of the outer periphery of energy production, this fledgling industry has moved more towards the centre of energy policy, although the industry still has a long way to go.

Basically, wind energy is an old technology; in fact, a technology that was largely abandoned with the introduction of other forms of power, especially fossil fuels. Yet, wind has been rediscovered in the last few decades. 'Rediscovered', however, is a misleading term. Modern wind power has undergone an interesting scientific development over recent decades, involving significant research input focusing, for instance, on the technology of wind turbines and intelligent wind power systems and their placement, all factors that qualify it as high-tech industry. Parallel to this progress, a commercial and organizational development has characterized the industry, linking different actors along the production chain and building new relations to scientific communities and public institutions, in and across nations. The local or national orientation is definitely not irrelevant, but new international horizons have opened (Ronit 2012).

The Danish wind turbine industry started in the wake of the energy crisis of the 1970s. Industrial development was pioneered by people with a zest for developing alternative and renewable sources of energy that were friendlier to the environment than traditional fossil fuels (Karnøe 1991). Big business was not involved in these early stages of innovation and industrial development. Accordingly, small and inexperienced firms had to find ways to leverage political decision-makers in a Danish context. The basic aim of the industry was to give these start-up firms better opportunities in relation to investment, research and development. This was not an easy task to accomplish as a strong tradition prevails in Danish industrial policy not to support specific firms and industries (Sidenius 1984). Although this strategy is imbued with rhetoric and exceptions, it can be hard to secure support for specific sections of business, and fledgling industries seem to have a particularly hard time.

In line with Danish traditions of business associability, the wind turbine industry soon undertook collective action, and in 1981 established 'Foreningen af Danske Vindkraftanlægsproducenter', later called Foreningen af 'Danske Vindmøllefabrikanter', and later still called 'Vindmølleindustrien' (in English: Danish Wind-Industry Association). First headquartered in the Danish province of Jutland and based completely outside the 'nerves of government', it relocated in 1994 to the Danish capital, a clear indication of the stronger focus on political action (Danish Wind Industry Association 2006).

Through the 1980s, it became evident that wind power was not just a utopian idea promoted by naïve entrepreneurs, but rather a Danish technological success story. Progress was notable from an environmental point of view, and also from a more traditional business perspective. Hence, the industry became little by little more attractive from the standpoint of government because wind energy could help solve environmental problems, and, much later, climate change problems, as well as the economy at large. Add to this the fact that the industry began to expand on foreign markets.

Although when taken in isolation and combination, these factors significantly improved the role of the industry and the public perception of wind energy, the industry continues to face many challenges on the domestic scene. Since the scepticism of the pioneer days has slowly evaporated, the industry has received broad acclaim for its achievements, although political support has been very uneven. The industry has thrived best under conditions in which export, industrial, and trade-related issues go hand in hand, and it cannot be taken for granted that the government will take specific care of and represent the industry in European contexts.

However, it also became clear that the domestic platform was too narrow and fragile to promote the industry, and efforts were made in a larger institutional context. The European Wind-Energy Association (EWEA) was already established by 1982. The formation of the new association was not much spurred by strong political ambitions from EU institutions to prioritize renewables or wind power in particular, and the goal of the association was rather to improve cooperation in the industry and raise public awareness more generally about the potentials of the industry. In those days the industry was still in its infancy, and although the very idea of switching to sustainable energy seemed promising, the supply of wind energy was comparatively limited. Under these conditions political leverage was constrained, but stronger political orientations and capacities were slowly built up. The EU has also scaled up its renewables policy in the last decade, including the adoption of directives enhancing the role of renewables in the internal energy market (European Union 2001, 2009). These measures are also important in improving the global position of the European wind industry.

The wind turbine industry through EWEA – and from 2000 also through the European Renewable Energy Council (EREC) – has endeavoured to promote wind energy and see it appear more strongly on the European agenda, partly through its own activities at the European level and partly through influencing governments by way of national associations at home. Still, however, the wind industry has to compete with more important and conventional forms of energy, the interests of which are also represented in Brussels – as well as through member states sceptical of the role of renewables and favouring traditional sources of energy. Significant achievements have been made, and 'the European Wind-Energy Association believes that the 2001 RES-E directive constitutes the world's most significant existing piece of legislation for renewable electricity, and is the key factor explaining the success of renewable energies, including wind, worldwide' (European Wind-Energy Association 2010a).

Recent developments have emphasized that renewables should be integrated more strongly into European energy policy. From the perspective of security policy, the EU should strive to become independent of Middle Eastern oil and Russian gas. The aspect of security in relation to energy supply that dominated in the past has, in many ways, returned. From the perspective of climate policy, it is also evident that energy consumption should be reduced and existing sources of energy gradually replaced by sustainable forms of energy, including wind power, to reduce CO_2 emissions. These new agendas have largely been beneficial, but this does not suggest that the scene has been taken over by renewables. It is essential that an active and coordinated effort be made to keep these agendas alive and create further incentives for the wind industry through European energy policy. If European energy policy more actively promotes sustainable energy and offers various incentives in order to introduce renewables, the demand for wind turbines will likely increase. Eventually, this increase would have some consequences for the further technological development of wind turbines, improve the competitiveness of the European wind turbine industry, and help it gain a stronger position in global markets. However, there is uncertainty as to which renewables should be encouraged and, therefore, predictability and planning in public policy is essential.

Although European developments are given due attention, wind energy is not just a European specialty. In other parts of the world also, interesting technological developments must be closely followed, and foreign markets must be addressed by expanding companies. Indeed, the economic and political contexts of the industry are of a global nature today, and a need for collective action beyond Europe is apparent.

In 2005, it was decided to organize in a global format through the Global Wind Energy Council (GWEC) to provide the industry with a stronger voice and to present wind energy as an alternative to conventional energy, but also to distinguish the industry from other branches in the renewables sector. In this way, the globalization of the industry – of research, development and production – was reflected in the industry's organization. Interestingly, the initiative to coordinate the different national and regional interests in a global forum came from the Danish Wind-Industry Association. It definitely gave this initiative greater weight: not only is the Danish wind industry one of the pioneers, but it is also present on global markets – in other words, it is a big industry from a small country.

The structure of the new global association is indeed telling: national and regional associations represent the wind industry in different parts of the world, indicating the regional element of the industry and of energy policy. Within a relatively short time, regional and national associations in major countries have sprung into existence in order to represent a new industry, including many new companies. Various regional issues bring cleavages into the global association, but the formation of a global outfit is a big step forward in coordinating the industry and in representing the industry in global forums. It shows that the industry has something to offer when it addresses global issues, in particular climate policy, which has become increasingly important for the industry and a key for its further development (European Wind-Energy Association 2010b). Indeed, changes in global climate policy will also have repercussions for European strategies and will provide arguments for a more ambitious renewables policy in Europe. Global achievements will encourage national developments in many countries where it is difficult or impossible to build strong enough domestic alliances to enhance the role of the renewables in energy supply.

The global organization of the industry is also required when constituting renewables policy as an amalgam of energy and environmental policy, but with its own specific agendas, conferences, committees, expert bodies and other elements typically characterizing a policy field. This institutionalization has recently led to the emergence of a new UN organization focusing on sustainable forms of energy, namely, the International Renewable Energy Agency (IRENA), set up in 2009 and based in Abu Dhabi. The opportunities for influencing global policy in this domain are significantly better whenever the industry is organized in a corresponding global framework.

Today, European integration also covers energy policy and the small area of wind power. In addition to political activities on the domestic scene, the Danish Wind-Industry Association is engaged in various political activities through its European association to enhance leverage with European institutions. European initiatives are important to the industry and are given high priority, but relatively soon after sustainable energy was addressed in Europe the field began to undergo a process of global institutionalization, with new organizations and forums on the public as well as on the private side. Without abandoning the European level, increased attention from the industry has been directed towards global policies; and for the Danish wind industry having a global economic and political orientation, the European scene is one out of several arenas, but not always the most important one.

Conclusions

Business must carefully assess when and where to represent interests and, accordingly, carve out appropriate strategies. Participation in domestic processes remains important, but, with European integration and institution-building, choices have become more complex, and uploading of interests offers many new choices. In this chapter, the patterns of interest representation in two Danish industries, Shipping and Wind Turbine, are studied: shipping is an old industry, now featuring a variety of private and public institutions as well as established principles, regulations and norms; whereas the wind turbine industry is very recent, with a young and limited institution-building component and a set of new policies. Yet, the two industries also share some interesting features: The operations of companies are not limited to domestic or regional markets but cover the global arena, and, although representing a small country, Danish shipping and wind turbine companies play a key role in the global make-up of these industries.

The variations and similarities in economic, organizational and political properties have strong impacts on the behaviour of these two industries. Politically, the Danish shipping industry is a very experienced player that has a rich tradition of combining actions at domestic and global levels; only later has it, with some reluctance, become involved in European issues. The main goal here is not to develop European maritime policy, but to stall it. Within a short time, the wind turbine industry has also learnt how to combine actions at different territorial levels; from first focusing on domestic issues it soon embraced the European scene, and a little later it globalized its activities. For both industries, however, it is evident that politics does not stop with Europe. Historically, the global scene has been decisive for shipping, and for the wind turbine industry global politics is becoming ever more important. Underlying different economic conditions and embedded in different institutional politics, the two industries display interesting variations. This does not suggest, however, that one strategy is superior and serves as an example to be followed. Both industries have achieved a number of successes, but whereas shipping has a global strategy and prefers limited interventions, the wind turbine industry has a more mixed strategy and also encourages public initiatives. In this regard, it is in some ways possible to rank them on a continuum between Europeanization and globalization.

The forms and avenues of interest representation discussed here are neither available nor relevant to all segments of Danish business, or to other interest groups for that matter, and it cannot be concluded that these two cases are illustrative of Danish business as a whole. For a number of industries, however, European engagement is not the final and most crucial level. It can even be a disturbing or a less important factor in the overall strategy of business. This pattern of associational behaviour is not just relevant to Danish business but applies to all industries in Europe that are present on global markets and that are characterized by global regulation.

Studies on business and other private interests in Europe are usually confined to the domestic and European levels, and European policies are often perceived as somewhat encapsulated, but business must be understood in broader contexts, a point particularly essential when analysing industries with a global outlook, of course. As we have seen, some processes of globalization actually pre-date European integration, some run simultaneously with the European project, and yet other globalization processes follow later and add a new layer to politics, and, accordingly, different patterns of behaviour must be scrutinized. In all cases, interest representation in Europe is typically part of a more complex scenario.

Note

1 According to the Register of Interest Representatives, established by the European Commission in 2008, a number of Danish actors are active on the European scene and exchange with the European Commission and the European Parliament in many contexts. They are not just working out of their Danish headquarters but have their own offices in Brussels, from where they seek access to European institutions. Currently, 65 organizations headquartered in Denmark have joined the voluntary register – this figure includes foreign and international organizations with a formal headquarter in Denmark, but there are some Danish organizations that, for various reasons, have not joined the register. Other smaller EU-countries display the following figures: Sweden 88; Finland 52; Ireland 40 (European Commission 2011). In addition to such direct strategies, a much larger number of Danish organizations are affiliated with European federations and speak with one voice. Indeed, this is the preferred strategy of the majority of Danish associations in and outside the business community.

11 The European 'rights revolution' and the (non) implementation of the citizenship directive in Denmark[1]

Marlene Wind

Introduction

When the Treaty of Rome was signed in 1957 it had no mention of human rights. After the Second World War, the division of labour seemed clear: the European Community should establish peace and prosperity in post-war Europe through economic cooperation, while the Council of Europe and the European Convention on Human Rights were to take care of this more normative dimension. Although William Mass has demonstrated that already the Treaty of Paris considered free movement rights,[2] the EEC – by its mere wording – had its focus on the market and only subsequently on market-related rights. Today, however, 'rights' have become an integral part of almost everything the EU does. The EU now has a binding Charter of Fundamental Rights and, with the Lisbon Treaty, even a fundamental rights Commissioner. It also has an Agency of Fundamental Rights that monitors the rights-situation in all of Europe. Finally, the EU has, for a long time, had quite a strong human rights focus in its accession and neighbourhood policy (conditionality) and in its foreign and development policies more generally.

Not everyone, however, would agree that human rights is the answer to all prayers as the EU crawls towards a maturing democracy. Joseph Weiler once said that 'you can give slaves rights but it still does not make them free' (Weiler 1999). Streit and Mussler are also critical. Speaking from an economist's perspective, they argue that the EU's social dimension (here understood as everything that does not focus on the market) only distracts attention away from the essentials of what the EU *should* be doing: deregulating and liberalizing (Streit and Mussler 1995: 14ff.). In their view, the EU was intended to constitute a 'market without a state', where competition between various regulatory systems would make any kind of centralized intervention superfluous (Streit and Mussler 1995: 14ff.). In a country like Denmark, with a very 'matter of fact' approach to the EU and where the Union – for the most part – has been seen as pragmatic towards the market, the Streit and Mussler argument has always been compelling. Denmark only entered the EU because the United Kingdom decided to do so (and because Denmark would have lost its important bacon market if it stayed outside) and has thus always played down the more value-based arguments for joining. Moreover, in Denmark – which has a very positivist legal tradition – human rights, strong activist courts and dynamic legal interpretations are a very foreign phenomena, which means that the Danish politicians, when Denmark joined the EC in 1973, strongly downplayed the fact that the Community was *not* an ordinary international law regime, but a semi-constitutional order based on the supremacy of European law and a strong Court.

Over the years, however, even Denmark has come to realize that what it considered to be 'just an internal market' can have strong 'sovereignty-implications'. One of the most spectacular examples in recent years (in a Danish context at least) was the Metock case and the fuss around the EU's citizenship directive, which hit Danish self-understanding like a rocket. It can be argued that it was not until 2008, when this case surfaced, that the Danes discovered that the EU is about more than ordinary diplomacy. It is, in other words, the EU's Internal Market rules which govern who may enter, stay and get family unification on Danish territory.

When trying to make sense of the European rights revolution and its impact on a small – but in human rights terms – self-conscious member state like Denmark, the most obvious place to start will be to look at the expansion of citizen rights as part of a general Europeanization process, which includes a European as well as a national perspective. The analysis here will not launch a full-fledged study of Denmark's reactions/accommodations to the rights revolution in Europe over the years, but focus more specifically on the Danish reaction to/implementation of that part of the citizenship directive that deals with family unification. This aspect is interesting for several reasons: most importantly it is illustrative of a reactive Danish approach to the development of a European rights regime. Moreover, it represents a hard case in the sense that it deals with Internal Market regulation, which traditionally has been heralded by Danish policy-makers. Moreover, Denmark is normally described as a 'dutiful complier' to European law and regulation, which means that when a directive has been accepted in the Council of Ministers, complacency and full adaptation is expected (Falkner *et al.* 2005; Kelstrup *et al.* 2008: 325). As seen below however, this is not how to best describe the situation surrounding the implementation of the citizenship directive – despite the fact that it was Denmark who hosted the EU presidency and thus chaired the meetings when the directive was negotiated. Before moving on to the directive and the illustration of Denmark as a very reactive player, it is appropriate to take a brief look at the development of the EU's free movement rules more generally.

Turning factors of production into EU citizens[3]

Over the past half-century, the right to free movement has been one of the most basic principles of Community law (Craig and de Búrca 2003). In the early years of Community history, there was an image of the migrating worker as a *factor of production* who was expected to contribute to a more prosperous European economy. This kind of 'market citizenship', as Michelle Everson has named it, clearly only referred to a rather limited category of member state nationals (Everson 1995: 73; Wind 2009a). However, this image was gradually replaced by an idea of the migrating worker as a *human being* who, together with his or her family, has a legitimate right to reside and work in another member state without being discriminated against (Craig and de Búrca 2003: 701). With the Amsterdam Treaty in 1999, the Schengen cooperation was merged with the general legal and institutional framework of the EU.[4]

While the Rome Treaty set out to create a single market with no internal barriers, the fundamental right to settle and take on employment in another member state was only gradually made possible. Until 1968,[5] it was thus difficult to exercise the right to free movement, since all EC citizens had to apply for work and residence permits individually. In 1973, private businessmen and their families were granted the same rights to free movement as ordinary workers,[6] which represented a new and much broader interpretation of the concept of 'worker'. At the same time, the Community also ensured that labour mobility was supported by social security measures. Of most importance is regulation 1408/71, which coordinated the social security policy of the member states facilitating that workers seeking employment in another member state were able to bring earned social benefits etc. with them (Martinsen 2005a: 93).[7] Moreover, the families of migrating workers acquired full access to the national school system and universities, as well as social welfare, on an equal footing with nationals. The same was the case for national health-care systems and insurance policies. The dictum was that member states could organize their social security systems and their labour markets as they pleased, but not discriminate between nationals and non-nationals when the latter took up legal residence in the host state.

With the 1992 Maastricht Treaty, Union citizenship replaced the idea of 'the worker' as the main recipient of rights in the Internal Market. The argument was that the EU should not only be a Community for migrating labour – it should include all citizens: the unemployed, the handicapped, the self-employed the pensioner, the student, etc. (Wind 2009a). In 1992, however, the citizenship concept already created controversy. Was it meant to emerge into a true citizenship status? Was it ever to replace national citizenship? From 1997, the Amsterdam Treaty made it explicit that Union citizenship should not replace but merely *supplement* national citizenship – which meant that the Danish opt-out to the citizenship clause in the Maastricht Treaty (adopted in the Edinburgh agreement from 1993), became a unified European understanding of Union citizenship. What Denmark was exempted from in its opt-out was thus only one aspect of the citizenship provision, which says that it *should not replace national citizenship.* Denmark is not exempted from those aspects of the citizenship provision that deal with the Internal Market and, thus, the EU's free movement rules. In other words, no member state can be exempted from the core of the EU, which is, and remains, the Internal Market. The Union citizenship debate in Denmark is thus a very good example of the emergence of an EU right that Danes could benefit from, but really don't want.

Because Denmark held the rotating Presidency in the EU in 2002, it negotiated the citizenship directive which was finally adopted as 2004/38/EC

(EUR-Lex 2012b).[8] It can be argued that the directive put 'flesh on the bones' of Union citizenship, clarifying – once and for all – what rights Union citizens and their families have when they make use of their free movement rights. The directive thus codified previous regulation in this area together with ECJ case law regarding citizenship and social security rights. It was the general opinion that simplification was needed as the area of free movement and residence rights were regulated by nine directives and two regulations![9] With the new residence directive, any European citizen can take residence in another EU member state for up to three months without first acquiring a residence permit. Furthermore, after only five years of residence, a citizen (whether from another EU member state or a Third Country spouse of an EU citizen), will have full access to the social security rights of the host country. As made explicit in the directive, the migrating citizen and his/her dependent spouse, partner and children will, moreover, have a right to remain in the host country in case of death, divorce or termination of the contract of the primary right-holder. The directive was, however, not just a product of legislation but also – and perhaps most prominently – of previous case law. Since the ECJ has also played a prominent role in the shaping of the European rights revolution in the area of interest here, namely 'family unification', we will now take a brief look at the most important case law in this area.

The Court speaks up

The first important case was the Singh-case from 1990 (EUR-Lex 2012c). Here the ECJ established that since an EU worker has a right to bring her family with her when migrating to another EU member state, the worker shall of course also be allowed to return to her home state with her family (EUR-Lex 2012d). Where the Singh case concerned EU workers who had physically exercised their right to free movement, the Carpenter case made clear that even though you – as an EU citizen – do not exercise a trans-border activity (i.e. physically move to another EU country), you may nevertheless be able rely on the rights linked to the EU's free movement rules when it comes to family unification.[10]

In 2003, however, the ECJ delivered its Akrich judgment,[11] which must be considered a setback compared to the two previous cases. In Akrich, the Court reasoned that family unification with a Third Country National (TCN) spouse is conditioned on the spouse having been *a legal resident* of another member state prior to being unified with an EU citizen. Several legal experts have argued that the case 'was out of line' and thus clearly inconsistent with the Court's previous reasoning (in particular in the MRAX case),[12] when it comes to the prior legal residence requirement of TCN's (Currie 2009: 321; Lansbergen 2009: 287; Jacqueson 2010: 277–296). It has been suggested that the Akrich ruling was influenced by the enlargement negotiations where the EU's very liberal free movement rules caused some tensions in the member states (Currie 2009: 321). It is, however, hardly surprising that Akrich was popular among those member states who preferred stricter family unification rules. They referred to the case again and again when the Metock case controversy came up (Jacqueson 2010). This also happened in Denmark.[13]

In the Metock ruling, which is now examined in some detail below, the ECJ went one step further, removing the:

> [s]ecurity blanket of Akrich from the Member States, seemingly leaving them powerless to refuse claims of residency from TCN spouses of Union citizens, even in circumstances where they have previously been unlawfully present on the Member State's territory and regardless of when the marriage occurred.
>
> (Currie 2009: 311)

The Metock case – which explicitly refers to the citizenship directive adopted by the member states themselves – questions who will in future will actually be in charge of national immigration policies. After the Metock ruling, there seemed to be little room for manoeuvre left to the member states. It is now appropriate to take a closer look at the Danish implementation of the directive in order to detect those mediating variables that hindered a correct and timely transposition of the EU rules.

Danish (non) implementation

The directive was, as noted above, negotiated (in part) by the Danish Presidency in 2002. As mentioned earlier, it was meant to simplify and make the rules concerning free movement clearer and more transparent. The purpose of the directive reads in its preamble (paragraph 3) as follows:

> Union citizenship should be the fundamental status of nationals of the Member States when they exercise their right of free movement and residence. It is therefore necessary to codify and review the existing Community instruments dealing separately with workers, self-employed persons, as well as students and other inactive persons in order to simplify and strengthen the right of free movement and residence of all Union citizens.
>
> (EUR-Lex 2012b)

The Danish government received its mandate to adopt the directive in the EAC of the Danish parliament (the Folketing) in September 2003. Before that, it had been negotiated – with no objections in the EAC on 21 September 2001 and 8 November 2002. The directive was adopted by the Council and the European Parliament in 2004 and should be fully implemented in the member states before 30 April 2006.[14]

After the Danish centre-right minority government (supported by the right-wing Danish People's Party) resumed power in 2001, it tightened the Danish immigration rules significantly. The main argument was that there had been an explosion of immigrants during the Social Democratic leadership (from

1993–2001). One of the main focus areas of the incoming government was a tightening of access to family unification so that, for instance, refugees no longer had a legal *right* to be unified with their families. This does not mean that they could not acquire family unification at all, only that was no longer a *legal right* that they would have to apply for. Moreover, in the new law on immigration, from 2002[15] it was required that in order to obtain family unification an applicant should (according to the Danish law on immigration paragraph 9) demonstrate that: (1) he or she had not, within the past year, received social security funding from the state; (2) he or she was above 24 years of age; (3) he or she was in possession of a home of a 'reasonable' size; (4) the couple should prove to be clearly more closely affiliated to Denmark than to the country from which the spouse originated (unless the applicant had been a legal resident in Denmark for 28 years); (5) prove that the marriage was not between two individuals who had a family relation; and (6) that the applicant should not within a 10-year period have had a criminal record.[16]

The reasoning underpinning the controversial 24-year rule was based on an attempt to limit the number of forced marriages. Moreover, in 2007, it was made a condition for family unification that the applicant should pass a 'language- and knowledge-of-society-test'. Due to the stricter national immigration laws launched at the beginning of the 2000s, which were broadly supported by the voters, the Danish reaction to the previous years' ECJ case law, and later the citizenship directive, was extremely reluctant. Below, we will demonstrate how the reactions were played out. We will also see that Denmark (in this area) has been far from the 'obedient complier' that Gerda Falkner speaks of in terms of European compliance-patterns.

Employing the Europeanization approach to the Danish case, the following looks at the different mediating variables which created *barriers* to a correct implementation: in the literature, a distinction can be made between 'institutional capacity'; 'institutional tradition'; 'veto points' and 'compliance culture' (see Radaelli 2003; Kelstrup *et al.* 2008). This is illustrated in Figure 11.1 below, as a scale of compliance that denotes where transformation is the most radical adjustment in national law to European law and withdrawal is the opposite:

Most emphasis will be put on the veto-players, as these are clearly most relevant in this context.

Political capacity

When discussing *political capacity* in a Europeanization framework, the debate broadly deals with the ability of a member state to coordinate and smoothly transpose EU law into the national legal order regardless of issue area (Pedersen 2002: 193; Bøegh-Lervang and Madum 2010: 81). Danish public administration has, over the years, been significantly Europeanized partly due to the fact that there has been a solid consensus in the Danish parliament (from the Liberal Party to the Social Democratic Party) supporting Danish policy towards Europe (Nedergaard 2005: 58). Moreover, Denmark is a centralized state and the ministries

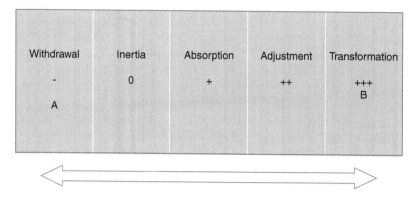

Figure 11.1 Scale of compliance (sources: Radaelli 2003; Kelstrup *et al.* 2008: 325).

thus have a great deal of control over implementation. It is often argued that Denmark has been a constructive player in EU policy-making processes (Adler-Nissen 2009a). Perhaps in an attempt to compensate for the so-called Danish opt-outs Denmark has – it is often argued – implemented EU legislation on time (Adler-Nissen 2009a).[17] In many respects, Falkner's hypothesis and evidence that sees Denmark as an obedient complier is thus not entirely off the mark (Falkner *et al.* 2005). When looking at the citizenship directive however, the misfit been national and European rules and values were simply so evident that it severely influenced the transposition of the directive into national law. This does not so much concern political capacity, but rather political institutional tradition and – as seen shortly – strong veto-players.

After the directive was adopted, Danish civil servants found themselves caught in a political 'double game' where the politicians silently supported the citizenship directive at the European level but, at the same time, placed heavy pressure on the national administration to make the EU rules on residence rights fit the attitudes of the majority in parliament. A majority supported a very strict ('tough and fair') immigration policy.[18] The civil servants had warned the EAC of the Danish parliament both in 2001 and in 2003 that: 'The directive will in its current form lead to changes in the immigration law [...]' and that 'The Directive is expected in its current form to lead to an expansion in the right to family unification'. However, nothing in the available documents suggests that the specific issue of requiring or not requiring 'prior legal residence in another EU member state', which was the core issue in the controversial Metock case law, was mentioned or debated at any point in the national or European negotiations. In fact, the big issue on everybody's lips in 2003–2004 was thus *not* family unification and prior legal residence of TCNs, but whether same sex marriages should be included in the citizenship directive or not (Ryborg 2008: 7).

Political tradition

If *political tradition* is examined, this dimension has also been categorized as 'the goodness of fit' hypothesis, illustrating how the national path in the family unification policy area fits with the European one. The misfits are quite obvious here. Not only because of the Danish opt-outs from the Maastricht Treaty, which mean that Denmark is not part of the supranational legislation in the JHA area (and many therefore believed that Denmark was automatically exempted from everything that dealt with family unification), but also because Denmark, since 2001, has been tightening its national immigration laws as described above.

However, Denmark is, of course, not exempted from regulation in the immigration field when it falls under the Internal Market. The discrepancy between Danish and EU family unification law has thus grown in recent years. Danish citizens' access to family unification under Danish law is, in other words, more limited than the access that a Danish citizen can rely on when applying EU rules i.e. the citizen directive. The only requirement here is that a Danish citizen will need to exercise 'a trans-border activity' in the Union. None of the restrictive Danish conditions as described above apply.

The paradox in this connection is, of course, that despite the much stricter Danish immigration policy, the Danish opt-out on JHA – (and the fact that the Social Democratic–Social Liberal Government had already introduced restrictions on family unification) – made the political parties express reservations when the European Commission launched its first draft of the citizenship directive in September 2001. When the new draft directive was debated in the Council a week after the Commission had tabled the proposal, the Danish delegates remained silent.[19] Moreover, between the first and second reading, the ECJ ruled in two cases, which expanded the family unification rights. The first was the Carpenter judgment, where the Court as mentioned above ruled that an EU citizen has a right to family unification without actually residing in another EU member state. The other was the Akrich case law, from 2003, which established that lawful residence in another EU member state was a precondition for a Third Country National to have family unification with an EU citizen. However, the Akrich case law also emphasized that EU law should pay due attention to Article 8 of the European Convention of Human Rights, which emphasizes respect for family life. Moreover, the ECJ emphasized (as noted above) in this case law, that the motive for making use of one's free movement rights was entirely irrelevant. To put it differently, it was irrelevant if an EU citizen moved to another EU member state with the specific motive to acquire family unification. Both cases were, however, interpreted very restrictively in Denmark by the Ministry of Justice. The Danish authorities/administration, which in this respect can be seen as *veto-players*, thus argued that the Carpenter case did not establish a general right for Danish citizens to have family unification after delivering services in another EU member state. Also rejected was the notion that Article 8 should play a significant role in the interpretation of family unification cases and that motive to move to another EU member state was irrelevant (Bøegh-Lervang and Madum 2010; Ryborg 2008). According to the Danish authoritative interpretation, moving to another member state merely to obtain family unification could be regarded as fraud and an attempt to circumvent the strict Danish immigration rules.

Veto players

When the citizenship directive was adopted, the governments were, as always, given two years to implement it. However, none of the governments in the EU did a good job in this respect, as reported by the Commission in its analysis from 2008. As noted below, Denmark – the 'usual complier' when it comes to EU law – moved very far in order to accommodate not the directive, but the immigration policy laid down by a majority in parliament. Generally, new studies have shown how Denmark, as a typical homogenous and consensus-seeking Nordic welfare state, is a good example of a classical majoritarian democracy that gives priority to the majority in parliament vis-à-vis the individual citizen (Wind et al. 2009; Føllesdal and Wind 2009). In majoritarian democracies (as opposed to constitutional ones) courts as protectors of human rights play a very limited role and there is no tradition for either judicial review or for citizens to take their own governments to court (Wind et al. 2009; Føllesdal and Wind 2009). In our case here, this may explain the rather one-eyed focus from the state authorities when it comes to pleasing the will of political majority, as opposed to the individual citizen, when it comes to EU rights.

In July 2008, a Danish national newspaper, *Berlingske Tidende*, thus revealed – in a three week long campaign – how the Danish authorities had withheld information about the new EU rights following from the directive giving citizens easier access to family unification (Wind 2008). 'Test-calls' to the Danish Immigration Service (Udlændingeservice) that journalists had recorded, demonstrated that civil servants abstained from informing about the possibility of using the EU rules when EU citizens sought family unification. The newspaper also showed how the Ministry of Integration's home page – which was meant to inform potential applicants for family unification – had been confusing for years; leaving out essential information on the possibilities of using the rules and rights of the directive. When asked about the 'misdoings', the civil servants explained (anonymously) to the newspaper that they deliberately left out the information about the EU rules due to instruction from the Minister and the Ministry's senior civil servants, who interpreted the EU rules and the directive as a 'loophole' and as a way of circumventing the much stricter Danish immigration and family unification law. There is, in other words, little doubt that the Ministry of Integration – sanctioned by the Minister and the Ministry of Justice (who normally acts as the authority when it comes to implementing EU rules) – acted as veto-players in this context.

The analysis presented in this chapter shows that the civil servants knew very well what they were doing. Being squeezed by an immigration critical majority and a Minister who wanted results, they thus obeyed orders (but warned about the illegality!) when the Minister, in 2004, administratively decided to change a praxis dating back to 1993. The practice had made explicit that not only workers, but also pensioners, the self-employed and students, were able to make use of the EU's free movements rights. The inclusion of these groups was in nice accordance with the introduction of the EU citizenship in the Maastricht Treaty – and though Denmark had an exception from the Citizenship clause, it did not – as mentioned earlier – have an opt-out from the part that deals with free movement of EU citizens. Nevertheless, in order to curb the worst 'undesirable effects' of the directive, the above-mentioned groups were excluded from being able to make use of the directive from 2004 to 2007. The Minister in place at the time Rikke Hvilshøj defended her new position in the Danish parliament saying that:

> [T]he government will of course always seek to explore whether it is possible to interpret EU rules in such a manner that it matches the government's policies. And are we met by initiatives which has the purpose of using EU law to undermine Danish immigration rules, we will obviously try to find out whether we – while upholding our EU law commitments – can counter such initiatives.[20]
>
> (EU-Oplysningen 2012c)

In 2006 however, the Commission criticized the practice and threatened to launch a case against Denmark. However, when Denmark finally got round to changing its practices in 2007, the Ministry abstained from revealing this to its prime 'customers' at its homepage. In sum, nobody was told that these groups were now allowed to make use of the EU rules to acquire family unification. Looking back at Figure 11.2, there is thus little doubt that a situation was faced where the Danish administrative level had not only omitted implementation of the Citizenship directive, but had directly countered the effect of the intended measure by excluding certain groups from their rights. We thus find ourselves on the left extreme, namely *withdrawal* when it comes to best describing the implementation of this aspect of the directive.

The Metock case

After the Danish newspaper had launched its campaign focusing primarily on the citizens who had been deprived of their rights due to the Danish implementation of the citizenship directive, the Metock case was handed down by the ECJ causing a new outcry in the Danish public debate. All of sudden focus shifted from the wrongdoings of the Ministry (and thus the state vis-à-vis innocent citizens who had to move to Sweden to acquire family unification in accordance with the EU rules), to the 'expansive' interpretation of the directive by the ECJ. All politicians in the Danish parliament, with the exception of those from the small Social Liberal Party, criticized the ECJ for its judgment, which was called everything from political to undemocratic and scandalous etc. But what was all the fuss really about? In Metock, the Court was duly asked by an Irish tribunal whether it was in accordance with the citizenship directive to require (as the Irish authorities had done) that a spouse to a Union citizen had to have resided legally in another member state in order to acquire family unification. The Court was very clear, explaining that this would not be in accordance with the citizenship directive and that, de facto, it had corrected the Court's Akrich ruling, stating the opposite. In the summary of the Metock case, the Court clarified the following:

> As regards family members of a Union citizen, no provision of Directive 2004/38 makes the application of the directive conditional on their having previously resided in a Member State. As Article 3 (1) of Directive 29004/38 states, the directive applies to all Union citizens who move to or reside in a Member State other than that of which they are a national, and to their family members.... *The definition of family members in point 2 of Article 2 of Directive 2004/38 does not distinguish according to whether or not they have already resided lawfully in another Member State.*
> (EUR-Lex 2012f: paragraph 1, author's emphasis)

The Irish court also asked the ECJ whether a spouse of an EU citizen could benefit from the rights of the directive irrespective of when and where the marriage had taken place. In the Metock case, which dealt with a group of people who had previously applied for – and had been rejected – asylum in Ireland, the applicants thus had a status as rejected asylum-seekers when they married their EU spouses in Ireland.

The ECJ emphasized that, following the directive, no limitation in the right of residence granted to family members under EU law was allowed. As Lansbergen put it: 'The Court considered that 'having regard to the context and objectives of Directive 2004/38, the provisions of that Directive cannot be interpreted restrictively' (Lansbergen 2009: 290). According to the ECJ, there was thus no requirement in the directive that a Union citizen must already have established a family *before* moving to another EU member state. Moreover, the Court also noted that having diverging national immigration/family unification rules under EU law could create barriers to the free movement of citizens. As Lansbergen puts it:

> [D]iverging national immigration rules governing the admission of non-EU national family members would mean that the conditions of residence for an EU citizen would vary between Member States [...] (and would MW) [...] not be compatible with the objective of establishing an internal market characterized by the abolition of obstacles to free movements of persons between Member States.
> (Lansbergen 2009: 290)

As noted above, the Metock judgement was interpreted by almost all political parties as an excessive and activist judgement. The Danish People's Party, on which the government depended for its majority in parliament demanded that the government should ask the European Commission to work towards amending the directive in order to reintroduce the Akrich requirement of 'prior-legal-residence'. The Danish People's Party also demanded a special national agreement, specifying how fraud with regard to EU rules could be combated and how the national immigration rules for non-EU citizens could be tightened even further. As the EU directive did not prevent any member state from fighting fraud and abuse with the family unification rules, the post-Metock initiative, launched by the government and the Danish People's Party, was merely symbolic and without any legal clout except for one important point: in line with this agreement, the Ministry today randomly checks 50 per cent of all EU family unification cases for fraud. And we are here speaking of cases where there is no particular suspicion of fraud.[21]

It is, nevertheless, fair to conclude that the government and the Danish People's Party have de facto, and rather silently, accepted that when it comes to family unification for EU citizens – and also TCNs – national rules no longer apply. After the communication about the Danish implementation problems with the European Commission, the Danish Immigration Service (which had been caught out in its flawed implementation of the EU's residence rules) reformed its web site, and it is today clearer about the family unification rights of EU citizens. Figuratively, the timeline can be illustrated in this way:

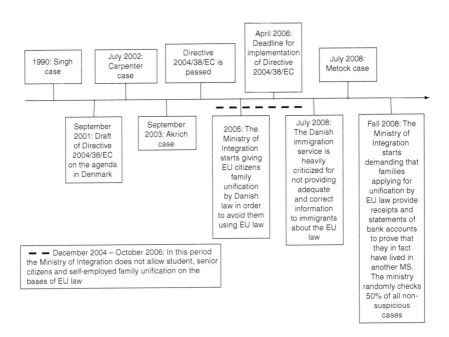

Figure 11.2 The Metock case.

Denmark as a reactive player

What does the case study presented in this chapter then tell us about Denmark and the European rights revolution? Quite a bit! Though Denmark has traditionally stood on a high note when it comes to promoting human rights and human values abroad, it has not been easy for a small majoritarian country like this to be confronted with the binding constitutional democratic principles of the EU. To give an example: none of those 300 couples who, in order to avoid the Danish 24-year rule and the other restrictions, moved to Sweden to be family unified (under the more liberal EU rules), pressed charges against the Danish government. There is little doubt that this tells us something about the lack of a tradition in Denmark (and the other Nordic majoritarian democracies for that matter) to use courts as a conflict resolution mechanism (Wind *et al.* 2009; Wind 2010). In the Nordic welfare states, conflicts are solved outside the courtroom. Denmark has – in common with the other Nordic countries (except Norway) – a tradition of not using judicial review by courts, and generally pays tribute to the principle of 'no one over or above the parliament' (Wind 2009b). This self-evidently makes it difficult to accept the implementation of court-produced supranational law. The Nordics like human rights, but they prefer rights to be the product of legislative proposals and not something produced by courts (Wind 2009b). Moreover, the national authorities are considered to be 'your friend', whose advice you take, and against whom you do not press charges (Wind *et al.* 2009). In this sense, ordinary citizens are far from those watch dogs of EU law that we see in many other EU member states (Cichowski 2007).

There is little doubt that the Danish story of the implementation of the citizen directive is a story of a dutiful complier member state that fell to earth from the stars. The empirical case study thus supports the thesis that where there is a fundamental misfit between national and European law, the transposition of EU law into the national legal order will be extremely difficult. It highlights the constraints upon, and tensions for, Denmark in balancing influence and autonomy in practice, and in handling the difficulties of downloading all aspects of EU business (see the Introduction to this volume). When it concerns the basic principles of protecting minority rights, the will of the majority – here through immigration/family unification rules – will supersede any other concerns.

The analysis above also illustrates how the expansion of citizen rights and EU competencies over time makes it more and more difficult for member states to govern classical national prerogatives like immigration. What not just the ECJ case law, but certainly also the Citizenship directive, tells us is that when it comes to immigration policies that are linked to the Internal Market and Union citizens, the EU has taken over and left very little, if any, discretion to the member states.

Conclusion

The emphasis on rights and values in recent decades has no doubt had a legitimizing goal for the EU as such. As Grainne de Búrca puts it:

> These values differ sharply and obviously from the Community's legacy of economic focus. Rights talk [...] denotes a certain moral content to Community law and policy, and thus offers a means of developing a moral and ethical foundation for the Community.
> (de Búrca 1995: 52)

Looking at the overall picture, the 'European rights revolution' can thus be seen as both a gradual evolution from 'worker to citizen' on the one hand, and a more classical human rights community on the other. While these two strands of rights have evolved independently, they have today merged into a Union citizenship with radical consequences for the member states – particularly when it comes to immigration control. Denmark is a case in point. As citizenship and Internal Market regulation have become more and more integrated – and also in the future are likely to include more and more policy areas from the JHA – it becomes increasingly difficult to be a small opt-out country with an immigration policy out of sync with the rest of Europe. Denmark may be the 'usual complier' when it comes to implementing general EU law; however, its strong focus on immigration control and national prerogatives – together with a weak tradition for protection of rights – may end up leaving it on the doorstep when the Union is taking yet another step in the direction of a rights and justice community.

Notes

1 Thanks to Niels Skærbæk, Centre for European Politics, Department of Political Science, University of Copenhagen, for research assistance and for his enormous help with the collection of data for this article.
2 As Mass puts it:
> Most commentators view the 'birth of Europe' as heralded by the Treaty establishing the European Economic Community, yet the earlier Treaty of Paris not only established the Community's basic institutional framework [...] but also established the first legal provisions concerning free movement of labour.
> (Mass 2003: 2)
3 This section builds in part on Section VI of Wind (2009a).
4 Today, around 500 million people live in the Schengen area. It covers 22 EU member states plus Iceland, Norway and Switzerland. Bulgaria, Cyprus and Romania do not yet apply the Schengen *acquis* fully, which is why checks on persons are still carried out at the internal borders with those three countries. The United Kingdom and Ireland have an opt-out in the abolition of internal border control. They thus only adhere to the provisions relating to police and judicial cooperation in criminal matters.
5 Regulation 1612/68 focuses on equal treatment and lists many substantial rights to workers and their families. 1251/70 goes further and protects – under certain conditions – workers' rights to remain in the territory of a member state in case of retirement, death, incapacity to work etc. after having been employed for a certain period of time in the host state.

The European 'rights revolution' 173

6 See also Directive 75/34 at EUR-Lex (2012a).
7 The Regulation applies to all legislation relating to the social security branches concerning sickness and maternity benefits, invalidity benefits, old age benefits, survivor's benefits, benefits in respect of accidents at work and occupational diseases, unemployment benefits, family benefits and death grants. It applies to general and special contributory and non-contributory social security schemes; however, it does not apply to medical or social assistance.
8 This Directive amends Regulation 1612/68 and annuls Directive 64/221, 68/360, 72/194, 73/148, 75/34, 75/35, 90/364. 90/365 and 93/96.
9 27 September 2001 was the first time that the Commission's preliminary draft to a citizenship directive was negotiated in the Council for Internal Market affairs.
10 The case concerned a British citizen living in Britain selling and adverts to journals in other EU member states. The British authorities had decided to expel Mr. Carpenter's Philippino wife because her tourist visa had expired. The case was handed over to the European Court in order to have clarified whether Mr. Carpenter could make use of the EU's free movement rules. The ECJ argued that even though Mr. Carpenter was not physically exercising his right to free movement, he was selling cross-border services and therefore able to rely on the Internal Market's rules of free exchange of services. The ECJ thus established that his ability to continue delivering cross-border services to other member states might be endangered if he was not allowed to live with his Philippino wife who took care of his children from a previous marriage. Delivering cross-border services is, in other words, just as legitimate as actual physical movement and residence when wanting to make use of the EU's more generous family unification rules.
11 See EUR-Lex (2012e: paragraph 55–57).
12 In the MRAX case [Case 2002 ECR I-6591] the ECJ emphasized that TCN spouses could come within the scope of Article 10 of Regulation 16/12 despite their country of origin.
13 See paragraph 49–50 in EUR-Lex (2012e). The more liberal or expansive part of Akrich concerned the question of whether it should be considered a circumvention of stricter national immigration rules when an EU citizen make use of the EU's free movement rules in order to acquire family unification. The ECJ reasoned that the *motive* for residing in another member state was entirely irrelevant. It could thus not be considered misuse of the EU's free movement rules when an EU citizen moved to another member state with the sole purpose of acquiring family unification.
14 Already at this stage (in 2001 and 2003) governmental civil servants warned the European Affairs Committee of the Danish parliament that 'The Directive in its current version will to a certain extent increase the possibilities to acquire family unification' (see joint note 13 September 2001; and joint note 12 September 2003).
15 See Retsinformation (2012).
16 Moreover, it was no longer possible to acquire a permanent legal residence for parents above 60 years of age.
17 It should be noted, however, that (Danish) implementation is an understudied field. Most available implementation studies focus merely on formal, and thus not on actual, implementation, which is a huge problem. When a country has been characterized as a dutiful complier, it tells us little about how the national and local administration have in fact implemented EU law in the national legal order. See Kelstrup *et al.* (2008) for a discussion of this issue.
18 The Danish civil servants knew what they were doing and knew that the citizenship directive would collide with the government's immigration policy (only supported in parliament by the government coalition parties and the Danish People's Party). This was evident in the communiqués they delivered to the European Affairs Committee of the Danish parliament (see Collective note, 13 September 2001; and Collective note 12 September 2003).

19 EUU, 2007–8 (2nd collection), E 57.
20 In Danish:

> [R]egeringen [vil] naturligvis altid undersoge, om det er muligt at fortolke EU-reglerne på den måde, som bedst understotter regeringens politik. Og bliver vi modt med initiativer, der har til formål at bruge EU-retten til at udhule danske udlændinge regler, så vil vi selvfolgelig undersoge, om vi indenfor EU-rettens rammer kan imodegå disse initiativer.
> (EU-Oplysningen 2012b)

21 Those applying for family unification through the EU rules are today required to supply receipts from their housing contracts and bank accounts to demonstrate that they are actually paying for housing in another member state.

12 EU-phoria or -phobia?

Danish public opinion about the EU

Andreas R. T. Schuck and Claes H. de Vreese

Introduction

The EU is undoubtedly facing a time of crisis and its future success and development crucially depends on public support by its citizens (Hobolt 2009). Thus, looking at public opinion towards the EU in the individual member states (and its considerable variation across countries) as well as its development over time, and potential impact and implications, merits further investigation. In this light, Danish public opinion about the EU has always been a particular interesting case, leaving EU officials and commentators behind with mixed feelings.

Danish public opinion about the EU

Since the Danish entry to the EC in 1973, following an exciting referendum, Danes have been known to possess mixed feelings about European integration and the EU. On the one hand, Danes today are among the most vigorous and loyal supporters of their country being member of the EU, with an impressive 66 per cent (as opposed to just a 49 per cent EU-wide average) judging EU membership to be 'a good thing' (see Figure 12.1). Furthermore, more than three out of four Danes (76 per cent) think that Denmark has benefitted from EU membership, a hefty 23 per cent above the EU-wide average (53 per cent). Over the last 20 years (since 1991), the difference between Danish and EU-wide public opinion on perceived benefits of EU membership has always been more than at least 10 per cent apart (18.5 per cent on average from 1991–2010). With regard to EU membership being 'a good thing', Danish numbers are (since 1997) above EU-wide average continuously (7 per cent on average from 1997–2010), even though they were higher in the early nineties compared to the late nineties in absolute terms.

On the other hand, however, Danes are not enthusiastically embracing just any facet of the EU and EU integration, resisting, for example, the adoption of the euro as a common currency in a national referendum. In 1992, the Treaty of Maastricht was voted down in a referendum, leading to the revised Edinburgh Agreement and several 'Danish exceptions' in the collaboration with the other member states. Danish public opinion about the EU is therefore rather mixed.

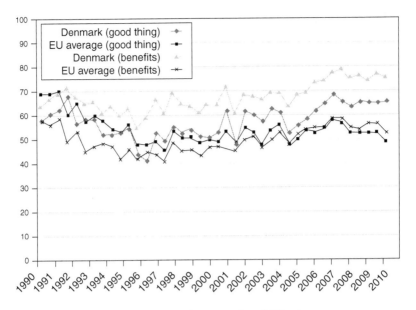

Figure 12.1 EU membership support in Denmark and EU-wide.

Note
Numbers are over-time trend lines based on Eurobarometer data (EB 33–73) indicating agreement to the statement that EU membership of one's country is 'a good thing' and that one's country has, on average, 'benefitted' from EU membership. Note that the EU-wide average numbers pertain to different numbers of countries given the past accession of new member states at different points in time.

This is also expressed in the confidence Danes display with regard to EU institutions. On the one hand, confidence in the EU and its institutions is rather high compared to other countries. On the other hand, confidence in the European Parliament, for example, is notably lower than the Danes' level of confidence in their own national parliament (see Figure 12.2). Whereas almost two-thirds of the Danes (63 per cent) tend to trust the European Parliament, EU-wide, less than half of their fellow European citizens do so (48 per cent). However, trust in their national parliament is still much higher (72 per cent) among Danes and has been so ever since these numbers have been measured. Thus, whereas European citizens on average trust the European Parliament more than their national parliaments, we see the reverse pattern in Denmark.

The same is true with regard to satisfaction with the way democracy works both in the EU and at home. Overall, Danes are satisfied with how democracy works in the EU (63 per cent) and more so than other Europeans (52 per cent on average) (see Figure 12.3). Since 2001, satisfaction with EU democracy among Danes is on average 11.4 per cent higher than the average satisfaction in other member states, whereas it has been below average in the years before. However, these numbers are still way below satisfaction with the way democracy works at

EU-phoria or -phobia? 177

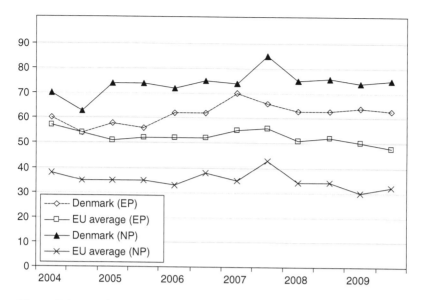

Figure 12.2 Trust in the European Parliament and national parliaments in Denmark and EU-wide.

Note
Numbers are over-time trend lines based on Eurobarometer data (EB 61–73) indicating levels of trust in the EU parliament and the national parliament.

home. Here, Danes display an impressive 94 per cent of satisfaction as opposed to just 58 per cent, on average, among other Europeans (30.4 per cent difference on average from 1997–2009). Furthermore, even though a growing share of national political decision-making is tied to Brussels nowadays, Danish democracy can still be regarded as robust, with clear increases in political interest, efficacy and trust in national political institutions (Christiansen and Togeby 2006).

As pointed out above, further developments of the EU are contingent on public support (now more than ever before). With the end of the era of permissive consensus, the future success of the EU hinges on public support by its citizens. Aside from national referenda on issues of EU integration, the 2007 Treaty of Lisbon for the first time established the opportunity for citizen initiatives on a European level. Europe is yet waiting for its first referendum initiated by European citizens but, as likely or unlikely as it might be to witness one in the foreseeable future, the opportunity alone already stresses the importance attached to public opinion about controversial European issues in the future and how they can be expected to be dealt with by EU officials. But aside from the referendum opportunity, and in light of the alleged democratic and communicative deficit of the EU (e.g. Anderson and McLeod 2004; Katz 2001; Rohrschneider 2002), it is impossible to ignore public opinion and public support as key

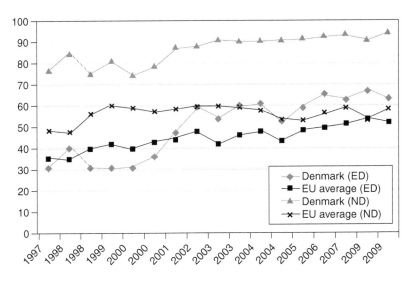

Figure 12.3 Satisfaction with the democracy in the EU and in one's own country in Denmark and EU-wide.

Note
Numbers are over-time trend lines based on Eurobarometer data (EB 47–73) indicating satisfaction with 'the way democracy works' in the EU and one's own country. Note that the EU-wide average numbers pertain to different numbers of countries given the past accession of new member states at different points in time. Also note that not for all years since 1997 data is available, and thus the distances between the different data points on the x-axis are not equal.

forces in shaping official future policy stances and trying to cope successfully with the challenges facing the EU.

Previous studies have proposed alternative explanations for why citizens support the EU and the success or failure of national referenda on issues of European integration. The scientific debate thereby oscillates between the importance attached to EU issue-related attitudes (i.e. first-order) (e.g. Svensson 2002) and domestic considerations such as government evaluations (i.e. second-order) (e.g. Franklin 2002; Franklin *et al.* 1994). The present study aims to make a contribution in assessing *how* and *to what extent* existing attitudes towards the EU can have an impact on the intention to vote 'no' in referenda on issues of EU integration above and beyond domestic, second-order considerations.

It is necessary to be very specific when speaking of public support for European integration as well as Euro-scepticism. This implies that there is a need to understand antecedents of both positive and negative EU attitudes. Denmark is a particularly interesting case study as regards the dynamics of EU referenda, and it has a long history of referenda on membership, various EU treaties and the common currency (see de Vreese and Semetko 2004 for an overview). Constellation of public opinion in Denmark therefore consititutes an important case to aid understanding of how existing EU attitudes play out in such referenda. The current study's context is provided by a hypothetical referendum scenario regarding the EU Constitutional Treaty. No actual referendum was held in Denmark on this issue, yet the context is still not entirely unrealistic. In 2005, a majority of voters rejected the European Constitution in France and the Netherlands, de facto marking the end of the ratification process. However, several other referenda in other countries, such as the United Kingdom and Denmark, were tentatively scheduled but obviously dependent on the outcomes of the preceding votes. The Dutch outcome, ultimately, contributed to the fact that no referendum was held in Denmark; however, the topic itself had been part of Danish public debate, and further referenda were still conducted (Luxembourg) regardless of the Dutch and French outcomes.

The study, presented in this chapter, is not so much interested in the question of what the outcome of such a referendum on the EU Constitution in Denmark would have been; rather the intention is to investigate the role of attitudes towards the EU vis-à-vis domestic considerations in explaining what people intended to vote. More specifically, the chapter analyses the role of Euroscepticism as a *mediator* for the influence of other political attitudes on the intention to vote 'no' in such a referendum; thereby tapping into the ongoing debate about the importance and role of the EU vs. other more general attitudes when people make up their minds about Europe. Denmark in this regard provides a particularly interesting context for such an investigation given that attitudes towards the EU ought to be particularly important here due to the four decades of continuing public debate regarding the EU and Denmark's status and relationship with it. Thus, it is expected that attitudes towards the EU will be particularly relevant in Denmark, and to matter above and beyond second-order explanations when people make up their minds about Europe. Finally, the findings are discussed in light of larger trends in Danish public opinion regarding the EU, and point out future implications.

The importance and role of EU attitudes

There are numerous predispositions and attitudes that are of particular importance when considering voting behaviour in referenda on issues of European integration. Both EU issue-related attitudes and more general political attitudes and domestic considerations have been proposed as key determinants for vote choice in EU referenda.

Several EU referendum studies have stressed the impact of issue-related factors and attitudes such as general *scepticism towards the EU* on vote choice (Siune and Svensson 1993; Svensson 2002). In referendum contexts in which involvement is high, citizens' voting decisions are more strongly orientated towards issue-related (i.e. EU-specific) considerations (see, for example, Garry *et al.* 2005; Hobolt 2005; Svensson 1994). Voters' pre-existing levels of support for the EU or European integration have indeed been shown to be one of the strongest predictors for vote choice in EU referenda, and also in a conservative multivariate test (de Vreese and Semetko 2004). A different stream of research, however, has emphasized that involvement in EU referenda is usually rather low, which attaches higher importance to considerations unrelated to the EU. In the context of such second-order type elections (Reif and Schmitt 1980; Schmitt 2005), citizens are perceived as more likely to direct their attention towards domestic issues and, for example, to use the referendum as an opportunity to rate the popularity of the incumbent government (Denver 2002; Franklin 2002; Franklin et al. 1995). However, rather than seeing EU-related factors, such as general Euro-scepticism, and domestic considerations or general political attitudes as competing alternatives for the explanation of referendum voting behaviour, it is suggested here that this represents an *integrated dynamic of mediation*. There is recent evidence suggesting that second-order explanations for voting behaviour in referenda and EU-issue voting have to be thought of as complementary rather than opposed to each other (Garry et al. 2005; Hobolt 2006). We suggest that EU attitudes are the factor *through which* other political attitudes and predispositions – unrelated to the specific referendum issue – exert an influence, at least partially, on voting intentions in EU referenda. Accordingly, general Euro-scepticism is integrated into our model of explaining vote choice in EU referenda as a potential *mediator*, which is expected to have a direct effect on voting intention, and which, in itself, may be determined by more general political attitudes and predispositions.[1] Thus, how might such a mediated relationship, as outlined above, aid understanding of voting behaviour in EU referenda? Previous research has shown that there is a link between incumbent support and pro-EU attitudes (for example, Ray 2003). Being in opposition to a government that promotes EU proposal(s) might thus translate into scepticism towards the EU itself and via this route exert an influence on the vote. Similarly, feelings of low political efficacy make it more likely for people to vote against a government proposal (Lowery and Sigelman 1981). Thus, having little faith in political elites that support a referendum proposal can be expected to result in increased scepticism towards the EU.

Other attitudes and predispositions are usually directly related to general EU support. Among these factors are feelings of national identity (Christin and Trechsel 2002; Denver 2002), 'national attachment' (e.g. Kritzinger 2003) or related concepts like 'national pride' (Carey 2002) or 'nationalism' (Oscarsson and Holmberg 2004). These concepts have all been shown to relate negatively as regards support for advanced EU integration. National identity can be expected to affect levels of Euro-scepticism and, through this route, also affect vote choice in EU referenda. The perception of economic benefits is another factor that has been shown to affect public support for the EU (Anderson and Reichert 1996; Jenssen et al. 1998) and, via this route, also has the potential to influence what people vote for in a referendum. Furthermore, since pronounced left and right political orientations can be linked to lower levels of support for EU integration as compared to centrist ideological preferences, political ideology is also included in our analysis (Oscarsson and Holmberg 2004). Political interest is another factor that is usually associated with more positive attitudes towards Europe (Siune et al. 1994). Finally, fear of immigration and fear of globalization is expected to exert an influence on vote choice in EU referenda. Being afraid of immigration contributes to people voting 'no' in referenda on EU integration issues (de Vreese and Boomgaarden 2005). Fear of globalization, however, is a relatively new factor introduced in a recent study (Schuck and de Vreese 2008). In this chapter, we build on the work of Oscarsson and Holmberg (2004), who show that being 'cosmopolitan' was related positively to voting 'yes' in the 2003 Swedish euro- referendum (see Miles 2004 and 2005a).[2] In addition, they found that 'internationalism' (support for an internationalist society with fewer borders between people and countries) was positively related to voting 'yes'.

Thus, in this chapter, it is expected that both factors, namely fear of immigration as well as fear of globalization, are linked to Euro-scepticism and exert their influence on the vote, at least partially, via the suggested indirect route. This translates into the mediated dynamic, resulting in our research hypothesis: *Euro-scepticism is a mediator for the influence of other political attitudes and predispositions on the intention to vote 'no' in EU referenda.* To test this hypothesis, data is made available from a survey conducted by GfK (Denmark).[3] The extent to which Euro-scepticism mediates the effect of the other predictors was formally assessed with a series of Sobel tests.[4]

Results

As Model 1, in Table 12.1 below, shows and in line with our expectations, fear of immigration, fear of globalization and national identity, as well as low levels of political efficacy, are all related to higher levels of Euro-scepticism. Political interest and government evaluation, as well as education and right political ideology, are not related to Euro-scepticism. Instead, leaning to the political left, as opposed to the centre, and gender (female) translates into higher levels of Euro-scepticism different to economic expectations that show no relationship.

In a next step, the same factors that account for Euro-scepticism (Model 1) are shown to also account, to a large extent, for the intention to vote 'no' in a potential referendum on the EU Constitution (Model 2a in Table 12.1). When adding Euro-scepticism to the model (Model 2b in Table 12.1), a large effect of Euro-scepticism is detectable on the intention to vote 'no', while most of the coefficients for the other variables decrease in magnitude. This gives a first indication of the mediating role of Euro-scepticism (see Schuck and de Vreese 2008).

A series of Sobel tests indeed confirms our previous findings according to which Euro-scepticism mediates the effect of most of the above variables (see Figure 12.4).[5] In addition, age has an independent significant negative effect on the intention to vote 'no', meaning that with age the likelihood of an intention to vote 'yes' increases. Also the effect of government evaluation on vote choice intention remains independent. However, Euro-scepticism is by far the strongest predictor for the intention to vote 'no'. In addition to the independent effect of age and government evaluation, political efficacy, left political ideology and fear of globalization also have effects on the intention to vote 'no'; however these

Table 12.1 OLS regression predicting Euro-scepticism (model 1) and logistic regressions (models 2a and 2b)

	Predicting Euro-scepticism Model 1 (OLS)	Predicting vote intention ('no') Model 2a (Logistic)	Predicting vote intention ('no') Model 2b (Logistic)
Education	0.005 (0.024)	0.118 (0.099) 1.126	0.078 (0.122) 1.081
Age	0.001 (0.001)	−0.014** (0.005) 0.986	−0.020** (0.007) 0.980
Gender (female)	0.138*** (0.042)	0.355* (0.170) 1.426	0.079 (0.208) 1.082
Political ideology (left)	0.252*** (0.058)	1.069*** (0.243) 2.911	0.714* (0.288) 2.043
Political ideology (right)	0.066 (0.053)	0.564** (0.218) 1.757	0.347 (0.273) 1.414
Political efficacy	−0.092*** (0.020)	−0.386*** (0.081) 0.680	−0.314** (0.098) 0.730
Government disapproval	0.030 (0.020)	0.527*** (0.090) 1.694	0.528*** (0.107) 1.695
Fear of immigration	0.188*** (0.021)	0.388*** (0.089) 1.474	−0.059 (0.111) 0.943
Fear of globalization	0.190*** (0.020)	0.560*** (0.082) 1.571	0.292** (0.103) 1.323
Political interest	−0.041 (0.034)	0.105 (0.144) 1.111	0.259 (0.177) 1.295
National identity	0.366*** (0.041)	1.070*** (0.174) 2.888	0.279 (0.215) 1.322
Negative economic expectations	0.004 (0.023)	−0.018 (0.092) 0.982	−0.045 (0.112) 0.956
Euro-scepticism	–	–	2.339*** (0.189) 10.376
Adjusted R square	0.34	–	–
Nagelkerke Pseudo R-Square	–	0.41	0.64
Percentage correctly classified	–	75%	84%
N	1121	869	868

Notes
The table explains the intention to vote 'no' if a referendum on the EU Constitution were to be held in Denmark. Cell entries are unstandardized coefficients and standard errors (in parentheses) for Model 1 and log odds, standard errors (in parentheses) and odds ratios for Models 2a and 2b.
* $p \leq 0.05$; ** $p \leq 0.01$; *** $p \leq 0.001$ (two-tailed).

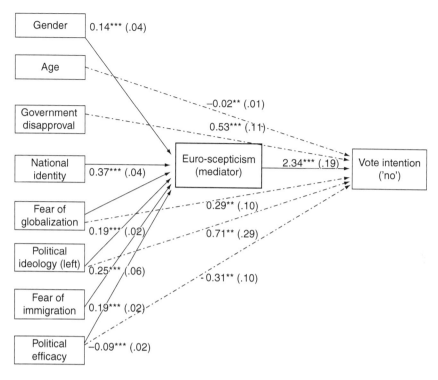

Figure 12.4 Mediation model for the effect on vote intention ('no')

Note
Coefficients are unstandardized coefficients for the relationships between the socio-demographic and political attitude variables and Euro-scepticism (OLS) and log odds for the relationships between age, government disapproval, fear of globalization, national identity, and Euro-scepticism and vote intention ('no') (logistic regression). In all analyses, standard errors are in parentheses. * $p \leq 0.05$; ** $p \leq 0.01$; *** $p \leq 0.001$ (two-tailed).

three effects are not fully independent but are all *partially* mediated by Euro-scepticism as well. The effect of national identity is also mediated.

Discussion

Public opinion regarding the EU in Denmark is highly ambivalent. On the one hand, Danes display strong support for EU membership and believe that their country has benefitted overall. On the other hand, they resist joining the euro and they show higher trust in their own national institutions. Given the Danish referendum experience and a long history of discussing European topics and issues in public attitudes towards the EU, rather more than mere second-order domestic considerations, are relevant when Danes make up their minds about Europe. The current study provides evidence for this by demonstrating what factors influence levels of scepticism regarding the EU among Danish citizens and how such attitudes become important within the context of the EU Constitutional Treaty in 2005 and a hypothetical referendum on this topic. In particular, our findings suggest that sceptical attitudes towards Europe are the strongest factor explaining why Danes would opt to vote against the treaty. Thus, EU-specific considerations matter to Danes – more than is typically suggested by the second-order literature on referendum voting behaviour, and in line with other research explaining voting behaviour in EP elections in Denmark specifically (de Vreese and Tobiasen 2007). This is in accordance with findings regarding the Dutch 2005 referendum on the EU Constitution, that also show that EU attitudes have been the driving force in explaining the 'no' vote (Lubbers 2008; Schuck and de Vreese 2008).

Furthermore, these findings are indicative of a considerable level of involvement in the topic on side of the public that typically makes EU-specific attitudes more salient in a referendum-voting context (Hobolt 2005). Our findings suggest conceptualizing Euro-scepticism as a *mediator* for the effects of other, more general political attitudes on voting intention in EU referenda. The effects of most of the other key predictors in our analysis have been either fully or partially mediated by Euro-scepticism and have exerted their influence on intended vote choice via this indirect route. However, attitudes unrelated to 'Europe' and/or the referendum issue also mattered. For example, in contrast to the Dutch case, government evaluations exerted an independent, yet less pronounced, influence on what Danes intended to vote. The present study focused on the mediating role of Euro-scepticism in explaining vote intention in EU referenda on the EU Constitutional Treaty. Rather than seeing EU attitudes and domestic considerations as competing alternatives for the explanation of voting behaviour in EU referenda, future studies should expand on the link between the two and address the dynamics, identified in this study, by conceptualizing Euro-scepticism as a mediator for the influence of other political attitudes. Comparing the Danish with the Dutch case can enable different conclusions to be drawn. First of all, conceiving of EU attitudes as a mediator and thus combining first- and second-order perspectives into one integrated model holds up in both cases and seems to provide a viable path for future research. It not only helps to understand that both processes are taking place at the same time, and to what extent, but it also provides a standard model allowing for comparative research, i.e. assessing the differential role and impact of EU attitudes vis-à-vis other explanations for referendum voting behaviour across time and space. There are also some more theoretical implications and questions that arise as a result of this study. The role of Euro-scepticism was investigated, both as an outcome variable as well as a mediator, in order to understand voting behaviour in EU referenda. However, with more people taking an interest in topics such as EU integration or further integration (e.g. Turkey) the EU might become electorally more important in the future. Thus, Euro-scepticism might become an antecedent variable to aid understanding of electoral behaviour in national elections (de Vries 2007) and also for satisfaction with the incumbent government.

Danish public opinion is an important case to learn from for other countries and for the EU. First of all Danish public opinion has induced clear and measurable effects on Denmark's role in the integration process and referendum outcomes that have affected Denmark's (non-)participation in certain EU policy areas. Second, the Danish opinion structure shows the multi-dimensionality of EU atttitudies and that a simple question of pro or con integration is no longer sufficient (see also Hobolt and Brouard 2011). In this chapter, a composite measure of scepticism was incorporated that includes multiple dimensions and shows how other effects work through this scepticism. EU attitudes are multifaceted and research has to take into account that support for, or scepticism towards, the EU can vary according to the exact dimension under scrutiny. Consequently, if it is assumed that individual levels of support or scepticism vary depending on the exact dimension this attitude refers to, then we can also assume different predispositions and preceding attitudes explaining levels of EU support or scepticism (Boomgaarden *et al.* 2011). This allows further development of the model tested in the current study by, for example, further specifying which EU attitude dimension is carrying the effect of other more specific political attitudes and predispositions, and which one matters the most in explaining referendum voting behaviour. This again also allows for interesting comparative investigations, i.e. looking at which attitude dimensions play more or less of a role in which country and in which referendum context. The results of such detailed analysis then can be explained more thoroughly comparing the particular characteristics of these national and referendum-specific contexts. Given the multifaceted nature of Danish public opinion regarding the EU, Denmark does provide a prime example for such an investigation into the differential role of different attitude dimensions, given its varying levels of support for different aspects of the EU and European integration.

Several limitations are acknowledged regarding our study design. The most obvious refers to the hypothetical scenario that represented the context of this study, and the fact that no actual referendum actually took place. Even though the topic has been on the public agenda and discussed in the media (and a referendum was scheduled to take place pending the outcomes of the other preeceding votes in France and the Netherlands) there was no real campaign as in the other countries. This could have depressed the importance of some (i.e. more domestic) considerations at the expense of others (for example, EU-specific). However, the proposed mechanism (operationalizing Euro-scepticism as a mediator for the influence of other attitudes and predispositions) is supported by the respective analysis and findings that indicate striking similarity (in terms of, for example, explained variance or the factors whose effects are mediated by Euro-scepticism) with other contexts (e.g. Schuck and de Vreese 2008). Nevertheless, caution is necessary as regards comparison of the differential impact of the more specific political attitudes vis-à-vis EU attitudes, given the hypothetical nature of the vote for the Danish case and the absence of Danish referendum campaigns. Nevertheless, the present study advances understanding of the shape and importance of Danish public opinion with regard to the EU and its future development in light of challenges lying ahead. Whereas it has often been seen as a problem that people would feel indifferent about the EU, it turns out that EU attitudes seem to matter more than previous research suggests – especially in Denmark, with its longstanding tradition of elite discourse about Europe and its previous referendum experience.

This again has implications for the future of the EU integration project as well as, more theoretically, for the nature of EU elections and referenda. Citizens might not necessarily vote against the contents of any proposed treaty in EU referenda; but rather use the opportunity to express their general scepticism towards the EU (see Lubbers 2008; Schuck and de Vreese 2008). Whereas previous research suggested that people use the opportunity of EU elections and referenda mainly to punish their national governments and base their voting decision largely on domestic (national) considerations and not the actual issue at stake, the EU itself might move towards becoming a target of the 'punishment trap' (Schneider and Weitsman 1996). Citizens might increasingly often use the opportunity of a referendum for a popularity rating of 'Europe' and thus not vote on the concrete issue at stake, but rather punish the EU, as such, on the basis of a conglomerate of different negative attitudes or a diffuse overall scepticism towards it. Danish public opinion and voting behaviour in EU referenda clearly bear witness to this taking place. In this sense, Danish public opinion, and the Danish electorate, has played in important role in shaping Danish further participation in the EU, and improving the quality of EU-related debates in Denmark. For the future of collaboration in Europe, public legitimacy is essential and understanding the nature and structure of public opinion is of great importance. The Danish case is important, not only for Denmark, but also for the EU.

Appendix A: overview of variables

Gender: Male=0 (49.1 per cent); female=1 (50.1 per cent).

Age: Measured in years ($M=46.30$, $SD=17.85$).

Education: Four levels of education from lowest to highest (Danish originals): (1) Folkeskole (7–9 klasse): 11.4 per cent; (2) 16–19 års alderen: 33.7 per cent; (3) Mellemlang uddannelse: 30.3 per cent; (4) Lang videregående/under uddannelse: 24.6 per cent.

Political interest (index): Two items on index scale reaching from: (1) low interest to (4) high interest: (1) 'How much interest do you have in politics in general?'; (2) 'How much interest do you have in political subjects that have to do with the EU?' ($M=2.29$, $SD=0.70$).

Political efficacy: One item reaching from: (1) strongly agree to (5) strongly disagree. Low scores represent low levels of efficacy, high scores represent high levels of efficacy: 'The political parties are only interested in my vote and not in my opinion' ($M=2.53$, $SD=1.11$).

Left political ideology: Self-placement on left–right scale where 1=left and 10=right ($M=5.82$, $SD=2.35$); recoded as 1 to 3 =left=1; otherwise=0.

Right political ideology: Self-placement on left–right scale where 1= left and 10=right (*M*=5.82, *SD*=2.35); recoded as 8 to 10=right=1; otherwise=0.

National identity: One item reaching from: (1) only European; (2) first European and then Danish; (3) first Danish and then European; to (4) only Danish (*M*=3.34, *SD*=0.55).

Fear of immigration: One item reaching from: (1) strongly agree to 5 strongly disagree: 'Denmark have to accept more asylum seekers' (*M*=3.81, *SD*=1.25).

Fear of globalization: One item reaching from: (1) strongly disagree to (5) strongly agree: 'Because of globalization many jobs will be lost in Denmark' (*M*=3.00, *SD*=1.15).

Economic expectations: One item reaching from: (1) strongly disagree to (5) strongly agree: 'The Danish economy will get worse over the next 12 months' (*M*=3.55, *SD*=1.06).

Government disapproval: One item reaching from: (1) strongly agree to (5) strongly disagree: 'Today's government is doing a good job' (*M*=2.69, *SD*=1.35).

Euro-scepticism: Multiple items index scale reaching from: (1) low level of scepticism to (5) high level of scepticism: (1) 'People have different opinions about Europe: What is your opinion about the EU?'; (2) 'It would be bad for Denmark to participate in the Euro'; (3) 'EU enlargement is progressing too quickly'; (4) 'Turkey should become member of the EU' *(reversely coded)* (*M*=3.36, *SD*=0.83).

Vote intention: Very likely or likely to vote 'no'=1 (37.8 per cent); very likely or likely to vote 'yes' (38.4 per cent)=0; undecided about vote intention=0 (23.5 per cent).

Notes

1 We first tested this idea in the Dutch context (see Schuck and de Vreese 2008) and now further pursue these propositions in Denmark. Given the special characteristics of Danish public opinion, as outlined above, and the country's extensive history with discussing and voting on EU issues, we expect EU attitudes to be of special importance in Denmark and the dynamic we suggest to be particularly pronounced in the Danish context.
2 Covering the following dimensions: attitudes towards immigration, foreign aid, and the building up of a multi-cultural society.
3 The survey was fielded from 29 September until 10 October 2005. The response rate was 75 per cent (AAPOR RR1), *n*=1,208. More information regarding the sample is available from the authors upon request. For the specific wording of all items and the descriptives for all variables listed in Table 12.1, see Appendix A. For more details regarding the analysis see Schuck and de Vreese (2008).
4 We use the Sobel test equation: $a*b/\text{SQRT}(b^2*s_a^2+a^2*s_b^2)$ where a=raw (unstandardized) regression coefficient for the association between independent variable and mediator, s_a=standard error of a, b=raw coefficient for the association between the mediator

and the dependent variable (controlling for the independent variable), and s_b = standard error of b (for an introduction to mediation analysis and the Sobel test see e.g. Baron and Kenny 1986; Goodman 1960; MacKinnon *et al.* 1995; Sobel 1982). Whereas the Sobel test is appropriate for large sample sizes (as in our study), other methods such as bootstrapping should be applied to formally assess mediation in smaller samples (see e.g. Preacher and Hayes 2004).

5 Euro-scepticism × Fear of immigration – Sobel test statistic: 7.25, $p<0.001$; Euro-scepticism × Political efficacy – Sobel test statistic: −4.31, $p<0.001$; Euro-scepticism × Fear of globalization – Sobel test statistic: 7.54, $p<0.001$; Euro-scepticism × National identity – Sobel test statistic: 7.24, $p<0.001$; Euro-scepticism × Gender – Sobel test statistic: 3.18, $p<0.001$; Euro-scepticism × Political ideology (left) – Sobel test statistic: 4.10, $p<0.001$.

13 Public administration, civil servants and implementation

Dorte Sindbjerg Martinsen

Introduction

European integration has introduced new and gradually intensified demands to the whole spectrum of public administration. Previous research has shown that almost all policy areas are affected by EU regulation, albeit to varying degrees (Blom-Hansen and Grønnegård Christensen 2003). The national executive – and hence the administration – is involved in all parts of the EU policy cycle (Kassim 2003), and thus is actively undertaking downloading and uploading activities (see the Introduction to this volume). National civil servants give expert advice when policies are drafted. They represent one decision-maker out of 27 when policies are adopted. In the final stages of the policy cycle, they implement decisions and respond when national compliance is evaluated. In fulfilling these responsibilities, the national administration plays a key role. The public administration constitutes a key actor concerning all parts of EU affairs, as it delivers expert advice, decides under flexible mandates and implements our EU obligations.

This chapter examines how the Danish public administration responds to the EU. First, it does so via a more general account of the role played in the EU policy cycle, but subsequently narrows the focus to consider the implications of when EU policies are implemented. Second, it examines implementation of EU obligations within two policy areas; healthcare and the environment. The two policy areas have been selected because the Danish engagement in supranational regulation has traditionally differed. Denmark has traditionally had strong reservations against EU intervention in welfare policies such as healthcare (Martinsen 2005a), and has thus been perceived as something of a 'foot-dragger' in this regard (see the Introduction to this volume); yet it has, on the other hand, acted proactively when it comes to environmental regulation and has also been seen as a 'pace-setter' (see the Introduction to this volume) and/or 'green leader' (Börzel 2000; Liefferink and Andersen 1998).

The analysis finds that for both policy areas, the administrative autonomy to implement has been considerable, but depends on the political, judicial and societal checks and balances that the executive encounters when transposing EU obligation into national acts and practices. Furthermore, the analysis substantiates that whereas Danish compliance with EU obligations is high when it comes to formal transposition and official scoreboards, the sufficiency of implementation becomes contestable and deficits identifiable regarding practical application. De facto compliance depends on external checks and balances with administrative autonomy as well as the ability of societal actors and institutions to scrutinize how the civil service interprets and acts upon its EU obligations.

The public administration and EU governance

The national public administration is omnipresent in the EU policy cycle. National civil servants advise and act as experts in relation to new initiatives taken by the Commission. They are key actors in the Council's decision-making process, representing their member state in the working groups, in COREPER and sometimes representing their minister at Council meetings. When EU directives, regulations or case law by the ECJ are implemented back home, national bureaucrats continue to be key actors. In addition, national civil servants participate in the Commission's comitology committees. In sum, the national public administrators take part in all stages of the continuous policy-making process of the EU. There are thus good reasons to 'rediscover bureaucracy' in EU studies (Olsen 2005) or join in on the 'public administration turn in integration research' (Trondal 2007).

The many arenas of national administrative participation in EU governance imply that to view the national and European administrative orders as separate misguides our understanding of the degree of bureaucratic Europeanization (see the Introduction to this volume). Whereas there may be no structural convergence between national administrative polities in the EU 27 (Kassim *et al.* 2000; Trondal 2007), tasks, policies and responsibilities between the national and the EU administration are highly interwoven (Miles, 2011a; 2011b). In order to grasp how the EU and the national executive intersect, it may be useful to distinguish between the *Brussels segment* and what happens when 'Europe hits home' (Börzel and Risse 2000), i.e. when national administrators are to *implement* and assure *compliance* with EU obligations. That is the distinction between the 'upload' and the 'download' of EU policies (see the Introduction to this volume).

Bureaucratic segmentation in Brussels

The many committees of EU governance integrate national civil servants and the EU core executive, i.e. the European Commission (Egeberg *et al.* 2003). The committees are stable and active features of EU governance at all stages of EU policy-making. Danish civil servants are part of a Brussels segment of multi-level administration, where they enter the European capital as representatives of national points of view, but meet, interact, argue, learn, adapt and socialize with their European counterparts (Trondal 2007: 964). Egeberg *et al.* (2003: 30) find that such interaction evokes multiple preferences, roles and identities, instead of either clear-cut national or supranational ones. In their study, they find that the institutional autonomy varies across committees. Civil servants act more as representatives from back home in the Council's working groups and the Comitology committees than when participating in the Commission's expert committees.[1] However, all committees produce multiple loyalties for the invited actors and are constitutive parts of the emerging multi-level administration, located in Brussels but where Europeanized views, problem-solving understanding and loyalties are brought back home on return (Egeberg et al. 2003: 30). EU committees are indeed sites where individual civil servants are Europeanized.

Denmark's membership of the EC in 1973 meant that the public administration was confronted with a demand to adapt of a scale not seen before (Grønnegård Christensen 2003: 63). Since then, EU obligation has only grown – in scope and depth. However, contrary to the 'hollowing out of the state' thesis (Rhodes 1997), this development does not seem to have disempowered the Danish executive. A new EU related bureaucratic order has come into place (Olsen 2007). Instead, it is found that, over time, membership of the EC and increased integration has extended the role and power of the Danish government and the Danish central administration (Pedersen et al. 2002). Part of the explanation is that EU policies often have a rather technical content that may prevent substantial intervention from a large set of political and societal actors. EU policies tend to appear complex, detailed and rather technical, which invites more expert participation and deliberation among experts (Martinsen and Beck Jørgensen 2010). Danish membership has produced more administrative tasks, and the Danish public administration has seen greater resources transferred to it as a result hereof (Grønnegård Christensen 2003: 58). Furthermore, Danish EU administration is found to be rather centralized and coordinated (Nedergaard 2005: 380–382; see also Chapter 14). This points to the fact that the Danish central administration constitutes a powerful actor for Denmark's participation in the daily EU policy process – both in formal and informal channels. It, however, participates in a 'multiple institutional embeddedness' with varying degrees of institutional autonomy (Egeberg et al. 2003), which makes compromised and shared policy-making the operating dynamic of the bureaucratic segmentation in Brussels. In this way, administrative autonomy is both considerable and compromised. Administrative *autonomy* constitutes a prerequisite for both influencing EU policies and the way this *influence* is carried out (See the Introduction to this volume).

Implementation of EU policies and compliance

According to Bardach (1977), implementation is 'the continuation of politics by other means', and the study of implementation, thus, addresses who controls the allocation of resources after a policy has been decided. EU implementation concerns the effectuation of EU decisions and how such decisions are transcended into outputs and outcomes. The implementation of Community law and policies has been interpreted as a potential second stronghold of national control, where national actors may attempt to 'claw back' what they may have lost during the European decision-making process (From and Stava 1993; Mény *et al.* 1996: 7). According to Article 4 (ex. article 10) of the 2007 Lisbon Treaty, member states are responsible for the implementation of EU policies. The post-legislative phase of policy-making may thus be where member states regain, or retain, control over the impact of policy and where multiple institutional embeddedness is replaced by more unitary, hierarchical administrative structures. The first and, eventually, most decisive actors in the implementation phase of EU policies are the government and the national civil servants.

From classic implementation theory, it is known that there are 'decision points' that are critical to the impact and control of policies in the implementation process. A 'decision point' arises when the consent of actors must be obtained in order to proceed with (further) implementation and may hinder efficient and/or successful implementation (Pressman and Wildavsky 1973: xxiv). In Europeanization theory, 'decision points' are conceived as 'veto points' or positions. Veto points arise at various stages in the policy-making process where agreement is required for policy change to take place (Haverland 2000: 85). Whereas the number and composition of veto-players in EU implementation varies from process to process, the public administration has the recurrent role as veto-player, proposing to the minister how the EU act shall be formally transposed and practically applied (Bursens 2002).

Moreover, regarding implementation, administrative *autonomy* varies and, thus, so does the independent *influence* that the administration may exert on implementation. First of all, the national bureaucracy is not a single united actor (Beck Jørgensen 2003), but is likely to have heterogeneous preferences on correct and sufficient implementation. Second, the degree to which a policy area is politicized or remains rather technical affects administrative autonomy, as the politicized area is likely to be more closely supervised by the government, the parliament and societal actors. Finally, administrative autonomy is likely to be reduced when regulating policy areas with strong and vested societal interests. By and large, the degree of administrative autonomy will depend on checks and balances from other institutions and actors.

EU acts will specify the date when the supranational decisions have to be implemented. However, this is far from the end of sufficient compliance. Subsequently, a second round of the post-legislative phase may set off, in which de facto compliance may be questioned and examined. During this process, the European Commission and the ECJ may play a key role in 'pushing' full implementation of policy through identifying and monitoring restrictive application or non-compliance by the national government (Börzel 2000; Tallberg 2003). National stakeholders, including citizens and interest groups, may be their allies, pointing out an implementation deficit and thus 'pulling' the impact of EU regulation. While in the short-to-medium run, national governments and bureaucracies exert a dominant influence over implementation, the combination of supranational mechanisms of enforcement and decentralized management mechanisms are decisive to ensure compliance in the longer run (Tallberg 2002). The combination of supranational enforcement and decentralized management mechanisms have been discussed to ensure considerable efficient EU implementation: 'This twinning of cooperative and coercive instruments in a "management-enforcement ladder" makes the EU exceedingly effective in combating detected violations, thereby reducing non-compliance to a temporal phenomenon' (Tallberg 2002: 610).

Although non-compliance may be temporal, its occurrence is a continuous challenge to the EU system and its output legitimacy. Börzel *et al.* (2010) find that powerful member states are the most likely non-compliers with European law, whereas small member states with efficient bureaucracies are the best compliers. The explanation is found to be that those smaller member states lack the political power to resist compliance pressure from the EU. They do not have sufficient political resources to confront the Commission with what contradicts domestic institutional legacies or national interests. Instead they generally choose to obey. Member states' political power and government/administrative capacity are thus found to be decisive explanatory factors to compliance patterns (Börzel *et al.* 2010). Political power is constituted by economic size and EU voting power (Börzel *et al.* 2010: 13), whereas government and administrative capacity consists of resources *and* the bureaucracy's ability to mobilize and channel resources into compliance (Börzel *et al.* 2010: 7–14). If resources are dispersed among many public agencies and over different levels of government, the bureaucracy is likely to have difficulties in mobilizing and channelling such resources into compliance.

Figure 13.1 demonstrates that Denmark belongs to those member states that have least reported violations of EU law and equally least infringement procedures from the Commission. In 2008, it had 38 formal notices of eventual non-compliance referred to it by the Commission, but it had no referrals to the ECJ. By means of infringement procedures referred to the ECJ under Article 258 of the Lisbon Treaty, Denmark stands out as a best complier which, according to

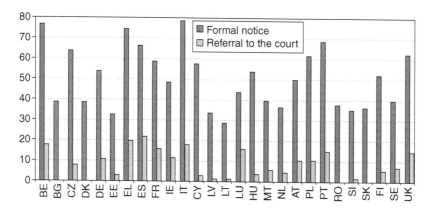

Figure 13.1 Infringement procedures against EU member states in 2008 (source: European Commission 2008b).

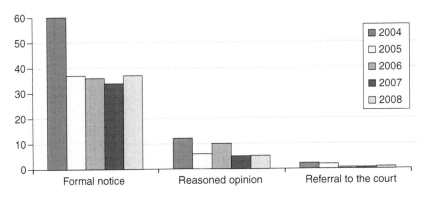

Figure 13.2 Infringement procedures against Denmark 2004–2008 (source: European Commission 2008b).

Börzel *et al.*, is explained by relatively low political power, but high administrative capacity (Börzel *et al.* 2010: 20).

Moreover, when Denmark's performance is examined in the context of receiving separate and formal notices, reasoned opinions and referrals to the ECJ, Denmark generally complies before an infringement procedure is taken to the latter. Whereas Denmark has a considerable number of formal notices and therefore infringement procedures initiated against it, it appears to comply before a matter ends up in the ECJ, as Figure 13.2 demonstrates.

Infringement procedures are, however, unlikely to be a sufficient measure of member states' compliance and are only likely to mirror the tip of the iceberg (Falkner *et al.* 2005). Underneath that tip, we are likely to find many more violations of EU law that the Commission does not discover or is informed about.

Implementing EU decisions in Denmark

In general, Denmark enjoys the reputation of best complier. In the study of Falkner *et al.* (2005), in which the authors have investigated implementation of a set of labour market directives in EU 15, Denmark is found to belong to a 'world of law observance'. Member states within this typology are guided by a compliance culture, according to which the goal to comply with EU obligation typically overrides domestic interests. Apart from Denmark, Sweden and Finland also belong to this world of compliance. Two other worlds exist: a 'world of domestic politics' and a 'world of neglect'. Within the former, obeying EU rules are at best one objective among others and within the latter compliance is no goal in itself (Falkner *et al.* 2005: 321–324).[2] The Falkner typology suggests that the Danish public administration has strongly internalized a norm or a culture, determining implementation behaviour and that – driven by this normative logic – Denmark generally implements irreproachably.

Also, earlier findings suggest high compliance standards in Denmark. Denmark may be highly EU-sceptic (Börzel *et al.* 2010), whilst still behaving as the teacher's pet when it comes to the implementation record:

> As a matter of policy, if a threatening in-court battle is unlikely to be won, the government seems to prefer to settle it by an out-of-court compromise. This will often be followed by pertinent new legislation being issued or other sorts of legal enactments which brings Denmark impeccably in line with its obligations.
>
> (Rasmussen 1988: 97)

However, it is argued here that it is important to distinguish between formal transposition and practical application (see Bursens 2002). Existing studies, as well as statistics comparing member states' implementation record, tend to concentrate on the *formal* transposition stage. That is the stage between the adoption of an EU act and the implementation date set out in that act, and thus where the national executive informs the Commission on its implementation measures. Formal transposition is thus a stage where the executive's means of implementation are least contested as they tend to be defined by, and for, the government and central administration. The sufficiency of formal transposition has not yet been tried out in practice.

Formal transposition: when administrative autonomy rules

It is important here to emphasize that formal transposition in Denmark is mainly a governmental and administrative act that tends not to involve any direct parliamentary control. First of all, this means that administrative transposition is not contested and, second, it may in part explain why Danish implementation stands out as highly efficient. As legal adviser to the Danish government, Karsten Hagel-Sørensen wrote:

> When Denmark not without reason boast about its very high transposition rate of [EU] rules, an important causal mechanism is that transposition to a large extent can be carried out administratively, whereas you in other countries as for example Italy traditionally have far stronger constitutional limits on delegation from the legislative power to the administration.
>
> (Hagel-Sørensen, 1994: 115, author's translation)

In general, EU directives continue to be transposed by means of executive order. This implies that the minister and his/her administration are responsible for the implementation, and the Danish parliament (the Folketing) is not involved as a legislative power. The parliament becomes involved when an act is transposed by means of a law, debated and processed in the parliament (Blom-Hansen and Grønnegård Christensen 2003: 72–73). The means of transposition are demonstrated by the study of Blom-Hansen and Grønnegård Christensen within the long time span of 1973–2003 (Blom-Hansen and Grønnegård Christensen 2003).

Table 13.1 Transposition form of EU directives (percentage)

Year of adoption	Law	Executive order	Circular	N = 100%
1973 and earlier	23	77	1	137
1974–1983	19	74	7	309
1984–1993	25	72	4	867
1994–2003	28	70	2	2,244

Source: Blom-Hansen and Grønnegård Christensen 2003: 71.

When implementation takes place in a largely secluded administrative space without systematic checks and balances, the administration's discretionary power and the power to define are likely to become considerable. Thus Kallestrup finds that the manoeuvrable scope for the minister and the civil servant acting on his/her behalf has not diminished as a result of EU integration, but continues to be extensive (Kallestrup 2005, 2008). Until national implementation is eventually questioned by supranational (or non-governmental) national institutions and actors, such extensive manoeuvrable scope remains intact. In most matters, EU implementation thus remains within the exclusive portfolio of the Danish civil service. Studies of implementation beyond formal transposition may, however, point out a different picture, questioning the Danish reputation as best complier.

Implementing EU healthcare rights

From 1998 to 2010, the ECJ laid down that healthcare is a service within the meaning of the Treaty, which shall in principle circulate freely (Martinsen 2005b, 2009). In its ongoing case law interpretations, the judiciary has laid down that the free movement principles apply to all healthcare services independent of how that healthcare service is financed or which healthcare system provides it. Jurisprudence has clarified that under certain conditions national restrictions to cross-border healthcare are justified, but here the ECJ distinguishes between non-hospital care and hospital care. Free movement applies without restrictions to non-hospital care, essentially meaning any form of outpatient care/ambulatory care that can be taken care of without hospitalization, i.e. without spending at least 24 hours in hospital. Regarding hospital care, member states may make access to treatment in another member state subject to certain conditions. The ECJ finds it justifiable that member states make the right to treatment subject to first having that right authorized by the competent healthcare institution. But the ECJ also sets out that the national authority is obliged to issue the authorization if the same treatment cannot be provided without undue delay back home and the decision whether to authorize or not has to be based on international medical science and not purely national considerations.

The judicial policy-making process from 1998 to 2010 is characterized by bits and pieces. Judicial interpretation departs from considering very specific healthcare goods and services with very specific conditions for their provision to gradually consider healthcare in more general terms. Concerning implementation, the Danish civil service has enjoyed considerable scope to re-interpret, formulate and communicate how the wording of the ECJ impacts on Danish healthcare policy (Martinsen and Vrangbæk 2008). The scope of administrative autonomy will be analysed below, i.e. the scope to re-interpret and lay down a national understanding of what constitutes a service within the meaning of the Treaty.

The Danish government was one of the first governments to react to the early rulings of 1998. The government chose to set up an inter-ministerial working group of expert civil servants, commissioned to analyse the implications of the judgments for Danish health policy. The working group acknowledged that the cases had implications for healthcare systems other than that of Luxembourg and were not limited to glasses and dental treatment. The Danish report, however, contained a narrow definition of what constitutes a 'service', which remained the Danish re-definition of 'service', although later contradicted by new case law of the ECJ. To be a service according to the meaning of Treaty Article 50 (article 57 TFEU) the Danish civil service argued that there needs to be an element of private pay and profit involved:

> It is the view of the working group that if, on the other hand, the treatment had been taken care of by the public hospital sector, the Treaty's Article 49 would not have applied. The reason is that Article 50 defines services as services normally carried out in return for remuneration [...]. Characteristic for a service is thus that a service provider offers a service in return for remuneration.
>
> (Ministry of Health 1999: 23)

As part of the Danish way of narrowing down the definition of 'service', it could keep the large majority of Danish healthcare services outside the definition, since they are provided as benefits in kind, free of charge and thus with no direct remuneration. The early jurisprudence by the ECJ resulted in a smaller amendment of Danish healthcare policy, implemented by executive order,[3] and according to which persons insured under Group 2 could have medical treatment from a general practitioner as well as a specialist doctor in another member state, whereas persons insured under Group 1 could purchase dental assistance, physiotherapy and chiropractic treatments with subsequent fixed-price reimbursement from the relevant Danish institutions.

When Denmark submitted its opinion in the 2001 Geraets-Smits and Peerbooms case before the ECJ, it replicated its narrow definition of 'service', and argued that one precondition for a service to be a service within the meaning of the Treaty was that there must be an element of private pay and that the service must be provided with a view to making a profit (InfoCuria 2012a: paragraphs 76–78). Although the ECJ overruled the Danish definition in the sense that it overruled the argument that a 'service' requires an element of private pay and one of profit, Denmark did not change its point of view and did not extend the scope of outpatient treatment that could be provided in another member state.

However, an internal departmental note from 2004[4] clearly points out that the sufficiency of Danish implementation was disputed inside the Department of Health. Although externally, the public administration seemed to agree and find a consensus, it acted less as a unitary actor internally. The note set out explicitly that the Danish understanding of a service within the meaning of the Treaty could no longer be sustained, and that in the light of the recent case law[5] the Danish implementation of EU law was too narrow. The minister, at that time, Lars Løkke Rasmussen, had duly been informed by Danish bureaucracy; nevertheless no change occurred externally. In later answers to parliamentary questions, the narrow definition of 'service' was restated (see answers to parliamentary questions no. 4965, 4967 and 4969, 17 May 2006).

Internal dispute and criticism inside the civil service did not suffice as pressure to adapt. Instead practical application to EU law required external checks and balances outside the departmental corridors. In 2003, a case before the Danish National Social Appeals Board (Ankestyrelsen) commenced. One of the Danish municipalities had refused to reimburse a patient with Group 1 healthcare insurance in Denmark his cost for provided outpatient/ambulatory care in Germany. In the first case before the Social Appeals Board,[6] the Board supported the refusal, reasoning that the cost of care provided by a specialist doctor in Germany could not be reimbursed since a service within the meaning of the Treaty required an element of private pay and one of profit. The Board thus leaned on the definition of the Ministry, without considering it any further. The patient, however, complained to the Danish ombudsman. The ombudsman entered the case, and exchanged viewpoints with both the Ministry and the Social Appeals Board. Against this background, the Board decided to take the case up again. This resulted in a revised decision three years later,[7] in which the Social Appeals Board found that specialist treatment for insured persons under Group 1 constitutes a service within the meaning of the Treaty. It thus contradicted the maintained definition of the Ministry of Health, reasoning that the ECJ had a broader view on what defines an EU-related service than the Danish re-definition from 2000 an onwards.

The new statement by the board did not, however, lead to the Ministry reconsidering its implementation practice. In May 2007, the Danish ombudsman proceeded with his inquiries and questioned the Ministry on why it had not changed its executive order of June 2000 to include a broader view on access to healthcare services in another EU member state. The ombudsman also reminded the Ministry that the National Social Appeals Board ranked as the highest national administrative instance in interpreting and laying down the definition of service within the meaning of the Treaty. The ministry finally responded and changed the executive order as of 1 December 2008[8] to also cover specialist treatment in another member state for Group 1 individuals insured in Denmark.

With a time lag of more than eight years, Danish application in law and practice stands out as anything but best compliance. Instead it appears to be self-reliant, defensive and, for a considerable period of time, rather immune to internal and external criticism. It required institutionalized checks and balances, with authorized mandates to inquire into administrative practices, to rectify the implementation balance that lasted for almost a decade. In this case, the Danish ombudsman became the turning point.

Implementation of EU environmental regulation

Analysing practical applications and implementation deficits appears more common than general statistics on formal transposition would lead us to believe. When it comes to EU environmental regulation, Denmark has had the self-perception to be among the leading member states. The role of leader of best practice has often been stated by the Danish Ministry of the Environment; 'In many years, Denmark has had a high environmental profile in the EU [...] therefore Denmark has pressed for high environmental standards and been very active, when it comes to the environment in EU' (Danish Environmental Protection Agency 2002: 20).

However, concerning implementation, the Danish role is more disputable. In the following, practical applications will be examined concerning the EU directive on the conservation of natural habitats and of wild fauna and flora, also known as the habitats directive.[9] According to the Directive, EU member states are to point out areas where wild flora and fauna can be conserved in order to preserve biodiversity.

In Denmark, the directive was implemented by executive order in 1998, where the Ministry pointed out 194 natural habitats.[10] This formal transposition resulted in various very critical evaluations. The Danish Nature Council (Naturrådet) found the implementation severely insufficient, not sufficiently setting out positive protection by means of conservation planning and not containing rules regarding general protection within appointed habitats. The implementation deficit implied that protection of nature, even within the assigned habitats, would not necessarily be favoured if other activities (as for example enterprises, construction or agriculture) threatened biodiversity or general conservation of the areas (Pagh 2001).

The Ministry of the Environment initiated its own evaluation and requested the Legal Adviser to the Danish government (Kammeradvokaten) to prepare a judicial report on the implementation. The report came out in summer 2002, and was highly critical. It found Danish implementation to be insufficient, among other aspects, in the light of the dynamic development of EU law.[11]

> But it has to be assumed that it [the Directive] not only concerns an obligation to establish areas, but also to ensure effective protection of those areas. In this regard the member states are obliged to ensure that considerable deteriorations of the areas or disturbances of the species, they are appointed to conserve, are avoided.
>
> (Kammeradvokaten 2002: 21, author's translation)

Although notable implementation deficits were identified by the adviser, the Ministry decided not to inform the Danish parliament of the critical report. Information on the report, however, leaked and in December 2002, a member of the Socialist People's Party questioned the minister on whether or not he had received a judicial assessment of the Danish implementation of EU environment rules (*Berlingske Tidende* 2002). Meanwhile, the Danish Forest and Nature Agency, under the Ministry of the Environment had requested the consultancy firm Rambøll to analyse what the implementation of the habitats directive and the directive on the conservation of wild birds[12] would cost. The estimated amount was received by shock – and then silence. It was estimated that the implementation would cost between 1.7 and 2.6 billion Danish kroner, i.e. €344–347 million, between 2003 and 2012 (parliamentary question S5439 to the Danish Minister of Environment, 9 September 2004, see EU-Oplysningen 2012d). The Danish Forest and Nature Agency received the report by July 2002, but decided not to inform the Commission, and the Danish parliament, on the estimated costs until December 2002. It was later held that the government had decided to keep silent until after the yearly negotiations on the national budget (*Berlingske Tidende* 2002).

Moreover, the national non-governmental organizations (NGOs) intervened considerably in the practical application of the habitats directive. They came to constitute important national agencies that discovered and informed the European Commission on implementation deficits. In 2003, the Danish Ornithological Society (Dansk Ornitologisk Forening) complained to the Commission about what they found to be insufficient protection of the important bird area in Southern Jutland, 'Tøndermarsken' (Andersen and Iversen 2006). Also the Danish Society for Nature Conversation, Danmarks Naturfredningsforening, sent complaints (Andersen and Iversen 2006: 91–92). These complaints contributed to the Commission sending a formal notice[13] to the Danish government in 2003 (Ministry of Foreign Affairs 2005; Andersen and Iversen 2006: 81). Against this background, the Danish Ministry of the Environment chose to appoint supplementing habitats as of 1 July 2003 (see Danish Nature Agency 2012). All in all supplementing habitats were pointed out five times, the latest in 2009. The Commission is, however, still not satisfied with the implementation of the directive and continues to examine the Danish case (Udenrigsministeriet 2009; Ritzaus Bureau 2010; Flensborg Avis 2010).

In the case of the environment, Danish implementation has not gone smoothly and Denmark has not proven to be a best complier when it comes to practical application. Instead, the public administration has interpreted its EU obligations in a way that is much too limited. In the medium run, between the formal transposition of the directive in 1998, and until approximately 2002, implementation remained an uncontested governmental matter, administered by the civil service. In this period administrative autonomy was high. However, as a result of external evaluations, implementation was brought under intensified scrutiny and the government was gradually forced to adapt in a way that was more in line with its EU obligations. This substantiates that compliance estimated by means of practical application is a much more inefficient and complicated process than formal transposition and best compliance scoreboards lead us to believe. To ensure practical application demands external checks and balances that recurrently question and control the de facto sufficiency of national implementation. In the case of environmental regulation, the Danish parliament and NGOs played such key role, reducing the administrative autonomy of the Danish executive.

Concluding remarks

The national public administration stands out as omnipresent in the EU policy cycle, having a significant say from the initiation to the evaluation of supranational decisions. The bureaucracy proves to be key actor at all stages and there are good reasons to 'rediscover bureaucracy' (Olsen 2005) in the EU institutional order.

Whereas national civil servants may fly into Brussels as representatives of national points of view, they adapt and socialize with their European counterparts. Identities and preferences within the bureaucratic segment in Brussels have thereby become overlapping and multiple. This has a significant impact on administrative autonomy and influence. On the one hand, administrative autonomy is considerable, as civil servants are the continuous actors in EU policy-making. EU integration has not disempowered the bureaucracy, but, on the contrary, has made it the irreplaceable actor in the EU- related bureaucratic order. On the other hand, administrative autonomy is compromised as the national civil servant participates in a multiple institutional embeddedness, and the more Europeanized the civil servant becomes, the more he/she is obliged to think and act on behalf of Europe – and take that view back home.

Implementation is different and poses different demands on bureaucratic behaviour. Formal transposition is one thing. Here administrative autonomy seems to rule. Danish implementation is mainly made by means of executive orders. This implies that the decision on how to comply is largely taken in a secluded administrative space. Compliance scoreboards continue to portray Denmark as best complier, and as long as Denmark continues to do this well, there is no immediate reason for the Commission to question formal transposition. However, the reputation as best complier and obedient European may only partially portray Danish compliance.

As the two case studies analysed in this chapter demonstrate, practical application is where implementation also becomes a more muddy business in Denmark. Practical application suggests that the public administration may far from always prioritize compliance over domestic interests. The efficient bureaucracies of small member states (Börzel *et al.* 2010) may not necessarily assure high compliance. Their bureaucratic ethos is far from neutral, but actually strives to preserve national autonomy, more loyal to the preferences of their ministers and the legacies of their national institutions than to EU obligations. The two case studies also substantiate that, in practical applications, external checks and balances become essential. In this stage of EU policy-making, sufficient implementation comes to depend on the extent to which institutionalized checks and balances and societal actors are oriented towards the EU system as well as the extent to which they are capable of and willing to evaluate national practices in the light of EU law and policies. Their partaking in a multiple institutional embeddedness becomes as essential, when it comes to effectuating supranational decisions, as it is to policy initiation and decision-making.

Analysing the role of the public administration and the implementation process provides insights into at least two of the dimensions raised in the introduction to this volume. Administrative autonomy varies across policy areas and stages in the policy cycle. As a result thereof, the independent influence that civil servants may exert on how and to what degree Europe is effectuated, varies too. When it comes to the two cases examined in this chapter, high administrative autonomy equals high influence in the Danish civil service on the reach of Europe into Danish society and concrete EU rights. Administrative autonomy and influence are, however, reduced the more other institutions and actors step in as mechanisms of checks and balances. The extent of policy change and the impact of Europe thus seem to depend not only on administrative power and capacity, but also on the engagement of the national legislature and societal actors. This proves that the EU political system and its impact has matured to such a degree that the same mechanisms are at play as when domestic political systems and their policy cycles are considered.

Notes

1. This finding contrasts (in part, at least) the earlier one by Jorges and Neyer, where participation in the Commission's Comitology committees were found to make national civil servants functional representatives of a Europeanized administration, where roles and perceptions transfer from the national to the supranational level (Joerges and Neyer 1997).
2. Germany, Austria, the United Kingdom, the Netherlands, Belgium and Spain belong to the 'world of domestic politics' whereas Ireland, Italy, Greece, Portugal, Luxembourg and France belong to the 'world of neglect' (Falkner et al. 2005: 330–340).
3. The policy reform entered into force by executive order, BEK no. 536, 15 June 2000.
4. Internal unofficial departemental note from the Ministry of Interior and Health, 22 March 2004.
5. I.e. the cases C-157/99 Geraets-Smits and Peerbooms, 2001 and C-372/99 Müller-Fauré and van Riet, 2003.
6. Case before the National Social Appeals Board, 31 October 2003.
7. Case before the National Social Appeals Board, 29 September 2006, SM S-2–06.
8. The policy reform entered into force by executive order, BEK no. 1098, 19 November 2008.
9. Council Directive 92/43/EEC of 21 May 1992 on the conservation of natural habitats and of wild fauna and flora.
10. Executive order, BEK no. 782, 1 November 1998.
11. Referring to the case law of the European Court of Justice, see InfoCuria (2012b) and EUR-Lex (2012g).
12. Council Directive no. 79/409, 2 April 1979 on the conservation of wild birds.
13. The formal notice questioned the Danish implementation of article 6. 2–4 of the habitats directive (Ministry of Foreign Affairs 2005: 32).

14 EU coordination processes in Denmark

Change in order to preserve[1]

Peter Nedergaard

Introduction

The coordination of EU decision-making processes varies from member state to member state. On the one hand, it firmly demonstrates how policies and administrative procedures intertwine. On the other, it is also a simple way of conveying the degree to which the EU represents an overcrowded and fluid environment for actors.

The reason for the national variations in EU coordination is partly attributed to the use of different methods of coordination, and in particular: (1) variations of usage in terms of the horizontal dimension, (i.e. the allocation of units within the coordination process), and; (2) partly because these variations depend on the vertical dimension, (i.e. whether the member state practises a centralized or decentralized method of EU coordination (Kassim *et al.* 2000: 6)). These EU characteristics require and call for a coordination chain that extends – in chronological order – from within each ministry through interministerial coordination of both a vertical and horizontal nature to coordination between the executive and legislative power (Wright 1996) – and thus impacts upon understanding of uploading and downloading in the Danish case (see Introduction to this volume).[2] Many scholars have found this subject at the same time to be both rather intriguing and complicated to analyse (Kassim *et al.* 2000; Miles 2005a; Nedergaard 2005; Esmark 2008; Pedersen 2000; Trondal 2000).

Generally, all kinds of coordination can be defined as ways of creating an order, as far as certain elements are concerned, that is both different and interconnected. In the political world, both legitimacy and efficiency considerations are involved in all kinds of coordination. In addition, organizational rivalry is a natural ingredient in the coordination of political decision-making, as some institutions stand to gain from specific types of coordination, whereas others stand to lose. Another dividing line is, as identified in the Introduction to this volume, whether or not to use formal or more informal means of coordination. In spite of the fact that informally-based coordination is of paramount importance due to highly embedded bureaucratic cultures and routines, formally-based coordination tends to be the centre of attention in analyses in the field (March and Olsen 1989; Nedergaard 2005: 378). This chapter incorporates information about the informal means of coordination via interviews with selected respondents in the ministries as well as in the Danish parliament (the Folketing).[3] Whereas the advantages of the centralized model might seem obvious, at least from an intergovernmentalist perspective, one can speculate over the reasons for the decentralized model: is it a sign of a deliberate functionalist wish for sector-based integration, or is it in fact due to a lack of coordinating skills (Kassim et al. 2000: 1–19)?

All EU member states have developed special administrative procedures in order to handle their national interests in the EU decision-making process. It is possible to distinguish between coordination through external centralization or external decentralization, depending on whether or not a member state attempts to upload and speak with one consistent voice in the EU decision-making process. In contrast, internal centralization or internal decentralization deals with the centralization or decentralization *within* the individual member states, i.e. between the Ministry of Foreign Affairs on the one hand and the sectorial ministries on the other.

Some member states have chosen a relatively centralized model, such as the creation of strong EU coordination procedures held together by special administrative units. Others have preferred a more decentralized model, implying that the individual administrative units look after their own EU affairs, and only take into consideration what is going on in other policy domains to a certain extent.

Traditionally, Denmark is regarded as a typical example of a member state belonging to the centralized camp, together with other member states such as France, the United Kingdom, the Netherlands, Poland, Belgium and Spain. On the other hand, member states such as Germany, Italy, Luxembourg, Ireland, Austria, Greece and Portugal are seen as members of the decentralized category.[4] It is characteristic of the decentralized category, that the coordination of EU decision-making takes place under various forms of formal and informal hearing procedures. Often, most coordination is carried out via ad hoc meetings between the involved ministries.

An analysis of the principles of EU coordination in Denmark follows in the next section, followed by an evaluation of EU coordination in Denmark in chronological order beginning with a case in a ministry and ending with a coordinated EU position after negotiations in the Danish parliament. In other words, the structure follows the parliamentarian governance chain in reverse order. In the third section, the role of the ministries in Danish EU coordination is evaluated, while in the fourth section, the three administrative layers involved in the preparation of a Danish governmental position in the EU coordination process are analysed. The fifth section provides an analysis of the functioning of the parliamentarian democratic control of Denmark's EU decision-making through the EAC of the Danish parliament. In the sixth section, the influence of the Danish parliament and the EAC in Danish EU coordination is examined. The conclusion follows in the seventh section.

Principles of Danish EU coordination

Traditionally, it is assumed that centralized EU coordination in Denmark stems partly from Danish scepticism towards stronger integration in the EU (i.e. centralization used as an instrument to stop further integration) and partly from the country's tradition for minority governments (i.e. centralization used as an instrument to ensure a parliamentarian majority behind the government's position in the Council of Ministers and its subgroups). In this respect, this may illustrate the blurring of international and domestic priorities as identified in the Introduction. In addition to these legitimacy-based arguments, it has been claimed that centralized EU coordination has contributed to a (normally) efficient implementation of EU directives as part of Danish legislation.

At the beginning of Denmark's membership of the EU, a doctrine of Danish EU coordination was put forward in the Danish parliament by former Minister of Foreign Affairs, K. B. Andersen:

> It is important to keep in mind as a central point that Danish policy positions has to be presented in negotiations against foreign partners in a coordinated fashion where the balance of – however, not necessary – coincident interests are found beforehand in a cooperative work at the domestic level. In order to solve this task not only close cooperation is needed between the Ministry of Foreign Affairs, other parts of government and other bodies and institutions. It is also required that a constant coordination takes place at all levels within the Ministry of Foreign Affairs.
> (Folketingstidende 1973–1974 Tillæg A: 986)

As this chapter seeks to clarify, this doctrine of external centralization has served as a *leitmotif* for Danish EU coordination ever since. The original inspiration for the Danish centralized system of EU coordination came from the French system (Pedersen 2000: 221).

In the first years of Denmark's membership of the EC, there was not only a rigorous external centralization, but also a strong internal and formal centralization of the Danish EU coordination process under the auspices of the Ministry of Foreign Affairs (Grønnegård Christensen 1980: 185). The instruments of Danish EU policy (see the Introduction to this volume) were thus highly centralized. Around 1980, a certain degree of internal decentralization occurred from the Ministry of Foreign Affairs to the sectoral ministries because of the increasing numerical weight of, for example, EU directives as regulations stemming from the EU decision-making process (Grønnegård Christensen *et al.* 1994). This process accelerated in the aftermath of the Single European Act and the Internal Market programme from the mid 1980s. However, this has not changed the fact that externally, Denmark's EU coordination (and thereby the instruments of Danish EU policy) is still, to a great degree, centralized.

Ministries and Danish EU coordination

The sectoral ministries for agriculture, employment and business, for instance, are initiators in the EU decision-making phase, which occurs immediately after the Commission has published a new proposal. These ministries are responsible for the hearings of other public bodies and private interest organizations concerning all new proposals coming out of Brussels.

The sectoral ministries also send Danish representatives to working party meetings in Brussels held under the auspices of the Secretariat of the Council of Ministers, unless the ministries' own attachés (who are, however, formally employed by the Ministry of Foreign Affairs) at the Permanent Representation in Brussels take part in these meetings. Negotiations here are based on instructions from the relevant ministry. They also instruct relevant negotiators at the Permanent Representation on A-points[5] at COREPER, while the Ministry of Foreign Affairs instructs the Representation on B-points[6] at COREPER based on input from the sectoral ministries. Last, but certainly not least, the sectoral ministries are represented by their own ministers at the meetings of the Council of Ministers (Ministry of Foreign Affairs 2010a).

All these factors contribute to the sectorization or internal decentralization of Danish EU coordination in spite of the overall external centralization. By sectorization in this regard, is meant that policy positions concerning EU proposals are mainly formulated in the sectoral ministries and their network.[7] In contrast to most cases of EU coordination in the member states that are characterized by either a government that speaks with one voice in Brussels or sectorization (Kassim *et al.* 2000: 2), Danish EU coordination encompasses both. According to this author's investigations (see also Pedersen 2000; Nedergaard 2005), the main reason for this unusual correspondence is a strong politico-administrative culture in Denmark supporting consensus.[8] Sectorization also leads to alliances between the ministries, their civil servants and their traditional interest groups (the so-called iron triangles) being kept intact when it comes to EU decision-making. The sectorization or internal decentralization of Danish EU coordination has its advantages as competence and decision-making power are kept together. However, the downside is that bureaucratic politics (i.e. institutional rivalries between the various bureaucratic units due to interests based upon linkages with differing groups outside the ministries) will probably flourish more than under an internally centralized system.

At the same time, it has to be mentioned that the sectorization is still balanced by the omnipresent coordinative function played by the Ministry of Foreign Affairs. Civil servants from this ministry are represented at all levels throughout the Danish decision-making process. In addition, the Ministry of Foreign Affairs is formally in charge of all connections to the Danish Permanent Representation in Brussels where, for instance, all attachés and counsellors seconded from the sectoral ministries are situated. Every Monday, a video conference is held between the management of the Ministry of Foreign Affairs in Copenhagen and the management of the Permanent Representation in Brussels about the upcoming Council of Ministers' meetings of the week.[9]

The Ministry of Foreign Affairs is also responsible for the coordination of the EU Committee (EU udvalget), and acts as secretariat for the government's Foreign Affairs Committee (see below). All contacts with the EAC of the Danish parliament concerning, for example, procedural questions, documents and scheduling, are also the responsibility of the Ministry of Foreign Affairs. In addition, it is solely responsible for the preparations of all initiatives as far as the European Council's meetings are concerned, even though a ministerial committee headed by the Prime Minister's Office prepares the meetings in the European Council (see below). Generally, Danish EU coordination has been characterized as a 'police patrol' system with the Ministry of Foreign Affairs assuming the policing role (Pedersen 2000: 226).

The anticipation is that the sectoral ministries will act as obedient citizens. Only in cases where they do not 'toe the line' does the Ministry of Foreign Affairs step in (cf. its police patrol-role).

Preparing EU decisions in the Danish coordination system

Network of committees

From an institutional point of view, EU coordination in Denmark, including coordination at the parliamentary level, consists of an interlinked network of committees between the various ministries, which is organized on four levels. The most important institutions are the committees with civil servants in the ministries (the Special Committees), the coordinating committee in the Ministry of Foreign Affairs (the EU Committee), the government's Foreign Affairs Committee, and the Danish parliament's EAC, cf. Figure 14.1.

In Denmark, EU coordination begins in these so-called EU Special Committees ('Specialudvalg'), established under the auspices of the various sectoral ministries. Then the EU Committee of the Ministry of Foreign Affairs takes

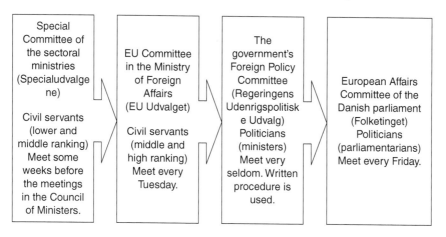

Figure 14.1 Model of Danish EU coordination.

over. Afterwards, the government's Foreign Affairs Committee, comprising the ten most important ministers in the government, has the final decision-making power. Lastly, the EAC of the Danish parliament assigns the minister with a mandate before the meeting of the Council of Ministers. These EU coordination steps, taking place in Copenhagen, correspond to three levels of coordination in Brussels: the working parties of the Council of Ministers (Special Committees), the COREPER (the EU Committee) and the Council of Ministers (the government's Foreign Affairs Committee and the parliament's EAC).

There are 34 EU Special Committees under the sectoral ministries. The chairmanship and secretariats are in the hands of the most relevant ministry. The Special Committees form the core of the internally decentralized Danish EU coordination, as it is here that by far the most time is spent on EU coordination. It is in these committees that most of the inter-ministerial coordination takes place as both the Ministry of Foreign Affairs and the ministries with adjacent tasks are represented.[10] Interest organisations are also represented in the Special Committees when relevant (i.e. in Special Committees dealing with economic-political subjects). The objective of the work in the EU Special Committees is mainly: (1) to identify the content and the scope of the proposal, and; (2) to prepare a Danish governmental position for the EU Committee at the next level in the coordination process (Ministry of Foreign Affairs 2010). Most Special Committees meet on a regular basis three or four weeks before the meeting of the Council of Ministers.

Special Committees

Normally, the reading (in the Special Committees) of the proposals coming out of Brussels begins at the same time as in the Council of Ministers' working parties in Brussels. Within a few weeks, a draft position paper is produced by the secretariat of the Special Committee. Together with the actual proposal, it is sent out to members of the committee for consideration. The Special Committees are the forums for distributing hearings in order to have all points of views on the table. In addition, there are many important contacts and a great deal of networking between all stakeholders concerning the specific proposal.[11]

On the basis of responses from, for example, ministries and other interested organisations, a so-called framework paper ('rammenotat') is prepared. This establishes a detailed Danish governmental position four to six weeks after a proposal has been presented. This paper provides guidelines for negotiations in the working parties in Brussels, and it is always approved by the relevant Special Committee. As far as its content is concerned, it corresponds to the so-called document with an annotated agenda ('notat med kommenteret dagsorden') prepared immediately before the meeting of the Council of Ministers, where all the points on the agenda are presented and discussed (Nedergaard 2005: 398–399).

However, documents with an annotated agenda differ from a framework paper by having – at the end of each point on the agenda – a sentence stating that it is recommended that Denmark works for 'xx' or endorses 'yy'.[12]

Sometimes, an EU case is only submitted to the Special Committee once. However, it is often necessary to have more meetings because of further developments in negotiations in the working parties under the Council of Ministers, or because of specific problems that possibly require a renewed Danish policy position. In many cases, however, cases are also handled by written procedure.[13]

EU cases are often very technical in character and this presupposes a certain degree of technical expertise among the participants dealing with them. This is one explanation for the important role of the Special Committee in the Danish EU coordination system. Another is the desire for consensus based upon a tight external and internal political, case-related and interest-related coordination (Nedergaard 2005: 400–401).

The Special Committees are the institutional key to the strength of the Danish EU coordination consensus machine. Hence, they also play an essential role in ensuring the wider legitimacy of the overall Danish EU coordination system due to the fact that consensus decision-making is seen as more legitimate than non-consensus decision-making.

It is very seldom that recommendations from the Special Committees are changed later in the EU coordination process in Denmark. According to investigations by Nedergaard (2005) and informants from the Ministry of Foreign Affairs (2010), more than 95 per cent of the recommendations from the Special Committees are kept intact, around 4 per cent are changed in the EU Committee and less than 1 per cent (normally only one–two cases per year) are changed by the government ministers in their Foreign Affairs Committee. This does not mean that there are no differences of opinion in the Special Committees.

In most cases, the strong politico-administrative consensus norm of the Danish ministries prevails. Hereby, bureaucratic politics are also kept under control as 'consensus' is 'good' and 'conflict' is 'bad' in the perception of the ministries' top management. Therefore, the recommendations from the Special Committees normally represent balanced compromises that are usually kept intact while being processed by the EU coordination process. It is usually only in cases of disagreement in the Special Committee that the EU Committee or (very seldom) the government's Foreign Affairs Committee are actively involved in a case.[14]

The EU Committee

The next step in the EU coordination process is the EU Committee under the auspices of the Ministry of Foreign Affairs. If the Ministry of Foreign Affairs plays a policing role in the Danish EU coordination system, the EU Committee is certainly the police department. This committee meets every Tuesday morning at 11.00 a.m. and the meetings take less than one hour. The points on the agenda are mainly the upcoming meetings of the Council of Ministers.

At the meetings of the EU Committee, the members (i.e. representatives from all relevant ministries, typically at the level of Head of Division or lower and from the Prime Minister's Office and with a high ranking official from the

Ministry of Foreign Affairs as chairperson) discuss both the content and the recommendations for the upcoming meetings of the EAC and the Council of Ministers.

The EU Committee is a link between the substantial and thorough case handling in the Special Committees and the political decisions that can only be taken by the government and the subsequent representation in the parliament's EAC. On the other hand, the EU Committee has not become the high-ranking committee that it was supposed to be when Denmark joined the EC in 1973. Instead, its representatives from the various ministries (sometimes chairpersons of the Special Committees or with close connections to the chairpersons of the Special Committee) are Heads of Divisions[15] or Chief Consultants, and not permanent secretaries as originally planned (Pedersen 2000; Nedergaard 2005). However, if there are unsolved problems after the meetings, either the permanent secretaries or the ministers will get in touch via telephone in order find a solution on the possible disagreements. Again, the norm is that consensus should prevail before the next phase of the EU coordination process. It is seen as a failure of the civil service if there is no consensus at this point in the coordination process.[16]

The Foreign Affairs Committee

The government's Foreign Affairs Committee represents the highest level in the inter-ministerial EU coordination system (Ministry of Foreign Affairs 2004), with the formal legitimacy and power to sanction the government's position before the meeting of the Council of Ministers. The Minister of Foreign Affairs chairs the Committee, and the secretary is the chairperson of the EU Committee. When it meets, it does so on Thursdays, i.e. two days after the meetings in the EU Committee and the day before the meeting of the parliament's EAC on Friday. In practice, the Foreign Affairs Committee convenes only very rarely and cases are normally handled by written procedure. At the same time, the Foreign Affairs Committee is by no means unimportant (besides its role as the official sanctioning of the Danish government's position) in a country like Denmark where coalition governments are the general rule. Even through the written procedure, coalition partners can again oversee what is taking place in the ministries as far as EU coordination is concerned.[17]

In principle, it is only in the government's Foreign Affairs Committee that the Danish policy position is defined; this is then presented to the parliament's EAC the following day. As mentioned above, in almost all instances, the recommendations from the Special Committee and the EU Committee are confirmed. These policy positions also represent the Danish negotiating mandate in the Council of Ministers unless the EAC in the Danish parliament objects and demands changes.

Besides sanctioning the government's policy position before a meeting of the Council of Ministers, there are also EU cases that are treated independently by the government's Foreign Affairs Committee. These cases can be divided into two main groups. First, the committee provides general policy guidelines, for example, on EU budgetary problems, on reforms of the CAP and on the 2012 Danish EU Presidency. Second, there are often specific EU cases that demand the attention of the government, such as a Treaty infringement action underway in the Commission towards Denmark (Nedergaard 2005: 407).

The European Affairs Committee and the Danish parliament

The EAC is established by the Danish parliament's party groups and for the Danish party groups. The Danish parliament's EAC consists of 17 members (and 11 alternating members), and reflects the strength of the political parties in the parliament,[18] i.e. a government that enjoys the support of a majority in the parliament also, in principle, has the backing of a majority in the EAC. However, no matter which parties are in the (coalition and minority) government, in practice, it does not necessarily follow from the political parties' general support of a government that they will support the government in concrete EU cases. Political parties to the left (the Unity List – the Red–Green Alliance and Socialist People's Party) as well as the populist Danish People's Party are often relatively sceptical towards new proposals for more EU integration coming out of Brussels. No matter the colour of the government, it normally has to look for the necessary political backing from the centre-right or centre-left political parties (the Social Democratic Party, the Social Liberal Party, the Liberal Party or Conservative Party). This is where the EAC distinguishes itself from the other committees of the Danish parliament.

The government submits most EU cases directly to the EAC in order to obtain a mandate based on an oral presentation by the minister, taking into consideration the recommendations in the document with the annotated agenda in order to orient the committee. The government does not ask for a direct mandate in the EAC in cases where one is required. Instead, it acts in accordance with the position presented by the minister unless the chairperson of the Committee notes that a majority of the members are against it. However, not all ministers get the mandates they ask for. According to interviewed respondents, in 15–20 per cent of such cases, the Committee refuses to deliver.[19] Then the minister has to come back again, most probably after some negotiations and briefings with some of the members of the EAC.

All EU cases are first submitted to the Special Committees of the parliament before a mandate is given to the minister in the EAC. In this regard, some committees have traditionally been more active in the handling of EU cases than others. The parliament's Environmental Committee ('Miljø- og Planlægningsudvalget'), the Judicial Committee ('Retsudvalget'), and the Agricultural Committee ('Landbrugsudvalget') have for years been actively involved in EU affairs with the aim of submitting recommendations to the parliament's EAC. Due to the 2007 Lisbon Treaty and the Danish parliament's new role in scrutinizing whether or not the subsidiarity principle is observed, the chairperson of the EAC has strengthened the secretariat of the Committee so that all Special Committees of the parliament can become actively involved.

The EAC is responsible for, as one of its functions, the legitimization of the government ministers' positions in the EU decision-making system. In addition, the Committee probably also contributes to the wider legitimacy of the EU decision-making process in general, as it is an institution in which directly-elected parliamentarians are involved in the process.

In Denmark, historically, the EAC is a concrete expression of the desire by the parliament to control the EU decision-making process that is predominantly handled by the executive. The committee in its present form was established in 1972 to prepare Denmark for membership of the EC.[20] In the 1972 Danish Accession Act, it is stated that the government shall inform the Danish parliament's EAC of proposals for Council decisions which apply directly in Denmark or in which implementation requires the participation of the Danish parliament.

It was only after the first report from the EAC in 1973, that the requirements of this information to the parliament were more clearly specified (Jensen 2003: 36). In questions of 'considerable importance' (væsentlig betydning), the government shall orient the EAC. These consultations shall respect both the influence of the parliament and the freedom of the government to negotiate. In decisions of 'wider scope' (større rækkevidde) the government shall have the acceptance of a mandate for the negotiations in the Council of Ministers (Ministry of Foreign Affairs 2010a). These obligations have been clarified and extended over the years through subsequent reports from the EAC. Nevertheless, these qualifications mean that the government has to estimate whether or not a specific EU case should be submitted to the committee for a mandate or just for orientation; normally, however, the government plays safe.

According to the Danish constitution, there is no guarantee that the Danish parliament should have any influence on the government's EU policy. Hence, when Denmark entered the EC, there was a political need to create an institution that could – in accordance with the parliamentarian principle – ensure that a majority of Danish parliamentarians could influence the (minority) government's EU policy. Hereby, such a construction could also give impetus to greater legitimacy of Danish EU policy more generally that was in demand due to the relatively large resistance to EU membership in the country (Nedergaard 2005: 412).[21] This was the background for the position of the EAC. It was, however, not until it was questioned in a concrete case at the beginning of March 1973, right after the Danish EC membership on 1 January 1973, that the EAC obtained the role on a parliamentarian basis before the negotiations in the Council of Ministers.

At the meeting of the EAC, the minister presents his or her views as to the Danish governmental position concerning the points on the agenda at the Council of Minister's meetings in the coming week. After some discussion between the minister and the Committee members, the chairperson of the Committee summarizes the debate and points out what the minister has promised. If nobody objects, the minister has his or her mandate on these conditions. Only on rare occasions does an actual vote take place; for example, if the minister does not withdraw a proposal for a mandate that does not have the backing of a majority in the Committee according to the judgment of its chairperson.[22]

The new EU decision-making procedures imply that a greater number of de facto decisions are, in reality, taken at an earlier stage than before;[23] for example, in connection with a first reading agreement with the European Parliament. However, negotiating mandates are avoided for so-called A-items on the agenda in the Council of Ministers. In practice, however, and according to the author's informants,[24] negotiation positions for relevant B-items on the agenda are, in most cases, also presented in the weeks before the final negotiations in the Council of Ministers (sometimes for the second time because the case has evolved).

As mentioned, the EAC ensures the formal parliamentarian legitimacy to accept proposals and vote in the Council of Ministers. However, questions have often been asked about the possibilities for the Committee to actually control the behaviour of the Danish minister in the Council of Ministers. On the one hand, the Council of Ministers' meetings take place behind closed doors when it comes to actual negotiations and voting (they are open for television coverage when ministers make presentations). On the other hand, ministers send minutes, detailing what has happened (especially with regard to the Danish governmental position), no later than five days after the respective meeting has taken place. These can be compared with the stenographic minutes from the relevant meeting of the EAC in the Danish parliament.

The influence of the European affairs committee on Danish EU coordination

In accordance with the classical definition by Dahl (1957), influence may be defined as meaning that actor A has influence on B, if, and only if, B behaves in ways that B would not have behaved in if he/she was not under influence stemming from A. Based on this definition, in principle, the EAC has a major influence. It can change the government's position on EU cases and thereby ensure that a majority of parliamentarians are behind the future implementation of EU directives. This enhances the efficiency of the implementation process. This is even more important as a considerable amount of Danish legislation stems from EU directives.

According to the author's informants, who possess long experience in working with the EAC, the general assessment is that the Committee has become more politicized and active in recent years. It could thus be argued that it has even increased its influence when taking into account that a 'no' from the EAC no longer necessarily means a 'no' to the piece of legislation on the negotiating table, due to the fact that qualified majority voting has become the formal rule of decision-making in the Council of Ministers (even though there is a strong norm that one should strive for consensus). Against that backdrop, the influence of the EAC seems to be considerable.

The government accepts the binding mandates because minority governments are the general rule in Danish politics (to a larger degree than in some other EU member states). Potentially, the government risks accepting EU rulings which will not be adopted later on by the Danish parliament unless the government has a firm foundation for its EU policy positions. Hence, the mutual interest of both the EAC and the government in the binding mandates.

The other face of the important and influential EAC is that of a committee that still most often arrives with the decisive weapon of ensuring mandates late in the decision-making process, and hence only has limited influence on the content of the EU negotiations before they arrive before the Council of Ministers.

In addition, generally speaking, national parliaments have been taken more seriously by EU actors over the years. The influence of national parliaments (and thereby not least the EAC) has been strengthened with the 2007 Lisbon Treaty (EU-Oplysningen 2008b) and they have gained a new role in the EU (especially with regard to the subsidiarity principle) and in their cooperation with the European Parliament. The new role assigned to the national parliaments is that they – after the submission of a new proposal from the Commission – should announce within eight weeks whether or not they agree that the subsidiarity principle is being observed.

Conclusion

In spite of the evolving EU coordination process, important elements of Danish EU coordination remain the same. The doctrine on Danish EU coordination presented by K. B. Andersen in 1973 is intact: Danish governmental positions with regard to EU issues are still presented in a highly coordinated fashion. External centralization remains an essential feature of the process. In this respect, the Danish parliament's 'gate-keeper' role vis-à-vis the government concerning mandates for negotiations in the Council of Ministers is essential.

This also demonstrates that in spite of the many neofunctionalist processes taking place within the EU integration process (cf. Haas 1958; Lindberg 1963; Niemann and Schmitter 2009; Tranholm-Mikkelsen 1991), Danish EU coordination is still perceived within a general contextual framework of intergovermentalism. There remains, then, potential for tension between influence and autonomy motivations within Danish EU coordination processes as outlined in the Introduction to this volume.

At the same time, the desire for autonomy has certainly increased the influence of the EAC of the Danish parliament. It could be claimed that Denmark has practised influence-maximizing behaviour through autonomy-maximization. Or perhaps it would be fairer to say that the Danish EU coordination system is a sign of a somewhat hesitant state participating in what is an ongoing federalizing process of the EU.

Over the years, the Danish EU coordination process has been in a permanent state of change, though centred on some core principles. Internally, the EAC of the parliament has gradually strengthened its role and increased its legitimacy.

Internal strength has, to some extent, been undermined by an external weakening due to the development of new (and more 'federal') EU decision-making procedures. However, considering the EU decision-making procedures (and the informal consensus norm), the EAC is probably as strong as ever. Also, the sectoral ministries have secured growing significance within the EU coordination process because of the fact that the Special Committee has become the core of an increasing, all-encompassing EU coordination process. It represents the institution where networks of, for instance, civil servants, interest groups and representatives, are working, and thus offers real possibilities for successful Danish uploading and downloading of preferences towards the EU.

Notes

1 This manuscript has certainly benefitted from the discussions and comments made at the seminar at Schæffergården on 29–30 September 2010. The author appreciates not least the comments made by Ian Manners, Knud Erik Jørgensen, Lee Miles, Rebecca Adler-Nissen, Caroline Grøn and Anders Wivel. The chapter in an updated version was also discussed at an internal research seminar at the Department of Political Science at the University of Copenhagen on 27 January 2011. From this seminar, the author is grateful for comments from Henrik Jensen, Mads Dagnis Jensen and Karina Kosiara-Pedersen. Lena Brogaard was a research assistant on this project.
2 This chapter only analyses the decision-making process. The implementation process is also important with regard to EU coordination, but it is left out. Danish EU coordination at the European level (especially from the Danish Permanent Representation) is also left out of the analysis in order to limit the scope of the chapter. Danish EU coordination in Brussels is included here only if it has a direct impact on Danish EU coordination at the domestic level. See Kassim *et al.* (2001) for at treatment of national coordination of EU policy at the European level.
3 The data collected for this piece stems from a large number of public documents from the Ministry of Foreign Affairs (with the overall responsibility for Danish EU coordination) and from the Danish parliament. In addition, a number of interviews have been carried out with key informants about the subject: Member of the Danish parliament and chairperson of the European Affairs Committee, Anne Marie Meldgaard (October 2010), Head of Division Martin Bresson, the Ministry of Business and Economics (June 2010), Chief Consultant Lise Bøgh Hansen, the Ministry of Foreign Affairs (September 2010), and Chief Consultant Lotte Linnet, Ministry of Food, Agriculture and Fisheries (September 2010).
4 Cf. Lise Bøgh Hansen, Ministry of Foreign Affairs.
5 A-points are points on the agenda of the upcoming meeting of the Council of Ministers, where all member states agree and where there is a written procedure as far as the decision-making in the Council of Ministers is concerned.
6 B-points are points on the agenda of an upcoming meeting of the Council of Ministers where member states are not in agreement.
7 I regard sectorization and internal decentralization as synonymous.
8 Cf. Lise Bøgh Hansen, Ministry of Foreign Affairs, and Anne Marie Meldgaard, the Danish parliament.
9 Cf. Lise Bøgh Hansen, Ministry of Foreign Affairs.
10 The Ministry of Finance is also represented in most Special Committees.
11 Cf. Lise Bøgh Hansen, Ministry of Foreign Affairs and Martin Bresson, Ministry of Business and Economics.
12 In some of the Special Committees these recommendations are not made public.
13 Cf. Lise Bøgh Hansen, Ministry of Foreign Affairs.
14 Cf. Lise Bøgh Hansen, Ministry of Foreign Affairs.
15 Some of the most important ministries in EU affairs (e.g. the Ministry of Business and Economics) are sometimes represented by a Head of Department.

16 Cf. Lise Bøgh Hansen, Ministry of Foreign Affairs and Martin Bresson, Ministry of Business and Economics.
17 Cf. Anne Marie Meldgaard, the European Affairs Committee of the Danish parliament.
18 Hence, according to the author's informants, there are no problems with absentees. All members attend – or send their alternates.
19 Cf. Anne Marie Meldgaard, European Affairs Committee of the Danish parliament, and Lise Bøgh Hansen, Ministry of Foreign Affairs.
20 However, the European Affairs Committee have roots that go back to the committee set up in 1961 to prepare the Danish negotiations with the EC (Jensen 2003: 33–34).
21 In the referendum on the Danish membership of the EC, on 2 October 1972, 63.2 per cent voted 'yes' while 36.6 per cent voted 'no'.
22 Cf. Anne Marie Meldgaard, European Affairs Committee of the Danish parliament.
23 Of course, the de jure decisions are taken much later.
24 Cf. Martin Bresson, Ministry of Business and Economics and Lise Bøgh Hansen, Ministry of Foreign Affairs.

15 Not quite a painful choice?
Reflecting on Denmark and further European integration[1]

Lee Miles

Introduction

If not before (and clearly since) the days of the EU agreement on the 'Danish compromise' at the 1992 Edinburgh European Council Summit, and the later Danish approval of the 1992 TEU the second time around in a public referendum in 1993, the Danish elite and public have been operating through the prism of 'differentiated integration' (see also Miles 2010a). As the Introduction to this volume discusses, Danish policy-makers have to contend and operate within the confines of a rather specific kind of domestic politics governed, at least officially, by the 'four Danish opt-outs' on EU Citizenship, EMU, the evolving ESDP and what was once called JHA. At the same time, and as the chapters in this volume by Marcussen (on EMU) and Adler-Nissen (on JHA questions) illustrate, the Danish political elite have been involved in a careful pursuit of Danish preferences and influence within the still relatively elite circles of EU decision-making, that sometimes seems to be beyond the confines of the official parameters of the domestic-orientated Danish opt-outs. As argued elsewhere (Miles 2003a, 2003b), Danish political elites and policy-makers have done much to ensure that they are 'unofficially fused' into the complexities of EU decision-making, even in those areas falling under the vestiges of Danish opt-outs. Nevertheless, in some domains, Danish EU policy remains decisively influenced by the official and domestically important profiles of the four opt-outs (Larsen 2011). Attempts over the last decade by the (then) Liberal-Conservative Government (from 2000–2011), to begin a process of building domestic support for the abandonment of the Danish opt-outs, were largely unsuccessful in changing the public mood. Albeit to a limited extent, Danish policy-makers in favour of closer further integration have not been able to drive forward Danish public debates to the point where notions of change have become overwhelmingly convincing.

Yet, how can this be understood, and can concepts drawn from FPA that seek to 'bridge the gap' between theory and practice provide conceptual utility (see George 1993). In particular, can FPA concepts that focus on notions of 'policy change' provide additional tools for understanding Danish policy towards the EU? This seems especially pertinent given that Danish EU policy remains constrained by the operational conditioning of the Danish opt-outs, and, thus, Danish policy towards the EU will be influenced by them. It is conditioned by, and within, the realms of incremental, elite-oriented political manoeuvring operating inside and around the edges of the parameters of the Danish opt-outs. It seems then, that Danish EU policy will refrain from addressing the continuation of the Danish opt-outs 'full on', with the elite not seeking to convince Danish public opinion of the merits of abandoning the tailored differentiated integration pathways directed by the Danish opt-outs.

This chapter therefore undertakes three tasks. First, it outlines (by drawing upon the FPA literature) the utility of Welch's (2005) work on 'Painful Choices' as a means of understanding why policy change has been so difficult at the level of general Danish EU policy. Second, it combines this with notions of a fusion perspective (Miles 2005a) to provide a more tailored understanding of how Danish policy-makers follow a 'clustered fusion' approach (Miles 2011a, 2011b) to handling differentiated integration in the Danish context. Third, the chapter then considers the challenges for Danish policy-makers in pursing such a differentiated strategy in the longer term and what it implies for the successful pursuit of Danish uploading of preferences to the EU supranational level.

Conceptualizing Danish EU policy: from an FPA perspective

While Hill (2004: 160) has often stressed that there is plenty of life left in national foreign policy, it is important to recognize the complexities of Danish EU policy and thus, to some extent, locate this chapter study. Taking a similar departure to that of Larsen (2005: 5), there is a need to concentrate on the *substance* of Danish EU policy, and to highlight that Danish EU policy is conducted within and/or through the EU (Larsen 2005: 8). Put simply, it may still be possible, although now within certain limitations, to 'study national foreign policy of EU member states and the way it is conducted: that there is still a separable analytical category even in the context of the EU' (Larsen 2005: 8). As White (2001: 39) also argues, it is now important (even with the reforms envisaged in the 2007 Lisbon Treaty that establishes, for example, an EU External Action Service), so that three forms of European foreign policy (involving Denmark) may be studied analytically – namely Community, Union and national foreign policies.[2] Nevertheless, such assumptions need to also recognize that the distances between these separable categorizations are closing, and that the term 'foreign policy' of EU members is 'deceptively difficult to define' (Beach 2012: 1).

Most of all, policy-making at the nation state level, and thus the conduct of what was once firmly called 'national foreign policy', is exceedingly vulnerable to ever greater levels of blurring in the light of Europeanization (see Ladrech 2010; Gross 2009; Wong and Hill 2011) and the fusing of the activities of elites and policy-makers across regional, national and supranational domains (see Miles 2005a, 2010b, 2011a, 2011b). While it may still be pushing it a little to talk about the EU as a 'democratic republic of Europe' (Jørgensen 1997), there do seem to be strong grounds to, at least in the context of this book, see Danish EU policy as including aspects akin to an instance of a 'fusing foreign policy', where European and national variables are now highly interwoven and increasingly blurred. Whatever the scenario, it is certainly important to recognize that Europeanization in terms of foreign policy has represented:

> a transformation in the way national foreign policy is constructed, in the ways in which professional roles are defined and pursued and in the consequent internalization of norms and expectations arising from a complex system of collective European policy making.
>
> (Tonra 2000: 229)

Nevertheless, this chapter is principally concerned with Denmark and the EU and from this perspective, it is still important to recognize the integral preferences and roles of national actors as well as the national EU policies of member states. If, as usual, Europeanization is often understood 'as a process of foreign policy convergence', in which there is greater interaction between EU actors (institutions, politicians and diplomats) and those from the member states (in this case Danish actors) over agency, targets and directions of change (Wong and Hill 2011: 4), then there is still an important rationale for understanding the choices and actions of national actors, like those in Denmark. As Malici (2008: 5–6) argues, although the ambitions of EU member states may be often articulated via the common EU institutions and framework, the Union's ambitions and activities, especially in the domains of EU foreign policy, still rely quite heavily 'on more or less voluntary national decisions and contributions'. From this perspective, the EU can be seen as a 'shared mental model' (Malici 2008: 6) where national and EU actors are sharing (and fusing – see Miles 2011a, 2011b) activities and competencies, but this is contingent on the minds, hearts and will of national decision-makers, like those in Denmark, to 'help make it happen'.

Hence, it is still highly desirable to evaluate the policy choices of Danish EU actors, and the preferences of national policy-makers, since Danish actors are contributing towards the 'definition of a situation', the diagnostics propensities about a particular decision problem and the prescriptive propensities towards a decision-problem (Malici 2008: 6). Put another way, Danish national EU policy has been defined through the prism of: (1) a given situation – namely that the EU since the 1992 TEU has displayed characteristics that may lead to a Federal Europe or a least a more overtly supranational entity that will have substantial political implications for Danish sovereignty; (2) that although Danish policy-makers have accepted the nuances of EU supra-nationality, they also recognize the key diagnostic propensities that there are many elite Danish actors and a substantial part of the domestic population that remain opposed to this, and; (3) have agreed the Danish opt-outs as a set of operational parameters and prescriptive propensities that both define Danish participation in the EU in a formal sense, and provide limited prescriptions on how Danish EU policy and interaction with the EU will take place in the future (see Adler-Nissen's contribution to this volume). On this basis then, and in order to capture some of the nuances surrounding the complexity of this situation, this chapter draws upon empirical observations made not just through this particular author's ongoing research on Denmark and European integration, but also those of fellow contributors writing chapters in this volume.

Much of the analysis that examines Danish EU policy through the lenses of Europeanization and FPA would seem to highlight a remarkable consistency within Danish EU policy (see also Kelstrup in Chapter 2 of this volume). In vertical terms – or as the Introduction to this volume would better portray it in terms of uploading and downloading – Danish elite actors and policy-makers have been highly successful as 'pace-setters' in some supranational EU policy domains, such as EU environmental policy. They have been active participants in many aspects of the EU supranational policy portfolios (see Chapter 3 on Danish participation in the SEM and the CAP) as well being adept at increasingly taking into account the changing and rather dynamic structural context of the emerging foreign policy and external relations of the EU. In horizontal terms, Danish political elites and policy-makers have become more skilful at cross-loading and domestic coordination, providing a wider array of actors, organs of government, and even executive-legislature and national-regional relations – with expertise and contacts ranging from agriculture to migration policy. They have developed their own trans-border and EU relations, and enhanced the requirement for effective national coordination. It could be argued that the existence of the four Danish opt-outs has actually provided a stable and differentiated policy environment and common 'rules of the game' governing the channels of both vertical (uploading and downloading) and horizontal (cross-loading) coordination undertaken by Danish actors.

What then can the realms of FPA offer if the changing scenarios of Danish EU policy might require substantial shifts or changes in Danish EU policy behaviour? This question has been attempted before, with notable FPA-derived evaluations to be found in the works of Kelstrup (1992), Larsen (2005) and Manners and Whitman (2000), to name just a few.[3] Nevertheless, given that the focus of this chapter is more reflective, one potential, if rather ignored, port of call may be to examine the works of Welch (2005) and more specifically, the notion of the 'loss-aversion' theory of foreign policy change. Although, of course, there are grave dangers in seeking to apply a universal principal of foreign policy change, the notion, as forwarded by Welch (2005: 8) that foreign policy is most likely to change dramatically 'when leaders expect the status quo to generate continued painful losses' seems highly appropriate. Most important for this context, Welch (2005: 8) argues that states (i.e. Denmark) 'will not alter their behaviour simply to try to realize some marginal gain'. As Mintz (2003: 3) has also argued, as part of his 'non-compensatory principle' of political decision-making, which incidentally forms a core part of the polihueristic theory of FPA, decision-makers 'rarely choose an alternative that will hurt them politically', which leads to some potential policy alternatives being very quickly eliminated as policy options, and remaining out of view (Mintz and DeRouen Jr. 2010: 35). The clearest signals of an impending change are desperation, stridency and distress. The choice for change will often carry with it a risk of even greater loss – a risk of loss so great that, in many cases, no rational actor would accept it. The choice for change, in short, 'is commonly a painful choice'.[4] Welch (2005: 46) contends that foreign policy change is most likely to occur:

> when decision makers perceive that their current policies are incurring painful costs: that a failure to change policy is virtually certain to result in further painful costs: and that at least one option open to them holds forth the possibility of an acceptable outcome, even if that acceptable outcome is not highly likely.

All this requires some operationalizing of initial concepts – namely: (1) establishing a reference point (see Tversky and Kahneman 1992) (say Denmark's existing position as an EU full member) and in this regard, Denmark will be regarded as holding the status of being a 'near core insider' in being, in many ways, part of the political and economic core of the EU, and yet, for political reasons, refraining from being fully involved in certain political aspects of its development, and certainly remaining outside the core of the Franco-German axis (Miles 2005c); (2) the decision makers' subjective assessment of the status quo vis-à-vis the reference point and whether it is satisfactory or not (say Denmark's position within the EU as a full member and Danish policy-makers' assessments of the impact upon it. And in addition, of its position outside key integrative initiatives, such as its not being a full member of the euro and formally outside the eurozone, which led to the establishments of formal opt-outs to parts of key EU Treaties). This is what Welch (2005: 55) refers to in relation to 'whether decision-makers are operating within a gains frame or a loss frame', as well as: (3) the identification of a favoured alternative option or not (say the removal of one or more of the existing opt-outs in the future, with or without a formal referendum). In essence then, Welch is trading 'in terms of conditional likelihoods' (Welch, 2005: 68). Yet, for this discussion of Denmark and the EU, and more specifically the continued existence of a Danish policy towards the EU shaped within the parameters of the formal Danish opt-outs, the notion of 'painful choices' in how to structure Danish policy with or without the opt-outs has a certain resonance.

Reflecting on Danish participation in the EU

The starting reference point of this discussion must be to accept that after 40 years of full membership, Danish elite actors are largely integrated into EU structures and frameworks. However, there remains considerable domestic opposition among certain Danish political parties, interest groups and especially the general public towards further integration, and thus there is a gap (or at least an asymmetry) between elite and public discourse and activities towards the EU. Of course, there is a need to show caution here, and an immediate need to recognize that government policy 'is not launched in a vacuum' (Larsen 2005: 45), and thus elite considerations will be somewhat differentiated, although still interlinked. It is important, for example, to highlight that certain elite preferences towards integration may be driven by the potential benefits and costs that may be accrued for key political actors in terms of rather specific and actor-oriented notions of enhancing individual power and influence, e.g. for Danish policy-makers or respective political parties, while domestic debates may frame discussions of the costs and benefits of Europe more generally in terms of benefits and costs of participation for the country at large (see Miles 2005c). These calculations may also follow differing temporal logics, and there have been numerous instances, say on the question of the Single European Market in the late 1980s, or on issues of Danish participation in EMU in 2000, where elite views have been out of kilter with the general thrust of public opinion at the time. Hence, this asymmetry between Danish elites and public opinion is, albeit to a limited extent, affected by differentiated spatial and temporal dynamics.

Yet, as previously argued (Miles 2003a; 2003b), the Danish political elite have often acted as 'unofficial fusionists', showing selective, but still strong preferences for supra-nationalism in some EU policy areas and willing to fuse national competencies with EU ones in a limited number of fields – referred to elsewhere as 'fusion clusters' (see Miles 2011a, 2011b). To return to the arguments of Kelstrup (see Chapter 2), the starting reference point is now that in 2013, any 'integration dilemma' is often less explicit, constrained and has become increasingly selective and confined to certain policy fields as Danish policy-makers have become very effective operators within EU frameworks. Rather paradoxically then, the Danish reference point assumes a mixed or differentiated position on the part of Danish EU policy, whereby there has been: (1) the development of clustered 'fused foreign policy activities' (Miles 2011a, 2011b) where Danish national policy positions are integrated, supranational-orientated and often pace-setting in key EU policy domains, within the confines of those differentiated channels of further integration permissible (Miles 2011a, 2011b) and not constrained by the existence of the Danish opt-outs; (2) the development of elite strategies, as identified by, for example, Marcussen and Adler-Nissen to informally maximize the influence of Danish policy preferences in those domains covered by the opt-outs, and; (3) with the advances in further integration, no matter how differentiated, and as envisaged in the 2007 Lisbon Treaty, it seems likely that, as Adler-Nissen shows in the realms of JHA, these existing elite strategies will be less effective as a means of pursuing Danish policy preferences over time. From the perspective of Welch, new decision points will emerge in the near future.

Evidence that this triple reference point existed dates back at least formally to around 2000, when the Liberal-Conservative coalitions came to power under the premiership of Fogh Rasmussen, although political events, either domestic and/or external were to complicate any implementation of this position. As discussed elsewhere in this book, preparations were put in place to begin the process of securing their removal via the calling of a public referendum. Officially, the Liberal-Conservative Government has been planning to hold a referendum on abolishing the opt-outs (or more specifically the euro opt-out) since around 2004.

Moreover, as argued by Larsen (2010: 184), the government was also keen to simultaneously ensure that any decision on their removal would remain in the hands of the Danes themselves. Thus, the Danish governmental position during the negotiations of the Constitutional Treaty was 'to maintain the opt-outs' and, consequently, the proposed 2004 Constitutional Treaty contained four protocols dealing with the Danish exemptions. However, the circumstances of the French and Dutch rejections of the 2004 Constitutional Treaty, followed by the agreement among the EU governments to inaugurate a 'reflection period', and then the negotiations culminating in the revised 2007 Treaty of Lisbon, meant that such plans were continually delayed (Miles 2010a). Yet the negotiations on the 2007 Lisbon Treaty did actually lead to a formal change in the status of the Danish opt-outs, which are now recognized at the EU level not as completely set, but rather applicable on an individual, case-by-case basis.

However, the Prime Minister was consistent in doubting the viability and credibility of the Danish opt-outs and argued that the intention of his governments was to see their eventual removal. In his speech of 22 November 2007, after winning the 2007 parliamentary election, Fogh Rasmussen announced that the government would organize one or more referenda on abolishing the opt-outs before the next parliamentary election in 2011, although it remained unclear as to whether the referendum would consider the removal of all four opt-outs as a 'job-lot' or on a case-by-case basis. At that time, the referendum was originally expected to be held in the autumn of 2008; although once again this was delayed following the Irish rejection of the 2007 Treaty of Lisbon. A further attempt on the part of the Fogh Rasmussen government happened in early 2009, when the Prime Minister announced his expectation of a referendum on Denmark's participation in the third stage of EMU, adopting the single currency and joining the eurozone in 2010, and that he expected that it would be possible to satisfy the concerns of Danish Eurosceptic parties, like the Socialist People's Party. Yet these plans were again put into question when the Prime Minister left office in 2009 in order to take up the post of NATO Secretary-General.

Although it may have been the case that the Liberal-Conservative Government, and Fogh Rasmussen himself, may have generally held the position that the removal of the opt-outs could be viewed through a 'gains-frame', external events at various points in time continually put the overall gain under question, and certainly did not make it so overwhelming as to remove consideration of loss. Hence, the necessary pursuit of foreign policy change via the removal of the opt-outs was never truly demonstrated sufficiently within the inner circles of the Liberal-Conservative Government. In other words, this brief review of the Fogh Rasmussen years in office indicates that there was never sufficient evidence in order to remove 'decision-makers' fears that continuing with the status quo will generate ever more painful losses' (Alden and Aran 2012: 12). Or as Welch (2005: 46) would probably argue, there were never sufficient prospects to convince the Prime Minister to go the extra mile and call the respective referendum/referenda since there was never sufficient likelihood of 'disproportionate gain' to motivate foreign policy change. Indeed, there remained a constant awareness within the Fogh Rasmuseen government of the uncertain political costs that could be involved in seeing through such foreign policy change, since the former Social Democratic Prime Minister, Poul Nyrup Rasmussen, had lost a public referendum on the single currency in 2000, which had been widely seen to then add substantially to his political problems and ultimately his electoral loss to the non-socialists in 2001. Alongside this, the growing uncertainty about external events tended to produce, over time, a more cautious attitude, whereby Fogh Rasmussen and the Liberal-Conservative Government were willing to sustain any inherent costs of maintaining the existing governmental position rather than conduct foreign policy change to avoid any future losses (Welch 2005: 46).

Fogh Rasmussen's successor, Lars Løkke Rasmussen, announced that the opt-outs would only now be put to a referendum 'when the time is right', which raised doubts about the new Prime Minister's commitment to pursuing his predecessor's policy. This could be taken as evidence of the removal of the opt-outs increasingly being seen through a loss rather than a gains-frame over time. The issue was, to some extent, addressed only when the external stage was appropriate, when the new Prime Minister (in a meeting with Commission President Jose Manuel Barroso in mid 2009) affirmed his hope that at least a referendum on Danish adoption of the single currency, and thereby the removal of the Danish euro opt-out, would take place before the 2011 parliamentary election. This was in spite of the support of the leaders of the three largest opposition parties (Helle Thorning-Schmidt, Villy Søvndal and Margrethe Vestager) that suggested holding a referendum on the removal of the opt-outs in relation to defence and JHA in March 2010. Yet nothing really came to pass. Governmental and public attention turned externally, as the Liberal-Conservative Government became increasingly dominated by an implicit 'loss-framing' mind-set, and governmental attention focused very much on managing the evolving financial and then euro crisis, and internally, towards handling declining public support for the coalition government.

There was however, one brief phase where the concepts of loss aversion and conducting change were in line. For the government, two aspects of averting loss via change became increasingly intertwined in the last phases of rule by the Liberal-Conservative Coalition. First, during negotiations on an EU Competitiveness Pact in early 2011 (and as a response to the ongoing, worsening European sovereign debt crisis) Prime Minister Løkke Rasmussen proposed to hold a referendum on the opt-outs before June 2011 in order to have a mandate to participate in the negotiations over the Competitiveness Pact, and thus to help to formulate an institutional response within the eurozone and the single currency to which the Danish krone was pegged. Here, it could be argued that the Prime Minister was willing to move to the next step to avoid losses being incurred by the existing pegging, by permitting Denmark to fully participate in, and be a major contributor (both in political and financial terms) towards, any large coordinated EU response to the euro crisis. There is evidence here of the Danish government being willing to 'embrace' political and economic risk (Welch 2005:

45–46). Second, there was a specific domestic-oriented 'conditional likelihood' that supported change via a referendum – namely that the Prime Minister saw this as a strategy to possibly highlight differences between the governing coalition and the largest opposition parties that (apart from the removal of the opt-out on foreign and defence policy) did not agree on the removal of two of the other opt-outs, and to address the Prime Minister's and the coalition's increasing unpopularity. From a domestic perspective, foreign policy change via the pursuit of a referendum was now favoured, since it might remove existing losses and realize political and electoral gains politically. In this way, the Prime Minister himself viewed that his own leadership was possibly being undermined, and thus fulfilled, as Welch (2005: 49) argues, one of the features of loss-aversion theory, that change can be proposed 'when leaders themselves perceive themselves to be in the domain of losses'. Yet, rather ironically, this proposal met with opposition, not just from within the coalition but also within his own party, as critics argued that any referendum might be turned into a protest vote against the increasingly unpopular Prime Minister and the Liberal-Conservative Government.

With the victory of the left-wing coalition led by Social Democrat Thorning-Schmidt in September 2011, the new government announced that it also planned to hold referenda, but this time on the defence opt-out (where there was cross party agreement) and on either abolishing the JHA opt-out or modifying it to allow the country to opt into parts of it (see Chapter 5 by Adler-Nissen). However, this position was soon softened in the light of the continuing external problems of the euro and the euro crisis, with the new Prime Minister stipulating that this might imply no referendum before the end of this governmental term. Once again, the external situation has tended to reinforce a 'loss-framing' view that existing losses are unlikely to be addressed via a referendum-sanctioned change to join the euro. Thus, the gains are deemed to be uncertain, and could even induce even greater losses. This, combined with ongoing calculations on the part of the new government that the pursuit of change is unlikely to produce discernible electoral benefits, means that a referendum is unlikely to be pursued during this term of office.

Conclusions

Given this reference point in 2013, it seems that the likelihood of a referendum on the removal of the majority of the opt-outs is relatively distant, with the present trajectory being that a referendum on even one of these is going to be challenging for any Danish government. However, as Marcussen, Wivel and Adler-Nissen demonstrate in this volume, this situation may be bearable simply because of the success of Danish political elites in participating in EU structures, and fusing (on a selectively supranational basis) into the EU policy-making machinery, even in those policy dimensions and spheres where the Danish opt-outs apply. But, as Adler-Nissen argues in her chapter, the effectiveness by Danish elites in offsetting any costs associated with the opt-outs, especially in the JHA domains, may become increasingly harder, and thus in the field of JHA, not least in the post-11 September world, the losses incurred without policy change may become more unbearable over time. However, in a differentiated EU, that has, after all, become a normal *modus operandi* for the Union, it is probably wise to think in terms of policy change in differentiated areas, where the losses are calculated even more narrowly. 'Gains frames' and 'loss frames', as understood in terms of loss-aversion policy change, will need to be calculated and understood even more carefully in the context of Danish EU policy, especially in relation to specific opt-outs.[5] In this scenario, it is perhaps more appropriate to view Denmark in the EU through the prism of a selectively supranational and fused Denmark with fewer opt-outs, than the often superficial discourse about 'opt-out Denmark'.

Notes

1 The author would like to thank Hans Lödén and fellow editor, Anders Wivel for their constructive comments on earlier drafts of this chapter.
2 According to White (2001: 39), under the banner of 'European Foreign Policy', then there are three component forms: *Community foreign policy* covers policy processes surrounding external action in the context of the competence of the Commission in trade and development operations with third parties and agriculture; *Union foreign policy* concerns the CFSP framework and its later configurations and of course *National foreign policy*. According to Wong and Hill (2011: 3), 'EU foreign policy', which is narrower in focus, is 'the sum and interaction of the "three strands" of Europe's "external relations system"' consisting of: (1) the national foreign policies of the member states; (2) EC external trade relations and development policy; and (3) the Common Foreign and Security Policy of the EU.
3 It is also important to acknowledge that the focus is very much on Danish EU policy behaviour and that change is not a unitary concept (see Hermann 1990). As Brun Pedersen (2012) has demonstrated, Danish foreign policy activism towards NATO should be seen as representing 'differences of degree' (cf. Wivel 2005b), and although there may have been differing conditions attached to Danish participation in NATO at various points (see Doeser 2011; Mouritzen and Olesen 2010), Denmark has remained a loyal NATO member, which has also had implications for elite and public attitudes towards European integration and an EU defence identity.
4 Welch's (2005: 45–46) 'Loss-aversion theory of foreign policy change' is based on three propositions, namely: (1) there is broadly, greater policy stability in states that are more highly bureaucratized, and on this basis foreign policy change should be less frequent in highly bureaucratic states with democratic regimes (i.e. Denmark); (2) that any decision to undertake significant policy change implies a recognition that existing policy is somehow flawed and that certain premises of existing policy are wrong. On this basis, foreign policy change 'requires policy-makers to admit error, take responsibility or embrace risk', and this is usually shunned if at all possible in normal circumstances. Hence, all other things being equal, foreign policy change will be most likely when policy fails either repeatedly or catastrophically or when leaders become convinced that it will imminently do so; and (3) people are more sensitive to losses than they are to equivalent gains, and thus they will shun risks in the domain of gains, and that they will accept risks to avoid losses. On this basis, leaders are more likely to pay the inherent costs of (and embrace the inherent risks in) foreign policy change to avoid losses than to realize gains of equivalent magnitude. Equally, only prospects of disproportionate gain are likely to motivate foreign policy change.

5 A further avenue of research using these 'loss aversion' approaches could be, for example, Denmark's Arctic policy, where there are often obvious demonstrations of Danish national self-interest in pursuing claims of territory, waters and other resources and rights, and where there will be differing Danish priorities towards the execution of Danish policy preferences inside or outside EU frameworks and via a once-Danish inspired 'EU Arctic window'.

16 A smart state handling a differentiated integration dilemma?
Concluding on Denmark in the European Union

Lee Miles and Anders Wivel

Denmark has traditionally been portrayed as an outlier when it comes to European integration (see Larsen 2011: 93). Depicted as an 'anxious' or 'reluctant' European (Miljan 1977) and a member of the 'other', i.e. Nordic, European Community (Turner and Nordquist 1982), this respective view has been commonplace both at the elite and at the public level within Denmark and among discussions within other states on Denmark (see Branner and Kelstrup 2000; Hansen 2002; Kelstrup, Martinsen and Wind 2012: 415–444).[1] Yet, this volume tells a slightly different and more complex story of Denmark and the European Union, and seeks to present a more nuanced appreciation of Denmark in the European Union. At the governmental level, Denmark's official political commitment to the European integration process has varied over the years (cf. Larsen 2005), but pragmatism and selective engagement have – with few exceptions – been permanent features of Denmark's approach to European integration since 1973. At the same time, playing the game of differentiated integration in a Union characterized by increasing political, economic and cultural diversity, and functional, spatial and temporal dimensions (see Dyson and Sepos 2010b), Denmark has accepted Europeanization (see Graziano and Vink 2007) as a fundamental condition for policy-making, even in policy areas affected by the Danish opt-outs (see Miles 2010a; Pedersen 2000; Larsen 2011). As Larsen argues (2005: 203), almost all areas of Danish policy have some sort of EU dimension. The country could be regarded as 'a committed member – with opt-outs!' (Larsen 2011: 93).

As illustrated by several contributions to this volume, Europeanization and differentiation do not preclude pragmatism, and the development of a more diverse European Union has, to some extent, normalized and ameliorated the effects of selective engagement (cf. Diedrichs *et al.* 2011). In effect, while preserving its pragmatic approach to the European integration process, and in order to maintain semblances of domestic consensus (see Pedersen 2000: 232), Denmark has increasingly pursued a dualist strategy in the EU: preserving, at least officially, the (formal) reservations granted by the Edinburgh Agreement and staunchly defending an intergovernmentalist position in regard to EU's

Concluding on Denmark in the European Union 229

institutional development, while, at the same time, allowing for intensified cooperation in some policy areas and actively participating (both formally and informally) in day-to-day negotiations and workings of the Union based on a permissive understanding of the opt-outs. In this respect, Denmark shows similarities with certain other Nordic states in often managing the twin pressures of Euro-scepticism and adaptation (Laursen 2010).

This chapter explores the dualism of the Danish approach to Europe in three steps. First, using the chapters of this volume as a springboard, it assesses how Danish dualism is played out in different policy areas and through different institutional settings in the EU; and it identifies three defining characteristics of the dualistic Danish approach to Europe. Second, these characteristics are compared to the findings of the current literature on small states in the EU, focusing in particular on the so-called 'smart-state' approach. Finally, the chapter concludes with reflections on the Danish experience and outlines the prospects pertaining to future Danish EU engagement.

Defining Danish dualism

Small states seek to further their interests by trying to preserve as much autonomy as possible, while influencing the actions of the great powers upon which their security and survival ultimately depend. They seek to expand their influence over the great powers mainly through international organizations, but this participation typically reduces their own political autonomy (Goetschel 1998: 17). The European Union presents small states with a particularly intense version of this autonomy/influence dilemma, because European integration entails cooperation across a very broad spectrum of policy areas, challenges autonomy more fundamentally by use of supranational decision-making and increases the costs of opting-out by being an ever-more inclusive monopoly provider of political integration in Europe (cf. Kelstrup 1993; Petersen 1998; Wivel 2005a). At the same time, differentiated integration helps to ameliorate this 'integration dilemma' by allowing for multiple positions along a continuum of integration, thereby normalizing a position of less than full integration. The success of a small state in uploading into (and in impacting upon) the EU, and in managing these simultaneous pressures of EU downloading, are largely dependent upon the intelligence and effectiveness of national political elites in addressing these two aspects of autonomy and influence (Miles 2002: 95), and, in particular, on devising strategies that effectively prioritize national, political and administrative resources to take advantage of the decentralized institutional landscape of the EU (Wivel 2005a, 2010).[2] Thus, whereas the elites of some small member states choose to stress more fully the benefits of participating fully in all aspects of the integration project, contributing actively towards its developments and thereby maximizing influence, those of other small member states highlight the value of continual safeguarding of selected political bastions (monetary policy, migration policy and defence policy in the case of Denmark); thereby preserving a greater degree of autonomy, yet foregoing the chance of influencing affairs in certain policy areas (cf. Mouritzen and Wivel 2005; Wallace 1999).

This volume has illustrated that whereas the tension between autonomy and influence continues to play an important role in Denmark's relations with the European Union, formal institutional affiliations tell only part of the story on how Denmark has handled this challenge. On the one hand, since 1973, all Danish governments have formulated their general approach to Europe in the context of the integration dilemma. As argued by Kelstrup in Chapter 2, this general approach has developed through five phases: selective and reluctant engagement from 1973–1986; a more positive attitude from 1986–1992, seeing the EU as a necessary part of Denmark's strategy for preserving the Scandinavian welfare state in a globalizing international order; a short phase of shock and adjustment in 1992–1993 following the rejection of the Treaty on the European Union by the Danish electorate and resulting in the Edinburgh Agreement with four Danish opt-outs from the original treaty; a return to a more selective engagement from 1993–2001, but with an acceptance among a majority in the political elite and the electorate that pragmatism now included acceptance of increased majority voting and intensification of European integration in some areas even if they touched on symbols of national autonomy (such as the Schengen Agreements); and, finally, from 2001, the Danish approach to Europe has been a low priority for government and has been dominated by considerations of domestic politics combining the acceptance of the EU opt-outs with the acceptance of differentiated integration (cf. Chapter 2). This pragmatic approach, reflecting the continuing importance of the integration dilemma between influence and autonomy, was continued even after the change of government in 2011. Thus, the Danish EU Presidency in 2012 was focused on effective and low-cost problem solving, rather than on visions about Europe's future. In effect, all five phases represent variations upon a theme: the pragmatic balancing between the preservation of national autonomy and maximizing influence through institutional engagement. At the same time, Denmark's approach to Europe through all five phases is best characterized as reactive: Denmark followed Britain into the European Union in 1973 and changes in the Danish position were primarily due to external developments such as the Single European Act and the Treaty of the European Union.

This duality is reflected in Danish behaviour in central EU institutions. When Denmark has uploaded preferences in the Council, these have typically defended the institutional status quo against developments further challenging national autonomy. As noted by Brun Pedersen in Chapter 7, Danish Council policy has combined 'foot-dragging' and the formal defence of political bastions against further institutional integration with active participation in the informal everyday politics of the Council and attempts to exploit the existing institutional framework of the Council, e.g. by being actively involved in the everyday negotiations of COREPER and the working groups. Despite the Commission's reputation as the protector of small-state interests (Bunse *et al.* 2005; Geurts 1998), Denmark has traditionally had a rather reluctant attitude towards the Commission, because as a supranational EU institution, it has been a symbol of the potential threat to Danish autonomy resulting from participation in the integration process. Therefore, as Grøn argues in Chapter 8, Danish actors have traditionally attempted to avoid interacting with the Commission and even aimed at delimiting its role. Thus, Danish actors have typically seen a need to shelter against Commission downloading and have used formal channels of influence as an emergency break.

However, at the same time, Danish civil servants have actively pursued informal strategies, often using technical arguments, in order to upload Danish interests to the European level. The European Parliament possibly has an even worse reputation in Denmark than the Commission, with numerous press reports painting a picture of incompetence and excessive use of taxpayers' money. This view of the Parliament is, to some extent, reflected in recruitment patterns and lack of interest in the Parliament by the political elite. Still, Rasmussen finds that official Danish institutions cooperate with MEPs, mostly informally and on an ad hoc basis, in uploading Danish interests and ideas to the European level in order to preserve Danish autonomy and influence. Concurrent with these efforts, the work of the members of the European Parliament (MEPs) is relatively well coordinated with that of the national government and parliament, compared to many EU member states. This makes sense as the chapter shows that Danish MEPs continue to differ from their colleagues from other member states on key issues, and sometimes promote political agendas that are more compatible with Danish domestic society than that of their respective party political parliamentary groups.

The duality of the Danish approach is reflected in Danish behaviour in some of the most central policy areas affected by Danish EU membership, such as the internal market and agricultural policy as well as justice and home affairs, EMU and defence policy; i.e. the three policy areas on which Denmark has obtained an opt-out.

Regarding the CAP and the Internal Market, these policy areas continue to play an important role in Danish EU policy, but, as shown by Nedergaard in Chapter 3, in a different way now than previously. When Denmark first joined the EU, the CAP was used as a major selling point, because of its importance for Danish agriculture and the importance of Danish agriculture for the Danish economy. In addition, a significant part of the Danish electorate had emotional ties to agriculture, as their families had left the countryside only a generation or two earlier. Today, the combination of CAP reforms, the dwindling importance of Danish agriculture to the Danish economy, and a more diverse array of interest groups concerned with the production and distribution of agricultural products in Denmark (including environmental groups undermining the dominance of agricultural interests) has resulted in a normalization of the Danish approach to EU agricultural policy. Likewise, whereas Internal Market Policy in the 1980s became an ideological battleground on the grand design of the European Union, Nedergaard shows how former idealistic arguments for and against have now been replaced by real pragmatism. Like agricultural policy, Internal Market Policy has become normalized. Indeed, these observations also confirm the views of Miles (2011b) that there are now notable instances of Danish participation in the EU where Danish policy-makers are extensively 'fused' into the EU policy-making system, with Internal Market Policy representing an example of 'clustered fusion', where national adaptation is extensive and where Danish preferences are fully immersed into EU Internal Market Policy.

Yet, do the opt-outs prevent normalization of politics in an EU context? On the face of it, it seems that they do. The Danish opt-outs define the baseline for Danish policy options in each of the affected policy areas and are the starting point for any formal political statement regarding Denmark's position on the EU's policy on EMU, JHA and defence. However, Marcussen (in Chapter 4 on the EMU), Adler-Nissen (in Chapter 5 on justice and home affairs), and Wivel (in Chapter 6 on defence policy) point to the dual nature of elite-level administration of the Danish reservations. On the one hand, for political and administrative decision-makers, the opt-outs constitute a legal as well as a political binding that restricts the Danish action space. On the other hand, the political and administrative elites share a permissive understanding of the restrictions imposed by the opt-outs, allowing them to participate in informal EU discussions on most issues related to the cases directly affected by the opt-outs. Certainly, the findings in this book also confirm the view of Larsen (2011: 109) that Denmark can be characterized as a 'committed participant in EU foreign policy'.

Formally, the opt-outs define the legitimate space for Danish participation in the affected policy areas. In that sense, they transport policy options at the Union level to Danish policy choices like a light tube transporting the light to its designated location. However, when looking at the administration of the opt-outs, another analogy conveys what is going on more accurately. Rather than a light tube, the opt-outs affect policies like a prism reflects the light. It bends in all kinds of different – and sometimes unexpected – ways. Due to the opt-outs, formal politics are stuck in the exceptional and somewhat crude distinction between autonomy and influence, and structural change is only possible in the event of a referendum that allows for an abolishment. However, as Miles illustrates in Chapter 15, day-to-day politics have been normalized, and the challenges of conducting informal and formal Danish policy within the formal confines of the opt-outs have not proved that 'painful' for Danish policy-makers. Denmark informally uploads preferences to the European level and may influence policy changes.

Implementation has been normalized as well. In Chapter 13, Martinsen shows how administrative autonomy varies across policy areas and stages in the policy cycle. As in domestic politics, it is highly dependent on the engagement of the national legislature and societal actors. However, as argued by Wind in Chapter 11, domestic politics may occasionally push Denmark's approach to Europe back to exceptionalism, as has been the case in citizenship and migration issues. Also, Danish EU coordination remains organized after the same centralized intergovernmentalist model as it has been since 1973, with the European Affairs Committee of the Danish parliament and the Foreign Ministry continuing to play central roles. Again, however, dualism seems to be at play. As argued by Nedergaard in

Chapter 14, the centralized EU negotiation system has provided Denmark with legitimate political and administrative procedures for participating in an ongoing federalizing process of the European Union. Thus, rather than creating tension between influence and autonomy, these procedures have allowed Denmark to maximize influence by maximizing autonomy. As shown by Schuck and de Vreese in Chapter 12, the co-existence – even mutual reinforcement – of autonomy and influence fits with Danish public opinion on EU membership, with support for membership and assessment of EU membership as beneficial for Denmark being well above the EU average. At the same time, Danes trust their national institutions more than EU institutions and continue their resistance to selected aspects of the integration process. Concurrent with the findings of the volume in general, Schuck and de Vreese suggest that EU attitudes and domestic considerations should not be viewed as competing alternatives for the explanation of voting behaviour in EU referenda.

In sum, the contributions to this volume point to four defining characteristics of the dualist Danish approach to European integration. First, the Danish approach is essentially pragmatic. Danish policy-makers have seized opportunities to maximize influence when they have occurred even in policy areas formally restricted by the opt-outs, which they have interpreted in a permissive way allowing them to participate in the everyday deliberations of European Union politics as long as policy was not directly affected by the Edinburgh Agreement. Furthermore, as Marcussen in Chapter 3, and Adler-Nissen in Chapter 4, demonstrate, Danish policy-makers have at times been rather creative in exercising such permissiveness and in enabling, in a pragmatic way, Danish participation even in policy fields where the opt-outs could be deemed operational. Second, this pragmatic pursuance of influence has been by way of depoliticizing issues related to the European Union, thereby allowing for a gradual normalization of most policy areas. Perhaps most remarkably, the opt-out areas, which were highly politicized as a consequence of the Maastricht referendum and the ensuing public debates over the future of Europe and Denmark's place in it, have been managed in a permissive way that has only rarely attracted political attention. As Miles illustrates in Chapter 15, any pain accruing from managing the opt-outs has become rather bearable for Danish policy-makers. In addition, institutional issues, that have traditionally played an important role in the EU policies of Denmark and other small states, have been depoliticized as well. Thus, Danish policy-makers agreed to qualified majority voting in the Council, increased influence for the European Parliament and the undermining of the importance of the rotating Council Presidencies (a traditional showcase for small states) without much public attention or debate. Indeed, this is all the more surprising given that Danish policy-makers had been rather adept at utilizing Council presidencies to enhance the image of Denmark in the past and did 'lead from the periphery' (Miles 2003c). Danish policy-makers have only (and rarely) been stuck in the integration dilemma and forced to choose between autonomy and integration, when domestic politics have not allowed for depoliticizing. Citizenship and border policies were important exceptions to pragmatic normalization of the

Danish approach to the EU because they were so closely related to migration, which played a major divisive role in Danish politics throughout the 1990s and 2000s.

Pragmatic depoliticizing of most policy areas allowed for an incremental Danish approach to European integration, a third characteristic of Danish dualism. Thus, whereas official Danish EU policy has undergone little change since the early 1990s with – on the one hand – policy-makers ritually repeating their respect for the outcome of previous referenda and therefore the opt-outs, and – on the other hand – voicing their concern that these bindings reduce Danish influence, the same policy-makers have actually pursued an influence maximizing strategy in day-to-day politics. For instance, as noted by Brun Pedersen in Chapter 7, constitutional bargaining and successive rounds of EU enlargements have gradually eroded Danish Council 'bastions'. Danish policy-makers have pragmatically adapted to integration dynamics in order to manage the dilemma of integration and to avoid marginalization of Denmark. Finally, Denmark's approach to Europe is reactive, a fourth characteristic of Danish dualism. The opt-outs lead to a natural focus on defending autonomy, which logically leads to a reactive position vis-à-vis new developments in the EU. Even outside opt-out areas, Denmark has rarely acted as a pace-setter and when it has – i.e. leading the way in post-Cold War defence and security reforms as pointed out by Wivel in Chapter 6, or pursuing private sector interests as shown by Ronit in Chapter 10 – pace-setting has been a question of pursuing Danish interests in a globalized world order rather than agenda-setting in the EU.

Learning from the Danish experience: from small state policy to smart state strategy?

Danish dualism is pragmatic, depoliticized, incremental and reactive. In that way, Danish EU policy resembles the behavioural characteristics often seen as typical for small states in international relations: a tendency to pragmatically adapt to their external environment, and to seek influence through membership of international institutions in order to cushion the effects of international anarchy (Amstrup 1976: 178; Antola and Lehtimäki 2001: 13–20; Archer and Nugent 2002: 2–5; Christmas-Møller 1983: 40; Hey 2003: 2–10; Knudsen 2002: 182–185; Panke 2010c: 15; Steinmetz and Wivel 2010: 4–7). At the same time, this volume documents the success of Danish dualism, which can be partly seen as both a reflection of the 'smart strategies' of Danish policy-makers and of the effectiveness with which Danish elites are now immersed or possibly 'fused', on a selective and differentiated basis, into the EU system (Miles 2011b). The protection of bastions of national autonomy and active participation in order to maximize influence is conducted in parallel, and points to a differentiation and potential amelioration of the integration dilemma.

In day-to-day EU politics, there is rarely a clear-cut choice between autonomy and influence. Rather it is well documented in parts of the EU literature that, while the two may intuitively be seen as conflicting goals, they can be used by national policy-makers to reinforce each other. Thus, Andrew Moravcsik, shows how the public identification of national 'win-sets' may be used strategically as a bargaining tool at the supranational level, which can be used to influence the composition of the overall agreement (Moravcsik 1998: 60–67; cf. Putnam 1988). However, we would expect the strategic use of win-sets to be a significantly stronger tool for big EU member states than for small EU member states: small states can only rarely threaten to block the agreement, because blockage would lead to stronger repercussions for the small state than for the EU (cf. Moravcsik 1993). Hence, small states only rarely use their veto power (Thorhallsson and Wivel 2006). For this reason, small states choose a slightly different strategy. Rather than identifying win-sets that may be used to influence the overall composition of an agreement at the EU level, they define political bastions denoting selected issues, where their national interests or domestic preferences are particularly intense (Mouritzen 1997; Mouritzen and Wivel 2005). Bastions serve a double purpose for small member states: they signal to the domestic audience that the political elite is willing to defend core values against supranational infringements, and they signal to the other member states, and politicians and civil servants, operating at the EU level what is negotiable and what is not. From this starting point, bastions of autonomy may be used to define the baseline for negotiating influence at the supranational level and for getting the domestic legitimacy to do so.

From that perspective, Danish EU policy may fit the stereotype of pragmatic, depoliticized, incremental and reactive small state behaviour, but at the same time this may be seen as a viable road to maximising influence in the EU. A recent wave of literature on how small states maximize influence in the EU focuses on so-called smart state strategies (cf. Arter 2000; Joenniemi 1998; Wivel 2005a, 2010; Grøn and Wivel 2011). A smart state strategy has three fundamental characteristics. First, goals and means must be highly focused and sharply ordered in accordance with preferences. Small states do not have sufficient resources to pursue a broad political agenda with many different goals. They must therefore focus their resources and signal their willingness to negotiate and compromise on issues that are not deemed to be of vital importance. Second, small states must present their initiatives as being in the interest of the Union as a whole, i.e. a common interest. Thus, political initiatives, at least at the formal level, from small EU member states should avoid conflict with existing EU initiatives or political proposals from any of the big EU member states. Ideally, they should be presented as specific contributions to a general development as opposed to a change of policy or attempt to slow it down. Finally, small states launching policy initiatives should seek to mediate between the different great power interests in order to achieve consensus. This will allow the small state agenda-setting powers not otherwise at their disposal.[3] Smart state strategies are most often seen as activist and high-profile (such as the Finnish Northern Dimension-initiative or the role played by Denmark and Sweden in EU enlargement with Central and Eastern European countries), but if being smart is essentially about maximizing influence in accordance with the three defining characteristics of the smart state strategy, then low-profile and reactive – or even inactive – strategies may be just as valuable depending on the conditions for policy-making. Thus, foot-dragging or fence-sitting policies (on some policy issues) may be seen as signalling bastions, and not as dissatisfaction with the entire integration process.[4] In this way, a delicate mix of pace-setting, fence-sitting and foot-dragging by Danish policy-makers can be understood as a logical response to the demands of differentiated integration, which has become the norm for the evolution of the EU (Miles 2010a). It might be wise, then, to also think about small state strategies as including an integral blend of differentiation, with differentiated degrees of reactivity and proactivity on the part of policy-makers, in which they may pursue both formal and formal strategies as part of representing a smart small state.

The recent literature on small EU member states suggests that these states tend to rely on soft bargaining strategies (Dür and Mateo 2010; Steinmetz and Wivel 2010; Thorhallsson and Wivel 2006), but it tells us little about the particular content of these strategies. However, drawing on Grøn and Wivel's recent theoretical discussion of smart state strategies in the EU, and looking at the findings of the present volume from a smart state perspective, Danish EU policy may be seen as an example of a small member state acting as a lobbyist (Grøn and Wivel 2011), pursuing an ever more complicated mix of formal and informal channels of access and communication in a fusing EU (see Miles 2011a, 2011b), in order to compensate for the weakening of traditional channels of small state influence. Just as corporate actors can utilize their expert knowledge, so can states, and just as some interest group lobbyists work from a well-defined political brief, so do politicians and civil servants from a state with well-defined political bastions (Grøn and Wivel 2011). States may utilize their knowledge of a specific issue area or domestic interest group and public opinion, typically working to influence the Commission, the Parliament and COREPER working groups. When pursuing a lobby strategy, domestic administrative competencies are particularly important, i.e. the prioritization of EU work by lead ministries, effective cooperation between the small states' Permanent Representation and the lead ministries, and procedures for solving conflicts between ministries (Panke 2010c). Also, experience with new policy areas (e.g. climate policy) and technical expertise have proved highly valuable administrative competences when pursuing a lobby strategy in the Danish case. This potent mix of Danish experiences help us to at least partly understand why Danish policy-makers have yet to go the extra mile and achieve the removal of the opt-outs over the last decade, since Danish informal and formal lobby strategies have been able to use them to reduce any 'pain' (see Chapter 15) accruing from Denmark's asymmetrical status in the EU.

Differentiating the integration dilemma

Playing the game of differentiated integration in a Union characterized by increasing political, economic and cultural diversity, the Danish political elite have been involved in a careful pursuit of Danish influence within the still relatively elite circles of EU decision-making, that sometimes seems to be beyond the confines of the official parameters of the domestic-orientated Danish opt-outs. The starting point for this policy has been formal and public identification of political bastions in the form of the Danish opt-outs on justice and home affairs, monetary policy and defence and the national Danish EU coordination process, including the Danish parliament and several sector ministries under the political coordination of the government and the administrative coordination of the Foreign Ministry.

This policy points to a necessary differentiation of the integration dilemma. The classical integration dilemma literature points to a fundamental trade-off between autonomy and influence (e.g. Kelstrup 1993, 2000a; Pedersen 1998; cf. Goetschel 1998). We find this trade-off in its purest form when a state is about to enter the EU: national autonomy is traded for influence on EU politics through membership. However, the trade-off is complex and not easily unpacked. Above all, the pressures of the integration dilemma become increasingly more nuanced and differentiated, and are demonstrated in ever more complex strategies, and mixes of complex strategies, as a state adapts over time to EU membership, becomes ever-more fused into the EU system, and is confronted by the demands of differentiated integration as a normal part of EU development (Miles 2010b, 2011a, 2011b). For instance, an outsider with strong economic and political ties to the EU will be dependent on EU policies even though it is excluded from those policies by institutional membership. Conversely, most EU insiders have defined political bastions protecting autonomy, while still pursuing influence inside an increasingly differentiated EU.

Denmark is a notable case of this potent combination, whereby policy-makers identify political bastions of autonomy and simultaneously pursue selective supra-nationalism. This volume shows that a differentiated EU leaves a surprisingly large action space for a member state like Denmark, where managing the pressures of any integration dilemma and participating in a fusing (yet also differentiated) integration process, may not be that incompatible in practice. Thus, even though the Danish opt-outs are typically seen as defining a narrow action space for Danish EU policy-making and influence (e.g. Dansk Institut for Internationale Studier 2008), one important finding of this volume is that the formal restrictions are less damaging when pursuing influence than the literature has suggested so far, and that the identification of political bastions may even be used in an effort to maximize influence. A second important finding is that EU policy-making takes place in a context of global and domestic politics and that the integration dilemma can rarely be seen in isolation from these contexts. A third important finding, following from these two, is that what is important for policy outcomes is not the existence of an integration dilemma as such, but rather the differentiation of dilemmas across different policy areas, embedded within different institutional settings and played out at different levels of decision-making. To be sure, this does not point to the obsolescence of the integration dilemma, but it does leave us with an altogether more optimistic scenario for combining autonomy with influence within the realms of EU politics.

Notes

1 For instance, Kelstrup, Martinsen and Wind find that Danish European policy may be understood as a continuation of Denmark's traditional defensive small state posture and that this is surprising given the activist turn in Danish foreign policy in general and the the institutional environment in the EU, which provides fertile ground for small state acitivism (Kelstrup *et al.* 2012: 425–426; cf. Petersen 2006). See also, Kelstrup's discussion of the historical development of Denmark's policy in the EU and Wind's discussion of the (non-)implementation of the citizen directive in Denmark in this volume.
2 See also the discussions of the opportunities and challenges of small states in the EU in Steinmetz and Wivel (2010) and Thorhallsson and Wivel (2006).
3 For elaborations and discussions of these three defining criteria, see Grøn and Wivel (2011) and Wivel (2010).
4 The evidence on Danish public opinion provided by Schuck and Vreese in Chapter 12 suggests that this may be true in the Danish case. The Danish electorate finds that Danish EU membership is highly useful, but that bastions must be defended and that Danish political institutions are vital in doing so.

Appendix A

The results of the Danish Parliamentary Elections 1971–2011

APPENDIX A

	SDP	SLP	CP	CD	STP	SPP	DCP	DPP	CS	CDP	LP	LS	PP	UL	LA	Others	Participation
1971	37.3% (70)	14.4% (27)	16.7% (31)	–	1.7% (0)	9.1% (17)	1.4% (0)	–	–	1.9% (0)	15.6% (30)	1.6% (0)	–	–	–	0.3% (0)	87.2%
1973	25.6% (46)	11.2% (20)	9.2% (16)	7.8% (14)	2.9% (5)	6.0% (11)	3.6% (6)	–	–	4.0% (7)	12.3% (22)	1.5% (0)	15.9% (28)	–	–	0.0% (0)	88.7%
1975	29.9% (53)	7.1% (13)	5.5% (10)	2.2% (4)	1.8% (0)	5.0% (9)	4.2% (7)	–	–	5.3% (9)	23.3% (42)	2.1% (0)	13.6% (24)	–	–	0.0% (0)	88.2%
1977	37.0% (65)	3.6% (6)	8.5% (15)	6.4% (11)	3.3% (6)	3.9% (7)	3.7% (7)	–	–	3.4% (6)	12.0% (21)	2.7% (5)	14.6% (26)	–	–	0.9% (0)	88.7%
1979	38.3% (68)	5.4% (10)	12.5% (22)	3.2% (6)	2.6% (5)	5.9% (11)	1.9% (0)	–	–	2.6% (5)	12.5% (22)	3.7% (6)	11.0% (20)	–	–	0.4% (0)	85.6%
1981	32.9% (59)	5.1% (9)	14.5% (26)	8.3% (15)	1.4% (0)	11.3% (21)	1.1% (0)	–	–	2.3% (4)	11.3% (20)	2.7% (5)	8.9% (16)	–	–	0.2% (0)	83.2%
1984	31.6% (56)	5.5% (10)	23.4% (42)	4.6% (8)	1.5% (0)	11.5% (21)	0.7% (0)	–	–	2.7% (5)	12.1% (22)	2.7% (5)	3.6% (6)	–	–	0.1% (0)	88.4%
1987	29.3% (54)	6.2% (11)	20.8% (38)	4.8% (9)	0.5% (0)	14.6% (27)	0.9% (0)	–	2.2% (4)	2.4% (4)	10.5% (19)	1.4% (0)	4.8% (9)	–	–	1.7% (0)	86.7%
1988	29.8% (55)	5.6% (10)	19.3% (35)	4.7% (9)	–	13.0% (24)	0.8% (0)	–	1.9% (0)	2.0% (4)	11.8% (22)	0.6% (0)	9.0% (16)	–	–	1.5% (0)	85.7%
1990	37.4% (69)	3.5% (7)	16.0% (30)	5.1% (9)	0.5% (0)	8.3% (15)	–	–	1.8% (0)	2.3% (4)	15.8% (29)	–	6.4% (12)	1.7% (0)	–	0.9% (0)	82.8%
1994	34.6% (62)	4.6% (8)	15.0% (27)	2.8% (5)	–	7.3% (13)	–	–	–	1.9% (0)	23.3% (42)	–	6.4% (11)	3.1% (6)	–	1.0% (1)	84.3%
1998	35.9% (63)	3.9% (7)	8.9% (16)	4.3% (8)	–	7.6% (13)	–	7.4% (13)	–	2.5% (4)	24.0% (42)	–	2.4% (4)	2.7% (5)	–	0.4% (1)	86.0%
2001	29.1% (52)	5.2% (9)	9.1% (16)	1.8% (0)	–	6.4% (12)	–	12.0% (22)	–	2.3% (4)	31.2% (56)	–	0.6% (0)	2.4% (4)	–	0.0% (0)	87.1%
2005	25.8% (47)	9.2% (17)	10.3% (18)	1.0% (0)	–	6.0% (11)	–	13.3% (24)	–	1.7% (0)	29.0% (52)	–	–	3.4% (6)	–	0.4% (0)	84.5%
2007	25.5% (45)	5.1% (9)	10.4% (18)	–	–	13% (23)	–	13.9% (25)	–	0.9% (0)	26.2% (46)	–	–	2.2% (4)	2.8% (5)	0.0% (0)	86.6%
2011	24.8% (44)	9.5% (17)	4.9% (8)	–	–	9.2% (16)	–	12.3% (22)	–	0.8% (0)	26.7% (47)	–	–	6.7% (12)	5.0% (9)	0.1% (0)	87.7%

Sources: Folketinget (2012) *Folketingsvalgene 1953–2011*. available HTTP: www.ft.dk/Folketinget/Oplysningen/Valg/~/media/Pdf_materiale/Pdf_download_direkte/Folketingets%20Oplysning/Folketingsvalgene%20 1953–2011.pdf.ashx (accessed 26 October 2012).

Notes

The figures in parentheses are the number of seats. The abbreviations for the parties used in the table are as follows: SDP – the Social Democratic Party; SLP – the Social Liberal Party; CP – the Conservative Party; CD – the Centre Democrats; STP – the Single-Tax Party; SPP – the Socialist People's Party; DCP – the Danish Communist Party; DPP – the Danish People's Party; CC – Common Stance; CDP – the Christian Democratic Party; LP – the Liberal Party; LS – the Leftist Socialists; PP – Progress Party; UL – the Unity List – Red-Green Alliance; LA – Liberal Alliance. The dates of the Danish elections: 21 September 1971; 4 December 1973; 9 January 1975; 15 February 1977; 23 October 1979; 8 December 1981; 10 January 1984; 8 September 1987; 10 May 1988; 12 December 1990; 21 September 1994; 11 March 1998; 22 November 2001; 8 February 2005; 13 November 2007; 16 September 2011. The threshold in Denmark is 2.0 per cent.

Appendix B

The composition of Danish governments 1971–2011

APPENDIX B

Government/Prime Minister	Period	Composition
Jens Otto Krag III	11 October 1971–5 October 1972	The Social Democratic Party
Anker Jørgensen I	5 October 1972–19 December 1973	The Social Democratic Party
Poul Hartling	19 December 1973–13 February 1975	The Liberal Party
Anker Jørgensen II	13 February 1975–30 August 1978	The Social Democratic Party
Anker Jørgensen III	30 August 1978–26 October 1979	The Social Democratic Party and The Liberal Party
Anker Jørgensen IV	26 October 1979–30 December 1981	The Social Democratic Party
Anker Jørgensen V	30 December 1981–10 September 1982	The Social Democratic Party
Poul Schlüter I	10 September 1982–10 September 1987	The Conservative Party, the Liberal Party Centre Democrats, the Christian Democratic Party
Poul Schlüter II	10 September 1987–3 June 1988	The Conservative Party, the Liberal Party Centre Democrats, the Christian Democratic Party
Poul Schlüter III	3 June 1988–18 December 1990	The Conservative Party, the Liberal Party, the Social Liberal Party
Poul Schlüter IV	18 December 1990–25 January 1993	The Conservative Party and the Liberal Party
Poul Nyrup Rasmussen I	25 January 1993–27 September 1994	The Social Democratic Party, the Centre Democrats, the Social Liberal Party, the Christian Democratic Party
Poul Nyrup Rasmussen II	27 September 1994–30 December 1996	The Social Democratic Party, the Centre Democrats and the Social Liberal Party
Poul Nyrup Rasmussen III	30 December 1996–23 March 1998	The Social Democratic Party and the Social Liberal Party
Poul Nyrup Rasmussen IV	23 March 1998–27 November 2011	The Social Democratic Party and the Social Liberal Party
Anders Fogh Rasmussen I	27 November 2011–18 February 2005	The Liberal Party and the Conservative Party
Anders Fogh Rasmussen II	18 February 2005–23 November 2007	The Liberal Party and the Conservative Party
Anders Fogh Rasmussen III	23 November 2011–5 April 2009	The Liberal Party and the Conservative Party
Lars Løkke Rasmussen	5 April 2009–3 October 2011	The Liberal Party and the Conservative Party
Helle Thorning-Schmidt	3 October 2011–	The Social Democratic Party, the Social Liberal Party and the Socialist People's Party

Source: Folketinget (2012) *Regeringer 1953–2011*, available at: www.ft.dk/Dokumenter/Publikationer/Tal%20og%20Fakta/Regeringer.aspx (accessed 26 October 2012).

Bibliography

Adler-Nissen, R. (2008) 'Organized duplicity? When states opt out of the European Union', in R. Adler-Nissen and T. Gammeltoft-Hansen (eds) *Sovereignty Games: Instrumentalizing State Sovereignty in Europe and beyond*, New York: Macmillan.
Adler-Nissen, R. (2009a) *The Diplomacy of Opting Out: British and Danish Stigma Management in the EU*, PhD-thesis, Copenhagen: University of Copenhagen.
Adler-Nissen, R. (2009b) 'Behind the scenes of differentiated integration: circumventing national opt-outs in justice and home affairs', *Journal of European Public Policy*, 16(1): 62–80.
Adler-Nissen, R. (2009c) 'The European security and defence policy: from distant dream to joint action', in P. D. Thruelsen (ed.) *International Organisations: Their Role in Conflict Management*, Copenhagen: Royal Danish Defence College.
Adler-Nissen, R. (forthcoming) *Diplomacy, Sovereignty and European Integration: Opting Out of the European Union*, book manuscript under review.
Adler-Nissen, R. and Gammeltoft-Hansen, T. (2008) 'Retsforbeholdet: Et forbehold ude af kontrol?', *Økonomi & Politik*, 81(3): 35–43.
Adler-Nissen, R. and Gammeltoft-Hansen, T. (2010) 'Straitjacket or sovereignty shield?', in N. Hvidt and H. Mouritzen (eds) *Danish Foreign Policy Yearbook*, Copenhagen: Danish Institute for International Studies.
Agence Europe (17 November 1997) *Agence Europe*, published 17 November 1997.
Agence Europe (24 November 1997) *Agence Europe*, published 24 November 1997.
Agence Europe (10 December 1997) *Agence Europe*, published 10 December 1997.
Agence Europe (11 December 1997) *Agence Europe*, published 11 December 1997.
Agence Europe (12 December 1997) *Agence Europe*, published 12 December 1997.
Agence Europe (17 July 2000) *Agence Europe*, published 17 July 2000.
Agence Europe (10 September 2004) *Agence Europe*, published 10 September 2004.
Agence Europe (24 October 2008) *Agence Europe*, published 24 October 2008.
Alden, C. and Aran, A. (2012) *Foreign Policy Analysis: New Approaches*, London: Routledge.
Amstrup, N. (1976) 'The perennial problem of small states: a survey of research efforts', *Cooperation and Conflict*, 11(3): 163–182.
Andersen, J. G. (2002) 'Danskerne, Europa og det 'demokratiske underskud': Den 'stille revolution' i danskernes forhold til EU', in T. Pedersen (ed.) *Europa for Folket? EU og det danske Demokrati*, Aarhus: Aarhus University Press.
Andersen, J. G. (2011) 'Økonomiske kriser: Danmark fra økonomisk mirakel til økonomisk problembarn', in M. Marcussen and K. Ronit (eds) *Politik, forvaltning og kriser – de internationale udfordringer*, Copenhagen: Hans Reitzels Forlag.

Bibliography

Andersen, S. R. and Iversen, N. M. (2006) *Hvordan påvirker EU national politik? – Et studie af europæisering som resultat af implementering af arbejdsmarkeds- og miljøpolitiske direktiver i Danmark*, master-thesis, Copenhagen: University of Copenhagen.

Anderson, C. and Reichert, S. (1996) 'Economic benefits and support for membership in the EU: a cross-national analysis', *Journal of Public Politics*, 15(3): 231–249.

Anderson, P. and McLeod, A. (2004) 'The great non-communicator? The mass communication deficit of the European Parliament and its press directorate', *Journal of Common Market Studies*, 42(5): 897–917.

Antola, E. and Lehtimäki, M. (2001) 'Small states in the EU', unpublished, Jean Monnet Centre of Excellence – Turku University.

Archer, C. (2005) *Norway outside the European Union*, London: Routledge.

Archer, C. and Nugent, N. (2002) 'Introduction: small states and the European Union', *Current Politics and Economics of Europe*, 11(1): 1–10.

Arregui, J. and Thompson, R (2009) 'States' bargaining success in the European Union', *Journal of European Public Policy*, 16(5): 655–676.

Arter, D. (2000) 'Small state influence within the EU: the case of Finland's northern dimension initiative', *Journal of Common Market Studies*, 38(5): 677–697.

Attina, F. (1990) 'The voting behaviour of European Parliament Members and the problem of the Europarties', *European Journal of Political Research*, 18(4): 89–114.

Auken, M. (2008) 'Et Parlamentet for Verdensborgere!', in P. Nedergaard (ed.) *Fra Fælles Forsamling til Folkestyre*, Copenhagen: Europa-Parlamentets Informationskontor.

Bardach, E. (1977) *The Implementation Game: What Happens after a Bill Becomes a Law*, Cambridge: MIT Press.

Baron, R. and Kenny, D. (1986) 'The moderator–mediator variable distinction in social psychological research: conceptual, strategic, and statistical considerations', *Journal of Personality and Social Psychology*, 51: 1173–1182.

Beach, D. (2010) *Magten blandt medlemsstater i EU's lovgivningsproces*, available online at: http://magasineteuropa.dk/?p=1269 (accessed 18 March 2012).

Beach, D. (2012) *Analyzing Foreign Policy*, Houndmills: Palgrave Macmillan.

Beck Jorgensen, T. (2003) 'Forvaltningsinternationalisering i dag. En oversigt over former og udbredelse', in M. Marcussen, and K. Ronit (eds) *Internationalisering af den Offentlige Forvaltning i Danmark*, Aarhus: Aarhus University Press.

Benedetto, G. (2005) 'Rapporteurs as legislative entrepreneurs: the dynamics of the co-decision procedure in the European Parliament', *Journal of European Public Policy*, 12(1): 67–88.

Benz, A. (2004) 'Path-Dependent institutions and strategic veto players: national parliaments in the European Union', *West European Politics*, 27(5): 875–900.

Bergman, T. (1997) 'National parliaments and EU affairs committees: notes on empirical variation and competing explanations', *Journal of European Public Policy*, 4(3): 373–387.

Berlingske Tidende (2000a) 'LO: OMU-nej koster 35.000 job', published 11 April 2000.

Berlingske Tidende (2000b) 'Storbanker stotter Lykketoft', published 31 August 2000.

Berlingske Tidende (2002) 'Naturpleje: Ministerium skjulte viden', published 8 December 2002.

Berlingske Tidende (2006) 'Fogh imod EU's rejsecirkus', available online at: www.b.dk/danmark/fogh-imod-eus-rejsecirkus (accessed 21 March 2012).

Berlingske Tidende (2009a) 'Stotten til Euroen i frit fald', published 11 February 2009.

Berlingske Tidende (2009b) 'Kun få danskere mærker krisen', published 22 June 2009.

Bibliography 245

Berlingske Tidende (2011) 'Danskerne mere euroskeptiske', published 11 February 2011.
Blom-Hansen, J. and Grønnegård Christensen, J. (2003) *Den Europæiske Forbindelse*, Aarhus: Magtudredningen.
Bøegh-Lervang, M. and Madum, L. (2010) *'Dobbeltspil? – en analyse af europæiseringen af dansk familiesammenføringspolitik'*, master-thesis, Copenhagen: University of Copenhagen.
Bonde, Jens-Peter (1993) *Unionen efter Maastricht og Edinburgh*, Copenhagen: Notat og Regnbuegruppen.
Boomgaarden, H., Schuck, A. R. T., Elenbaas, M. and de Vreese, C. H. (2011) 'Mapping EU attitudes: conceptual and empirical dimensions of Euro-scepticism and EU support', *European Union Politics*, 12(2): 241–266.
Børsen (2009) *Løkke: afstemning inden næste valg*, published 13 May 2009.
Børsen (2011) *Løkke åbner for debat om euro-forbehold*, published 10 February 2011.
Börzel, T. A. (2000) 'Why there is no "southern problem": on environmental leaders and laggards in the European Union', *Journal of European Public Policy*, 7(1): 141–162.
Börzel, T. A. (2002) 'Pace-setting, foot-dragging and fence-sitting: member state responses to Europeanisation', *Journal of Common Market Studies*, 40(2): 193–214.
Börzel, T. A. and Risse, T. (2000) 'When Europe hits home: Europeanization and domestic change', *European Integration online Papers (EIoP)*, vol. 4.
Börzel, T. A., Hofmann, T., Panke, D. and Sprungk, C. (2010) 'Obstinate and inefficient: why member states do not comply with European Law', *Comparative Political Studies*, 43(11): 1363–1390.
Bouwen, P. (2004) 'Exchanging access goods for access: a comparative study of business lobbying in the European institutions', *European Journal of Political Research*, 43: 337–369.
Bowler, S. and Farrell, D. M. (1995) 'The organizing of the European Parliament: committees, specialization and co-ordination', *British Journal of Political Science*, 4(1): 124–142.
Bowler, S., Farrell, D. M. and Katz, R. S. (1999) *Party Discipline and Parliamentary Government*, Columbus: Ohio State University Press.
Branner, H. (2000) 'The Danish foreign policy tradition and the European context', in H. Branner and M. Kelstrup (eds) *Denmark's Policy Towards Europe After 1945: History, Theory and Options*, Odense: Odense University Press.
Branner, H. and Kelstrup, M. (eds) (2000) *Denmark's Policy Towards Europe After 1945: History, Theory and Options*, Odense: Odense University Press.
Brighi, E. (2005) *Foreign Policy and the International/Domestic Nexus: The Case of Italy*, unpublished thesis, London School of Economics.
Brighi, E. and Hill, C. (2008) 'Implementation and behaviour', in S. Smith, A. Hadfield and T. Dunne (eds) *Foreign Policy*, Oxford: Oxford University Press.
Browning, C. S. (2007) 'Branding Nordicity: models, identity and the decline of exceptionalism', *Cooperation and Conflict* 42(1): 27–51.
Brun Pedersen, R. (2012) 'Danish foreign policy activism: differences in kind or degree?' *Cooperation and Conflict*, 37(3): 331–349.
Brundtland, A. (1965) 'The Nordic balance: past and present', *Cooperation and Conflict* 1(1): 30–63.
Bulmer, S. (2007) 'Theorizing Europeanisation', in P. Graziano and M. P. Vink (eds) *Europeanisation: New Research Agendas*, Houndmills: Palgrave.
Bulmer, S. and Lequesne, C. (2005) *The Member States of The European Union*, Oxford: Oxford University Press.

Bunse, S., Magnette, P. and Nicolaïdis, K. (2005) *Is the Commission the Small Member States' Best Friend?*, Report 9/2005, Stockholm: SIEPS.

Bursens, P. (2002) 'Why Denmark and Belgium have different implementation records: on transposition laggards and leaders in the EU', *Scandinavian Political Studies*, 25(2): 173–195.

Carey, S. (2002) 'Undivided loyalties: is national identity an obstacle to european integration?', *European Union Politics*, 3(4): 387–413.

Carlsnaes, W. (2002) 'Foreign policy', in W. Carlsnaes, T. Risse, and B. A. Simmons (eds) *Handbook of International Relations*, London: Sage.

Christiansen, F. J. and Pedersen, R. B. (2011) 'Europeanization and coalition management in minority parliamentary systems', in M. Wiberg and T. Persson (eds) *Government in the Nordic Countries at a Crossroad*, Stockholm: Santérus Förlag.

Christiansen, T. M. and Togeby, L. (2006) 'Power and democracy in Denmark: still a viable democracy', *Scandinavian Political Studies*, 29(1): 1–24.

Christin, T. and Trechsel, A. (2002) 'Joining the EU? Explaining public opinion in Switzerland', *European Union Politics*, 3(4): 415–443.

Christmas-Møller, W. (1983) 'Some thoughts on the scientific applicability of the small state concept: a research history and a discussion', in O. Höll (ed.) *Small States in Europe and Dependence*, Vienna: Wilhelm Braumüller.

Cichowski, R. (2007) *The European Court and Civil Society: Litigation, Mobilization and Governance*, Cambridge: Cambridge University Press.

Cohen, B. J. and Subacchi, P. (2008) 'Is the euro ready for "prime time?"', in *Chatham House Briefing Paper (IEP BP 08/03)*, London: Chatham House.

Commission of the European Communities (1985) *White Paper on the Completion of the Internal Market (COM (85) 310)*, Brussels: Commission of the European Communities.

Commission of the European Communities (1986a) *Council Regulation of 22 December 1986 Applying the Principle of Freedom to Provide Services to Maritime Transport between Member States and Member States and Third Countries*, Brussels: Commission of the European Communities.

Commission of the European Communities (1986b) *Council Regulation of 22 December 1986 Laying Down Detailed Rules for the Application of Articles 85 and 86 of the Treaty to Maritime Transport*, Brussels: Commission of the European Communities.

Commission of the European Communities (1986c) *Council Regulation of 22 December 1986 on Unfair Pricing Practices in Maritime Transport*, Brussels: Commission of the European Communities.

Commission of the European Communities (1986d) *Council Regulation of 22 December 1986 Concerning Coordinated Action to Safeguard Free Access to Cargoes in Open Trade*, Brussels: Commission of the European Communities.

Conservatives (2010) *William Hague: Britain's Foreign Policy in a Networked World*, available online at: www.conservatives.com/News/Speeches/2010/07/William_Hague_Britains_Foreign_Policy_in_a_Networked_World.aspx (accessed 5 July 2010).

Coombes, D. (1970) *Politics and Bureaucracy in the European Community: A Portrait of the Commission of the E.E.C.*, London: George Allen and Unwin Ltd.

Corbett, R., Jacobs, F. and Shackleton, M. (2005) *The European Parliament*, 6th edition, London: John Harper.

Corbett, R., Jacobs, F. and Shackleton, M. (2007) *The European Parliament*, 7th edition, London: John Harper.

Costello, C. (2009) 'Metock: free movement and "normal family life" in the Union', *Common Market Law Review*, 46: 587–622.

Craig, P. and de Burca, G. (2003) *EU Law: Text, Cases, and Materials*, 4th edition, Oxford: Oxford University Press.

Crooks, E. and Parker, G. (2003) 'Single currency forum freezes out non-euro states', *Financial Times*, published 29 April 2003.

Currie, S. (2009) 'Accelerated justice or a step too far? Residence rights of non-EU family members and the court's ruling in Metock', *European Law Review*, 34(2): 310–326.

Dahl, R. A. (1957) 'The concept of power', *Behavioral Science*, 2(3): 205–215.

Damgaard, E. (2000) 'Parliament and government', in P. Esaiasson and K. Heidar (eds) *Beyond Westminster and Congress: The Nordic Experience*, Columbus: Ohio State University Press.

Danish Agency for the Modernisation of Public Administration (2010) *Ansættelse som national ekspert*, available online at: http://perst.dk/Udvikling%20og%20ledelse/ Talent%20og%20Karriereudvikling/International%20karriere/Karriere%20i%20EU/ Dine%20karrieremuligheder%20i%20EU/Ansaettelse%20som%20national%20 ekspert.aspx (accessed 21 March 2012).

Danish Agency for the Modernisation of Public Administration (2011) *International karriere*, available online at: http://perst.dk/Udvikling%20og%20ledelse/Talent%20 og%20Karriereudvikling/International%20karriere.aspx (accessed 21 March 2012).

Danish Broadcasting Corporation (2008) *Topchefer er ligeglade med Euroen*, available online at: www.dr.dk/Nyheder/Penge/2008/07/21/072905.htm?rss=true (accessed 11 March 2012).

Danish Defence Commission (1998) *Fremtidens Forsvar: White paper of the 1997 Defence Commission*, Copenhagen: Danish Ministry of Defence.

Danish Environmental Protection Agency (2002) *Fælles miljø, fælles ansvar – Danmark og EU*, Copenhagen.

Danish Government (1993) *Principper og perspektiver i dansk udenrigspolitik: dansk udenrigspolitik på vej mod år 2000*, Copenhagen: Danish Ministry of Foreign Affairs.

Danish Government (2003) *En verden i forandring. Regeringens bud på nye prioriteter i Danmarks udenrigspolitik*, Copenhagen: Danish Ministry of Foreign Affairs.

Danish Government (2004) *En verden i forandring – nye trusler, nye svar. Redegørelse fra regeringen om indsatsen mod terrorisme*, Copenhagen: Danish Ministry of Foreign Affairs.

Danish Government (2006) *The Borderless World – The Foreign Ministry and Globalisation*, Copenhagen: Danish Ministry of Foreign Affairs.

Danish Government (2010) *Et mere åbent og sikkert indre marked – A More Open and Safe Single Market*, available online at www.evm.dk/~/media/oem/pdf/2010/publikationer-2010/2010/EBS-Handlingsplan-Klar-pdf.ashx.

Danish Ministry of Foreign Affairs (2009) *Undenrigsministeriets oversigt: Danmark og EU-domstolen i 2009*, Copenhagen: Danish Ministry of Foreign Affairs.

Danish Nature Agency (2012) *Natura 2000*, available online at: www.naturstyrelsen.dk/ naturbeskyttelse/natura2000/ (accessed 9 April 2012).

Danish Shipowners' Association (1984) *Frit hav*, Copenhagen.

Danish Shipowners' Association (2010) *Dansk Skibsfart 2010*, Copenhagen.

Danish Wind Industry Association (2006) *Vindmølleindustrien gennem 25 år – Vindformation*, Copenhagen.

Danmarks Statistik (2008) *Data fra 60 år i tal – Danmark siden 2. Verdenskrig*, available online at: www.dst.dk/pukora/epub/upload/12433/tresaar.pdf (accessed 11 March 2012).

248 Bibliography

Danmarks Statistik (2011) *Statistikbanken*, available online at: www.statistikbanken.dk/ (accessed 10 December 2011).

Dansk Folkeparti (2004) *Dansk Folkepartis Valggrundlag til Europaparlamentet 2004*, available online at: www.danskfolkeparti.dk/sw/frontend/show.asp?parent= 18717&menu_parent=22669&layout=0 (accessed 18 April 2012).

Dansk Institut for Internationale Studier (2008) *De danske forbehold over for Den Europæiske Union: Udviklingen siden 2000*, Copenhagen: Dansk Institut for Internationale Studier.

Dansk Udenrigspolitisk Institut (2000) *Udviklingen i EU siden 1992 på de områder der er omfattet af de danske forbehold*, Copenhagen: Dansk Udenrigspolitisk Institut.

de Búrca, G (1995) 'The Language of Rights and European Integration' in G. More and J. Shaw (eds) *New Legal Dynamics of the European Union*. Oxford: Oxford University Press.

de Vries, C. (2007) 'Sleeping giant: fact or fairytale? How European integration affects national elections', *European Union Politics*, 8(3): 363–385.

de Vreese, C. and Boomgaarden, H. (2005) 'Projecting EU referendums: fear of immigration and support for European integration', *European Union Politics*, 6(1): 59–82.

de Vreese, C. and Semetko, H. (2004) *Political Campaigning in Referendums: Framing the Referendum Issue*, New York: Routledge.

de Vreese, C. and Tobiasen, M. (2007) 'Conflict and identity: explaining turnout and anti-integrationist voting in the Danish 2004 elections for the European Parliament', *Scandinavian Political Studies*, 30(1): 87–114.

Denver, D. (2002) 'Voting in the 1997 Scottish and Welsh devolution referendums: information, interests and opinions', *European Journal of Political Research*, 41: 827–843.

Det Okonomiske Råd (2000) *Dansk Økonomi*, annual report, Copenhagen: Det Okonomiske Råd/Formandskabet.

Det Okonomiske Råd (2009) *Dansk Økonomi*, annual report, Copenhagen: Det Okonomiske Råd/Formandskabet.

Diedrichs, U., Faber, A., Tekin, F. and Umbach, G. (2011) (eds) *Europe Reloaded: Differentiation or Fusion?*, Baden-Baden: Nomos.

Doeser, F. (2011) 'Domestic politics and foreign policy change in small states: the fall of the Danish "Footnote Policy"', *Cooperation and Conflict*, 46(2): 222–241.

Drachmann, H. (1994) 'Ritt må slås for miljopost', *Politiken*, published 3 October 1994.

Due-Nielsen, C. and Petersen, N. (1995) 'Denmark's foreign policy since 1967: an introduction', in C. Due-Nielsen and N. Petersen (eds) *Adaptation and Activism*. Copenhagen: DJOF.

Dür, A. and Mateo, G. (2010a) 'Choosing a bargaining strategy in EU negotiations: power, preferences, and culture', *Journal of European Public Policy*, 17(5): 680–693.

Dyson, K. (1994) *Elusive Union: The Process of Economic and Monetary Union in Europe*, London: Longman.

Dyson, K. and Quaglia, L. (2010) *European Economic Governance and Policies, Volume I: Commentary on Key Historical and Institutional Documents*, Oxford: Oxford University Press.

Dyson, K. and Sepos, A. (2010a) 'Differentiation as design principle and as tool in the political management of European integration', in K. Dyson and A. Sepos (eds) *Which Europe? The Politics of Differentiated Integration*, Houndmills: Palgrave.

Dyson, K. and Sepos, A. (2010b) (eds) *Which Europe? The Politics of Differentiated Integration*, Houndmills: Palgrave.

Bibliography 249

Egeberg, M. (2006) 'Executive politics as usual: role behaviour and conflict dimensions in the College of European Commissioners', *Journal of European Public Policy*, 13(1): 1–15.

Egeberg, M., Schaefer, G. and Trondal, J. (2003) 'The many faces of EU Committee governance', *West European Politics*, 26(3): 19–40.

Eising, R. (2007) 'The access of business interests to EU institutions: towards elite pluralism?', *Journal of European Public Policy*, 14(3): 384–403.

Elbjørn, K. and Wivel, A. (2006), 'Forståelsesbrevet', in D. Gress and K. Elbjørn (eds) *20 begivenheder der skabte Danmark*, Copenhagen: Gyldendal.

Eliason, L. (2001) 'Denmark: small state with a big voice', in E. E. Zeff and E. B. Pirro (eds) *The European Union and the Member States*, London and Boulder: Lynne Rienner Publishers.

Eschenburg, T. (1955) *Herrschaft der Verbände?*, Stuttgart: Deutsche Verlags-Anstalt.

Esmark, A. (2008) 'Tracing the national mandate: administrative Europeanization made in Denmark', *Public Administration*, 86(1): 243–257.

EUbusiness (1 July 2011) *Denmark Reintroduces Custom Control at its Borders*, published 1 July 2011.

EU-Oplysningen (2004) *Politisk aftale om Danmark i det udvidede EU*, available online at: www.eu-oplysningen.dk/emner/reformtraktat/ft/ftdebatter/debat/dokument/ (accessed 11 March 2012).

EU-Oplysningen (2006a) *Referenda*, available online at: www.euo.dk/euo_en/dkeu/referenda/ (accessed 11 March 2012).

EU-Oplysningen (2006b) *Folkeafstemning om EF-pakken*, available online at: www.eu-oplysningen.dk/dkeu/dk/afstemninger/afstemning/1986/ (accessed 17 August 2010).

EU-Oplysningen (2008a) *Ny Dansk Europapolitisk Aftale*, available online at: www.eu-oplysningen.dk/nyheder/euidag/2008/februar/euuaftale/ (accessed 18 March 2012).

EU-Oplysningen (2008b) *Ændrer Folketingets rolle sig med Lissabon-traktaten*, available online at: www.euo.dk/spsv/off/alle/gultkort/ (accessed 18 April 2012).

EU-Oplysningen (2009) *Hvor kan jeg se resultaterne af de danske valg til Europa-Parlamentet?*, available online at: www.eu-oplysningen.dk/spsv/off/alle/valgtilEP/ (accessed 11 March 2012).

EU-Oplysningen (2012a) *Danish Opt-Outs*, available online at: www.euo.dk/emner_en/forbehold/ (accessed 11 March 2012).

EU-Oplysningen (2012b) *The Edinburgh Agreement*, available online at: www.euo.dk/fakta_en/denmark/edinburgh/ (accessed 17 March 2012).

EU-Oplysningen (2012c) *Om familiesammenføring*, available online at: www.eu-oplysningen.dk/dokumenter/ft/paragraf_20/samling/2006_2007/1235/?print=1 (accessed 31 March 2012).

EU-Oplysningen (2012d) *Om de totale udgifter til forvaltning af de internationale naturbeskyttelsesområder frem til 2012*, available online at: www.eu-oplysningen.dk/dokumenter/ft/paragraf_20/alle/20045439/ (accessed 31 October 2012).

EurActive (2009) 'Barroso II brings nine women on board', *EurActive*, published 25 November 2009.

EUR-Lex (2012a) *Council Directive 75/34/EEC of 17 December 1974 Concerning the Right of Nationals of a Member State to Remain in the Territory of Another Member State After Having Pursued therein an Activity in a Self-Employed Capacity*, available online at: http://eur-lex.europa.eu/smartapi/cgi/sga_doc?smartapi!celexplus!prod!DocNumber&lg=en&type_doc=Directive&an_doc=1975&nu_doc=34 (accessed 31 March 2012).

250 Bibliography

EUR-Lex (2012b) *Directive 2004/38/EC of the European Parliament and of the Council of 29 April 2004 on the Right of Citizens of the Union and Their Family Members to Move and Reside Freely within the Territory of the Member States Amending Regulation (EEC) No 1612/68 and repealing Directives 64/221/EEC, 68/360/EEC, 72/194/EEC, 73/148/EEC, 75/34/EEC, 75/35/EEC, 90/364/EEC, 90/365/EEC and 93/96/EEC*, available online at: http://eur-lex.europa.eu/LexUriServ/LexUriServ.do?uri=CELEX: 32004L0038:en:NOT (accessed 31 March 2012).

EUR-Lex (2012c) *The Queen v Immigration Appeal Tribunal and Surinder Singh, ex parte Secretary of State for Home Department*, available online at: http://eur-lex.europa.eu/smartapi/cgi/sga_doc?smartapi!celexplus!prod!CELEXnumdoc&numdoc=61990J0370&lg=en (accessed 31 March 2012).

EUR-Lex (2012d) *Mary Carpenter v Secretary of State for the Home Department*, available online at: http://eur-lex.europa.eu/smartapi/cgi/sga_doc?smartapi!celexplus!prod!CELEXnumdoc&lg=en&numdoc=62000J0060 (accessed 31 March 2012).

EUR-Lex (2012e) *Secretary of State for the Home Department v Hacene Akrich*, available online at: http://eur-lex.europa.eu/LexUriServ/LexUriServ.do?uri=CELEX: 62001J0109:EN:HTML (accessed 31 March 2012).

EUR-Lex (2012f) *Blaise Baheten Metock and Others v Minister for Justice, Equality and Law Reform*, available online at: http://eur-lex.europa.eu/LexUriServ/LexUriServ.do?uri=CELEX:62008J0127:EN:HTML (accessed 31 March 2012).

EUR-Lex (2012g) *Case C-117/00*, available online at: http://eur-lex.europa.eu/LexUriServ/LexUriServ.do?uri=CELEX:62000CJ0117:EN:HTML (accessed 9 April 2012).

Europaudvalget (2003) *Bilag 551 af 31. januar 2003*, Copenhagen: Europaudvalget/Folketinget.

European Commission (2000a) *Reforming the Commission. A White Paper – Part I (COM(2000) 200 Final/2, 5.4.2000)*, Brussels: Commission of the European Communities.

European Commission (2000b) *Reforming the Commission. A White Paper – Part II Action Plan (COM(2000) 200 Final/2, 5.4.2000)*, Brussels: Commission of the European Communities.

European Commission (2005) *EAGGF Section Guarantee: Annual Payments Made to MS as Recorded Since 1963*, available online at: http://ec.europa.eu/budget/documents/2009_en.htm?submenuheader=2#table-3_2 (accessed 10 December 2011).

European Commission (2006) *Green Paper: European Transparency Initiative (COM (2006) 194 final)*, Brussels: European Commission.

European Commission (2008a) 'EMU@10: successes and challenges after 10 years of economic and monetary union', in *European Economy (2/2008)*, Brussels: Directorate-General for Economic and Financial Affairs.

European Commission (2008b) *Commission Staff Working Document. Accompanying document to the Report from the Commission 26th Annual Reprot on Monitoring the Application of Community Law (2008)*, available online at: http://ec.europa.eu/community_law/docs/docs_infringements/annual_report_26/en_sec_statannex_vol.1clean.pdf (accessed 2 April 2012).

European Commission (2009) *Strategic Goals and Recommendations for the EU's Maritime Transport Policy until 2018 (COM(2009) 8 final)*, Brussels: European Commission.

European Commission (2010a) *Agricultural Policy Perspectives – Member States Factsheets – May 2010*, available online at: http://ec.europa.eu/agriculture/fin/budget/index_en.htm (accessed 10 December 2011).

European Commission (2010b) *Archives for the Progress in Notification of National*

Bibliography 251

Measures Implementing Directives, available online at: http://ec.europa.eu/community_law/directives/archmme_en.htm (accessed 17 August 2010).

European Commission (2010c) *Communication from the Commission to the European Parliament, the Council, the European Economic and Social Committee and the Committee of the Regions: Commission Work Programme 2010: Time to act (COM(2010) 135 final)*, Brussels: European Commission.

European Commission (2011) *Register of Interest Representatives*, available online at: https://webgate.ec.europa.eu/transparency/regrin/welcome.do?locale=en (accessed 4 April 2011).

European Commission (2012a) *Public Opinion*, available online at: http://ec.europa.eu/public_opinion/cf/showchart_column.cfm?keyID=5&nationID=2,16,&startdate=1973.09&enddate=2011.05 (accessed 11 March 2012).

European Commission (2012b) *Seconded National Experts*, available online at: http://ec.europa.eu/civil_service/job/sne/index_en.htm (accessed 21 March 2012).

European External Action Service (2011) *Overview of the Missions and Operations of the European Union July 2011*, available online at: http://consilium.europa.eu/eeas/security-defence/eu-operations.aspx?lang=en (accessed 9 September 2011).

European Union (2001) *Directive 2001/77/EC of the European Parliament and of the Council of 27 September 2001 on the Promotion of Electricity Produced from Renewable Energy Sources in the Internal Electricity Market*, Brussels: European Union.

European Union (2009) *Directive 2009/28/EC of the European Parliament and of the Council 23 April 2009 on the Promotion of the Use of Energy from Renewable Sources and Amending and Subsequently Repealing Directives 2001/77/EC and 2003/30/EC*, Brussels: European Union.

European Union (2010) *Consolidated Version of the Treaty of the European Union*, available online at: http://eur-lex.europa.eu/LexUriServ/LexUriServ.do?uri=OJ:C:2010:083:0013:0046:EN:PDF (accessed 21 March 2012).

European Union (2012) *Decision-Making in the European Union*, available online at: http://europa.eu/about-eu/basic-information/decision-making/index_en.htm (accessed 21 March 2012).

European Wind-Energy Association (2010a) *EWEA Briefing on Commission Communication – 'Analysis of Options to Move Beyond 20% Greenhouse Gas Emission Reductions and Assessing the Risk of Carbon Leakage'*, available online at: www.ewea.org/fileadmin/ewea_documents/documents/publications/position_papers/EWEA_Position_on_moving_beyond_20_percent.pdf (accessed 9 April 2012).

European Wind-Energy Association (2010b) *Key Aspects of the Renewable Energy Directive*, available online at: www.ewea.org/index.php?id=197 (accessed 17 December 2010).

Everson, M. (1995) 'The legacy of the market citizen', in G. More and J. Shaw (eds) *New Legal Dynamics of the European Union*, Oxford: Clarendon Press.

Falkner, G., Treib, O., Hartlapp, M. and Leiber, S. (2005) *Complying With Europe? EU Harmonisation and Soft Law in the Member States*, Cambridge: Cambridge University Press.

Farrell, D. and Scully, R. (2007) *Representing Europe's Citizens? Electoral Institutions and the Failure of Parliamentary Representation*, Oxford: Oxford University Press.

Farrell, D., Hix S., Johnson, M. and Scully, R. (2006) *EPRG 2000 and 2006 MEP Surveys Dataset*, available online at: www.lse.ac.uk/collections/EPRG/ (accessed 21 March 2012).

Farrell, H. and Héritier, A. (2004) 'Interorganizational negotiation and intraorganizational power in shared decision making: early agreements under co-decision and their impact

Bibliography

on the European Parliament and Council', *Comparative Political Studies*, 37(10): 1184–1212.

Featherstone, F. and Radaelli, C. (eds.) (2003) *The Politics of Europeanization*, Oxford: Oxford University Press.

Fich, O. (2008) 'Er Europa-Parlamentet EU's demokratiske dimension?', in P. Nedergaard (ed.) *Fra Fælles Forsamling til Folkestyre*, Copenhagen: Europa-Parlamentets Informationskontor.

Financial Times (2008) *Sarkozy in drive to hold ECB to account*, published 20 July 2008.

Finer, S. E. (1966) *Anonymous Empire: A Study of the Lobby in Great Britain*, London: Pall Mall Press.

Flensborg Avis (2010) *EU truer Danmark med retssag om Tondermarsken*, published 28 April 2010.

Folketinget (1978) '*Forespørgsel vedr. landbrugspriserne for 1978–79 den 17. maj 1978*', Copenhagen: Folketingstidende 1977–1978, column 9958–10049.

Folketinget (1988) '*Forespørgsel om EF's indre marked den 25. november 1988*', Copenhagen: Folketingstidende 1988–1989, column 2605–2666.

Folketinget (2003a) '*Beretning om eksportrestitutioner for fersk og frosset svinekod afgivet af Udvalget for Fødevarer, Landbrug og Fiskeri den 19. juni 2003*', Copenhagen: Folketinget.

Folketinget (2003b) '*Besvarelse af Folketingets Europaudvalgs spørgsmål 46 af 21. januar 2003 af Udenrigsministeriet og Økonomi- og Erhvervsministeriet den 4. februar 2003*', Copenhagen: Folketinget.

Folketinget (2003c) '*EU-direktiv om overtagelsestilbud, Folketingets Erhvervsudvalg den 28. november 2003*', Copenhagen: Erhvervsudvalget/Folketinget.

Folketinget (2005) '*Forespørgsel nr. F10 om servicedirektivet den 24. november 2005*' Copenhagen: Folketingstidende 2005–2006, column 1356–1600.

Folketinget (2007a) '*Betænkning over Forslag til folketingsbeslutning om udarbejdelse af strategi for afvikling af EU's landbrugsstotte*', Copenhagen: Folketingstidende 2006–2007, column 1482–1484.

Folketinget (2007b) '*Folketingsbeslutning om udarbejdelse af strategi for afvikling af EU's landbrugsstotte*', Copenhagen: Folketinget.

Folketinget (2007c) *1. Behandling af beslutningsforslag nr. B75: Forslag til folketingsbeslutning om udarbejdelse af strategi for afvikling af EU's landbrugsstotte*, Copenhagen: Folketingstidende 2006–2007, column 5813–5828.

Folketinget (2011) *Viderestilling til tidligere folketingssamlinger*, available online at: http://webarkiv.ft.dk/?/samling/arkiv.htm (accessed 12 September 2011).

Folketinget (2012) *Folketingsvalgene 1953–2011*, available online at: www.ft.dk/Folketinget/Oplysningen/Valg/~/media/Pdf_materiale/Pdf_download_direkte/Folketingets%20Oplysning/Folketingsvalgene%201953–2011.pdf.ashx (accessed 26 October 2012).

Folketinget (2012) *Regeringer 1953–2011*, available online at: www.ft.dk/Dokumenter/Publikationer/Tal%20og%20Fakta/Regeringer.aspx (accessed 26 October 2012).

Follesdal, A. and Wind, M. (2009) 'Introduction – Nordic reluctance towards judicial review under siege', *Nordic Journal of Human Rights*, 27(2): 131–142.

Franklin, M. (2002) 'Learning from the Danish case: a comment on Palle Svensson's critique of the Franklin Thesis', *European Journal of Political Research*, 41(6): 751–758.

Franklin, M., Marsh, M. and Wlezien, C. (1994) 'Attitudes toward Europe and referendum votes: a response to Siune and Svensson', *Electoral Studies*, 13: 117–121.

Franklin, M., van der Eijk, C. and Marsh, M. (1995) 'Referendum outcomes and trust in

government: public support for Europe in the wake of Maastricht', *West European Politics*, 18: 101–117.
From, J. and Stava, P. (1993) 'Implementation of Community law: the last stronghold of national control?', in S. S. Andersen and K. A. Eliassen (eds) *Making Policy in Europe – The Europeification of National Policy-making*, London: Sage Publications.
Gammeltoft-Hansen, T. (2007) 'The extraterritorialisation of asylum and the advent of protection lite', in *DIIS Working Paper (2007/2)*, Copenhagen: Danish Institute for International Studies.
Gammeltoft-Hansen, T. (2009) 'Familiesammenføring: Vejledning fra Kommissionen', *Ugebrevet Europa*, published 2 July 2009.
Garry, J., Marsh, M. and Sinnott, R. (2005) '"second-order" versus 'issue-voting' effects in EU referendums: evidence from the Irish Nice treaty referendums', *European Union Politics*, 6(2): 201–221.
Geddes, A. (2000) *Immigration and European Integration: Towards Fortress Europe?* Manchester: Manchester University Press.
Georgakakis, D. (2010) 'Tensions within Eurocracy? A socio-morephological view', *French Politics*, 8(2): 116–144.
George, A. L. (1993) *Bridging the Gap: Theory and Practice in Foreign Policy*. Washington, DC: United States Institute of Peace Press.
Geurts, C. (1998) 'The European Commission: a natural ally of small states in the EU institutional framework?', in L. Goetschel (ed.) *Small States Inside and Outside the European Union*, Dordrecht: Kluwer Academic Publishers.
Givens, T. and Luedtke, A. (2003) 'EU immigration policy: from intergovernmentalism to reluctant harmonization', in T. A. Börzel and R. A. Cichowski (eds) *The State of the European Union: Law, Politics and Society*, Oxford: Oxford University Press.
Global Policy Forum (2003) *Europe and America Must Stand United*, available online at: www.globalpolicy.org/component/content/article/168/36565.html (accessed 26 August 2011).
Goetschel, L. (1998) 'The foreign and security policy interests of small states in today's Europe', in L. Goetschel (ed.) *Small States Inside and Outside the European Union*, Dordrecht: Kluwer Academic Publishers.
Goetz, K. H. (2010) 'The temporal dimension', in K. Dyson and A. Sepos (eds) *Which Europe? The Politics of Differentiated Integration*, Houndmills: Palgrave.
Goodman, L. (1960) 'On the exact variance of products', *Journal of the American Statistical Association*, 55: 708–713.
Graziano, P and Vink, M. P. (eds) (2007) *Europeanisation: New Research Agendas*, Houndmills: Palgrave.
Green-Pedersen, C. (2012) 'A giant fast asleep? Party incentives and politicization of European integration', *Political Studies*, 60(1): 115–130.
Greenwood, J. (2007) *Representing Interests in the European Union*, 2nd edition, Houndmills: Macmillan.
Greenwood, J., Grote, J. R. and Ronit, K. (1992) *Organized Interests and the European Community*, London, Newbury Park, New Delhi: Sage.
Grøn, C. H. (2010) *Same Procedure as Last Year? An Analysis of Trust/Control Constellations in Personnel Management in the European Commission*', PhD-thesis, Copenhagen: University of Copenhagen.
Grøn, C. H. and Wivel, A. (2011) 'Maximizing influence in the European Union after the Lisbon Treaty: from small state policy to smart state strategy', *Journal of European Integration*, 33(5): 523–539.

Gronnegård Christensen, J. (1980) *Centraladministrationen: organisation og politisk placering*, Copenhagen: Samfundsvidenskabeligt Forlag.

Grønnegård Christensen, J. (2003) 'Den fleksible og robuste forvaltning', in M. Marcussen and K. Ronit (eds) *Internationalisering af den offentlige forvaltning i Danmark. Forandring og kontinuitet*, Aarhus: Aarhus University Press.

Gronnegård Christensen, J., Germer, P. and Pedersen, T. (1994) *Åbenhed, offentlighed og deltagelse i den danske EU-beslutningsproces*, Copenhagen: Rådet for Europæisk Politik.

Gross, E. (2009) *The Europeanization of National Foreign Policy: Continuity and Change in European Crisis Management*, Houndmills: Palgrave Macmillan.

Grote, J. R., Lang, A. and Schneider, V. (eds) (2008) *Organized Business Interests in Changing Environments. The Complexity of Adaptation*, Houndsmills: Palgrave.

Haahr, J. H. (1992) 'European integration and the Left in Britain and Denmark', *Journal of Common Market Studies*, 30(1): 77–100.

Haahr, J. H. (1993) *Looking to Europe: The EC Politics of the British Labour Party and the Danish SDP*, Aarhus: Aarhus University Press.

Haas, E. B. (1958) *The Uniting of Europe: Political, Social and Economic Forces 1950–57*, London: Library of World Affairs.

Hækkerup, P. (1965) *Danmarks udenrigspolitik*, Copenhagen: Fremad.

Hærens Operative Kommando (2008) *Internationalt Engagement*, available online at: www.forsvaret.dk/HOK/omhaeren/historie/INT%20Engagement/Pages/Ledelse.aspx (accessed 12 September 2011).

Hagel-Sorensen, K. (1994) 'Fællesskabsretten som del af dansk ret', in J. Rosenlov and K. Thorup (eds) *Festskrift til Ole Due*, Copenhagen: Gads Forlag.

Hanreider, W. (1971) *Comparative Foreign Policy*, New York: MacKay.

Hansen, L. (2002) 'Sustaining sovereignty: the Danish approach to Europe', in L. Hansen and O. Wæver (eds) *European Integration and National Identity. The Challenges of the Nordic states*, London and New York: Routledge.

Hausemeer, P. (2006) 'Participation and political competition in committee report allocation: under what conditions do meps represent their constituencies?', *European Union Politics*, 7(4): 505–530.

Haverland, M. (2000) 'National adaptation to European integration: the importance of institutional veto points', *Journal of Public Policy*, 20(1): 83–103.

Hayes-Renshaw, F., van Aken, W. and Wallace, H. (2006) 'When and why the council of ministers votes explicitly', *Journal of Common Market Studies*, 44(1): 161–194.

Heisbourg, F. (2000) 'Europe's strategic ambitions: the limits of ambiguity', *Survival*, 42(2): 5–15.

Hermann, C. F. (1990) 'Changing course: when governments choose to redirect foreign policy', *International Studies Quarterly*, 34(1): 3–21.

Heurlin, B. (2001) 'Danish security policy over the last 50 years – long-term essential security priorities', in B. Heurlin and H. Mouritzen (eds) *Danish Foreign Policy Yearbook 2001*, Copenhagen: Danish Institute of International Affairs.

Heurlin, B. (2007) 'Det nye danske forsvar: Denationalisering, militarisering og demokratisering', in B. Heurlin (ed.) *Nationen eller Verden? De nordiske lands forsvar i dag*. Copenhagen: DJOF Forlag.

Hey, J. A. K. (2003) 'Introducing small state foreign policy', in J. A. K. Hey (ed.) *Small States in World Politics*, Boulder: Lynne Rienner.

Hill, C. (2002) *The Changing Politics of Foreign Policy*, Houndmills: Palgrave Macmillan.

Hill, C. (2003) *The Changing Politics of Foreign Policy*, Houndmills: Palgrave.

Bibliography 255

Hill, C. (2004) 'Renationalising or regrouping EU foreign policy since 11 September 2001', *Journal of Common Market Studies*, 42(1): 143–163.

Hix, S. (2002) 'parliamentary behaviour with two principals: preferences, parties, and voting in the European Parlaiment', *American Journal of Political Science*, 46(3): 688–698.

Hix, S. (2005) *The Political System of the European Union*, Basingstoke: Palgrave.

Hix, S. and Lord, C. (1997) *Political Parties in the European Union*, London: Routledge.

Hix, S., Noury, A. and Roland, G. (2005) 'Power to the parties: cohesion and competition in the European Parliament, 1979–2001', *British Journal of Political Science*, 35(2): 209–234.

Hix, S., Noury, A. and Roland, G. (2006) 'Dimensions of politics in the European Parliament', *American Journal of Political Science*, 50(2): 494–511.

Hix, S., Noury, A. and Roland, G. (2007) *Democratic Politics in the European Parliament*, Cambridge: Cambridge University Press.

Hobolt, S. B. (2005) 'When Europe matters: the impact of political information on voting behaviour in EU referendums', *Journal of Elections, Public Opinion, and Parties*, 15(1): 85–110.

Hobolt, S. B. (2006) 'Direct democracy and European integration, *Journal of European Public Policy*', 13(1): 153–166.

Hobolt, S. B. (2009) *Europe in Question. Referendums on European Integration*, Oxford: Oxford University Press.

Hobolt, S. B. and Brouard, S. (2011) 'Contesting the European Union? Why the Dutch and the French rejected the European Constitution', *Political Resarch Quarterly*, 64(2): 309–322.

Holbraad, C. (1991) *Danish Neutrality*, Oxford: Clarendon Press.

Holm, Hans-Henrik (2002) 'Danish foreign policy activism: the rise and decline', in B. Heurlin and H. Mouritzen (eds) *Danish Foreign Policy Yearbook 2002*, Copenhagen: Danish Institute for International Studies.

Hooghe, L. (2007) 'Several roads lead to international norms, but few via international socialization: a case study of the European Commission', in J. T. Checkel (ed.) *International Institutions and Socialization in Europe*, Cambridge: Cambridge University Press.

Howarth, D. (2009) 'The European Central Bank: the bank that rules Europe?', in K. Dyson and M. Marcussen (eds) *Central Banks in the Age of the Euro: Europeanization, Convergence and Power*, Oxford: Oxford University Press.

Hoyland, B. (2006) 'Allocation of co-decision reports in the fifth term of the European Parliament', *European Union Politics*, 7(1): 30–50.

Hudson, V. M. (2005) 'Foreign policy analysis: actor-specific theory and the ground of international relations', *Foreign Policy Analysis*, 1(1): 1–30.

Hug, S. and König, T. (2002) 'In view of ratification: governmental preferences and domestic constraints at the Amsterdam Intergovernmental Conference', *International Organization*, 56(2): 447–476.

InfoCuria (2012a) *Case C-157/99*, available online at: http://curia.europa.eu/juris/document/document.jsf?text=&docid=46529&pageIndex=0&doclang=en&mode=req&dir=&occ=first&part=1&cid=1530739 (accessed 30 October 2012).

InfoCuria (2012b) *Case C-103/00*, available online at: http://curia.europa.eu/juris/document/document.jsf;jsessionid=9ea7d0f130d58de15518c2c9414da3b7e575140a0485.e34KaxiLc3eQc40LaxqMbN4Oa3aNe0?text=&docid=46672&pageIndex=0&doclang=EN&mode=doc&dir=&occ=first&part=1&cid=189372 (accessed 9 April 2012).

Information (1999) *Danske EU-politikere skal særbeskattes*, available online at: www.information.dk/29893 (accessed 21 March 2012).
Information (2009) *Mickey Mouse er ved at blive voksen*, available online at: www.information.dk/192398 (accessed 21 March 2012).
Information (2000) *Skræmmekampagne ultra-light*, published 22 September 2000.
International Maritime Organization (2010) *Comprehensive List of all IMO Treaties*, London: International Maritime Organization.
Jacqueson, J. (2010) 'Metock as a shock? The struggle between rights and sovereignty', in H. Koch, K. Hagel-Sorensen, U. Haltern and J. H. H. Weiler (eds) *Europe: The New Legal Realism*, Copenhagen: DJOF.
Jakobsen, P. V. (2009), 'Small states, big influence: the overlooked Nordic influence on the civilian ESDP', *Journal of Common Market Studies*, 47(1): 81–102.
Jensen, A. D. and Jespersen, M. H. T. (2003) *'Folketingets debat om EU-forbeholdene'*, master-thesis, Copenhagen: University of Copenhagen.
Jensen, H. (2003) *Europaudvalget – et udvalg i Folketinget*, Aarhus: Aarhus University Press.
Jensen, M. D., Rasmussen, A. and Willumsen, D. M. (2009) *Europa-Parlamentet*, Copenhagen: Thomson Reuters.
Jenssen, A., Pesonen, P. and Gilljam, M. (eds) (1998) *To Join or Not to Join: Three Nordic Referendums on Memberships in the European Union*, Oslo: Scandinavian University Press.
Jessen, C. K., Tang, U. and Nielsen O. B. (2009) 'EU onsker Connie H, men Lokke tover', *Berlingske Tidende*, published 21 October 2009.
Jorgensen, K. E. (1997) 'PoCo: the diplomatic republic of Europe', in K. E. Jorgensen, (ed.) *Reflective Approaches to European Governance*, Houndmills: Macmillan.
Joenniemi, P. (1998) 'From small to smart: reflections on the concept of small states', *Irish Studies in International Affairs*, 9: 61–62.
Joerges, C. and Neyer, J. (1997) 'From intergovernmental bargaining to deliberative political processes: the constitutionalisation of comitology', *European Law Journal*, 3(3): 273–299.
Johnson, D. and Turner, C. (2006) *European Business*, London: Routledge.
Jyllands-Posten (1999) *Dansk EU-post til debat*, published 10 July 1999.
Jyllands-Posten (2009) *S: EU's rejsecirkus skal stoppes*, available online at: http://jp.dk/indland/indland_politik/article1696669.ece (accessed 21 March 2012).
Jyllands-Posten (2012) *Danske topchefer vil ikke have euro*, published 3 January 2012.
Kaeding, M. (2004) 'Rapporteurship allocation in the European Parliament', *European Union Politics*, 5(3): 353–571.
Kaeding, M. (2005) 'The world of committee reports: rapporteurship assignment in the European Parliament', *The Journal of Legislative Studies*, 11(1): 82–104.
Kallestrup, M. (2005) *Europæisering af Nationalstaten*, Copenhagen: DJOF Forlag.
Kallestrup, M. (2008) 'EU-retten og de nationale aktorers politiske rolle', in B. E. Olsen and K. E. Sorensen (eds) *Europæisering af Dansk Ret*, Copenhagen: DJOF Forlag.
Kammeradvokaten (2002) *Notat om Implementering af Habitatsdirektivet (J.nr.: 40–1735 HS/BIE/ANI/nor, 28. november 2002)*, Copenhagen: Kammeradvokaten.
Karnoe, P. (1991) *Dansk vindmolleindustri – en overraskende international succes: Om innovationer, industriudvikling og teknologipolitik*, Copenhagen: Samfundslitteratur.
Kassim, H. (2003) 'Meeting the demands of EU membership: the Europeanization of national administrative systems', in K. Featherstone and C. Radaelli (eds) *The Politics of Europeanization*, Oxford: Oxford University Press.

Kassim, H. (2004) 'A historic accomplishment? The Prodi Commission and administrative reform', in D. Dimitrakopoulos (ed.) *The Changing European Commission*, Manchester: Manchester University Press.

Kassim, H. and Menon, A. (2004) 'EU Member states and the Prodi Commission', in D. Dmitrakopoulos (ed.) *The Changing European Commission*, Manchester: Manchester University Press.

Kassim, H., Peters, B. G. and Wright, V. (eds) (2000) *The National Co-Ordination of EU Policy: The Domestic Level*, Oxford: Oxford University Press.

Kassim, H., Menon, A., Peters, B. G. and Wright, V. (eds) (2001) *National Co-Ordination of EU Policy: The European Level*, Oxford: Oxford University Press.

Katz, R. (2001) 'Models of democracy: elite attitudes and the democratic deficit in the European Union', *European Union Politics*, 2(1): 53–80.

Keating, M. (2010) 'The Spatial Dimension', in K. Dyson and A. Sepos (eds) *Which Europe? The Politics of Differentiated Integration*, Houndmills: Palgrave.

Kelstrup, M. (1990) 'the process of Europeanization: on the theoretical interpretation of present changes in the European regional political system', *Cooperation and Conflict*, 25(1): 21–40.

Kelstrup, M. (ed.) (1992) *European Integration and Denmark's Participation*, Copenhagen: Copenhagen Political Studies Press.

Kelstrup, M. (1993) 'Small states and European political integration: reflections on theories and strategies', in T. Tiilikainen and I. D. Petersen (eds) *The Nordic Countries and the EC*, Copenhagen: Copenhagen Political Studies Press.

Kelstrup, M. (2000a) 'Danish integration policies: dilemmas and options', in H. Branner and M. Kelstrup (eds) *Denmark's Policy towards Europe After 1945: History, Theory and Options*, Odense: Odense University Press.

Kelstrup, M. (2000b) 'Integration policy: between foreign policy and diffusion', in H. Branner and M. Kelstrup (eds) *Denmark's Policy Towards Europe After 1945: History, Theory and Options*, Odense: Odense University Press.

Kelstrup, M. (2006) 'Denmark in the process of European integration: dilemmas, problems and perspectives in Danish integration policy', in J. L. Campbell, J. A. Hall and O. K. Pedersen (eds) *National Identity and the Varieties of Capitalism: The Danish Experience*, Montreal and London: McGill-Queen's University Press.

Kelstrup, M., Martinsen, D. S. and Wind, M. (2008) *Europa i forandring – en grundbog om EU's politiske og retlige system*, Copenhagen: Hans Reitzels Forlag.

Kelstrup, M., Martinsen, D. S. and Wind, M. (2012) *Europa i Forandring*, 2nd edition, Copenhagen: Hans Reitzels Forlag.

King, A. (1976) 'Modes of executive-legislative relations: Great Britain, France and West Germany', *Legislative Studies Quarterly*, 1(1): 11–36.

Kjær, K. U. (2004) 'EU's familiesammenføringsdirektiv og dansk ret', in *Ægtefællesammenføring i Danmark (udredning nr. 1)*, Copenhagen: The Danish Institute for Human Rights.

Knudsen, A.-C. L. (2009) *Farmers on Welfare: The Making of Europe's Common Agricultural Policy*, Ithaca: Cornell University Press.

Knudsen, O. F. (2002) 'Small states, latent and extant: towards a general perspective', *Journal of International Relations and Development*, 5(2): 182–198.

Kölliker, A. (2010) 'The functional dimension', in K. Dyson and A. Sepos (eds) *Which Europe? The Politics of Differentiated Integration*, Houndmills: Palgrave.

Kreppel A. (2000) 'Rules, ideology and coalition formation within the European Parliament: past, present and future', *European Union Politics*, 1(3): 340–362.

258 Bibliography

Kreppel A. (2002) *The European Parliament and Supranational Party System: A Study in Institutional Development*, Cambridge: Cambridge University Press.

Kreppel, A. and Tsebelis, G. (1999) 'Coalition formation in the European Parliament', *Comparative Political Studies*, 32(8): 933–966.

Kritzinger, S. (2003) 'The influence of the nation-state on individual support for the European Union', *European Union Politics*, 4(2): 219–241.

Kurpas, S., Grøn, C. H. and Kaczyński, P. (2008) *The European Commission After Enlargement: Does More Add Up to Less?*, Brussels: CEPS.

Laatikainen, K. V. (2003) 'Norden's eclipse: the impact of the EUs common foreign and security policy on Nordic cooperation in the United Nations', *Cooperation and Conflict*, 38(4): 409–441.

Ladrech, R. (2010) *Europeanization and National Politics*, Houndmills: Palgrave Macmillan.

Landbrugs- og Fiskeriministeriet (1995) *Hvordan fungerer EU's Landbrugspolitik?* Copenhagen: Departementet, Landbrugs- og Fiskeriministeriet.

Lansbergen, A (2009) 'Metock, implementation of the citizens' rights directive and lessons for EU citizenship', *Journal of Social Welfare & Family Law*, 31(3): 285–297.

Larsen, H. (1997) *Foreign Policy and Discourse Analysis: France, Britain and Europe*, Routledge: London.

Larsen, H. (2000) 'Danish CFSP policy in the post-Cold War period: continuity or change?', *Cooperation and Conflict* 35(1): 37–63.

Larsen, H. (2005) *Analysing the Foreign Policy of Small States in the EU: The Case of Denmark*, Houndmills: Palgrave.

Larsen, H. (2009) 'Danish foreign policy and the balance between the EU and the US: the choice between Brussels and Washington after 2001', *Cooperation and Conflict* 44(2): 209–230.

Larsen, H. (2011) 'Denmark – a committed member – with opt-outs', in R. Wong and C. Hill (eds) *National and European Foreign Policies*, Routledge: London.

Larsen, J. V. (1994) 'EU-duel bag lukkede dore', *Berlingske Tidende*, published 30 October 1994.

Lassen, N. (2007) '*Centrale EU-direktiver vedrorende asyl- og ophold: På hvilke områder er der ringere standarder i Danmark?*', Copenhagen: Dansk Flygtningehjælp.

Laursen, F. (ed.) (2002) *The Amsterdam Treaty National Preference Formation, Interstate Bargaining and Outcome*, Odense: Odense University Press.

Laursen, F. (ed.) (2008) *The Rise and Fall of the Constitutional Treaty*, Leiden/Boston: Martinus Nijhoff Publishers.

Laursen, F. (2010) 'The Nordic countries: between scepticism and adaptation', in M. Carbone (ed.) *National Politics and European Integration: From the Constitution to the Lisbon Treaty*, Cheltenham: Edward Elgar.

Liefferink, D. and Andersen, M. S. (1998) 'Strategies of the 'green' member states in EU environmental policy-making', *Journal of European Public Policies*, 5(2): 254–270.

Lijphart, A. (1971) 'Comparative politics and the comparative method', *American Political Science Review*, 65 (3): 682–693.

Lindberg, B. (2008a) *Fit for European Democracy? Party Discipline in the European Parliament*, PhD-thesis, Uppsala: University of Uppsala.

Lindberg, B. (2008b) 'Are political parties controlling legislative decision-making in the European Parliament? The case of the services directive', *Journal of European Public Policy*, 15(8): 1185–1205.

Lindberg, B., Rasmussen, A. and Warntjen, A. (2009) 'Party politics as usual? The role

of political parties in EU legislative decision-making', *Journal of European Public Policy*, 15(8): 1107–1126.
Lindberg L. (1963) *The Political Dynamics of European Economic Integration*, Stanford, CA: Stanford University Press.
Lord, C. J. (2006) *The Aggregating Function of Political Parties in EU Decision-Making*, available online at: http://europeangovernance.livingreviews.org/Articles/lreg-2006-2/download/lreg-2006-2Color.pdf (accessed 21 March 2012).
Lowery, D. and Sigelman, L. (1981) 'Understanding the tax revolt: eight explanations', *American Political Science Review*, 75: 963–974.
Lubbers, M. (2008) 'Regarding the Dutch "nee" to the European Constitution. A test of the identity, utilitarian and political approaches to voting "no"', *European Union Politics*, 9(1): 59–86.
McElroy, G. (2001) 'Committees and party cohesion in the European Parliament', *Party Politics*, 12(6): 691–714.
McElroy, G. (2002) *Committees and Party Cohesion in the European Parliament*, available online at: www2.lse.ac.uk/government/research/resgroups/EPRG/EPRGworkingPapers.aspx (accessed 21 March 2012).
McElroy, G. (2006) 'Committee representation in the European Parliament', *European Union Politics*, 7(1): 5–29.
McElroy, G. (2007) 'Legislative politics', in K. E. Jørgensen, M. Pollack, and B. J. Rosamund (eds) *Handbook of European Union Politics*, London: Sage.
MacKinnon, D., Warsi, G. and Dwyer, J. (1995) 'A simulation study of mediated effect measures, *Multivariate Behavioral Research*, 30(1): 41–62.
Magnette, P. and Nicolaïdis, K. (2005) 'Coping with the Lilliput Syndrome: large vs. small member states in the European Union', *European Public Law*, 11(1): 83–102.
Magnúsdóttir, G. L. (2009) *Small States' Power Resources in EU Negotiations – the Cases of Sweden, Denmark and Finland in the Environmental Policy of the European*, PhD-thesis, Reykjavik: University of Iceland.
Malici, A. (2008) *The Search for a Common European Foreign and Security Policy*, Houndmills: Palgrave.
Mamadouh, V. and Raunio, T. (2003) 'The committee system: power, appointments and report allocation', *Journal of Common Market Studies*, 41(2): 333–351.
Manners, I. (2000) *Substance and Symbolism: An Anatomy of Cooperation in the New Europe*, Aldershot: Ashgate.
Manners, I. and Whitman, R. (eds) (2000) *The Foreign Policies of European Union Member States*, Manchester: Manchester University Press.
March, J. and Olsen, J. P. (1989) *Rediscovering Institutions: The Organizational Basis of Politics*, New York: the Free Press.
Marcussen, M. (2005) 'Denmark and European monetary integration: out but far from over', *Journal of European Integration*, 27(1): 43–63.
Marcussen, M. (2008) 'The Danish central bank – the reluctant European', in *CEP Working Paper Series (2008/1)*, Copenhagen: University of Copenhagen.
Marcussen, M. (2009) 'United in diversity: EMU as a differentiation project', in R. Caesar, H. Kotz, W. Kösters and D. Schwarzer (eds) *Governing the Eurozone: Looking Ahead After the First Decade*, Berlin: Stiftung Wissenschaft und Politik.
Marcussen, M. (2010) *Den danske model og globaliseringen*, Copenhagen: Samfundslitteratur.
Marcussen, M. and Dyson, K. (2010) 'Transverse integration in European economic governance: between unitary and differentiated integration', *Journal of European Integration*, 32(1): 17–39.

Marcussen, M. and Kaspersen, L. B. (2007) 'Globalization and institutional competitiveness', *Regulation and Governance*, 1(3): 183–196.

Marcussen, M. and Zolner, M. (2001) 'The Danish EMU referendum 2000: business as usual', *Government and Opposition*, 36(3): 379–402.

Marks, G. and Hooghe, L. (2001) *Multi-Level Governance and European Integration*, Lanham: Rowman & Littlefield.

Marshall, D. (2010) 'Who to lobby and when: institutional determinants of interest group strategies in European Parliament committees', *European Union Politics*, 11(4): 553–575.

Martinsen, D. S. (2005a) 'The Europeanization of welfare – the domestic impact of intra-European social security', *Journal of Common Market Studies*, 43(5): 1027–1054.

Martinsen, D. S. (2005b) 'Towards an internal health market with the European Court', *West European Politics*, 28(5): 1035–1056.

Martinsen, D. S. (2009) 'Conflict and conflict management in the cross-border provision of healthcare services', *West European Politics*, 32(4): 792–809.

Martinsen, D. S. and Beck Jorgensen, T. (2010) 'Accountability as a differentiated value in supranational governance', *The American Review of Public Administration*, 40(6): 742–760.

Martinsen, D. S. and Vrangbæk, K. (2008) 'The Europeanisation of healthcare governance – implementing the market imperatives of Europe', *Public Administration*, 86(1): 169–184.

Mass, W. (2003) 'Creating European citizens: the genesis of European rights', paper presented at European Union Studies Association Biennial Conference on Creating European Citizens, Nashville, March 2003, available online at: http://aei.pitt.edu/6520/ (accessed 29 March 2012).

Mattila, M. (2004) 'contested decisions: empirical analysis of voting in the European Union Council of Ministers', *European Journal of Political Research*, 43(1): 29–50.

Mattila, M. (2008) 'Voting and coalitions in the council after the enlargement', in D. Naurin and H. Wallace (eds) *Unveiling the Council of the European Union – Games Governments Play in Brussels*, Basingstoke: Palgrave Macmillan.

Mattila, M. and Lane, J. E. (2001) 'Why unanimity in the council? A roll call analysis of council voting', *European Union Politics*, 2(1): 31–52.

Mény, Y., Muller, P. and Quermonne, J.-L. (1996) *Adjusting to Europe – The Impact of the European Union on National Institutions and Policies*, London: Routledge.

Messmer, W. M. (2003) 'Taming Labour's party MEPs', *Party Politics*, 9(2): 201–218.

Meynaud, J. (1958) *Les Groups de Pression en France*, Paris: Armand Colin.

Michelmann, H. J. (1978) *Organizational Effectiveness in a Multinational Bureaucracy*, Westmead: Saxon House.

Miles, L. (1996) *The European Union and the Nordic Countries*, London: Routledge.

Miles, L. (1998) 'Sweden and the IGC: testing the membership diamond', *Cooperation and Conflict*, 33(3): 339–366.

Miles, L. (2001) 'Sweden in the European Union: changing expectations', *Journal of European Integration*, 23(4): 303–333.

Miles, L. (2002) 'Small states and the European Union: reflections', *Current Politics and Economics of Europe*, 11(2): 91–98.

Miles, L. (2003a) 'Evaluating the Danish EU presidency' in P. Carlsen and H. Mouritzen, (eds) *Danish Foreign Policy Yearbook 2003*, Copenhagen: Danish Institute of International Studies.

Miles, L. (2003b) 'The fusion perspective revisited', *Cooperation and Conflict*, 38(3): 291–298.

Miles, L. (2003c) 'Leading from the periphery?', *Cooperation and Conflict*, 38(3): 281–282.
Miles, L. (2004) (ed.) 'Symposium on the 2003 Swedish euro referendum: international responses', *Cooperation and Conflict*, 39(2): 151–203.
Miles, L. (2005a) *Fusing with Europe: Sweden in the European Union*, Aldershot: Ashgate.
Miles, L. (2005b) 'Introduction: euro-outsiders and the politics of asymmetry', *Journal of European Integration*, 27(1): 3–23.
Miles, L. (2005c) 'The North', in H. Mouritzen and A. Wivel (eds) *The Geopolitics of Euro-Atlantic Integration*, London: Routledge.
Miles, L. (2009) 'A fusing Europe? Insights for EU governance', in M. Dougan and S. Currie (eds) *50 Years of the European Treaties: Looking Back and Thinking Forward*, Oxford: Hart Publishing.
Miles, L. (2010a) 'Nordic Europe', in K. Dyson and A. Sepos (eds) *Which Europe? The Politics of Differentiated Integration*, Houndmills: Palgrave.
Miles, L. (2010b) 'When a fusing Europe and a globalizing world meet', in J.-W. Wunderlich and D. J. Bailey (eds) *The European Union and Global Governance*, London: Routledge.
Miles, L. (2011a) 'Thinking bigger: fusion concepts, strengths and scenarios', in U. Diedrichs, A. Faber, F. Rekin, and G. Umbach (eds) *Europe Reloaded: Differentiation or Fusion?*, Baden-Baden: Nomos.
Miles, L. (2011b) 'National adaptation and fusion in the Nordic states', in H. Høibraaten and J. Hille (eds) *Northern Europe and the Future of the European Union*, Berlin: BWV - Berliner Wissenschaftsverlag.
Miljan, T. (1997) *The Reluctant Europeans – The Attitudes of the Nordic Countries Towards European Integration*, London: C. Hurst & Company.
Mintz, A. (2003) 'Integrating cognitive and rational theories of foreign policy decision making: a poliheuristic perspective', in A. Mintz, (ed.) *Integrating Cognitive and Rational Theories of Foreign Policy Decision Making*, Houndmills: Palgrave Macmillan.
Mintz, A. and DeRouen Jr. (2010) *Understanding Foreign Policy Decision Making*, Cambridge: Cambridge University Press.
Ministry of Agriculture (1983) *Betænkning fra Udvalget vedrørende landbrugets økonomiske vilkår og udvikling. En fremtidig landbrugspolitik – nogle mere langsigtede perspektiver*, Copenhagen.
Ministry of Agriculture and Fisheries (1995) *Hvordan fungerer EU's landbrugspolitik*, Copenhagen.
Ministry of Food, Agriculture and Fisheries (2010) *Towards a New Common Agricultural Policy: Comments from the Danish Government to the Commission's Public Debate*, Copenhagen.
Ministry of Foreign Affairs (2004) *Retningslinier for den danske EU-beslutningsprocedure*, Copenhagen.
Ministry of Foreign Affairs (2005) *Oversigt over traktatkrænkelsessager og retssager, hvori Danmark var involveret i 2004, journalnummer 400.C.2–0, 18. april 2005*, Copenhagen.
Ministry of Foreign Affairs (2009) *Danmark og EU-Domstolen i 2009. Årlig oversigt over retssager ved EU-Domstolen, som Danmark er involveret i, og traktatkrænkelsessager mod Danmark*, available online at: www.um.dk/NR/rdonlyres/0D2C2D19-A70B-4F8B-8850–0513045016AB/0/DanmarkogEUDomstoleni2009.pdf (accessed 9 April 2012).

Ministry of Foreign Affairs (2010a) *Introduction to the Danish EU Decision-Making Process by Thomas Lehmann and Lise Bøgh Hansen of 17 May 2010*, Copenhagen.

Ministry of Foreign Affairs (2010b) *Handlingsplan: Et mere åbent og sikkert indre marked*, Copenhagen.

Ministry of Health (1999) *Consequences of the European Court of Justice Rulings in the Decker/Kohll Cases – Statement by the Working Group*, Copenhagen: Danish Ministry of Health.

Moller, J. O. (2003), 'Maastricht-traktaten og Edinburgh-afgorelsen', in *Danmark 30 år i EU – et festskrift*, Copenhagen: Gyldendal.

Molle, W. (2006) *The Economics of European Integration: Theory, Practice, Policy*, Farnham: Ashgate Publishers.

Monar, J. (2007) 'Justice and home affairs', *Journal of Common Market Studies*, 45(1): 107–227.

Monti, M. (2010) *A New Strategy for the Single Market at the Service of Europe's Economy and Society: Report to the President of the European Commission José Manuel Barroso*, Brussels.

Moravcsik, A. (1993) 'Preferences and power in the European Community: a liberal intergovernmentalist approach', *Journal of Common Market Studies*, 31(4): 473–524.

Moravcsik, A. (1998) *The Choice for Europe: Social Purpose and State Power from Messina to Maastricht*, Ithaca: Cornell University Press.

Moravcsik, A. and Nicolaidis, K. (1998) 'Keynote article: federal ideals and constitutional realities in the Treaty of Amsterdam', *Journal of Common Market Studies*, 36: 13–38.

Mouritzen, H. (1988) *Finlandization: Towards a General Theory of Adaptive Politics*, Aldershot: Avebury.

Mouritzen, H. (1995) 'The Nordic model as a foreign policy instrument: its rise and fall', *Journal of Peace Research*, 32(1): 9–21.

Mouritzen, H. (1996) 'Denmark', in H. Mouritzen, O. Wæver and H. Wiberg (eds) *European Integration and National Adaptations*. Commack: Nova Science Publishers.

Mouritzen, H. (1997) *External Danger and Democracy: Old Nordic Lessons and New European Challenges*, Aldershot: Ashgate.

Mouritzen, H. (2007) 'Denmark's super atlanticism', *Journal of Transatlantic Studies*, 5(2): 155–169.

Mouritzen, H. and Olesen, M. R. (2010) 'The interplay of geopolitics and historical lessons in foreign policy: Denmark facing German post-war rearmament', *Cooperation and Conflict*, 45(4): 406–427.

Mouritzen, H. and Wivel, A. (eds) (2005) *The Geopolitics of Euro-Atlantic Integration*, London: Routledge.

Mouritzen, H., Wæver, O. and Wiberg, H. (eds) (1996) *European Integration and National Adaptations*, Commack: Nova Science Publishers.

Napel, S. and Widgren, M. (2010) Strategic versus non-strategic voting power in the EU Council of Ministers: the consultation procedure, available online at: www.vwl4.uni-bayreuth.de/de/research/publications/2011/Strategic_vs__Non-strategic_Voting_Power_in_the_EU/SMP_in_ConsultationRevised.pdf (accessed 18 March 2012).

Naurin, D. and Lindahl, R. (2008a) '*Out in the Cold? Euro-Outsiders Inside the Council of Ministers*', paper prepared for presentation at the International Studies Association's 49th Annual Convention, San Francisco.

Naurin, D. and Lindahl, R. (2008b) 'East-north-south: coalition building in the Council before and after enlargement', in D. Naurin and H. Wallace (eds) *Unveiling the Council*

of the European Union – Games Governments Play in Brussels, Basingstoke: Palgrave Macmillan.
Neack, L. (2003) *The New Foreign Policy: US and Comparative Foreign Policy in the 21st Century*, Lanham: Rowmand & Littlefield.
Nedergaard, P. (1992) 'Agricultural policy', in L. Lyck (ed.) *Denmark and the EC Membership Evaluated*, London: Pinter Publishers.
Nedergaard, P. (1995) 'The political economy of CAP reform', in F. Laursen (ed.) *The Political Economy of European Integration*, The Hague: Kluwer Law International.
Nedergaard, P. (2005) *Organiseringen af Den Europæiske Union. Bureaukrater og Institutioner: EU-Forvaltningens Effektivitet og Legitimitet*, Copenhagen: Handelshøjskolens Forlag.
Nedergaard, P. (2006) 'The 2003 reform of the Common Agricultural Policy: against all odds or rational explanations?', *Journal of European Integration*, 28(3): 203–223.
Nedergaard, P. (2009) *Business and Politics in the European Union*, Copenhagen: DJØF.
Nielsen, R. L. and Pedersen, R. B. (2011) 'The Danish Left and the Constitutional/Lisbon Treaty: from vote/office seekers to policy pragmatists?', in M. Holmes and K. Roder (eds) *The Left and the European Constitution*, Manchester: Manchester University Press.
Niemann, A. and Schmitter, P. (2009) 'Neofunctionalism', in A. Wiener and T. Diez (eds) *European Integration Theory*, 2nd edition, Oxford: Oxford University Press.
Noreen, E. (1983) 'The Nordic balance: a security policy concept in theory and practice', *Cooperation and Conflict*, 18(1): 43–56.
Noury, A. (2002) 'Ideology, nationality and Euro-parliamentarism', *European Union Politics*, 3(1): 33–58.
Nugent, N. (2000) *At the Heart of the Union: Studies of the European Commission*, Houndmills: Macmillan.
Nye, J. S. (2004) *Soft Power: The Means to Success in World Politics*, New York: Public Affairs Books.
Olesen, T. B. and Laursen, J. (1994) 'Det europæiske markedskisma 1960–1972', in T. Swienty (ed.) *Danmark i Europa 1945–93*, Copenhagen: Munksgaard.
Olsen, G. R. (2011) 'How strong is europeanization, really? The Danish defence administration and the opt-out from the European Security and Defence Policy', *Perspectives on European Politics and Society*, 12(1): 13–28.
Olsen, J. P. (2005) 'Maybe it is time to rediscover bureaucracy', *Journal of Public Administration Research and Theory*, 16(1): 1–24.
Olsen, J. P. (2007) *Europe in Search of Political Order. An Institutional Perspective on Unity/Diversity, Citizens/Their Helpers, Democratic Design/Historical Drift, and the Co-Existence of Orders*, Oxford: Oxford University Press.
Oscarsson, H. and Holmberg, S. (2004) *Kampen om euron*, Göteborg: University of Göteborg.
Østergaard, M., Olesen, J. and Attrup, L. (2004) 'EU-kommissær: Outsider vandt over favoritten', *Jyllands-Posten*, published 3 August 2004.
Page, E. C. (1997) *People Who Run Europe*, Oxford: Clarendon Press.
Pagh, P. (2001) *Responsum om dansk gennemførelse af Habitatdirektivets Artikel 6 – om den danske implementering af EU's krav til bevarings og beskyttelsesforanstaltninger for de særlige bevaringsområder Danmark har udpeget i henhold til fugledirektivet (79/409) & habitatdirektivet (92/43)*, Copenhagen.
Panke, D. (2010a) *Small States in the European Union: Coping with Structural Disadvantages*, Aldershot: Ashgate.

264 Bibliography

Panke, D. (2010b) 'Small states in the European Union: structural disadvantages in EU policy-making and counter-strategies', *Journal of European Public Policy*, 17(6): 799–817.

Panke, D. (2010c) 'Good instructions in no time? Domestic coordination of EU policies in 19 small states', *West European Politics*, 33(4): 770–790.

Papagianni, G. (2001) 'Flexibility in justice and home affairs: an old phenomenon taking new forms', in B. de Witte, D. Hanf and E. Vos (eds) *The Many Faces of Differentiation in the EU*, Antwerp: Intersentia.

Pedersen, O. K (2002) 'Fire teser', in O. K. Pedersen (ed.), *EU i Forvaltningen. Broen fra Slotsholmen til Bruxelles*, Copenhagen: DJOF Forlag.

Pedersen, O. K. and Campbell, J. (2007) 'The varieties of capitalism and hybrid success. Denmark in the global economy', *Comparative Political Studies*, 40(3): 307–332.

Pedersen, O. K., Esmark, A., Frankel, C. and Hojbjerg, E. (2002) *EU i forvaltningen: Broen fra Slotsholmen til Bruxelles*, Copenhagen: Juristernes og Okonomernes Forlag.

Pedersen, R. B. (2009) *Danmark under traktaterne: Et casestudie af regerings- og parlamentsrelationer under forhandlingerne om Fælles Akten og Maastricht traktaten*, PhD-thesis, Aarhus: University of Aarhus.

Pedersen, T. (1996) 'Denmark and the European Union', in L. Miles (ed.) *The European Union and the Nordic Countries*, London: Routledge.

Pedersen, T. (1998) *Germany, France and the Integration of Europe: A Realist Interpretation*, London: Pinter.

Pedersen, T. (2000) 'Denmark', in H. Kassim, B. G. Peters and V. Wright (eds) *National Co-Ordination EU Policy: The Domistic Level*, Oxford: Oxford University Press.

Peers, S. (2006) *Justice and Home Affairs Law*, Oxford: Oxford University Press.

Permanent Representation of Denmark to the EU (2008) '*Europa-Kommissionen. EU-repræsentationens interne vejledning*', Copenhagen.

Petersen, N. (1995) 'Denmark and the European Community 1985–1993', in C. Due-Nielsen and N. Petersen (eds) *Adaption and Activism: The Foreign Policy of Denmark 1967–1993*, Copenhagen: DJOF Forlag.

Petersen, N. (1998) 'National strategies in the integration dilemma: an adaptation approach', *Journal of Common Market Studies*, 36(1): 33–54.

Petersen, N. (2004) *Europæisk og globalt engagement: Bind 6 i Dansk Udenrigspolitiks Historie*, Copenhagen: Danmarks Nationalleksikon.

Petersen, N. (2006) *Dansk Udenrigspolitiks Historie 6: Europæisk og Globalt Engagement 1973–2006*, Copenhagen: Gyldendal.

Petersen, N. H. (2003), 'Formuleringen af forbeholdene', in *Danmark 30 år i EU – et festskrift*, Copenhagen: Gyldendal.

Peterson, J. (1999): 'The Santer era: the European Commission in normative, historical and theoretical perspective', *Journal of European Public Policy*, 6(1): 46–65.

Pisani-Ferry, J., Aghion, P., Belka, M., Hagen, J. von, Heikensten, L. and Sapir, A. (2008) *Coming of Age: Report on the Euro Area (Bruegel Blueprint Series Volume 4)*, Brussels: Bruegel.

Politiken (2001) *Nyrups folk ramte mest ved siden af*, published 1 January 2001.

Politiken (2007a) *EU's rejsecirkus skal under lup*, available online at: http://politiken.dk/udland/ECE290765/eus-rejsecirkus-skal-under-ny-lup/ (accessed 21 March 2012).

Politiken (2007b) *EU's rejsecirkus belaster miljoet*, available online at: http://politiken.dk/udland/ECE291086/eus-rejsecirkus-belaster-miljoeet/ (accessed 21 March 2012).

Politiken (2009) *EU-politikere får markant lonhop*, available online at: http://politiken.dk/politik/article710889.ece (accessed 21 March 2012).

Politiken (2011) *Danmark: Ansatte i EU får alt for høj løn*, published 22 February 2011.
Pollack, M. (2003) *Delegation, Agency, and Agenda Setting in the European Community*, Cambridge: Cambridge University Press.
Preacher, K. and Hayes, A. (2004) 'SPSS and SAS procedures for estimating indirect effects in simple mediation models, *Behavior Research Methods, Instruments & Computers*, 36(4): 717–731.
Pressman, J. and Wildavsky, A. (1973) *Implementation: How Great Expectations in Washington are Dashed in Oakland*, Berkeley: University of California Press.
Putnam, R. (1988) 'Diplomacy and domestic politics: the logic of two-level games', *International Organization*, 43(3): 427–460.
Radaelli, C. M. (2003) 'The Europeanization of public policy', in K. Featherstone and C. M. Radaelli (eds) *The Politics of Europeanization*, Oxford: Oxford University Press.
Rasmussen, A. (2008a) 'The EU Conciliation Committee: one or several principals?', *European Union Politics*, 9(1): 87–113.
Rasmussen, A. (2008b) 'Party soldiers in a non-partisan community? party linkage in the European Parliament', *Journal of European Public Policy*, 15(8): 1164–1183.
Rasmussen, H. (1988) 'Denmark', in H. Siedentopf and J. Ziller, (eds) *Making European Policies Work – The Implementation of Community Legislation in the Member States*, London: Sage.
Rasmussen, M. K. (2007) '*Another Side of the Story: A Case Study of Voting Behaviour in the European Parliament*', master-thesis, Aarhus: University of Aarhus.
Rasmussen, M. K. (2008) 'Another side of the story: a qualitative case study of voting behaviour in the European Parliament', *Politics*, 28(1): 11–18.
Rasmussen, M. K. and Manners, I. (2008) 'Danes MEPs – a channel for Danish values?', in P. Nedergaard (ed.) *Fra Fælles Forsamling til Folkestyre*, Copenhagen: Europa-Parlamentets Informationskontor.
Rasmussen, M. V. (2005) '"What's the use of it?": Danish strategic culture and the utility of armed force', *Cooperation and Conflict*, 40(1): 67–89.
Raunio, T. (1997) *The European Perspective: Transnational Party Groups in the 1989–1994 European Parliament*, Aldershot: Ashgate.
Ray, L. (2003) 'reconsidering the link between incumbent support and pro-EU opinion', *European Union Politics*, 4(3): 259–279.
Reif, K. and Schmitt, H. (1980) 'Nine second-order national elections: a conceptual framework for the analysis of European election results', *European Journal of Political Research*, 8(1): 3–44.
Retsinformation (2006) *Cirkulære om lønudgifter til danske embedsmænd udsendt som nationale eksperter til EU-Kommissionen, EU's Ministerråd og Europa-Parlamentet*, available online at: www.retsinformation.dk/Forms/R0710.aspx?id=5932&exp=1 (accessed 21 March 2012).
Retsinformation (2010) *Lov om ændring af lov om afgift af spiritus m.m. (Ændringer som følge af EF's indre marked m.v.), Lov nr. 1917 af 19/12/1992*, Copenhagen.
Retsinformation (2012) *Lov om ændring af udlændingeloven og ægteskabsloven med flere love*, available online at: www.retsinformation.dk/Forms/R0710.aspx?id=28895 (accessed 31 March 2012).
Rhodes, R. A. W. (1997) *Understanding Governance: Policy Networks, Governance, Reflexivity, and Accountability*, Maidenhead: Open University Press.
Ringsmose, J. (2009) 'Paying for protection: Denmark's military expenditure during the Cold War', *Cooperation and Conflict*, 44(1): 73–97.
Ringsmose, J. and Rynning, S. (2008) 'The impeccable ally? Denmark, NATO, and the

uncertain future of top tier membership', in N. Hvidt and H. Mouritzen (eds) *Danish Foreign Policy Yearbook 2008*, Copenhagen: Danish Institute for International Studies.

Ritzaus Bureau (2010) *Truede fugle i Tondermarsken*, published 26 April 2010.

Rohrschneider, R. (2002) 'The democracy deficit and mass support for an EU wide government', *American Journal of Political Science*, 46(2): 463–475.

Ronit, K. (2000) 'Leading and following – private and public organizations in the evolution of global shipping', in H. J. Jacek (ed.) *Organized Business and the New Global Order*, London: Macmillan.

Ronit, K. (2012) 'Global strategies and policy arrangements: institutional drivers for innovation in the wind turbine industry', forthcoming in J. M. Bauer, A. Lang and V. Schneider (eds) *Innovation Policies and Governance in High-Technology Industries: The Complexity of Coordination*, Berlin and New York: Springer.

Rüdiger, M. (1994) 'Stagnation, 1973–79', in T. Swienty (ed.) *Danmark i Europa 1945–93* Copenhagen: Munksgaard.

Ryborg, O. V. (1998) *Det utænkelige nej...!*, Copenhagen: Informations Forlag.

Ryborg, O. V. (2008) 'VK gav gront lys for lempede familiesammenforingsregler i EU', *Mandag Morgen*, published 11 August 2008.

Sandholtz, W. and Zysman, J. (1989) '1992: recasting the European bargain', *World Politics*, 42(1): 95–128.

Saxi, H. L. (2010) 'Defending small states: Norwegian and Danish defence policies in the post-Cold War era', *Defence and Security Analysis*, 26(4): 415–430.

Saxi, H. L. (2011) 'Nordic (in)security', available online at: www.pnyxblog.com/pnyx/2011/9/2/nordic-insecurity.html (acessed 27 January 2012).

Schalk, J., Torenvlied, R., Weesie, J. and Stokman, F. (2007) 'The power of the Presidency in EU Council decision-making', *European Union Politics*, 8(2): 229–250.

Schmidt, V. (2006) *Democracy in Europe: The EU and National Politics*, Oxford: Oxford University Press.

Schmitt, H. (2005) 'The European Parliament elections 2004: still second-order?', *West European Politics*, 28(3): 650–679.

Schneider, G. and Weitsman, P. (1996) 'The punishment trap: integration referendums as popularity contests', *Comparative Political Studies*, 28: 582–607.

Schuck, A. and de Vreese, C. (2008) 'The Dutch no to the EU Constitution: assessing the role of EU skepticism and the campaign', *Journal of Elections, Public Opinion, and Parties*, 18(1): 101–128.

Schwartz, H. M. (2001) 'The Danish "miracle" luck, pluck, or stuck?', *Comparative Political Studies*, 34(2): 131–155.

Sidenius, N. C. (1984) 'Dansk industripolitik – beslutningsformer, interesser og statens relative autonomi', in G. R. Olsen, M. Ougaard and N. C. Sidenius (eds) *Stat, Statskundskab, Statsteori*, Aarhus: Politica.

Siune, K. and Svensson, P. (1993) 'The Danes and the Maastricht Treaty: the Danish EC referendum of June 1992, *Electoral Studies*, 12(2): 99–111.

Siune, K., Svensson, P. and Tonsgaard, O. (1994) 'The European Union: the Danes said 'no' in 1992 but 'yes' in 1993: how and why?', *Electoral Studies*, 13: 107–116.

Snyder, G. (1984) 'The security dilemma in alliance politics', *World Politics*, 36(4): 461–495.

Sobel, M. (1982) 'Asymptotic intervals for indirect effects in structural equations models', in S. Leinhart (ed.) *Sociological Methodology 1982*, San Francisco: Jossey-Bass.

Soetendorp, B. (1999) *Foreign Policy in the European Union*, London and New York: Longman.

Sørensen, C. (2007a) *Euro-scepticism: A Conceptual Analysis and a Longitudinal, Cross-Country Examination of Public Scepticism toward the European Union*, PhD-thesis, Copenhagen: University of Copenhagen.

Sørensen, C. (ed.) (2007b) *50 år med EU: Danske perspektiver*, Copenhagen: Dansk Institut for Internationale Studier.

Sørensen, V. (1994) 'Fra Marshall-plan til de store markedsdannelser 1945–59', in T. Swienty (ed.) *Danmark i Europa 1945–93*, Copenhagen: Munksgaard.

Starup, P. (2008) 'Europæiseringen af dansk familiesammenføringsret', in B. E. Olsen and K. E. Sørensen (eds) *Europæiseringen af dansk ret*, Copenhagen: DJØF Forlag.

Steinmetz, R. and Wivel, A. (eds) (2010) *Small States in Europe: Challenges and Opportunities*, Aldershot: Ashgate.

Streit, M. and Mussler, W. (1995) 'The economic constitution of the EC: from Rome to Maastricht', *European Law Journal*, 1(1): 5–30.

Strömvik, M. (1998) 'Fifteen votes and one voice? The CFSP and changing voting alignments in the UN', *Statsvetenskaplig Tidskrift*, 101(2): 181–196.

Svensson, P. (1994) 'The Danish YES to Maastricht and Edinburgh: The EC referendum of May 1993', *Scandinavian Political Studies*, 17(1): 69–82.

Svensson, P. (2002) 'Five Danish referendums on the European Community and European Union: a critical assessment of the Franklin Thesis', *European Journal of Political Research*, 41: 733–750.

Tallberg, J. (2002) 'Paths to compliance: enforcement, management, and the European Union', *International Organization*, 25(2): 173–195.

Tallberg, J. (2003) *European Governance and Supranational Institutions, Making States Comply*, London: Routledge.

Tallberg, J. (2006) *Leadership and Negotiation in the European Union*, Cambridge: Cambridge University Press.

Thomassen, J., Noury, A. and Voeten, E. (2004) 'Political competition in the European Parliament: evidence from roll call and survey analysis', in C. Marks and M. R. Steenbergen (eds) *European Integration and Political Conflict*, Cambridge: Cambridge University Press.

Thomson, R., Stokman, F. N., Achen, C. H. and König, T. (2006) *The European Union Decides*, Cambridge: Cambridge University Press.

Thorhallsson, B. and Wivel, A. (2006) 'Small states in the European Union: what do we know and what would we like to know?', *Cambridge Review of International Affairs*, 19(4): 651–668.

Togeby, L., Andersen, J. G., Christiansen, P. M., Jørgensen, T. B. and Vallgårda, (?) (2003) *Magt og demokrati i Danmark – hovedresultater fra Magtudredningen*, Aarhus: Aarhus University Press.

Tonra, B. (2000) 'Denmark and Ireland', in I. Manners and R. Whitman (eds) *The Foreign Policies of European Union Member States*, Manchester: Manchester University Press.

Tranholm-Mikkelsen, J. (1991) 'Neofunctionalism: obstinate or obsolete? a reappraisal in the light of the new dynamism of the European Community', *Millennium*, 20: 1–22.

Trondal, J. (2000) 'Multiple institutional embeddedness in Europe: the case of Danish, Norwegian, and Swedish government officials', *Scandinavian Political Studies*, 23(4): 311–341.

Trondal, J. (2007) 'The public administration turn in integration research', *Journal of European Public Policy*, 14(6): 960–972.

Trondal, J. (2008) 'The anatomy of autonomy: reassessing the autonomy of the European Commission', *European Journal of Political Research*, 47(4): 467–488.

Trondal, J., Van den Berg, C. and Suvarierol, S. (2008) 'The compound machinery of government: the case of seconded officials in the European Commission', *Governance*, 21(2): 253–274.

Turner, B. and Nordquist, G. (1982) *The Other European Community: Integration and Cooperation in Nordic Europe*, London: Weidenfeld and Nicholson.

Tuytschaever, F. (1999) *Differentiation in European Union Law*, Oxford: Hart Publishing.

Tversky, A. and Kahneman, D. (1992) 'Advances in prospect theory: cumulative representation of uncertainty', *Journal of Risk and Uncertainty*, 5(4): 297–323.

Umbach, G. and Wessels, W. (2009) 'Differentiation in the European system of central banks: circles, core, and directoire', in K. Dyson and M. Marcussen (eds) *Central Banks in the Age of the Euro: Europeanization, Convergence and Power*, Oxford: Oxford University Press.

Vedsted-Hansen, J. (2004) 'Denmark', in I. Higgens (ed.) *Migration and Asylum Law and Policy in the European Union: FIDE 2004 National Reports*, Cambridge: Cambridge University Press.

Vedsted-Hansen, J. (2008) 'Det retlige forbehold og personers mobilitet', in B. E. Olsen and K. E. Sorensen (eds) *Europæiseringen af dansk ret*, Copenhagen: DJOF Forlag.

Villaume, P. (1995) *Allieret med forbehold: Danmark, NATO og den kolde krig*. Copenhagen: Forlaget Vandkunsten.

Wæver, O. (1992) 'Nordic nostalgia: northern Europe after the Cold War', *International Affairs*, 68(1): 77–102.

Wæver, O. (1998) 'Integration as security: constructing a Europe at peace', in C. Kupchan (ed.) *Atlantic Security: Contending Visions*. New York: Council on Foreign Relations.

Wallace, H. (1997) 'At odds with Europe', *Political Studies*, 45(4): 677–688.

Wallace, W. (1999) 'Small European states and European policy-making: strategies, roles, possibilities', in W. Wallace *et al.* (eds) *Between Autonomy and Influence: Small States and the European Union*, Arena Report, 99(1), Oslo: ARENA – Centre for European Studies.

Weiler, J. H. H (1999) *The Constitution of Europe: 'Do the New Clothes Have an Emperor' and Other Essays on European Integration*, Cambridge: Cambridge University Press.

Welch, D. (2005) *Painful Choices: A Theory of Foreign Policy Change*, Princeton: Princeton University Press.

Wessels, W. (2001) 'Nice results: the millenium IGC in the EU's evolution', *Journal of Common Market Studies*, 39(2): 197–219.

Westlake, M. and Galloway, D. (2004) *The Council of Ministers*, London: John Harpers Publishing.

White, B. (2001) *Understanding European Foreign Policy*, Houndmills: Palgrave Macmillan.

Whittaker, R. (2005) 'National parties in the European Parliament – an influence in the committee system?', *European Union Politics*, 6(1): 5–28.

Wiberg, H. (1989) 'Danmark mellem Norden og Europa', in B. Heurlin and C. Thune (eds) *Danmark og Det Internationale System*, Copenhagen: Political Studies Press.

Willis, V. (1982) *Britons in Brussels: Officials in the European Commission and Council Secretariat*, London: European Centre for Political Studies and the Royal Institute for Public Administration.

Wind, M. (2008) *Hykleri og dobbeltspil*, available online at: www.cep.polsci.ku.dk/formidling/artikler/mw.rson.pdf/ (accessed 9 March 2012).

Wind, M. (2009a) 'Post-national citizenship in Europe. The EU as a rights generator', *Columbia Journal of European Law*, 15(2): 239–264.
Wind, M. (2009b) 'When Parliament comes first – the Danish concept of democracy meets the European Union', *Nordic Journal of Human Rights*, 2: 272–289.
Wind, M. (2010) 'The Nordics, the EU and the reluctance towards supranational judicial review', *Journal of Common Market Studies*, 48(4): 1039–1063.
Wind, M., Martinsen, D. S. and Rotger, G. P. (2009) 'The uneven legal push for Europe: questioning variation when national courts go to Europe, *European Union Politics*, 10(1): 63–88.
Winther, B. (1999) 'Danmark spiller sidst ud', *Berlingske Tidende*, published 30 June 1999.
Wivel, A. (2000) *The Integration Spiral*, Copenhagen: University of Copenhagen.
Wivel, A. (2005a) 'The security challenge of small EU member states: interests, identity and the development of the EU as a security actor', *Journal of Common Market Studies*, 43(2): 393–412.
Wivel, A. (2005b) 'Between paradise and power: Denmark's transatlantic dilemma', *Security Dialogue*, 36(3): 417–421.
Wivel, A. (2009) 'En småstat som stormagt? Globaliseringen af dansk sikkerhedspolitik', in M. Marcussen og K. Ronit (eds) *Globaliseringens udfordringer: Politiske og administrative modeller under pres*. Copenhagen: Hans Reitzels Forlag.
Wivel, A. (2010) 'From small state to smart state: devising a strategy for influence in the European Union', in A. Wivel and R. Steinmetz (eds) *Small States in Europe. Challenges and Opportunities*, Aldershot: Ashgate.
Wivel, A. (2012) 'Danmarks militære aktivisme', in K. S. Kristensen (ed.) *Danmark i krig*, Copenhagen: DJOF Forlag.
Wong, R. and Hill, C. (2011) (eds) *National and European Foreign Policies*, London: Routledge.
Wright, V. (1996) 'The national co-ordination of European policy-making: negotiations and quagmire', in J. Richardson (ed.) *European Union. Policy and Policy-Making*, London: Routledge.
Yordanova, N. (2011) 'The effect of inter-institutional rules on the division of power in the European Parliament: Allocation of Consultation and Co-decision Reports', *West European Politics*, 34(1): 97–121.
Yoshinaka, A., McElroy, G. and Bowler, S. (2010) 'The appointment of rapporteurs in the European Parliament', *Legislative Studies Quarterly*, 35(4): 457–486.
Zimmer, C., Schneider, G. and Dobbins, M. (2005) 'The contested Council: conflict dimensions of an intergovernmental EU Institution', *Political Studies*, 53(2): 403–422.

Index

Page numbers in *italics* denote tables, those in **bold** denote figures.

A-points 206, 215n5
'active' EU policy 21
actors-context interplay 6, 17
adaptation 3, 4, 14, 16, 26–7, 97, 102, 229, 232
Adler-Nissen, R. 56, 65–79, 84, 107, 165, 217, 219, 222, 225, 232, 233
Afghanistan 81, 92
age, and voting behaviour 181
Agence Europe 57, 58, 59
Agency of Fundamental Rights 159
agenda-setting 118
Agricultural Committee 211
agriculture 7, 12, 16, 23, 141, 231; employment in 32; exports 32, 33, 34; price support 34, 35, 36, 37; prices 32–3; subsidies 32, 34, 35, 36–7, 37–8; *see also* Common Agricultural Policy (CAP)
Akrich case (2003) 162, 166, 169, 170, 173n13
Alden, C. 223
Amsterdam Treaty (1998) 20, 68, 69, 86, 161; referendum *16*, 20
Amstrup, N. 234
Andersen, J. G. 25, 53
Andersen, K. B. 205, 214
Andersen, M. S. 189
Andersen, S. R. 200
Anderson, C. 180
Anderson, P. 177
Antola, E. 234
Arab Spring (2011) 65, 66, 73
Aran, A. 223
Archer, C. 234
Arctic policy 227n5
armed forces 7, 81, 83
Arregui, J. 104, 106

Arter, D. 235
asylum policy 66, 67, 68, 70–1, 72, 73, 75, 78, 169
Attina, F. 131
Auken, M. 130
Austria 202n2, 204
autonomy 9–10, 15, 17, 18, 72–6, 133, 143
autonomy/influence dilemma 9, 14, 21, 27, 52, 229–30, 232, 233, 234–5; and CAP 42; and Council of Ministers 95, 100; and Danish EU coordination processes 214; and European Parliament 127, 231; and internal market 42; and Justice and Home Affairs (JHA) 68–9, 78; and opt-outs (reservations) 14, 18–19, 27; and public administration 191, 192; *see also* integration dilemma

B-points 206, 215n6
Balkans wars 86
Baltic countries 86; *see also* Lithuania
Bank for International Settlements 55, 57
banking: central 55, 57; supervisory system 54; *see also* European Central Bank (ECB)
Bardach, E. 191
Barroso, J. M. 65, 224
Beach, D. 103, 218
Beck Jørgensen, T. 191, 192
'beggar thy neighbour' policies 39
Belgium 202n2, 204
belonging 8
Bendtsen, B. 41
Benedetto, G. 136
Benelux countries 84; *see also* Belgium; Luxembourg; Netherlands
Benz, A. 97

Index 271

Bergman, T. 130
Berlingske Tidende 48, 50, 51, 126, 167, 200
Bjerregaard, R. 112
Blom-Hansen, J. 189, 195
Bøegh-Lervang, M. 164, 166
Bonde, J.-P. 48, 49, 134
Boomgaarden, H. 181, 185
border controls 22, 29n10, 65, 66, 68, 69, 72, 233–4
Børsen 51, 52
Börzel, T. A. 3, 4, 5, 190, 192, 193, 194, 195, 201
Bouwen, P. 147
Bowler, S. 133, 134
Branner, H. 15, 16, 228
Brighi, E. 6, 7
Brouard, S. 185
Browning, C. S. 83
Brun Pedersen, R. 95–108, 230, 234
Brundtland, A. 83
Brussels II Regulation 70, 72
Brussels Treaty (1948) 84
Bulgaria 172n4
Bulmer, S. 3, 110
Bundesbank 51, 57
Bunse, S. 110, 230
Bursens, P. 195
Bush, G. W. 92
business interests *see* interest representation

Campbell, J. 52
Camre, M. 130
capabilities 6, 7
Carey, S. 180
Carpenter case 162, 166, 173n10
cartoon crisis (2006) 88
CE (Communauté Européene/Conformité Européene) marking 42, 46n20
central banking 54, 55, 57, 60
Centre Democrats *24, 129*
change: vs. continuity 10–11, 19, 31, 43–4, 44–5; *see also* policy change
Charter of Fundamental Rights 159
child custody 72
Christian Democrats *24, 129*
Christiansen, F. J. 97, 98
Christiansen, T. M. 177
Christin, T. 180
Christmas-Møller, W. 234
Christophersen, H. 48, 112
Cichowski, R. 171
citizenship 18, 159–74, 233–4

civil law 70–1, 71–2, 74
civil servants *see* public administration
civil society 7
climate policy 21, 156
coalition building 10, 101
coalitions, political party 97, 98, 100
Cohen, B. J. 59
Cold War 15, 80, 82, 83, 84, 85, 89, 93, 94n4
College of Commissioners 112
Comité des Associations d'Armateurs des Communautés Européenes (CAACE) 151
Comitology committees 190, 191, 202n1
Committee of Permanent Representatives (COREPER) 96, 107, 190, 206, 208, 230, 236
committees 190–1; and EU coordination in Denmark 207–15; European Parliament 134–6; *see also names of individual committees*
Common Agricultural Policy (CAP) 30–1, 32–8, 141, 231; and autonomy/influence dilemma 42; and change and continuity dimension 43, 44; 'classical' subsidies 34–5, 37; direct payments to farmers 35, 36; expenditures *36*, 37; Fischler reform (2003–2004) 35, 37; and informal channels of influence 42–3; MacSharry reform (1993–1994) 35, 37; and policy change versus structural change 44; price
support policy 34, 35, 36, 37
common currency *see* euro
Common Foreign and Security Policy (CFSP) 8, 86, 87–8, 88, 226n2
Common Market 30, 32
Common Security and Defence Policy (CSDP) 7, 21–2
compatibility-consensus 6
competitiveness 38, 52, 53
Competitiveness Pact 51, 54, 55, 60, 62, 224
compliance with EU obligations 190, 191–5, 198–9, 200–2
conscription 87
consensus culture, Council of Ministers 106
Conservative Party 17, 19, *24*, 40, 41, 52, 97, *98, 99, 129*, 130, 211
Constitutional Treaty 21, 105, 179, 181, 184, 223
contacts, MEPs 138, 139, 143
continuity vs. change 10–11, 19, 31, 43–4, 44–5

Index

Coombes, D. 110
coordination processes 203–16, 220, 232; centralized 205 (external 204, 214; internal 204); decentralized 206, 208; formally-based 203, 204; informally-based 203, 204; sectorization of 206
Copenhagen summit (2002) 88
Corbett, R. 127, 128, 130, 138
COREPER (Committee of Permanent Representatives) 96, 107, 190, 206, 230, 236
cosmopolitanism 181
Council of Europe 159
Council of Ministers 10, 42, 54, 88, 93, 95–108, 206, 208, 210, 213; consensus culture 106; formal influence in 101–3; group presidency idea 105; informal influence in 104; negotiations, activity and engagement in 106–7; parliament (Folketing)/political parties and 97–100; presidency 95, 96, 97, 104–6, 233; qualified majority voting (QMV) 96, 101, 102, 108n3, 233; reform 95, 96, 100–1, 107, 108n3; simple majority voting 101; unanimity voting method 95, 96, 101, 102 108n3 and 4; veto power 101, 102; voting power in 102–3
Country of Origin principle 41
Craig, P. 160, 161
criminal law cooperation 68, 69, 74–5, 78
'cross-loading' process 3, 6, 7, 10, 220
currency 7, 18, 23; devaluations 45n4; floating 54; foreign 34; and national identity/sovereignty 55; *see also* euro
Currie, S. 162, 163
Cyprus 172n4
Czech Republic 63

Dahl, R. A. 213
Damgaard, E. 97
Danish Association of Lawyers and Economists 115
Danish Defence Commission 86, 87
Danish Economic Council 48
Danish Environmental Protection Agency 199
Danish Forest and Nature Agency 200
Danish Immigration Service 170
Danish Nature Agency 200
Danish Nature Council 199
Danish Ornithological Society 200
Danish People's Party 21, 65, 67, 97, *98*, *99*, 163, 211; and border controls 29n10; and CAP 36, 43; and euro opt-opt 50,
52; and European Parliament elections *24*, *129*, 130; Euroscepticism 21, 22, 25; government dependence on support of 20, 22, 26, 28; and immigration policy 169–70; and Internal Market 46n18; and JHA opt-out 72; nationalism 27
Danish Shipowners Association 145, 150, 151, 152, 153
Danish Society of Nature Conservation 200
Danish Wind-Industry Association 145, 154, 156
Dansk Institut for Internationale Studier 55, 71, 76, 81, 89, 237
Dansk Udenrigspolitisk Institut 19
Danske Bank 50
de Búrca, G. 160, 161, 172
de Gaulle, C. 33, 34
de Vreese, C. 175–88, 233
de Vries, C. 184
debt crises 60
decision-making processes: coordination of 203–16; European Commission 116–24; non-compensatory principle 220
decision points 192
defence opt-out 81, 88–9, 93–4, 224, 225, 237
defence policy 12, 16, 18, 19, 80–94, 232, 234; *see also* Common Security and Defence Policy (CSDP)
Delors, J. 16, 39
democracy 18, 85, 86, 176–7, **178**
Denver, D. 180
DeRouen Jr., K. 220
Det Økonomiske Råd 50, 53
détente 16, 83, 94n4
Diedrichs, U. 228
differentiated integration 7–8, 13n5, 217, 218, 229, 230, 236–7; functional dimension 8; geo-strategic dimension 7; institutional-legal dimension 7; political-economic dimension 7–8; socio-cultural dimension 8; spatial dimension 8; temporal dimension 8
diplomacy 7
direct payments, CAP 35, 36
disarmament 83
divorce 72
'downloading' process 3, 4, 6, 7, 9, 67, 82, 84, 85, 93, 109, 147, 190, 203, 220, 229
Drachmann, H. 112
dualistic policy 14, 22–3, 25–6, 27–8, 96, 107–8, 228–9, 229–34
Dublin system on asylum 70
Due-Nielsen, C. 82

Olsen, G. R. 88, 89
Olsen, J. P. 190, 191, 201, 203
openness 18
opt-in, Justice and Home Affairs (JHA) 76–8
opt-outs (reservations) 8, 11, 20, 26, 28, 217–18, 219, 220, 221, 222, 225–6, 228, 229, 230, 232, 233, 234, 237; abolition of 222, 223, 224, 225, 236; and autonomy/influence dilemma 14, 18–19, 27; citizenship 18, 161, 217; defence 18, 81, 88–9, 93–4, 217, 224, 225, 237; Euro 12, 18, 21–2, 47–64, 217, 221, 222, 224; Justice and Home Affairs (JHA) 12, 18, 21, 28, 66, 67–9, 166, 217, 224, 225, 226, 237
Organisation for Economic Cooperation and Development (OECD) 56
Oscarsson, H. 180, 181
Østergaard, M. 112

'pace-setting' strategies 4, 6, 7, 10, 86, 93, 189, 220, 222, 234, 236
Page, E. C. 110, 114, 115
Pagh, P. 199
'painful choices' 218, 221
Panke, D. 106, 234, 236
parallel agreements 66, 70–1, 75
Paris Treaty 159
parliament (Folketing): and Council of Ministers 97–100; elections results (1971–2011) *240*; and EU policy implementation 195
Party of European Socialists (PES) 134
peace 85, 86, 87
Pedersen, O. K. 52, 164, 191
Pedersen, T. 83, 84, 85, 205, 206, 207, 210, 228, 237
Peers, S. 70
People's Movement against the EU 19, 23, 24, 29n5, 48, 128, *129*
Petersberg tasks 86
Petersen, N. 9, 15, 82, 95, 96, 100, 102, 111, 229
Petersen, N. H. 58, 87
Peterson, J. 112
Pisani-Ferry, J. 59
Poland 63, 107, 204
police cooperation 65, 68, 69, 73–6, 78
policy change 11, 44, 217–18, 220–1, 224, 226
policy positions, in European Parliament 132–4
political capacity 164–5

political efficacy 181
political ideology 180, 181
political interest 180, 181
political parties: and Danish Council of Ministers policy 91–100; representation in European Parliament *24*, 128, *129*, 130; *see also names of individual parties*
political tradition 166–7
Politiken 112, 126
Pollack, M. 147
Pompidou, G. 34
Portugal 202n2, 204
positive integration 5
positive sanctions 7
power: hard 7; informal 101; soft 7
power index 102–3
preferences, transmission of *see* 'uploading' process
Pressman, J. 192
prestige of euro-outsiders 55–6
price support, CAP 34, 35, 36, 37
prices, agricultural 32–3
Progress Party *24*, 25, 49, *129*
public administration 189–202; and implementation of EU policies 189
public opinion 25, 175–88, 221, 222, 233, 238n4
public sector 52
Putnam, R. 6, 235

Quaglia, L. 47
qualified majority voting (QMV) 77, 96, 101, 102, 108n3, 233

Radaelli, C. 3, 164
rapporteurships 134, 136–8
Rasmussen, A. 126–44
Rasmussen, H. 195
Rasmussen, L. L. 22, 51, 198, 224
Rasmussen, M. K. 131, 132, 133, 138, 139, 140, 141
Rasmussen, M. V. 87
Rasmussen, P. N. 19, 20, 49, 130, 134, 224
Raunio, T. 131, 136
Ray, L. 180
reciprocity principle 70
Red–Green Alliance 21, 97, *98*, *99*, 211
referenda *16*, 26, 177, 178–9, 183; Amsterdam Treaty (1998) *16*, 20; Constitutional Treaty 21, 179, 181, 184; Edinburgh Agreement (1983) *16*, 17, 18, 19; on EU membership 15, *16*, 34; euro participation *16*, 20, 50–2, 64, 175, 224; Justice and Home Affairs (JHA) opt-in

Index 277

McElroy, G. 127, 131, 134
McLeod, A. 177
Madum, L. 164, 167
Magnette, P. 104
Magnúsdóttir, G. L. 56
Malici, A. 219
Mamadouh, V. 136
Manners, I. 6, 67, 131, 138, 141, 220
March, J. 203
Marcussen, M. 47–64, 217, 222, 232, 233
maritime sector *see* shipping industry
Marks, G. 147
Marshall, D. 148
Martinsen, D. S. 161, 189–202, 228, 232
Mass, W. 159, 172n2
Mateo, G. 236
Mattila, M. 106, 107
Members of European Parliament (MEPs) 231; attitudes towards extending power of EP *132*; attitudes towards representation *133*; committee seats 134–6; contact patterns 138, 139, 143; numbers 128; office-holding 134–6; policy positions 132–4; rapporteurships 134, 136–8; voting behaviour 132, 139–41, *142*, 143
Menon, A. 110
Mény, Y. 192
Merkel, A. 60
Messerschmidt, M. 67
Messmer, W. M. 139
Metock case 22, 160, 163, 165, 168–70
Meynaud, J. 147
Michelmann, H. J. 110
Miles, L. 1–13, 62, 63, 71, 88, 104, 110, 147, 190, 203, 217–27, 228–38
militarization 89
military activism 80–1, 87, 89–92
military defence 82–3
Miljan, T. 228
Ministry of Commerce and Shipping 150
Ministry of Economic and Business Affairs 116, 120
Ministry of Environment 200
Ministry of Foreign Affairs 116, 205, 206, 207–8, 209, 210, 212, 237
minority government 97, 100, 205
Mintz, A. 220
missile defence 81
Mitterand, F. 39
Molle, W. 32
Monar, J. 66
monetary policy-making 60–2
Monti, M. 42, 44
Moravcsik, A. 102, 131, 235

Mouritzen, H. 7, 80, 85, 96, 101, 230
MRAX case 162
Mussler, W. 159

Napel, S. 101
national attachment 180
national compromise (1992–1993) 17–18, 19–20, 27, 28, 49
national identity 180, 181, 183
national interests 3
national pride 180
National Social Appeals Board 198
nationalism 21, 27, 28, 180
nationality, and activity in European Parliament 131
NATO 15, 16, 19, 80, 81, 82–3, 84, 85, 88, 89, 92
natural habitats, conservation of 199–200
Naurin, D. 56, 104, 106, 107
Neack, L. 6
Nedergaard, P. 30–46, 128, 164, 203–16, 232–3
negative integration 5
negative sanctions 7
negotiation 7; informal 10
neoliberalism 17, 30, 38, 39, 41
Netherlands 21, 67, 104, 106, 179, 186, 202n2, 204, 223
neutrality 15, 82, 94n2
Nice Treaty (2003) 61, 102, 103
Nicoladïs, K. 104
Nielsen, R. L. 98
Niemann, A. 214
non-compliance 193–4
non-governmental organizations (NGOs), environmental 43
NORDEK (Nordiskt Ekonomiskt Samarbete) 15
'Nordic balance' 83
Nordic Council 82
'Nordic' foreign policy identity 83
Nordquist, G. 228
Noreen, E. 83
Nørgaard, I. 39, 40, 41
North Atlantic Treaty Organization *see* NATO
Northern Dimension initiative 235
Norway 15, 172n4
Noury, A. 131
nuclear weapons 88
Nugent, N. 110, 234
Nyre, J. S. 7

Olesen, T. B. 30, 33, 34, 38, 39

International Monetary Fund (IMF) 55, 56, 62
International Renewable Energy Agency (IRENA) 156
internationalism 181
Iraq 21, 80–1, 89–90, 92; 'letter of eight' 81, 89, 94n1
Ireland 15, 123, 169, 202n2, 204; debt crisis 60
Italy 65, 202n2, 204
Iversen, N. M. 200

Jacqueson, J. 162, 163
Jakobsen, P. V. 88
Jelved, M. 50
Jensen, A. D. 49, 50
Jensen, H. 212
Jensen, M. D. 126, 128
Jenssen, A. 180
Jespersen, M. H. T. 49, 50
Jessen, C. K. 112, 113
Joenniemi, P. 235
Johnson, D. 32
Joint Operation Poseidon (2011–2011) 65
Jørgensen, K. E. 218
Judicial Committee 211
Juncker, J.-C. 57, 58
June Movement 19, *24*, 25, 128, *129*
Justice and Home Affairs (JHA) 4, 8, 65–79, 172, 222, 231, 232; opt-in possibility 76–8; opt-out 12, 18, 21, 28, 66, 67–9, 166, 217, 224, 225, 226, 237
Justice Party *129*
Jyllands-Posten 53, 113

Kaeding, M. 136
Kahneman, D. 221
Kallestrup, M. 196
Karnøe, P. 154
Kaspersen, L. B. 52
Kassim, H. 110, 114, 189, 190, 203, 204, 206
Katz, R. 177
Keating, M. 8
Kelstrup, M. 1, 9, 14–29, 27, 95, 102, 107, 160, 164, 220, 222, 228, 229, 230, 237
Kjær, K. U. 73
Knudsen, O. F. 30, 32
Kölliker, A. 8
König, T. 100
Kosovo 81
Kreppel, A. 127, 131
Kritzinger, S. 180
Kurpas, S. 111, 116, 122, 124

Laatikainen, K. V. 87
labour market 52, 55, 56, 161
Ladrech, R. 218
Landbrugs- og Fiskeriministeriet 36
Lane, J. E. 107
Lansbergen, A. 162, 169
Larsen, H. 81, 84, 88, 89, 217, 218, 220, 221, 228, 232
Larsen, J. V. 113
Lassen, N. 73
Laursen, F. 30, 33, 34, 38, 39, 100, 102, 105, 229
learning processes 5
Left Socialists *129*
legislation 3, 4, 101; hard and soft 5, 118
Lehtimäki, M. 234
Lequesne, C. 110
Liberal Alliance *24*, 52, *129*
Liberal Party 17, 19, 20, 40, 41, *98*, *99*, 164, 211; and Council of Ministers 97, 100; and Euro opt-out 49, 50, 52; and European Parliament elections *24*, *129*
liberalization 39, 40, 52
Libya 92
Liefferink, D. 189
Lijphart, A. 146
Lindahl, R. 56, 104, 106, 107
Lindberg, B. 131, 136
Lindberg, L. 214
Lisbon Treaty (2007) 21, 28, 42, 66, 92, 108, 159, 177, 211, 214, 218, 222, 223; and CAP 38, 42; and Council of Ministers 100, 101, 102, 103, 105; and Euro-group 58; and European Commission 111; and European Council 104, 105; and implementation of EU policies 192, 193; and Justice and Home Affairs (JHA) 68, 74, 76, 78
Lithuania 107
lobbying 10, 12, 125n1 and 6, 236
Lord, C. 127, 133, 139
loss-aversion theory 220, 224, 225, 226
Lowery, D. 180
Lubbers, M. 184, 186
Luedtke, A. 68
Luxembourg 202n2, 204
Luxembourg Summit (1997) 58
Lykketoft, M. 50

Maastricht Treaty (Treaty on European Union (TEU), 1992) 1, 17, 18, 54, 58, 81, 86, 89, 161, 168, 217, 230; referenda 16, 17, 18, 19, 28, 48–9, 67, 88, 128, 175, 233

Goetschel, L. 229, 237
Goetz, K. H. 8
gouvernance économique 54, 59
government: composition of (1971–2011) *242*; minority 97, 100, 205
Graziano, P. 2, 228
Greece 202n2, 204; debt crisis 60
Green-Pedersen, C. 97
Greens (E/EFA) 137
Greenwood, J. 147
Grøn, C. H. 10, 109–25, 231, 235, 236
Grønnegård Christensen, J. 189, 191, 195, 205
Gross, E. 218
Grote, J. R. 147
Guantanamo Bay 92

Haahr, J. H. 17, 102
Haas, E. B. 131, 148, 214
habitats directive 199–200
Hagel-Sørensen, K. 195
Hague, W. 114
Hækkerup, P. 82
Hanreider, W. 6
Hansen, L. 67, 228
hard law 5, 118
hard power 7
harmonization: civil law legislation 71–2; and Euro Area 62, 63; of excise duties and taxes 40
Hausemeer, P. 136
Haverland, M. 192
Hayes-Renshaw, F. 107
healthcare 161, 189, 196–9
Heisborg, F. 86
Helsinki Headline Goals 86
Héritier, A. 136
Heurlin, B. 81 82, 87, 89
Hey, J. A. K.
Hill, C. 6, 7, 218, 219, 226n2
historical background of EU membership 15–22
Hix, S. 127, 131, 139, 141, 148
Hobolt, S. B. 175, 179, 180, 184, 185
Hoffmeyer, E. 48
Holbraad, C. 81
hollowing out of the state thesis 191
Holm, H.-H. 80
Holmberg, S. 180, 181
Hooghe, L. 114, 147
Howarth, D. 60
Hoyland, B. 131
Hudson, V. M. 6
Hug, S. 100

human rights 80, 85, 86, 87, 89, 92, 159–74
Hvilshøj, R. 168

Iceland 172n4
identity 8, 23, 55; national 180, 181, 183
identity politics 21, 82, 84
ideology, political 180, 181
immigration, fear of 180–1
immigration policy 65, 66, 67, 68, 69, 72, 73, 75, 78, 160–74, 234
implementation of EU policies 189, 191–202, 232; environmental regulations 199–201; healthcare 196–9
Independence/Democracy (IND/DEM) group 132, 134, 137
industrial goods 30, *33*, 38
influence 17; of euro-outsiders 56–7; formal channels of 9–10, 101–3, 124, 203, 204, 236; informal channels of 9, 10, 42–3, 104, 124, 203, 204, 236; *see also* autonomy/influence dilemma
informal channels of autonomy/influence 9, 10, 42–3, 104, 124, 203, 204, 236
informal power 101
infringement procedures 193–4
instruments 6, 7
integration: negative and positive 5; *see also* differentiated integration; economic integration; integration dilemma
integration dilemma 1, 9, 13n6, 14, 18, 19, 21, 27–8, 68, 95, 96, 107, 222, 229, 230, 233, 234, 236–7
intelligence gathering 10
interest rates 51, 60, 62
interest representation 10, 42–3, 145–58, 236; coordination of interests 147, 148; and European Parliament 148
Intergovernmental Maritime Consultative Organization (IMCO) 151
intergovernmentalism 1, 10, 16, 67–8, 84, 85, 95, 100, 106, 214, 228–9
Internal Market 5, 12, 30–1, 38–42, 47, 52, 53, 54, 55, 160, 161, 166, 172, 205, 231–2; and autonomy 42; and change and continuity dimension 43, 44–5; and informal channels of influence 42, 43; and policy change versus structural change 44
International Chamber of Shipping 150–1
International Federation of Shipping 150
international law 83
International Maritime Organization (IMO) 151

European Security and Defence Policy (ESDP) 86, 88, 89, 93, 217
European Security Strategy 86
European Semester 54
European Stability Mechanism 54
European System of Central Banks (ESCB) 54, 60
European Transparency Initiative 111, 125n6
European United--Nordic Green Left (EUL/NGL) 132
European Wind-Energy Association (EWEA) 154, 155, 156
Europeanization 2–5, 13n3, 21, 68, 160, 164, 190, 191, 218, 219, 220, 228
Europol 73–6
Euroscepticism 15, 16, 18, 19, 21, 22–3, 25, 76, 111, 229; changing character of 25; public 178, 184, 185, 186 (as mediator in referenda voting behaviour 179, 180, 181, *182*, 184)
Everson, M. 160–1
Exchange Rate Mechanism II (ERM II) 51, 52, 53–4, 57
exchange rate policy 51, 52
excise duties 40
expert committees 191
export subsidies (restitutions) 32, 34, 35, 36–7, 37–8
exports: agricultural 32, 33, 34; distribution of *31*
External Action Service 218

Falkner, G. 160, 164, 165, 194
family law 70, 72
family reunification policy 22, 67, 72, 73, 74, 78, 160, 162–3, 164, 165, 166–7, 168–70
Farrell, D. 128, 132, 134, 136
Featherstone, F. 3
federalization 16, 55, 219, 233
'fence-sitting' strategies 4, 6, 7, 10, 236
FEOGA (Fonds Européen d'Orientation et Garantie Agricoles) 32, 35
Fich, O. 126, 130–1, 132, 138, 140
financial crisis (2008–2009) 51, 52–3, 54, 58–9, 92
financial system 52
Financial Times 58
Finer, S. E. 147
Finland 88, 94n2, 106; Northern Dimension initiative 235
Fischer Boel, M. 113
fixed exchange rate policy 51, 52

Fogh Rasmussen, A. 20, 21, 22, 105, 113, 222, 223, 224
Føllesdal, A. 167
Fontainebleu Summit (1984) 39
'foot-dragging' strategies 4–5, 6, 7, 10, 81, 96, 102, 108, 189, 230, 236
Foreign Affairs Committee 207, 208, 209, 210–11
Foreign Affairs Council 104
foreign currency 34
foreign policy 80–94, 96; change 217–18, 220–1, 223; loss-aversion theory 220, 224, 225, 226; as painful choice 218, 221
fusion perspective 218–19, 222
foreign policy analysis (FPA) 5–7, 13n3, 111, 217, 218–21; strategic-relational approaches 6
foreigners: policy towards 22, 28; *see also* asylum policy; immigration; immigration policy; refugee policy
formal channels of autonomy/influence 9–10, 101–3, 124, 203, 204, 236
framework papers 208
France 21, 32, 39, 43, 65, 84, 85, 86, 104, 106, 179, 204, 223
Franklin, M. 178, 180
free movement rules 5, 22, 30, 53, 65, 66, 73, 159, 160–2, 163–74, 196
Freedom, Justice and Security *see* Justice and Home Affairs (JHA)
From, J. 192
Frontex 65
fusion perspective 218, 222, 234

Galloway, D. 102, 106
Gammeltoft-Hansen, T. 73, 75
Garry, J. 179, 180
GDP growth 7
Geddes, A. 66, 68
General Agreement of Tariffs and Trade (GATT) 35
Georgakakis, D. 114
George, A. L. 217
Geraets-Smith and Peerbooms case (2001) 197–8
Germany 21, 32, 38, 47, 57, 59–60, 68, 84, 85, 103, 104, 202n2, 204
Geurts, C. 230
Givens, T. 68
Global Wind Energy Council (GWEC) 155–6
globalization 52, 63, 64, 88, 149, 158; fear of 180–1

Dür, A. 236
Dyremose, H. 48
Dyson, K. 7, 13n5, 47, 60, 62, 228

Ecofin Council 57, 58
Economic Council of the Labour Movement 50
Economic and Financial Committee (EFC) 58
economic integration 15, 17, 18, 23; *see also* Economic and Monetary Union (EMU); euro
Economic and Monetary Union (EMU) 8, 11, 12, *18*, 40, 222, 223, 231, 232; opt-out 12, 47–64, 217; political dimensions of 54–62; *see also* euro; Euro Area
economic policy-making 57–60
economy 63–4
Edinburgh Agreement (1993) 49, 161, 175, 228, 230, 233; referendum *16*, 17, 18, 19
Egeberg, M. 110, 112, 190, 191
Eising, R. 147
Elbjørn, K. 86
Eliason, L. 82
Ellemann-Jensen, U. 48
employer associations 41
employment 18, 32, 161
energy *33*, 145, 146, 153–6, 157
enlargement of the EU 88, 105, 107, 110, 235
Environmental Committee 211
environmental NGOs 43
environmental policy 4, 18, 21, 53, 56, 87, 156, 189, 199–201, 220
Eschenburg, T. 147
Esmark, A. 203
Espersen, L. 65
EU Committee 207–8, 209–10
EurActive 113
euro: opt-out 12, 18, 21–2, 47–64, 217, 221, 222, 224; political dimensions of 55; referendum *16*, 20, 50–2, 64, 175, 224
Euro Area (eurozone) 23, 51, 52, 59, 60, 223, 224; enlargement 61; fate of 62–3
euro-council 57, 58
euro crisis 76, 224, 225
Euro-group 57–60; Working Group 58
Euro Plus Pact 54, 55, 62
euro sclerosis 39
Eurojust 74
Europe 2020 initiatives 7, 54
European Affairs Committee (EAC) 37, 41, 124, 130, 138, 163, 207, 208, 210, 211–14, 215, 232

European Arrest Warrant 74
European Central Bank (ECB) 8, 51, 58, 60; Governing Council 60–2; collegiality 60; rotating voting rights 61
European Coal and Steel Community (ECSC) 84, 85
European Commission 10, 40, 59, 109–25, 147, 190, 192, 230–1; administrative practices 111–12; agenda-setting 118; career progression in 115; Concours (entry competition) 114, 115; Danish commissioners 112–13; decision-making process 116–24; draft copies of proposals 120–1; officials 113–16; Seconded National Experts (SNEs) 114, 115–16, 119, 125n11; staff salaries 111–12, 115
European Community Shipowners' Association (ECSA) 151, 152
European Convention on Human Rights 159, 166
European Council 10, 88–9, 92, 104, 105, 148, 207
European Court of Justice (ECJ) 3, 8, 10, 22, 192, 193, 194; and citizenship rights 162–3, 166, 168–9; and healthcare rights 196, 197–8
European Defence Agency 88
European Economic Community (EEC) 84
European Free Trade Association (EFTA) 15, 16, 33, 38, 39
European Maritime Safety Agency (EMSA) 153
European Monetary Institute (EMI) 57
European Monetary System (EMS) 49
European Parliament (EP) 42, 54, 58–9, 96–7, 126–44, 148, 176, 231, 233; attitudes towards extending powers of *132*; attitudes towards representation *133*; and CAP decision-making 38; committees 134–6; contact patterns of MEPs 138, 139, 143; direct elections 16, 23, *24*, 26, 126, 128; and interest groups 148; number of Danes in 128; office-holding 134–6; policy positions 132–4; political party representation in *24*, 128, *129*, 130; rapporteurships 134, 136–8; trust in 176, **177**; voting behaviour 132, 139–41, *142*, 143
European Political Cooperation (EPC) 16, 84, 85
European Renewable Energy Council (EREC) 155

76; Maastricht Treaty (1992) 16, 17, 18, 19, 28, 48–9, 67, 88, 128, 175, 233; on opt-opt abolition 222, 223, 224, 225; Single European Act (SEA) *16*, 17, 39; voting behaviour in 179–83, 184, 186
refugee policy 65, 66, 69, 72
Reichert, S. 180
Reif, K. 130, 180
reservation, policy of *see* opt-outs
residence rights 162
resources 6–7
Rhodes, R. A. W. 191
Ringsmose, J. 81, 82, 83, 92
Risse, T. 190
Rohrschneider, R. 177
Romania 172n4
Rome Treaty (1957) 30, 159
Ronit, K. 145–58, 234
Ryborg, O. V. 48, 165
Rynning, S. 81, 92

salaries, European Commission staff 111–12, 115
same sex marriages 165
sanctions 7
Sandholtz, W. 30, 38
Santer Commission 111
Sarkozy, N. 58
Saxi, H. L. 87, 92
Scandinavian Defence Union 82
Schalk, J. 104
Schengen Agreement 20, 65, 69–70, 78, 161, 172n4, 230
Schengen Information System 65
Schlüter, P. 48, 49, 130
Schmidt, H. T. 130
Schmidt, V. 3
Schmitt, H. 130, 180
Schmitter, P. 214
Schneider, G. 186
Schuck, A. 175–88, 233
Scully, R. 128
security policy 16, 20, 80–94, 234; *see also* Common Foreign and Security Policy (CFSP); Common Security and Defence Policy (CSDP)
Seeberg, G. 130
Semetko, H. 178, 179
Sepos, A. 7, 13n5, 228
September 11 terrorist attacks 87, 88
services 30, *33*, 38
Services Directive 41
Shapley–Shubik Index (SSI) 102–3
shipping industry 145, 146, 150–3, 157

Sidenius, N. C. 154
Sigelman, L. 180
simple majority voting 101
Singh case (1990) 162
Single European Act (SEA) 151, 205, 230; referendum *16*, 17, 39
Single European Market (SEM) 16, 17, 222
Siune, K. 179, 180
smart-state approach 229, 234–6
Social Democratic Party 17, 19, 97, *98*, *99*, 100, 164; and Euro opt-out 49, 50, 52; and European Parliament elections *24*, *129*, 130; and family reunification policy 22; and Internal Market 40
Social Liberal Party 17, 19, *24*, 40, 49, 97, *98*, *99*, *129*, 168, 211
social security rights 161, 162, 173n7
Socialist People's Party 17, 19, 97, *98*, *99*, 100, 211, 223; and Euro opt-out 48–9, 50, 52; and European Parliament elections *24*, *129*, 130; and family reunification policy 22; and Internal Market 40; and national compromise 18, 49
socialization 8
Soetendorp, B. 82
soft law 5, 118
soft power 7
Sørensen, C. 23, 111
Sørensen, V. 38
South Africa 84
sovereignty 15, 23, 55, 67, 68
Soviet Union 83; collapse of 86, 87
Søvndal, V. 224
Spain 202n2, 204
Special Committees 207, 208–9, 211, 215
Stability and Growth Pact 62
stability-oriented philosophy 47–8, 56
Starup, P. 73
Stava, P. 192
Steinmetz, R. 234, 236
Strauss-Kahn, D. 57
Streit, M. 159
Strömvik, M. 84
structural change 11, 44
Subacchi, P. 59
subsidiarity 18, 211, 214
subsidies, agricultural 32, 34, 35, 36–7, 37–8
supranationality 3, 4, 8, 14, 15, 16, 17, 18, 28, 30, 66, 67–8, 69, 70, 74, 75, 111, 112, 189, 192, 193, 219, 220, 222, 235, 237

Suvarierol, S. 110
Svensson, P. 178, 179
Sweden 52, 53, 54, 63, 80, 87–8, 104, 106, 107, 235
Switzerland 172n4

Tallberg, J. 104, 192, 193
taxation 40, 55
terrorism 66, 69, 70, 73, 74, 81, 87, 88
Thatcher, M. 39, 126
third country nationals (TCNs) 162, 165, 170
Third World 80
Thomassen, J. 131
Thomson, R. 104, 106
Thorhallsson, B. 101, 102, 105, 235, 236
Thorning-Schmidt, H. 65, 224, 225
Tobiasen, M. 184
Togeby, L. 25, 177
Tonra, B. 219
trade negotiations 35
trade unions 41, 53
Tranholm-Mikkelsen, J. 214
transparency 111, 125n6
transposition of EU rules 195–6, 201
Treaty on European Union (TEU) *see* Maastricht Treaty
Trechsel, A. 180
Trondal, J. 11, 114, 115, 190, 203
Tsebelis, G. 131
Turner, B. 228
Turner, C. 32
Tversky, A. 221
two-day rule 40

Umbach, G. 60, 61
unemployment 40, 48, 50
Unibank 50
Union for Europe of the Nations (UEN) 132, 137
United Kingdom 15, 33, 34, 39, 79n4 and 11, 86, 104, 106, 159, 172n4, 179, 202n2, 204; as euro-outsider 63; and European Commission 114, 118, 122; and exchange rate mechanism (ERM) 53; and Western European Union (WEU) 84
United Nations (UN) 15, 82, 83, 88, 89, 92, 153
United States 80–1, 84, 85, 89, 92, 93, 94
Unity List 21, 97, *98*, *99*, 211
'uploading' process 3–4, 6, 7, 9, 21, 82, 84, 96, 109, 113, 138, 142, 146, 147, 190, 203, 220, 229, 231
Uruguay Round of trade negotiations 35

value policy 28
value promotion 82, 84
van Rompoy, H. 59
Vedsted-Hansen, J. 70
Vestager, M. 224
veto players 167–8, 192
veto points 192
veto power 101, 102, 235
Vink, M. P. 2, 228
voting behaviour: and age 181; Euroscepticism as mediator in 179, 180, 181, *182*, 184; MEPs 132, 139–41, *142*, 143; in referenda 179–83, 184, 186
Vrangbæk, K. 197

Wæver, O. 85
Waigel, T. 57
Wallace, H. 68
Wallace, W. 82, 230
weapons of mass destruction 88
Weiler, J. H. H. 159
Weitsman, P. 186
Welch, D. 218, 220, 221, 222, 223, 224, 225, 226n4
Wessels, W. 10, 60, 61
Western European Union (WEU) 84, 86
Westlake, M. 102, 106
White, B. 218, 226n2
Whitman, R. 6, 220
Whittaker, R. 134
Wiberg, H. 84
Widgren, M. 101
Wildavsky, A. 192
Willis, V. 114
Wind, M. 159–74, 228
wind turbine industry 145, 146, 153–6, 157
Winther, B. 112
Wise-Men's institution *see* Det Okonomiske Råd
Wivel, A. 1–13, 80–94, 95, 96, 101, 102, 105, 228–38
women commissioners 113
Wong, R. 218, 219, 226n2
World Shipping Council 153
World Trade Organization (WTO) 35, 62
Wright, V. 203

Yordanova, N. 134, 136
Yoshinaka, A. 136
Yugoslavia 86, 92

Zimmer, C. 106
Zølner, M. 50, 52
Zysman, J. 30, 38